MEDIA AND COMMUNICATIONS - TECHNOLOGIES, POLICIES AND CHALLENGES SERIES

INFORMATION AND COMMUNICATION TECHNOLOGIES POLICIES AND PRACTICES

Media and Communications – Technologies, Policies and Challenges Series

Intelligibility Research and Communication Issues in Emergency Situations
Samuel A. Fletcher (Editor)
2010. ISBN: 978-1-61668-634-5
(Hardcover)

Intelligibility Research and Communication Issues in Emergency Situations
Samuel A. Fletcher (Editor)
2010. ISBN: 978-1-61668-732-8
(Online Book)

Videoconferencing: Technology, Impact and Applications
Adam C. Rayler (Editor)
2010. ISBN: 978-1-61668-285-9
(Hardcover)

Videoconferencing: Technology, Impact and Applications
Adam C. Rayler (Editor)
2010. ISBN: 978-1-61668-407-5
(Online Book)

Mediating Health: The Powerful Role of the Media
Deborah Begoray, Mimi Cimon and Joan Wharf Higgins
2010. ISBN: 978-1-61668-324-5
(Softcover)

Mediating Health: The Powerful Role of the Media
Deborah Begoray, Mimi Cimon and Joan Wharf Higgins
2010. ISBN: 978-1-61668-614-7
(Online Book)

Noise-Induced Hearing Loss in Youth Caused by Leisure Noise
Hannah Keppler, B. Vinck and I. Dhooge
2010. ISBN: 978-1-61668-200-2
(Softcover)

Noise-Induced Hearing Loss in Youth Caused by Leisure Noise
Hannah Keppler, B. Vinck and I. Dhooge
2010. ISBN: 978-1-61668-460-0
(Online Book)

Spectrum Issues for the New Communications Age
Caroline D. Underwood (Editor)
2010. ISBN: 978-1-61668-544-7
(Hardcover)

Spectrum Issues for the New Communications Age
Caroline D. Underwood (Editor)
2010. ISBN: 978-1-61668-725-0
(Online Book)

Video Encryption Technology and Application
Zhengquan Xu and Jing Sun
2010. ISBN: 978-1-61668-331-3
(Softcover)

Video Encryption Technology and Application
Zhengquan Xu and Jing Sun
2010. ISBN: 978-1-61668-734-2
(Online Book)

Information and Communication Technologies Policies and Practices
Almas Heshmati and Sun Peng (Editors)
2010. ISBN: 978-1-60876-671-0

MEDIA AND COMMUNICATIONS - TECHNOLOGIES, POLICIES AND CHALLENGES SERIES

INFORMATION AND COMMUNICATION TECHNOLOGIES POLICIES AND PRACTICES

ALMAS HESHMATI

AND

SUN PENG

EDITORS

Nova Science Publishers, Inc.

New York

For permission to use material from this book please contact us:
Telephone 631-231-7269; Fax 631-231-8175
Web Site: http://www.novapublishers.com

LIBRARY OF CONGRESS CATALOGING-IN-PUBLICATION DATA

Information and communication technologies policies and practices / editors, Almas Heshmati and Sun Peng.
p. cm.
Includes index.
ISBN 978-1-60876-671-0 (hardcover)
1. Information technology--Government policy. 2. Telecommunication policy. I. Heshmati, Almas. II. Peng, Sun.
HC79.I55I53577 2009
338.9'26--dc22
2009045946

Published by Nova Science Publishers, Inc. † New York

CONTENTS

PREFACE

Chapter 1 – The organization of this volume is as follows. In this introductory chapter, the readers are introduced to some basic facts about ICT policies and practices, as well as a summary of each individual chapter. The remaining parts are divided into 5 main areas which are ICT Policy Development, Contributions of ICT Industry, Performance in ICT Sector, E-Government, and Globalization and Technology Transfer. Each part contains several complementary and comprehensive chapters discussing the issues in a specific country or country groups and provides suggestions and policy implications. The key conclusions of each chapter are also summarized in the following sections.

Chapter 2 – This study is an in depth discussion of the industrial technology policy specializing in the Information Technology (IT) sector in Vietnam. The paper finds that the transition process from a planned economy to a free market economic system combined with privatization has been positively promoting the development of the IT industry in Vietnam. It shows that the focused incentive policy public program has played a key role in making the software field grow more than the hardware field. The higher requirements of capital, technology and infrastructure in the hardware specialization require a higher foreign direct investment (FDI) inflow and more state-owned enterprise (SOE) involvement. Although most software firms are SMEs (small and medium enterprises), the software firms have captured better domestic market shares compared with the hardware firms, which were dominated by foreign well-known hardware brand name producers, especially in the electronic sector.

Chapter 3 – This paper presents background information and the progress of the government effort on Cyber Security in Cambodia. Firstly, this study establishes a framework to assess the current effort of Cambodian government on cyber security. Secondly, the results of the assessment are used to develop policy implications, serving as a roadmap to secure a national online community. Furthermore, this paper discusses the process to establish a management and technical incident response capability of the national Computer Emergency Response Team to contain on-going cyber incidents.

Chapter 4 – Technology plays an increasingly important role in development, be it economic or social. In the prevailing world economic order the pervasive use of technologies has brought countries like Nepal to the crossroads between traditional approaches and a paradigm shift towards sustainable development by capitalizing innovations in information and communication technologies (ICT), particularly the Internet. It is imperative for Nepal to adopt an information technology-friendly business environment so that it can further boost domestic and international trade regime in the wake of its paramount willingness to be a competitive newest republic in the globe. This calls for coordinated efforts from both public and private sectors aimed at promoting e-commerce in Nepal. The contribution of small and medium-sized enterprises (SMEs) to the overall economic growth and the GDP is highly significant in Nepal, where SMEs constitute almost all establishments covered by censuses and contributes 63% of the value-added segment. SMEs are the major source of income, a breeding ground for entrepreneurs and a creator of jobs. Such SMEs' efficiency can be enhanced by ICTs which also reduce costs and broaden market reach, both locally and globally. Unfortunately, many such factors discourage SMEs from fully realizing the benefits of ICTs, including a lack of knowledge, resources and trust. This paper attempts to highlight how ICTs can enhance the export competitiveness of SMEs in Nepal, and thereby the prospects and challenges with policy implications in the changed context of building a 'new' Nepal.

Chapter 5 – Since the telecommunications sector plays an important role in the overall development of a country, much foreign direct investment (FDI) has been attracted to information and communication technology (ICT) sectors in many developed and developing countries in the world. Taking the importance of the issue into account, the main purpose of this study is to analyze the effect of the main telecommunication indicators which have a significant influence on the inflow of FDI to the host countries' ICT sector. One of the most popular techniques, stochastic frontier analysis (SFA), has been applied to the data of 161 countries during 1997–2005, obtained from the International Telecommunications Union (ITU) and World Development Indicator (WDI) Databases. Empirical results of the present study demonstrate that revenue generated from mobile communication services and the overall economic development of the country have a significant positive influence on FDI inflow to target countries.

Chapter 6 – Information and communications technology (ICT) has a great role in public sector operation, reform and governance. It can also help to improve the transparency and efficiency of the public sector, create network links across service delivery agencies, cut bureaucratic red tape and realize vast savings in the public budget which can be used in productive activities. ICT in the public sector can engage citizens as participants in the overall development for the future. The issues of cost, quality and efficiency are in general neglected due to the ineffectiveness of the organization, lack of experience and resources. IT is a new tool that can be used in the cost and quality control enhancement of efficiency. In Kurdistan Region of Iraq, most of the public services are provided publicly in a traditional way. This study demonstrates the possibility of providing these services in a separate or joint public-private partnership and by using ICT in their delivery. In particular, it proposes the use of ICT in the control of the cost, quality and efficiency of goods and services both in the public and private domains. Based on the current status concerning the privatization trend, quality and administration capacity, efficiency, the role of private sector, competition and regulations, we propose necessary policy measures to enhance the use of ICT to achieve these targets.

Chapter 7 – During the last 10 years, Korea has rapidly developed, particularly in the Information and Communications Technology (ICT) sector. This paper analyses the Total Factor Productivity (TFP) growth in Korea's ICT manufacturing industry. An econometric approach is employed to measure technical change in two different ways: using Time Trend (TT) and General Index (GI) models. The TT and GI models are estimated in form of both production and cost functions. The TT model captures technical change in terms of long term trend, but the trend hardly explains reality, especially when unexpected fluctuations like economic crisis take place. According to previous research, it has been proved that GI model performs better than the TT model. Twenty four Korean telecommunications equipment manufacture plants data from 1993 to 2003 is used in this paper. The results suggest that GI cost function model fits well to measure the rate of technical change. We observe both positive technical change and TFP growth rates in Korean ICT manufacturing industry. There might have been structural change and changes in return to scale in the industry through the Asian financial crisis.

Chapter 8 – As applications require a wider and more stable bandwidth, Internet service providers (ISPs) try to control application services, and it has caused the network neutrality debate. This paper categorizes application services into four groups according to the attributes of bandwidth-usage and latency-sensitivity. By estimating the efficiency of four groups, whether there is difference in efficiency among those four groups is tested so as to see the discrimination of ISP under the circumstance in which network neutrality is not kept. Efficiency which is comparable among companies with different production functions can be calculated using a meta-frontier production function. Based on the estimated result, when the degree of freedom changes under network neutrality regulations, we forecast the effect of the development of the application service area and evaluate the network neutrality regulation.

Chapter 9 – If we take an overview of enterprise reform in China during the last 30 years, we will find that this process has always been accompanied by the debate of ownership identity and ownership structure. Numerous pieces of research on the relationship between the efficiency and ownership structure in China have been undertaken, but the conclusions vary and even contradict each other. This dissertation will explore the unique characteristics of the ownership structure of Chinese companies, and illustrate the effects of ownership structure on the efficiency of companies and finally discuss how to adjust the ownership structure to improve their efficiency. Unbalance panel data for listed ICT companies from 2003 to 2007 are collected to conduct an empirical analysis of the relationship between performance and the ownership structure of firms. A two-step procedure is used. In the first step, data envelopment analysis (DEA) Window model is applied to measure the efficiencies of these companies. In the second step, the Tobit regression model is used to establish the relationship between efficiency and the ownership structure, to identify the determinants of efficiency and to estimate their impacts. A sensitivity analysis with respect to model specification is conducted. In addition, this dissertation attempts to provide an explanation for the conclusions drawn, and provides policy guidelines for future adjustments in the ownership structure. In conclusion, the results suggest that the proportions of state-owned and private corporate shares do not affect the efficiency of companies significantly. However, the ownership concentration exhibits a positive impact on the efficiency level of the sample ICT firms.

Chapter 10 – Telecommunications plays a major role worldwide with the aim of achieving a better social life for citizens and is one of the major factors contributing to economic growth. This study provides an efficiency analysis of mobile operators in Colombia, Venezuela, Chile and Brazil.

For the empirical analysis, the stochastic frontier functions approach is employed to analyze data from 10 mobile operators from the sample countries. Mobile operators in Colombia are compared with others from Venezuela, Chile, and Brazil. Panel data from 2005 to 2007 is used in the analysis.

The efficiency estimation for each operator over time shows that the level is affected by some firms and market characteristics such as: type of ownership, market share, type of technology and firm level wages. One of the main findings of this research is that smaller operators work at the same level of efficiency compared with their larger counterparts.

Chapter 11 – As the process of telecommunication liberalization and increased competition evolves, the situation of market competition and the structure of mobile operators differs considerably across the Middle East and North African (MENA) countries. This study attempts to analyze the effects of foreign ownership and the market share on the traffic and financial performance of mobile operators in MENA region. To achieve these objectives, we use panel data estimation methods to assess MENA mobile industry performances using an unbalanced panel data of 13 mobile operators observed over the period 2002-2007. The empirical analysis results, using fixed and random effect models, showed that both foreign ownership and a higher market share have a significant positive impact on traffic, revenues, returns on sales and returns on investment of mobile operators in the MENA region.

Chapter 12 – Information technology (IT) is a factor that has led to an improvement in the productivity and efficiency of the postal services organizations. This study aims to explain the degree of efficiency gained by the use technology of ICT and government support programs. These are used to test the hypothesis about the effect of technology and government support programs. The study is divided into two steps: the first step is an analysis of efficiency by using DEA, while the second step is a "Tobit Model" analysis used to estimate the influence of the determinant factors on the efficiency of postal offices. The empirical results show that IT capital investment has a positive impact on the efficiency of the service organization. The efficiency of postal services over time has been decreasing. The government and top management should be concerned about the necessary improvement in postal services management.

Chapter 13 – The purpose of this study is to compare the capacity or potential of governments in East and Southeast Asia in their utilization of E-government as an instrument to deliver public services to their citizens. The principal component analysis methodology is used to compute the E-government index. The index is used as a benchmark to compare the performance of developing and newly industrialized economies in delivery of public services. The overall index is compromised of three main components: ICT infrastructure, development information and finances indices. The E-government index level shows the capacity of each country's governments to deliver public services. The result is useful for identifying the weaknesses and strengths in their service provision. An attempt is made to suggest alternative approaches to achieve the goals and progress towards an advanced E-government-based service provision that enhances equality in opportunities.

Chapter 14 – So far there have been few studies dealing with e-Government in Cambodia, one of the Least Developed Countries (LDCs) with an emerging economy. This study can be considered as a first in the examination of e-Government challenges in Cambodia. The Government Administration Information System (GAIS), one of the leading e-Government projects in Cambodia, is a main setting for this study. The study categorizes e-Government challenges in LDCs into six main areas: infrastructure development; law and ICT policy; management; equity issues; the digital divide; and privacy and security. The findings indicate that even though the GAIS has been successful in its initiative objectives, it has faced various critical challenges as well. These challenges and a set of policy implications are discussed in the paper.

Chapter 15 – This study starts with a comprehensive literature investigation on the background of international trade theory, empirical studies of trade effects on economic growth and policies both in developed and developing countries. Then it focuses on the effects of instruments of trade policy, such as tariff, quota, and subsidy. The evolution of China's trade policy from the 1950s up to 2007 is also discussed, as well as the reform of the Chinese trade regime. WTO accession, which represents a new milestone in China's trade evolution, also provides China with the opportunity to share more and more advantages in the world market.

Finally, it provides a better understanding of the static and dynamic benefits from international trade which resulted from the reform of trade policy in China. It is found that China's specialization in assembly trade has given rise to a highly competitive and internationalized manufacturing sector, which has been the main channel of technology transfers, while the traditional export sector has lagged behind. The implication of policy and conclusions are drawn, concerning the determinants of China's trade regime as well. The future international trade patterns of China need to be adjusted to the change in the global market and domestic economic development.

Chapter 16 - Nepal is one of the least developed countries in the world with a minimal input to national development from its industrial sector. The pace of industrialization depends on the quality and the approaches followed by the nation in its implementation of designated policies. This paper tries to analyze the policy implementation achievement in three major factors that are identified as key factors impacting industrial economics of Nepal. These are intellectual property rights (IPR), foreign direct investment (FDI) and technology transfer. The three factors are both interrelated and interdependent. In this study we provide a descriptive analysis of the available data. This will include the current status of the policies and their implementation, identification of weaknesses in policy implementation. In addition provide recommendations for the way forward in the dealing with the existing problems concerning IPR, FDI and technology transfer in Nepalese context.

In: Information and Communication Technologies…
Ed: Almas Heshmati and Sun Peng
ISBN 978-1-60876-671-0

Chapter 1

INTRODUCTION TO INFORMATION AND COMMUNICATION TECHNOLOGY POLICIES AND PRACTICES

Almas Heshmati*[*1] *and Peng Sun*[2]
[1]Seoul National University
[2]LiaoNing Entry-Exit Inspection and Quarantine Bureau of China
and Seoul National University

1. INTRODUCTION TO THIS VOLUME ON ICT

With increased globalization and productive investment and cooperation, Asia has achieved a remarkable record of high and sustained economic growth. There are a number of key factors crucial to the Asian success. Besides private domestic investment and rapid growth in human capital, which are regarded as the principal engines of growth, information and communication technology (ICT) sectors and inward technology transfer strategy play an indispensable role in the employment generation, with an increased flow of foreign direct investment and productivity growth. Consequently, the study of ICT policies and practices is of vast importance and significance for the competitiveness of firms, relevant institutions and agencies, decision-makers, economists and investors around the world, as well as many international and non-governmental organizations.

This volume serves as an international forum focusing on the information and communication technology policies and practices which have led to the rapid and remarkable record of high and sustained economic growth of Asian countries since the middle of the second half of 20th century. It aims to provide an up-to-date and in-depth analysis of five factors crucial to the success of the ICT industry and technology transfer in some specific countries in Asia.

These factors include: the development of ICT policy, the contribution of ICT sectors to the economy, the productivity and efficiency of ICT sectors, E-government utilization in the

* Corresponding author E-mail: heshmati@snu.ac.kr

provision of public services, and the effectiveness of globalization and technology transfer. Each chapter's contribution to this volume is to be seen as a separate contribution to a certain factor from a national or regional point of view. All together, however, they provide a complete and comprehensive picture of the key successful factors in ICT development and technology transfer in Asia, as well as the long way ahead in the achievement of targeted goals of the individual countries studied.

The literature on ICT policy and practice is growing in its number of studies, yet it is far from being sufficient to provide a complete picture of the situation in Asian countries. Some of the literature is just a result of an inadequate analysis from a general point of view without an in-depth study at the regional or sectoral levels. This volume provides opportunities to access information on different aspects of ICT fields and technology transfer. Each individual chapter analyses a number of the key factors by using a diversified and multidisciplinary approach. Some of the chapters are divided by region, such as ICT policy development in different countries, while others look at various sectors within a country. However, all together they provide a detailed introduction of the recent developments in ICT policy and practice in most of the Asian countries, namely Korea, China, Cambodia, Vietnam, Nepal, Indonesia as well as Central Asian, Middle Eastern and North African and Latin American countries.

One unique characteristic of this volume is that the majority of the contributors are experts or scholars with a strong background in the ICT field. With their experiences as working as strategists and advisors to ministries and relevant institutions in the public sector or agents in emerging Asian economies, they provide an in-depth study of ICT policies and practices.

This volume also serves as a good complementary to the existing literature on ICT by utilizing up-to-date data and methodologies in the field. The deep and highly professional analyses in specific fields are among the key features of this book.

In terms of academic level, the volume brings researchers, academics and practitioners together with extensive coverage from policy making and implementation to evaluation in the ICT sector in countries covering a whole range of development levels. The target readers are: researchers, decision-makers, governmental and non-governmental organizations, undergraduate and graduate students, and the general public with an interest in ICT policy and practices at the sectoral, national, regional and global levels. It is a perfect basic textbook which could be used for teaching a course on ICT policy and practices at the intermediate level.

The organization of this volume is as follows. In this introductory chapter, the readers are introduced to some basic facts about ICT policies and practices, as well as a summary of each individual chapter. The remaining parts are divided into 5 main areas which are ICT Policy Development, Contributions of ICT Industry, Performance in ICT Sector, E-Government, and Globalization and Technology Transfer. Each part contains several complementary and comprehensive chapters discussing the issues in a specific country or country groups and provides suggestions and policy implications. The key conclusions of each chapter are also summarized in the following sections.

2. ICT Policy Development

National ICT policies, as a kind of industrial policy, are set to guide a country in its use of these tools to secure the benefits of the information economy for all users. In general, ICT policies deal with the issues related to information dissemination and use, as well as issues related to the spread and use of the technology itself. One of the main objectives of ICT policies is to ensure the greatest possible diffusion of ICTs to meet national needs, ambitions, specificities and concerns. Therefore, ICT policies must take into account all issues at local, national and international levels, as well as sectoral concerns.

On "ICT Policy Development", different aspects of ICT policies in Vietnam and Cambodia are discussed. In *Chapter 2*, Tran-Quy discusses the industrial technology policy specializing in the Information Technology (IT) sector in Vietnam. This study finds that the transition process from a planned economy to a free market economic system, combined with privatization has been positively promoting the development of the IT industry in Vietnam. It shows that the focused incentive policy public program has played a key role in making the software field grow more than the hardware field. The higher requirements of capital, technology and infrastructure in the hardware specialization require a higher foreign direct investment (FDI) inflow and the more active involvement of state-owned enterprises (SOEs). Although most of software firms are SMEs (small and medium enterprises), the software firms have captured domestic market shares better compared with the hardware firms, which were dominated by foreign well-known brand producers, especially in the electronic sector. In order to join the global value chain, the facilitation of production by multi-national enterprises in Vietnam would be a better option in terms of policy and its implications.

In *Chapter 3*, Cheang presents background information and the progress of government efforts on Cyber Security in Cambodia. This chapter establishes a framework to assess the current effort of Cambodian government on cyber security first and then the results of the assessment are used to develop policy implications, serving as a roadmap to secure a national online community. Furthermore, the author discusses the process to establish a management and technical incident response capability of the national Computer Emergency Response Team to contain on-going cyber incidents.

3. Contributions of ICT Industry

With the advancement in technology and the emergence of convergence in the ICT industry, which reflects the seamless convergence of digital processing and telecommunications, the sector has become more and more prevalent and it has a prominent role in contributing to economic growth and building the competitiveness capacity of a country.

The voluminous research literature points to the fact that ICT is playing a more and more important role in increasing the efficiency in internal business and in the enhancement of productivity. In particular, it reduces communication costs and provides links to local and global supply chains, and it facilitates capacity building through e-learning.

This part on "Contributions of ICT Industry" sheds light on how the ICT industry can contribute to national development in different ways.

In *Chapter 4*, Manandhar discusses the contribution of ICT industry to the export competitiveness enhancement of SMEs in Nepal. In the prevailing world economic order, the pervasive use of technologies has brought countries like Nepal to the crossroads between traditional approaches and a paradigm shift towards sustainable development by capitalizing innovations in ICT, particularly the Internet. Manandhar finds it imperative for Nepal to adopt an information technology-friendly business environment so that it can further boost domestic and international trade regimes in the wake of Nepal's paramount willingness to be a competitive newest republic in the globe.

This calls for coordinated efforts from both public and private sectors aimed at promoting e-commerce in Nepal. Nepal's SMEs provide the greatest amount of employment in the country. They need promising and capable technically-backed human resources and an ICT-induced business mechanism to be able to innovate new products and services and market them into new business destinations. The ICT policies should encourage the progressive expansion of enterprises and support services for entrepreneurship development and particularly promote technology capacity-building and innovation activities for enhancing the competitiveness of SMEs.

In *Chapter 5*, Mukhrumbaev discusses the effect of the main telecommunication indicators on the inflow of foreign direct investment (FDI) by using the stochastic frontier analysis (SFA) approach. Since the telecommunication sector plays an important role in the overall development of a country, much FDI has been attracted to ICT sectors in many developed and developing countries of the world. Taking the importance of the issue into account, the main purpose of this chapter is to analyze the effect of the main telecommunication indicators which have a significant influence on the inflow of FDI to the host countries' ICT sector. SFA has been applied to the data of 161 countries during 1997–2005, obtained from the International Telecommunications Union (ITU) and World Development Indicators (WDI) Databases. Empirical results demonstrate that revenue generated from mobile communication services and the overall economic development of the country have a significant positive influence on the FDI inflow to target countries.

In *Chapter 6*, Khayyat discusses the effects of IT on cost, quality and efficiency in provision of public services. It is found that ICT has a great role in the public sector operations, reform and governance. It can also help to improve the transparency and efficiency of the public sector, create network links across service delivery agencies, cut bureaucratic red tape and realizes vast savings in the public budget which can be used in more productive activities.

ICT in the public sector can engage citizens as participants in the overall development for the future. The issues of cost, quality and efficiency are in general neglected in most developing countries due to the ineffectiveness of the organization, lack of experience and complementary resources. IT is a new tool that can be used in the cost and quality control enhancement of efficiency. In the Federal Region of Kurdistan most of the public services are provided publicly in the traditional way.

This chapter demonstrates the possibility of providing these services in separate or joint public-private partnership and by using IT in their delivery. In particular, it proposes the use of IT in the control of cost, quality and efficiency of goods and services both in the public and private domains.

4. PERFORMANCE IN ICT SECTOR

For several decades, productivity and efficiency in production have been popular topics of both theoretical and empirical research. These issues are frequently used in the evaluation of the performance, concentrating on agriculture, banking, health and manufacturing sectors, and are relatively scarcely in ICT sectors. The growing importance of ICT sectors has induced increasing concern about its performance. With the development of econometrics, the availability of data and computer computation power, many complicated methods based on mathematical models have been introduced to analyze performance in terms of productivity and efficiency in the ICT sector.

As regards Productivity and Efficiency in the ICT sector, different methods are applied to assess the performance of the ICT sector in Asian countries. In *Chapter 7*, Kim made an analysis of productivity in Korean ICT manufacturing industry. This chapter analyses the total factor productivity (TFP) growth in Korea's ICT manufacturing industry by using an econometric approach to measure technical change in two different ways: using time trend and general index models. Twenty four Korean telecommunications equipment manufacturing plants data from 1993 to 2003 is used. The results show both positive technical change and TFP growth rates in the Korean ICT manufacturing industry. There might have been structural change and changes in return to scale have taken place in the industry through the Asian financial crisis.

As regards "Performance in ICT Sector", different methods are applied to assess the performance of ICT sector in Asian countries. In *Chapter 8*, Lee discusses the network neutrality and the efficiency of internet application service providers by a meta-frontier analysis. This chapter categorizes application services into four groups according to the attributes of bandwidth-usage and latency-sensitivity. By estimating the efficiency of four groups, whether there is difference in efficiency among those four groups is tested so as to see the discrimination of Internet service providers (ISP) under the circumstance in which network neutrality is not kept. Efficiency which is comparable among companies with different production functions can be calculated using a meta-frontier production function.

In *Chapter 9*, Wang and Heshmati discuss the relationship between efficiency and ownership structure based on the case of China's listed ICT companies. This chapter explores the unique characteristics of the ownership structure of Chinese companies, and illustrates the effects of ownership structure on the efficiency of companies and finally discusses how to adjust the ownership structure to improve their efficiency. Unbalanced panel data for listed ICT companies from 2003 to 2007 in China are collected to conduct an empirical analysis of the relationship between the performance and ownership structure of firms. A two-step procedure is used. In the first step data envelopment analysis (DEA) a Window model is applied to measure the efficiencies of these companies. Then, the Tobit model is used to establish the relationship between efficiency and ownership structure, to identify the determinants of efficiency and to estimate their impacts. A sensitivity analysis with respect to model specification is also conducted. The results suggest that the proportions of state-owned and private corporate shares do not affect the efficiency of companies significantly. However, the ownership concentration exhibits a positive impact on the efficiency level of the sample ICT firms.

In *Chapter 10*, Borja-Barrera and Heshmati make a comparison of efficiency of mobile operators in South America. This chapter provides a comparative efficiency analysis of mobile operators in Colombia, Venezuela, Chile and Brazil. For the empirical analysis, the stochastic frontier function approach is employed to analyze data from 10 mobile operators. Mobile operators in Colombia are compared with others from Venezuela, Chile, and Brazil. Panel data from 2005 to 2007 is used in the analysis. The efficiency estimation for each operator over time shows that the level is affected by firms and market characteristics such as: type of ownership, market share, type of technology and firm level wages. One of the main findings of this research is that smaller operators work at the same level of efficiency compared with their larger counterparts.

In *Chapter 11*, El-Rhinaoui and Heshmati discuss the impact of foreign ownership and market share on financial performance and the communication traffic of mobile operators in the Middle East and North Africa (MENA) region. This study attempts to analyze the effects of foreign ownership and the market share on the traffic and financial performance of mobile operators in the MENA region. To achieve these objectives, panel data estimation methods were applied to assess MENA mobile industry performances by using an unbalanced panel data of 13 mobile operators observed over the period 2002-2007. The result of the empirical analysis, using fixed and random effects models, showed that both foreign ownership and a higher market share have a significant and positive impact on traffic, revenues, returns on sales and returns on investment of mobile operators in the MENA region.

In *Chapter 12*, Iman-Santoso and Heshmati discuss IT and efficiency of the postal service in Indonesia. This study aims to explain the degree of efficiency gained by the use of ICT technology and government support programs. These are used to test a hypothesis about the possible effects of technology and government support programs. The study is divided into two steps: the first step is an analysis of efficiency by using DEA, while the second step is a "Tobit Model" analysis used to estimate the influence of the determinant factors on the efficiency of postal offices. The empirical results show that IT capital investment has a positive impact on the efficiency of the service organization. Efficiency of postal services over time has been decreasing. The government and top management should be concerned about the necessary improvement in postal services management.

5. E-GOVERNMENT

The use of information technology that allows free movement of information which overcomes the physical bounds of traditional paper-based systems is e-government. In order to deliver an increasing number of services in a cost effective manner, the government is required to provide services increasingly. One of the greatest tasks for a government to accomplish is to increase the efficiency of the delivery of public services to the citizens. It is important to examine the global scope of an e-government as well, because the relative development of these technologies in various countries will have a significant impact on the ability of these governments to function well and effectively.

The "E-Government" part contributes to the growing ICT literature in respect to ICT utilization for public service provision. In *Chapter 13*, Heshmati, Sun and Oh discuss the utilization of e-government in the delivery of public services in Asia. They compare the capacity or potential of governments in their utilization of e-government as an instrument to deliver public services to their citizens. The principal component analysis methodology is used to compute the e-government index. The index is used as a benchmark to compare the performance of developing and newly industrialized economies in delivery of public services. The overall index is comprised of three main components: ICT infrastructure, development information and finances indices. The e-government index level shows the service delivery capacity of each country's government. The result is useful for identifying the strengths and weaknesses in their service provision. An attempt is made to suggest alternative approaches to achieve the goals and progress towards an advanced e-government-based service provision that enhances equality in citizens' opportunities.

So far there have been few studies dealing with e-Government in Cambodia, one of the Least Developed Countries (LDCs) with an emerging economy. In *Chapter 14*, Sang discusses the e-Government challenges in Cambodia. This chapter categorizes e-Government challenges in LDCs into six main areas: infrastructure development; law and ICT policy; management; equity issues; digital divide; and privacy and security. The findings of the study indicate that, even though the Government Administration Information System (GAIS) has been successful in its initiative objectives, it has come up with various critical challenges as well.

6. Globaliztion and Technology Transfer

Technology, as the most evident driving factor of rapid economic growth, contributes to the building of human resources, increase in the productivity, and large production cost saving. In the last decades, most countries are focusing on the enhancement of technology capability through technology transfer from developed countries and local research and development (RandD) capacity development. There are different perspectives on technology transfer to developing countries in the literature. While the flow of FDI is important, involvement in global production and domestic technology development are regarded as the main sources of national RandD capacity.

In the part of "Globalization and Technology Transfer", the different perspectives on technology transfer to Asian developing countries and domestic technology enhancement are discussed. In *Chapter 15*, Sun discusses trade policy and its effects on China's economic growth. This study starts with a comprehensive investigation of the background of international trade theory, empirical studies of trade effects on economic growth and policies both in developed and developing country environments. Then it focuses on the effects of trade policy instruments, such as tariff, quota, and subsidies. The evolution of China's trade policy from the 1950s up to 2007, including the reform of Chinese trade regime, is discussed. China's Word Trade Organization (WTO) accession, which represents a new milestone in China's trade evolution, also provides China with the opportunity to increasingly share advantages in the world market. Finally, Sun attempts to provide a better understanding of the static and dynamic benefits from international trade which resulted from the reform of trade policy in China. It is found that China's specialization in assembly trade has given rise to a highly competitive and internationalized manufacturing sector, which has been the main channel of technology transfers, while the traditional export sector has lagged behind. The implication of policy and conclusions are drawn. It is suggested that the future international trade patterns of China need to adjust to the change in the global market and the domestic economic development.

In *Chapter 16*, Ghimire discusses regulatory policy factors impacts on industrial technology development in Nepal. Nepal is one of the poorest countries in the world with minimal input to national development from its industrial sector. The pace of its industrialization depends on the quality and implementation of designated policies. This chapter tries to analyze the policy implementation achievement in three major factors of industrial economics i.e. intellectual property right (IPR), foreign direct investment, and technology transfer. These factors are interrelated. With the descriptive analysis of the available data, the current status of the policies and their implementation, weaknesses in implementation and policy recommendations for ways forward are given. Account is made for the current political conditions facing Nepal concerning IPR, FDI and technology transfer.

In: Information and Communication Technologies... ISBN 978-1-60876-671-0
Ed: Almas Heshmati and Sun Peng

Chapter 2

AN ANALYSIS OF INDUSTRIAL POLICY OF IT IN VIETNAM

Nam Tran-Quy*
Ministry of Information and Communication of Vietnam
and Seoul National University

ABSTRACT

This study is an in depth discussion of the industrial technology policy specializing in the Information Technology (IT) sector in Vietnam. The paper finds that the transition process from a planned economy to a free market economic system combined with privatization has been positively promoting the development of the IT industry in Vietnam. It shows that the focused incentive policy public program has played a key role in making the software field grow more than the hardware field. The higher requirements of capital, technology and infrastructure in the hardware specialization require a higher foreign direct investment (FDI) inflow and more state-owned enterprise (SOE) involvement. Although most software firms are SMEs (small and medium enterprises), the software firms have captured better domestic market shares compared with the hardware firms, which were dominated by foreign well-known hardware brand name producers, especially in the electronic sector.

Keywords: IT industry, IT policy, market structure, software, hardware, Vietnam.

1. BACKGROUND TO THE VIETNAMESE ECONOMY

Vietnam is basically a transition economy from a planned economic system moving to a free market-oriented economic system. The process started in 1986 with a dramatic change at the beginning of the 1990s. Before unification in 1975 and after the Vietnam War, Vietnam

* E-mail: tqnam@temep.snu.ac.kr

was a very poor country because many of its economic infrastructures were badly destroyed during the war.

There was a turning-point in the form of a major change called "Renovation" or, in Vietnamese, "Doimoi" at the Convention of the Communist Party, led by General Secretary Nguyen Van Linh in 1986. This helped Vietnam to change gradually from a planned economy to a free market economic system. However, even though the revolution began as soon as 1986, the expected change only appeared to be more and more clear at the beginning of the 1990s with different forms of relationships and economic ties with foreign partners in many aspects of the national economy. In addition, one important change that occurred in 1994 was when the United States lifted its trade embargo on Vietnam which was imposed after the Vietnam War. This was despite the fact that the official normalization of the relationship between the two countries was first announced one year later. As a result, the renovation progress has helped Vietnam to achieve much success in recent years. The Vietnamese economy achieved the averaged growth rate around 8-9% annually during 1990s and around 7-8% in recent years. The rapid growth of exports is also remarkable after implementing a liberal and open trade policy. In 1990, the total exports were just about $2.4 billion but in 2007 they jumped to $47.5 billion (see Table 1).

The economic achievement of Vietnam in recent years has not been contributed to by only the public sectors, which are represented by many state-own enterprises (SOE), but also by active private sector corporations. The privatization program started at the end of the 1990s but the key impacts were realized first on the economic front around 2003. During these periods, the Vietnamese Central Committee of the Communist Party issued the Resolution of the Central Committee Assembly 9 of the Communist Party numbered IX, which indicated clearly the direction of the "renewal of state enterprises to improve productivity, especially to promote privatization", and the Law of State Enterprises in 2003 also reaffirmed the same statement to promote privatization and the progress of some state-owned enterprises in order to make these enterprises become productive. More concretely, government promulgated the Decree 187/2004/ND-CP specializing in the privatization of some state-owned enterprises in order to realize this determination. As the result, the number of completely state-owned enterprises was reduced and the number of private sector enterprises rose significantly.

Table 1. Basic statistics of the Vietnamese Economy (adjusted for inflation)

Year	GDP per capita ($)	GDP Growth	Export ($ bill)	Inflation rate
1986	731	3.4%	-	774.5%
1990	942	5.0%	2.4	36.0%
1995	1,446	9.5%	5.4	16.9%
2000	2,037	6.8%	14.5	-1.7%
2005	3,025	7.5%	32.5	8.0%
2007	3,503	7.4%	47.5	12.6%

Source: IMF, GSO (General Statistics Office).

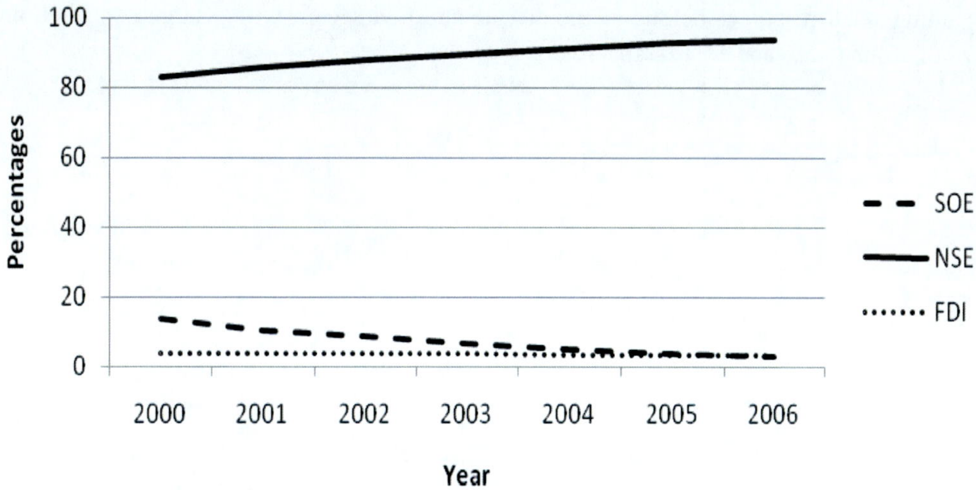

Source: General Statistics Office (GSO).

Figure 1. Growth of firm by type of ownership in Vietnam.

Figure 1 below shows the share of SOE firms, Foreign Direct Investment (FDI) firms and NSEs (Non-State Enterprises) and how these changed over the period of 2000–2006.

Because the indicators in Figure 1 show the percentages of different firms classified by types, not by size, it means that small firms with less than 10 employees also have the same weight as the larger firms with more than 1000 employees. Therefore, we can see the share of non-state enterprises (where private firms are the key component) is much higher than the share of FDI and SOE types, 90% vs. 10%.

What interested us here is the trend of the decrease or increase in the different types of firms in Vietnam during 2000-2006. This period prioritized high economic growth (see Table 1) and promoted privatization. In this regard, we can see that the share of SOEs has decreased sharply over time, while the share of NSEs, composed mainly of the private firms, increased during the same period. This figure was contributed to by the process of privatization and the change from public to private ownership. We can also see that the share of FDI companies seems to be stable during 2000–2006. In general, the private sector played a more significant and important role in achieving the stated Vietnamese economic goals. Since 2000 this condition is evidenced by a high GDP growth of around 7-8% per year.

Figure 2 below compares the ownership of firms by using the capital owned by these firms respectively. Figure 2.a shows that non-state-owned firms hold the highest share with 93%, while the public firms' share is just 2.82%. However, Figure 2.b shows that although the number of public firms is very small, they have a relatively much larger share of capital resources (52%). This fact shows the particular characteristics of the market in Vietnam, like other former socialist countries, in that the SOEs still played a very important role in the national economy. The importance of SOEs is obvious, but their performance is arguable. Dang-Xuan (2008) stated that state-owned enterprises are still a very cumbersome and low productive segment of the economy. He showed that state-owned enterprises governed by state representatives make a contribution corresponding to 40% of GDP, 30% tax remittances and 10% job creation but they use a much as 80% of state investment, 75% of fixed assets, 60% of total domestic lending and 70% of foreign debt (Dang-Xuan, 2008). Meanwhile the remaining small resources belong to the private and FDI sector, with a large contribution to GDP of around 45% and 15%, respectively.

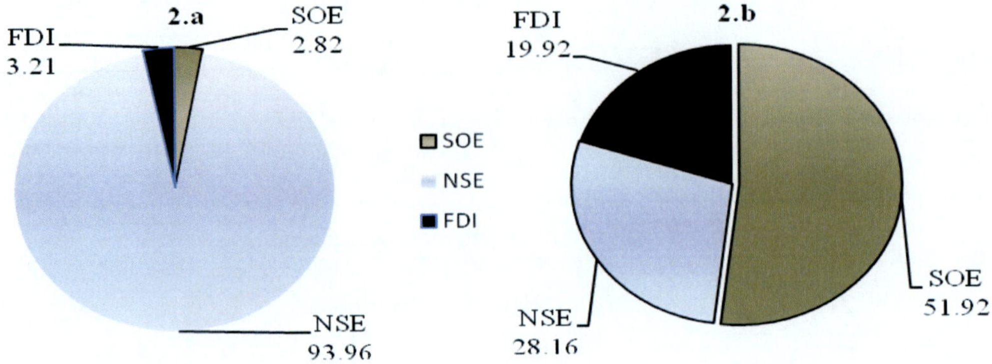

Source: GSO (2006).

Figure 2. (a) Share of Firm by Ownership; (b) Share of Firm Capital.

The largest share of capital resources in SOEs suggests strong state intervention in the Vietnamese economy. The literature says that state intervention is not always adverse for development, especially when it plays an important role in the initial stages of development to avoid market failure and help to build up an infant industry through promotion. The Japanese government also intervened heavily in the national economy after the Second World War (Okimoto, 1989). However, Japan illustrated that despite heavy state intervention, the size of the Japanese government is still small with a limited number of public servants. Most Japanese government power is concentrated in the Ministry of International Trade and Industry (MITI) serving as headquarters for the 'Japan, Incorporated' strategy (Okimoto, 1989) in order to unify, control and implement simultaneously industrial policy.

In Vietnam, the size of government seems to be large but, it is tending to shrink gradually. The number of Ministry and governmental agencies has tended to be downsized in recent years. In 2007, the National Assembly approved the reduction of the total number of Ministries from 26 to 22 and shrank the number of government agencies which were considered to be at the same level and equivalent to ministries from 12 to 8 agencies. The Vietnamese government is also trying to adapt new economic policy measures and to create a better business environment towards transition of the economy from an agricultural society to an industry and service sector society. In the 1980s, more than 90% of Vietnam's population was living and working in the agricultural sector, but now the share has dropped to around 70% of the labor force. In 2006 20.1% of the Vietnamese national GDP was generated by agriculture; 41.8% by industry; and 38.1% by the service sector. Source: GSO (2006).

2. Government Policy Towards IT Industry

In October 2000, recognizing the importance of IT development and application in the economy and society, the Political Committee of the Communist Party issued the Directive No-58/2000/CT-TW to pave the way for IT development in Vietnam. In order to implement this directive, the Vietnamese government promulgated a series of incentive policy measures towards the IT industry. Firstly, the Prime Minister signed Decision No. 128/2000/QD-TTg in 2000 to give the highest incentive policy to the software industry among all economic sectors (for details see Section 2.1). Then, based on the Law of Corporate Tax, the government issued Decree No. 164/2003/ND-CP to postulate corporate tax with high incentives favorable to the IT industry

There are some legal documents regarding the IT sector, most of which are incentive policy measures such as: the Decision of the Prime Minister No. 53/2004/QD-TTg on High-Tech Park policy; Decree No. 57/2006/ND-CP on 09/06/2006 by the Prime Minister on E-commerce, Decision of the Prime Minister No. 169/2006/QD-TTg issued on 17/07/2009 about the government procurement preferential toward the domestic IT investment and expenditure of the state-budgeted projects, Law of IT passed on June 22, 2006 by the National Assembly, Decree No. 26/2007/ND-CP on February 5, 2007 with details on implementing e-commerce using e-signature and certified e-signature, Decree No. 71/2007/ND-CP issued on May 3, 2007 concerning implementing in detail the regulations of IT Law in the IT Industry, Decision No. 51/2007/QD-TTg on April 12, 2007 on the Vietnam IT industry development program to 2010, and Decision No. 56/2007/QD-TTg on the Vietnam digital content industry's development program to 2010, to mention a few.

In general, all of the above listed government legal documents aimed to give the most incentive policies among the existing policies for IT industry and IT application in the economy and society. Because of the top-down government vertical structure, all political systems from central to local agencies at a provincial level share the same view and are determined to implement these policies to promote the IT industry nationwide. The establishment of the Ministry of Information and Communications (MIC) in 2002 which takes charge of the IT industry, telecommunications, broadcasting and postal services is also an indication of the high priority given to IT development in Vietnam.

According to the MIC definition, the IT Industry includes only 2 sectors, hardware (sub-sectors are computer, electronic, and telecommunication equipment) and software (sub-sectors are domestic and outsourcing software, the digital content industry, and the IT service industry). It is different from other countries' definition, even though Vietnam gets a major share of its revenue from the telecommunication service sector due to its large market provided by a large population (87 million people) but the government considers it not as an industrial sector, but only a part of the service sector. Regarding the IT industry in Vietnam, it has been developing very fast in recent years (see Table 2), especially after 2001 when the dot.com crisis emerged and the Vietnamese government promulgated the foreign direct investment law to promote an open market, international integration, and privatization.

The Vietnamese governmental policy concerning the IT industry is quite different from the telecommunications sector where public enterprises still dominate the telecom market and price setting is done by the government for vital telephone services. Thanks to the open policy, the IT industry in both software and hardware sectors has grown annually to a combined total of about 30% on average. The Vietnamese government encouraged the buying of domestic IT products through Directive 21/2001/CT-TTg circulated in 2001 for every domestic product in general and the Decision 169/2006/QD-TTg circulated in 2006 specialized in IT products procurement. Thanks to these kinds of policy, the domestic market share forms the main part of the software revenue (see Table 2, column 2).

Table 2. IT Industry Revenues ($mil)

Year	Software			Digital Content	Hardware	Total
	Domestic market	Outsourcing / Export	Total			
2002	65	20	85	-	550	635
2003	90	30	120	-	700	820
2004	125	45	170	-	760	930
2005	180	70	250	15	1150	1400
2006	255	105	360	65	1380	1740
2007	318	180	498	180	3080*	3700
2008	-	-	670	270	3560*	4500

Source: Combined by the author from source of: MIC (Ministry of Information and Communication) and HCA (2006, 2007, and 2008).

Note: * means hardware including household electronic appliances.

In 2008 the IT industry's revenue reached $4.5 billion (Nguyen-Trong, 2008), in which the hardware field (computer, electronic, and telecommunication equipment) contributed with $3.56 billion and the software field contributed $670 million (software domestic and export). Along with this exceptional achievement, the digital content industry received more than $270 million, increased by 50% compared with 2007 (see Table 4, column 5). Thanks to the main contribution of foreign-owned enterprises, such as Canon, Jujitsu, Hoya, LG, and Samsung, the hardware industry received a high level of revenue. In terms of software, the Vietnamese government's view it as the top priority for promotion, and it granted various incentive policies; therefore software growth achieved 35-40% growth annually (see Table 4, column 4). The growth rate is much higher than growth in the hardware industry. The share of software outsourcing increased rapidly in 2007 by more than 71%, meanwhile the domestic software/services market increased less but was still very impressive at 24% (calculated from Table 2, columns 2 and 3).

2.1. Software Industry Policy

The Vietnamese government considers the software industry to be characterized by low initial capital investment, high value-added, enhancing technological capabilities and it is suitable for the Vietnamese human capital, so the software industry became the top priority for development by government and business. One aspect of some facts that supports this view is that Vietnamese students perform well in the world competition at high school level in terms of IT competition, mathematics and physics by usually taking one or more gold medal annually. There are also other educational indices which show that Vietnam is standing at a high level relative to other countries with similar socioeconomic conditions. However, this view is challenged by several policy makers and experts. The opponents argue that high performance in school and competition in the market does not mean a strong position and performance in practice, especially in the IT industry which requires a high technological advancement. Anyway, many experts think that for Vietnam it is much harder to compete with countries with new and growing industries heavily dependent on high-tech and capital intensive production technology like manufacturing or heavy industry and instead it is better to focus on declining industries like the software industry.

Sharing this view, the Vietnamese government gave direction to support the software segment, therefore the software industry in Vietnam enjoys the highest incentive policy among all industrial sectors, especially in regard to the tax incentive postulated in Prime Minister decision numbered 128/2000/QD-TTg and then in Decree No. 164/2003/NĐ-CP, which details the Law of Corporate Tax. The incentive policy for software is outlined in the summary listed below:

- Businesses involved in software production and services, with both local and foreign investment, are exempted from corporate income tax for 4 years after generating their first taxable income and are deducted at 50% for the next 9 years.
- Preferential personal income taxation for people working in software industry.
- Zero Value Added Tax (VAT) applied to software products and services.
- Zero import tax for materials directly used in the software, zero import tax for materials directly used in the software production.
- Zero export tax for software products.

Other incentive policy measures related to the funding priority, the priority given to immigrants, VISA exemptions for foreign workers in telecommunication services. The details of the incentive policy are:

- Subsidy for internet access fees for enterprise operations in Software Parks
- Applied investment supporting by the state's applied investment supporting by the special state's development support fund
- Exempt from or reduced cost of using and renting land as well as from land tax.
- RandD activities: government support finance for RandD projects by deducting corporate tax
- Foreign experts enjoy a preferential policy concerning immigration procedures (through VISA exemption).

Thanks to these generous incentive policy measures, the software industry achieved a high growth rate of 35-40% annually (see Table 4, column 3), five times the growth of GDP (see Table 3). Meanwhile in China and India, two powerful software producing countries, the software growth is not much higher than the GDP growth (see Table 3). However, the share of software contributed to the GDP in Vietnam is very low compared with that of China and India. This shows that software does not play an important role in the national economy and it is still a very young infant industry despite the scale of targeted incentive policy measured.

In 2007, HCA (the Hochiminh Computer Association) reported that the share of IT services showed some noticeable figures. Following this data, the IT training received revenue of $15 million; digital content received $65 million, in which online game services contributed $13 million and value added services on mobile phones received $42 million, and online advertising on the Internet received $7 million in 2006 (HCA, 2007). The balance is shifting towards not only software, but also new industries such as the digital content industry.

Table 3. Software Industry's Comparison in Vietnam, China and India

Country	Software Revenue 2007 ($bill)	Software Revenue 2008 ($bill)	Software Growth Rate	GDP Growth	GDP in 2007 ($bill)	Software / GDP
Vietnam	0.498	0.67	35%	6.5%	70	0.71%
China	85	110	29%	9.3%	3280	2.59%
India	52	60	16%	7.9%	1100	4.73%

Source: Author combined from IMF, MIC Vietnam, MII China, NASSCOM India/

2.2. Hardware Industry Policy

The hardware sector also enjoys a high level of incentive support policies but it is not as high as that of the software industry. The hardware incentive policy does not have separate legal documents of its own since the beginning of 2000, although it has improved gradually in recent years with some key master plans and programs issued by the government. During this time, just for some special cases, the hardware firms have been able to get the same high incentive policy support as that of the software industry. For example, the hardware firms operating within high-tech zones or producing products which are on the priority list (colored televisions or computers, for example) were allowed by the government to enjoy the same level of incentive policy. As the statistics show in fact, software growth is higher than in the hardware industry in Vietnam (see Table 4, column 4). The heterogeneous incentive policy for hardware products and substantial requirements in the form of high technology and high initial capital investment which Vietnam lacked are factors that help to explain this relatively lower level of growth rate of the hardware industry compared to the software field.

Table 4. Growth of ICT Sub-sectors (in %)

Year	IT Industry	Software Growth	Hardware Growth	Digital Content	Telephone Subscribers	Internet Users
2002	-	-	-	-	28.17	30.00
2003	29.13	41.18	27.27		31.37	138.31
2004	13.41	41.67	08.57	-	39.80	104.81
2005	50.54	47.06	51.32	-	51.90	68.81
2006	24.29	44.00	20.00	333	78.54	37.09
2007	-	38.33	-	177	70.94	20.66
2008	21.62	34.54	15.58	50	75.22	17.59

Source: Author calculated from Source of MIC.

The IT industry growth in both hardware and software has a close link to the development of telephone and Internet services, because it creates a domestic market base for the industry. In the last decade Vietnam was one of the countries which had a higher growth of telephone subscriber and Internet users. Until December 2008, the total telephone subscribers in Vietnam reached 82 million. It is almost a rate of 1:1 among a population of 87 million. At the same time, the number of Internet users hit 20,834,401 (20 million). This growth creates a large market for IT firms to sell their products and services on the domestic market.

Table 4 shows the growth of the digital content industry accompanied by the growth of telephone and Internet users, which means domestic firms have captured most of the digital content domestic market. It is reasonable because these markets have a close link with their own countries' cultural environment while the foreign competitors face a harder challenge to compete with domestic companies. However, the fact that the growth of users both in telephone and Internet sectors are much higher than the growth of IT industry in general and hardware in particular, shows the fact that hardware firms have not captured well the domestic market and need to do much to get the expected result. In fact the high share of handsets, computers, especially laptops, which mostly include imported brand names such as Nokia, Samsung, Simen, Acer, IBM, Toshiba and others, means that the hardware market is still dominated by foreign companies. In other aspects the slow-down of Internet users' growth rate, along with the decreasing growth of the digital content industry, shows us the closed link between these two variables. The software industry also slowed down. The slowdown was accompanied by Internet users, while the growth of telephone subscribers remained stable with the hardware industry's development. This phenomenon is reasonable because the software industry usually has a close link with the Internet, while telecommunication services have a close link with hardware devices.

2.3. Electronics Industry

In Vietnam the electronics sector which is specialized for industrial purposes (for instance digital exchange in telecommunications) is also considered as one field that comprises the IT industry and some consumption products. The electronics sector was re-structured in 1994 just several years after the renovation process became reality in the 1990s. Before that time the electronics sectors were completely controlled by the state through the General Electronics Office belonging directly to the Prime Minister's office. However, the General Electronics Office was closed later in 1994. Before 1994, the electronics sector was seen as a low development and low productivity sector due to the weakness of the economic mechanisms.

Since reconstruction in 1994, the electronics sector has passed through 2 stages of development (Tran-Quang, 2008). The first stage is 1994–2000 with the main objective of providing consumer electronic products, such as television and radio, for the domestic market. The second stage has lasted from 2000 up to now with changes in the objectives of export orientation. In fact, it seems that the Vietnamese government looked into other successful cases in the electronics industry of neighboring countries, like Thailand and Malaysia before it decided to favor the electronics sector, but the period of time is different. Thailand and Malaysia focused on developing the electronics sector as early as the 1970s and then they benefitted from the wave of outsourcing electronic components from Japan which were considered to be low value-added by the Japanese corporations in the 1980s. Vietnam was a late-comer to this market when it joined it in the 1990s.

The fact that Vietnam tried to develop a sunset industry during the 1997 crisis period could make Vietnam face many more difficulties than usual. In fact the electronics industry was provided with some kind of protectionist policy, such as a high import tax barrier (although it has been lowered now due to AFTA, a free trade agreement among South East Asian countries), 0% import tax for equipment and production tools to produce electronic products domestically, 0-30% import tax for materials needed to be imported to serve domestic production. The corporate tax is as low as 0 – 15%, while in other sector it is as high as 28% (Tran-Quang, 2008).

With many efforts at progress in the electronics industry both in government and entrepreneurship, the electronics sector in Vietnam achieved some good results. The annual growth rate stands at 20-25%, with around 300 companies located in many countries. Notably 1/3 of them are foreign direct investment (FDI) companies which contribute much to the electronics sector. Within 10 years the total revenue from exports increased 10 times, by 1996 exports were $94 million and they reached $1.77 billion in 2006, $2.2 billion in 2007 and it is estimated that in 2008 the export revenue will be $2.5 billion. Although it has achieved a high total revenue, the electronic sectors reveals many inappropriate and weak points. The investment for RandD and the potential market is low, which makes Vietnamese companies dependent on the technology of foreign companies (Tran-Quang, 2008). Domestic firms are facing difficulties in competing with foreign famous brand products even just inside the internal Vietnamese market. Most consumers in Vietnam just look for an FDI brand name when they want to buy a new electronic product such as Samsung, LG, Sanyo, Sony or Panasonic. A survey carried out by VEIA (Vietnam Electronic Industry Association) of 64 companies shows that the companies which have the best incentive policies are not domestic companies as 70% of them are foreign companies (Tran-Quang, 2008). This survey also shows that most FDI companies in the electronics sector invested just 10 million dollars and most of this went to the assembly of simple components. The other point is the fact that whole FDI project in this sector is very short, just 10–15 years, which is a short period in the electronics field which needs a longer time to make long-term plan in producing expansion and technology transfer orientation.

In 2007, Vietnam became a member of WTO, so all the above tax preferential policy and other barriers will be gradually abandoned. The current situation has alarmed the government sufficiently for it to make domestic electronic firms stronger quickly. In the globalization era participation in the global value chain is the most important survival factor for any country instead of building its own industry sector alone. Thailand, Malaysia and other neighboring countries have transited to this direction already and Vietnam is not an exception to this trend in the globalization era.

3. The Relationship Between Industry and GDP Growth

In Vietnam government policy orientation is now moving toward the service sector and this is helping to increase the contributing share of this sector to GPD, while it is reducing the contributing share of the agricultural sector. Therefore, the share of the total industry sector to GDP is increasing over time (see Table 5, column 4). As a result, the share of the IT industry is also following this trend, accompanied by other industrial sectors which are following this direction by increasing their share of the GDP contribution annually (see Table 5, column 5).

Table 5. Share of Industry and IT industry in the GDP

Year	Total GDP (VND)	Total GDP (USD)	All Industry / GDP (%)	IT industry / GDP (%)
2002	535762	33.49	38	1.9
2003	613443	38.34	39	2.1
2004	715307	44.57	40	2.1
2005	839211	50.43	41	2.8
2006	974266	55.59	41	3.1
2007	1144015	61.38	41	6.1*
2008	1215287	75.95	44	5.9*

Source: Author calculated from GSO, MIC. 1$ =16000 VND.
Note: * means included household electronic appliances.

The contribution of the IT Industry to the Vietnamese GDP is increasing over time and now its share is around 6% of GDP including electronic appliances. In order to make a comparison we should look at the share of the IT industry in some famous developed countries 10 years ago. According to Graham et al. (2000), the contribution of the IT industry in the United States was 4.4% in 1997, France 3.5% in 1997, Germany 4.9% in 1990 and 3.8% in 1997, Canada 2.9% in both 1990 and 1997, and Italy 2.5% in 1997. Of course, the absolute revenue is not comparable with these very advanced countries, but these proportions of percentages show the same trends of the IT industry contribution in Vietnam. However, looking at neighboring countries in South East Asia, the share of the IT industry in GDP is much higher than in Vietnam, for instance in 1997 10% of GDP was accounted for by the IT industry in Thailand, and also, 31% in Malaysia (Graham et al., 2000). One of the reasons for the high share of the IT industry in Thailand or Malaysia is that they were front-runners in the first wave of the outsourcing of electronic products towards overseas countries by Japanese entrepreneurship in 1980s and achieved advantages of being the first-movers in South East Asia (see section 2.3).

Regarding growth the IT industry in Vietnam is on average 4-6 times higher than the average growth of GDP and 2 times higher than general industry (see table 6). This difference shows the importance of the IT industry as one of the locomotive sectors for promoting GDP growth in Vietnam.

Figure 2 below shows the instability of growth of the IT industry in general and the hardware sector in particular in Vietnam. The growth of GDP and other general industries are represented by a smoother and flatter line which describes the stable economic environment. Meanwhile, the highly fluctuating graph of the IT industry shows the unstable growth of the hardware sector.

Table 6. Industry and National Growth Rate Comparisons

Year	GDP Growth (%)	Industry Growth	IT Industry Growth	Software Growth	Hardware Growth
2002	7.08	14.80	-	-	-
2003	7.34	16.80	29.13	41.18	27.27
2004	7.79	16.60	13.41	41.67	08.57
2005	8.44	17.10	50.54	47.06	51.32
2006	8.23	17.00	24.29	44.00	20.00
2007	8.48	17.10	-	38.33	-
2008	6.23	14.60	21.62	34.54	15.58

Source: Author calculated from MIC, GSO.

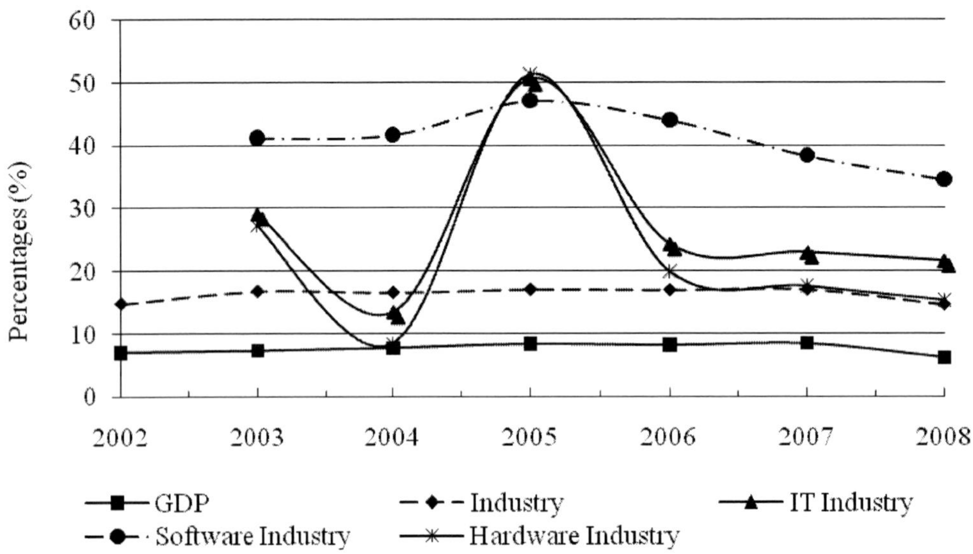

Figure 3. Growth Rate Comparison. Source: Author calculated from MIC, GSO.

But the software sector is still growing smoothly and it has shown stable growth for a long time. The peak of hardware growth happened in 2005 when the Intel Corporation decided to invest $1 billion in Vietnam by opening a new microchip testing factory in Hochiminh City.

Determinants of Industry Development

There are a number of determinants of the development of the IT industry in Vietnam, but among them 3 main factors have played a very important role. These are firm and market characteristics; human resources; and FDI inflow.

4.1. IT Firm and Market Characteristics

As explained previously in section 1, the Vietnamese government tends to promote privatization of several state-own enterprises and it encourages the private sector, so IT firms were not an exception. In fact, the IT industry has been privatized strongly since the last decade and the biggest IT Company now in Vietnam is the FPT Group which used to be state-owned enterprises under the Ministry of Science and Technology. Now FPT has become the strongest private IT firm in Vietnam.

Because the IT Industry in Vietnam was divided into two main fields, comprising the hardware and software industries, we will look at each of them respectively. In terms of the hardware industry, the engine for development fundamentally depended on FDI (Foreign Direct Investment) led by Japanese companies such as Canon, Fujitsu, Panasonic, Sony, Nidec and others.

Canon is the number one in terms of export revenue among hardware companies in Vietnam. The domestic companies also had significant achievements but they are less successful compared to FDI investor companies. Most domestic brand-name PC turnover was below $5 million; only two firms reached over $10 million. Growth of domestic firms such as FPT-Elead and CMS (local companies' main product is PC, notebook assembly) was 35.8% with turnover of $18.2 million whereas CMS stood at 49.5% with a turnover of $13.9 million in 2006.

However, the inadequate technology in domestic suppliers led to core components for assembling having to be imported from overseas.

As for the software industry, most of it consists of SME companies. There are only a few companies with more than 500 employees. A survey carried out by HCA in 2005 found that, in Hochiminh City, 82% of software companies have less than 50 employee, just 18% of them did have more than 50 employees. The biggest software company is FPT with total employees around 2,000 and total revenue in 2006 around $16 million. Other noticeable companies include TMA Solutions with 800 employees, Paragon Solutions Vietnam (PSV) with 600 employees, Silk Road with 420 employees, and Global Cyber Soft with 400 employees.

The successful Japanese market–orientation is significant. In 2008, according to JETRO, the Japanese IT firms consider Vietnam to be their third-best market after China and India for software outsourcing. Vietnam is now involved in almost 17% of Japanese firms' offshore outsourcing deals, estimated to be worth about 10-15 billion yen ($101-152 million) per year. Around 80 Vietnamese IT firms have been tied up with Japanese partners to provide software, but only a fourth of them get regular orders (Tran-Vu-Viet, 2008). Japanese IT is among the world's best, but it lacks young IT engineers since Japan has an aging population and Japanese firms have to pay high costs for programming at home. Therefore, they decided to turn to Asian countries like Vietnam and China where the cost of the labor force is just one third of that of Japan. The Vietnamese government soon recognized these opportunities after 2002 and the Ministry of Post and Telematics (now MIC) at that time acted tirelessly to pave the way for cooperation between Vietnamese and Japanese companies operating in the software sector.

4.2. IT Human Resource

The IT industry itself is in the high-tech sector which means firms need well-educated human resources to catch up with the rapid changes in technology. In software especially human resources play a very important role for success of any firm. The Law of IT, approved by the National Assembly in 2006, stated clearly the importance of IT human resources and the Ministry of Education and Training (MOET) granted certification to many IT Departments in Universities and opened several new colleges specified in IT education to provide good and large IT human resources. This policy has increased the number of universities where they educate IT engineers by almost double within 5 years (see Table 7).

Annually the number of graduates is around 10,000 but the quality of IT students is still not high and in some cases it is hard to meet the demands of IT firms. Despite the high requirements of universities for students to graduate, shown by the big gap between the input (newcomers) and output (graduated students) in recent years (see Figure 4), the CEOs of IT firms still complain about the quality of education at universities. This situation suggests that Vietnam still has a great deal of potential for developing further the IT industry, even though IT industry growth is now much higher than the average GDP and other industrial sectors' growth (see table 6). Improvement in the quality of education and products and services should a target for policies. Anyway, this weak point gives good potential room for government to enhance human resources to promote the IT industry. The Vietnamese government can focus on policy to improve the quality of the IT labor force to help in building up a better equipped industry for international competition.

Table 7. Graduates working in the IT sector

Major	IT, Informatics, Math			Electronic, Telecom		
Level	University	College	Vocational	University	College	Vocational
2002	55	80	33	20	6	-
2003	61	87	56	20	6	-
2004	74	107	97	22	6	-
2005	86	108	135	28	8	55
2006	93	125	187	32	15	67
2007	230 (total)		-	-	-	-

Source: MIC, MOET (Ministry of Education and Training).

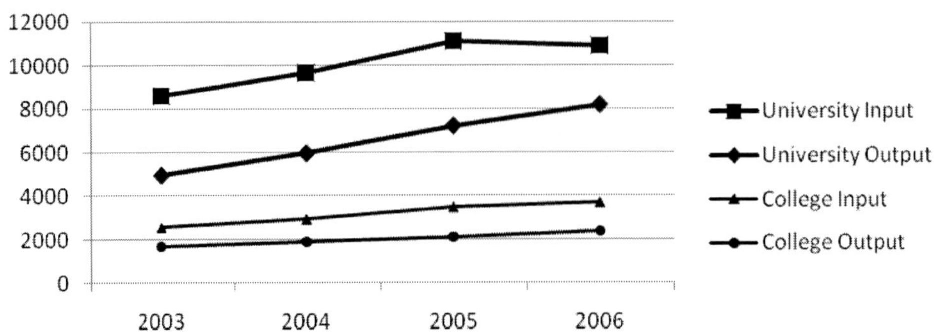

Figure 4. Gap between enrollment and graduation of IT Students.

4.3. FDI Inflow

Vietnam has been rising as a new star as one of the most attractive destinations for FDI inflow in Asia in recent years. The prominent advantages of Vietnam are the cheap labor force and large market due to its big population (87 million). Although there are some complaints about IT education and IT human resources quality, Vietnam still has a large number of highly skilled workers among the South East Asian countries. There are many foreign investors who praise Vietnamese labor for its very high quality and the low costs which have made Vietnam becoming a new attractive destination for FDI. Therefore, the inflow of FDI to Vietnam has been increasing rapidly in recent years with a record of $60 billion in 2008 (see Table 8, column 2, 3).

Table 8 shows that FDI capital is growing much faster than the growth rate of the IT industry. It seems that FDI inflow does not come into the IT sector, but this is not completely true. It is simply because the IT factories from FDI sources are still under construction, but in the future, the situation may change. In fact, the FDI share pours into real-estate and the steel-making industry has still the highest share in Vietnam. However, during the last few years, the Vietnamese government has actively attempted to attract high-tech FDI and persuade large multinational enterprises to open factories in Vietnam to get technological capability. As a result, in 2005 the Intel Corporation, the biggest microchip processor in the world, decided to invest $1 billion to open a testing factory in Hochiminh city, and now it is still under construction. In order to have such an achievement, the government made great efforts to persuade the president of Intel, Craig Barrette, to invest in Vietnam when he traveled to several countries to choose the most appropriate investment location. The Prime Minister himself met the president of Intel and talked with him about Vietnamese commitment. Finally, Vietnam was chosen and became a new point of the process in the production value chain of Intel in Intel's global value chain. At the same time other notable FDI projects, namely Samsung Electronics with its mobile phone factory project, and Hong Hai (from Taiwan) with a $5 billion project for a high-tech city in the North of Vietnam started in 2007.

Table 8. FDI Capital Inflow and IT Growth

Year	Total capital ($bill)	FDI Capital Growth (%)	IT Industry Growth (%)
2001	3142.8	-	-
2002	2998.8	-4.58	-
2003	3191.2	6.42	29.13
2004	4547.6	42.5	13.41
2005	6839.8	50.4	50.54
2006	12004.0	75.5	24.29
2007	21347.8	77.84	-
2008	60271.2	182.33	21.62

Source: Author calculated from Source of MII (Ministry of Planning and Investment).

In the software sector, Vietnam has emerged to become one of the top 10 favored countries for foreign partnerships in outsourcing software products (Kearney, 2009). In Asia outsourcing software development is the driving economic force of many emerging countries and India and China have already been recognized as the industry leaders and are very strong competitors for outsourcing software services. Despite their huge market share in offshore development, Vietnam is still quickly emerging as a software outsourcing destination with several specifications. In terms of outsourcing Vietnam is recognized as having lower costs compared with India and China. Compared to India developing software in Vietnam is between 1/3 and 1/7 times cheaper. Indian companies are entering the mature stage of the development cycle at a high level so costs are also much higher. This leads to a difference in costs between India and Vietnam and the gap will increase further over time. These cost advantages help Vietnam to be a cost effective development source for foreign companies. According to the forecast for 2010, Vietnam has a population of over 90 million people and over 60% of the population is under 30 years of age. The young generation is usually highly motivated by technological advancement and is helping Vietnam to become one of the highly globalised competitors in terms of software outsourcing (Gallaugher and Stoller, 2004).

For instance, GHP, German software companies located in Quang Trung Software Park in Vietnam is specializing in digitalizing data for broadcasting in Germany. Newspapers and magazines in Germany outsource their simple tasks, such as the web design of newspapers, the input of sport results, typing into digital files from raw materials, etc. to Vietnamese companies. In Vietnam, this kind of job costs only $150-200 per month, which is equivalent to only 1 day's pay in Germany but the quality is almost the same. The advantage for Vietnam is the time-zone difference between the two countries. Work is done in time in Vietnam and transferred to the German newspaper to be put on the paper printed the next day. A similar thing also happens between India and the United States' companies due to a favorable difference between the time-zones of the US and India.

For historical reasons many million Vietnamese American citizens now live in America. Many of them have succeeded in Silicon Valley and became important links between Vietnamese companies and US software companies. Some major companies such as TMA, Global Cyber Soft, and PSV have been founded and are headed, managed or occupied by major shareholders who are Vietnamese American citizens and these important figures help to bring outsourced job from the US to Vietnamese partners. In recent years, accompanied by the high growth rate of the economy, there are many Vietnamese people in the United States who want to return home for investment and most of them work in outsourcing areas for US giant companies.

The Japanese market orientation is also especially important to outsourcing to Vietnam. A similar culture plays an important role in the promotion of cooperation between businesses of the two countries. The hardware sector shows a lot of evidence that Japanese enterprises are moving some types of job to Vietnam. The Japanese Keiretsu, such as Sony, Fujitsu, Sumitomo and Hoya are opening their subsidiaries in Vietnam and these factories hire put lots of simple jobs to local companies. Hitachi is the main customer for outsourcing companies in the software sector for Vietnamese partners. Currently there are about 60 Vietnamese software companies doing outsourced jobs for the Japanese software market (Tran Vu-Viet, 2008) and Vietnam is now standing as number 3 among top favored countries for outsourcing by Japanese companies after India and China.

Concluding Remarks

Vietnam is basically a transition economy from a planned economy to a free market system and has made many achievements due to an open policy, international market penetration and the privatization of some SOEs which have contributed positively to IT industry development in Vietnam. The IT industry attained a higher growth rate than other industrial sectors and GDP, which shows the effectiveness of IT policy under specified industry promotion by incentive policy measures.

The quality and potential of its human resources need improving through an educational policy which may push the IT industry to grow at an even higher speed. The exploitation of special characteristics such as American Vietnamese citizens, its proximity to China or its closeness of culture with Japan may be among the key advantages for success in the case of Vietnam, and other developing countries may also have their own characteristics. The increasing inflow of FDI is not simply by country endowment, but is also a result of an active leadership which can attract high-tech multinational companies to transfer their technological capability to national firms. The policy implication also shares the view that the software industry, which is represented mostly by SME firms operating in the hardware sector, were better able to seize a larger share of the domestic market. However SMEs are facing difficulties in competing in the global market. Furthermore, the hardware industry, with its characteristic of being capital and technology intensive, seems to be dominated by FDI firms, but also the domestic market is dominated by foreign hardware brand names.

The lack of large scale enterprises (LSEs) in both the hardware and software sub-sectors in Vietnam caused weak competitiveness in the global market, which needed government support to remedy this weakness in the competitive globalization era. One of the good policy options for a developing country like Vietnam is to join the global value chain production of multi-national enterprises. The success in attracting the Intel Corporation to open a testing factory in Hochiminh City shows the advantages of the spillover effect which also made other high-tech companies follow Intel to set up production plants or become auxiliary component suppliers for Intel which as in the Vietnam case, had good policy implications for other developing countries.

References

Dang-Xuan T. (2008), Doanh nghiệp Nhà nước: Nền tảng hay bè mảng?, *The World and Vietnam Report*, http://www.tgvn.com.vn/printContent.aspx?ID=1143.

Gallaugher J. and Stoller G. (2004), Software Outsourcing in Vietnam: A Case Study of a Locally Operating Pioneer, *Journal on Information Systems in Developing Countries*, 17, 1, 1-18.

Graham, Vladimir, Pierre, Bénédicte and Masahiro (2000), OECD Information Technology Outlook 2000, http://www.oecd.org/dataoecd/30/56/1939833.pdf.

HCA (2006) Vietnam ICT Outlook 2006, *Vietnam Computer Electronics World Expo Conference*, Annually, Hochiminh City, Vietnam.

HCA (2007) Vietnam ICT Outlook 2007, *Vietnam Computer Electronics World Expo Conference*, Annually, Hochiminh City, Vietnam.

HCA (2008) Vietnam ICT Outlook 2008, *Vietnam Computer Electronics World Expo Conference*, Annually, Hochiminh City, Vietnam.

Kearney A.T. (2009), Global Services Location Index, *Published News from Ministry of Foreign Affair*, http://www.mofa.gov.vn/vi/nr040807104143 /nr040807105039 /ns090603095534.

Nguyen-Trong D. (2008), Vietnam IT Industry and the Orientation to the year 2010, *Global IT Policy and Technology Seoul Conference*, COEX, Seoul, Korea.

Okimoto D. I. (1989), *Between MITI and the Market: Japanese Industrial Policy for High Technology*, Stanford, California: Stanford University Press.

Tran-Quang H. (2008), Ưu đãi đầu tư cho công nghiệp điện tử: Những cái được và... mất!, http://www.vnmedia.vn/newsdetail.asp?NewsId=150573andCatid=35.

Tran-Vu-Viet A. (2008), Vietnam Software Industry and Potential Collaboration with Korean Companies on Outsourcing, *Global IT Policy and Technology Seoul Conference*, COEX, Seoul, Korea.

Website, GSO, General Statistics Office of Vietnam, www.gso.gov.vn.

In: Information and Communication Technologies... ISBN 978-1-60876-671-0
Ed: Almas Heshmati and Sun Peng

Chapter 3

STATE OF CYBERSECURITY AND THE ROADMAP TO A SECURE CYBER COMMUNITY IN CAMBODIA

Sopheak Cheang*

Cambodia Computer Emergency Response Team (CamCERT), NiDA, Office of the Council of Ministers and Seoul National University

ABSTRACT

This paper presents background information and the progress of the government effort on Cyber Security in Cambodia. Firstly, this study establishes a framework to assess the current effort of Cambodian government on cyber security. Secondly, the results of the assessment are used to develop policy implications, serving as a roadmap to secure a national online community. Furthermore, this paper discusses the process to establish a management and technical incident response capability of the national Computer Emergency Response Team to contain on-going cyber incidents.

Keywords: Cyber Security, Computer Emergency Response Team, Computer Security Incident Response Team, Cambodia, CamCERT

1. INTRODUCTION

Since the beginning of the new millennium, Cambodia has achieved considerable progress in promoting the use of ICT to improve the administration systems and services for her citizens and entrepreneurs. The most remarkable ICT project was the ambitious introduction of e-Government in 2002, which comprised of several programs, including the Government Administration Information System (GAIS) and the other cyber system for financial, banking, and customs (Phu, 2003). This proved that ICT has played more

* E-mail: sopheak@temep.snu.ac.kr

influential roles in the key sectors, and it provided the government with not only an effective administration system but also a better image.

Understanding this significance, government, as policymaker, has adopted a very friendly policy toward the development of information and communication technology (ICT) services in order to attract more investment and bring more competition (NiDA, 2003). The fruitful outcomes of this policy can be seen in price reductions, along with the expansion of the service to rural areas, and by transferring new technology. However, it seems that the dark side of this technology has been ignored by the government, the private sector, as well as citizens.

Cyber crimes and attacks are not new in this country, but they have mostly gone unnoticed and unpunished. There have been several reports on malicious viruses, and scam and fraud mail from Internet users, and also the efforts of ambitious local hackers, showing their hacking strength (Mom, 2008). Internet cafés have been a major source of virus spread, due to their limited cybersecurity measures. Hence, the Internet users, the majority of whom have considered cyber café as their major place for net surfing, have been at risk of virus infection themselves should they plug their USB flash drives into those computers.

The most ruthless cyber attack ever reported in Cambodia was the web hacking and defacement of the government websites. Recently, the website of the Ministry of Environment (www.moe.gov.kh) has been hacked by a team from Iran called the "Black Hats Team". This attack has tarnished the government image in the world cyber community. Other types of cyber crime, i.e., SQL injection and Distributed Denial of Service (DDoS) attack, have also targeted other ministries and government agency websites several times (Ou, 2008).

However, there have been no official reports of cyber attacks that target private companies offering online services, such as the Banks and Telecommunication Operators. It might be because private companies have a better equipped infrastructure to prevent cyber crimes. Most of the Internet Service Providers (ISP) have enough equipment, applications, and technicians to monitor network traffic, filter spam and prevent some malicious actions in cyberspace (Keuk, 2008).

The fact that most victims of cyber incidents were reluctant to report cases might be due to the perception that the impact of the incidents was not yet severe, and because of the absence of legal procedures and the limited capability of their enforcement. Though the issues have not been prioritized, the government considers that they should be contained. Consequently, a national working group on Information Security was founded in 2004 and later, it was converted into Cambodia's Computer Emergency Response Team (CamCERT) in 2007 (Council of Ministers, 2004), (Council of Ministers, 2007). However, since its formation, CamCERT has not yet worked up to its capacity as a national agency with the capability to stand against the cyber threat as the national Computer Emergency Response Team (CERT) in other countries.

As many Cambodians start to connect to the outside world, the risk of exposing their personal information and privacy to unintentional targets is getting higher. Though the cyber incidents have not been reported as having caused major damage financially to individual institutions or the Critical Infrastructure and Critical Information Infrastructure, prevention measures at national level should be established to avoid a future disaster, which is the motivation of this study.

This paper presents the status and the assessment of Cambodia's current efforts on cybersecurity in order to construct a strategic national framework to organize national efforts to combat the cyber threat. This framework could assist Cambodian policymakers to establish a roadmap to achieve its goal of a more secure Cambodian cyberspace. The paper is organized into five sections beginning with an introduction that covers the background of Internet security in Cambodia. Section 2 elaborates the vulnerabilities of the cyber threat and the motivation for establishing a counter-mechanism. Section 3 outlines the methodology of establishing a framework to assess the current status and the national efforts of cybersecurity. Section 4 provides the assessment, results and discussion on the status of cybersecurity in Cambodia, policy implications, and practical steps required to build the incident response capabilities of the national CERT are discussed, and section 5 concludes the paper.

2. Cyber Threats and The need for Counter Efforts

"Cybersecurity" has become a famous term since it was popularized by the International Telecommunications Union (ITU) as "the prevention of damage to, unauthorized use of, exploitation of, and—if needed—the restoration of electronic information and communication systems, and the information they contain, in order to strengthen the confidentiality, integrity and availability of these systems" (ITU-D, 2008). Due to its undeniable role in establishing trust and the safety of online communications, cybersecurity has become a vital part in the daily operation of each organization.

Pishva et al. (2007) supported this statement by pointing out that should the organizations have no proper Information Security Management System, they could become victims of malicious attacks, unauthorized access, and computer spywares and viruses. It would result in financial or credibility losses to the organizations. The British North American Committee (2007) estimated the cost of damage caused by misuse and viruses of global businesses between US$169 billion and US$204 billion in 2004, and the trend is rising sharply. The costs associated with spam in the United States, United Kingdom, and Canada in 2005 amounted to US$17 billion, US$2.5 billion, and US$1.6 billion, respectively. The damage can be caused by various forms of cyber attacks.

Kshetri (2005) classified Cyber attacks into two types: targeted and opportunistic attacks. In targeted attacks, specific tools are used against specific cyber targets. Opportunistic attacks, on the other hand, entail releasing worms and viruses that spread indiscriminately across the Internet. At this point, it must be emphasized that targeted attacks are more dangerous than opportunistic attacks and many of them have bigger financial ramifications.

Hellstrom (2007) noticed that for the public sectors, cyber crime appears in the form of hacking into government systems especially the Critical Information Infrastructure (CII) by stealing or destroying all the information or taking down the government websites by using a technique called Distributed-Denial of Service (DDoS) attack. The Critical Infrastructure, defined by ITU, is a composition of physical and virtual elements of national infrastructure, while CII is the service of providing ICT to the national infrastructure (ITU-D, 2008). CII and CI of the United States is the main target of cyber terrorism which can have serious consequences such as disrupting critical operations, causing loss of revenue and intellectual property, or loss of life (United Nations General Assembly, 2002).

Due to the possible grave damage caused by cyber crimes, cybersecurity has caught the attention of the world communities, both governmental and non-governmental institutions, and the need to introduce several counter measures (ITU-D, 2008), (United Nations General Assembly, 2002), (White House, 2003). In the United States, the National Strategy to Secure Cyberspace outlines the roles and missions of federal agencies to minimize disruption to critical information infrastructures and thereby protect the people, the economy, the essential human and government services, and the national security of the United States (White House, 2003). This policy, a model of cybersecurity policy in many countries, specified the need for an effective National Computer Security Incident Response Team (CSIRT) or Computer Emergency Response Team (CERT) capability and provided the strategic points of Public-Private-Partnership to secure cyber communities.

Historically the Computer Emergency Response Team and Coordination Center (CERT/CC) was formed by the Defense Advanced Research Project Agency of the United States at the Carnegie Mellon University in 1988 to serve as a single point of contact to provide a response to computer security incidents on the Internet, which is the first model of a CSIRT (West-Brown et al., 2003).

3. Methodology: Assessment Framework

This paper designs a framework to assess the effort of the government agencies to combat cyber incidents. The assessment is of the "on-going work" of the government, so that the unfulfilled or "left-over" tasks can be identified with policy implications based on the results of assessment.

Several studies (Grønlund, 2002), (Lee and Anderson, 2008), (World Bank, 2004) have outlined the necessity for evaluation of the government or public sector performance before the national policy or development framework can be formulated. The assessment or evaluation will provide not only in-depth information on the public sector performance, but also the "hole" or "shortage" in the government effort.

In the studies of Grønlund (2002), Gumansingh (2003), and the Pacific Council on International Policy (2002) evaluating e-Government progress, suggested that an assessment framework should be based on the following factors or components, including political will and information policy, Government Commitment, Relevant Legislation/Regulations/ Policies, Human Resource Development, Service Provision, Scope of Public-Private-Citizen Partnership and Efficiency and Efficacy of the system.

The most comprehensive and exclusive working paper on cybersecurity management is the ITU's framework on "A management framework for organizing national cybersecurity efforts" (ITU-D, 2008). It was the result of long term hard work of experienced cybersecurity experts of ITU and was undertaken to assist the member states in combating the cyber threat. Some of the key elements and tasks of ITU's framework were taken as assessment criteria that are summarized in Table.1.

The prime motivation for selecting this framework is the technical and practical merits of the key components that fulfill the three criteria (Riggins, 1999) - efficiency, effectiveness, and strategic benefits - which are the important factors in the design of an assessment framework. Secondly, ITU's framework, in addition to its dedication to cybersecurity, identified key components that have been used as factors for assessment in several studies in a similar area (Grønlund, 2002), (Gumansingh, 2003), (Pacific Council on International Policy, 2002).

Table 1. Criteria for assessment of national efforts in Cybersecurity

Elements	Tasks
1. Building a National Cybersecurity Strategy	*.Persuading top leadership* *.Forming a National Working Group*
2. Establishing a Government-Industry Partnership	*.Building trust between Government and industry* *.Assigning the scope/elements of cooperation*
3. Establishing a National Incident Management Capability	*.Improving Capabilities of national CSIRT in warning, defending, and coordinating with international governments and agencies against cyber attacks.*
4. Deterring Cybercrime	*.Establishing cyber law, regulations and law enforcement agencies*
5. Promoting a Culture of Cybersecurity	*.National awareness of Cybersecurity* *.Promoting public online services such as e-Government*

First element of the framework, a comprehensive *National Cybersecurity Strategy*, that includes a broad review of the adequacy of the current national practices, and a consideration of the role of all stakeholders, including governments, the private sector, and non-governmental organization, should be formed to assess the current state of the cyber threat and crimes and develop the program priorities. To achieve this goal, the government leaders should be persuaded to understand the importance of national action to combat the cyber threat. As stressed by Gumansingh (2003) and the Pacific Council on International Policy (2002), political will, policy, strategy, and government commitment are the key factors for evaluation. Lee and Anderson (2008) pointed out that the shortage of a national policy means a shortage of a unified plan of action and it could bring the development to nothing.

Another element of this framework is the *Government and Industry Partnership* that requires three elements, including a clear value proposition, clearly delineated roles and trust. Collaboration should be based on the mutual benefit that the government and industry sector could gain and the role that the government or the industry sector should play. Gumansingh (2003), the Pacific Council on International Policy, (2002), and the United Nations General Assembly (2002) also valued this partnership because, if the trust and scope of collaboration could be well-established, it would ensure financial and political support from industry to government.

Probably the most vital and urgent element of the framework is to establish a *National Incident Management Capability*. In this sense, a national institution should be created to serve as a focal point for securing cyberspace and the protection of CI and CII. A national CSIRT/CERT must be equipped with the capability for three vital tasks, including defending and responding to cyber attacks, coordinating government agencies and civilians on cyber incidents, and the cooperation and point of contact between government agencies, industry and international partners. Killcrece (2004) and West-Brown et al. (2003) compared the vital roles of an effective of national CSIRT/CERT, to the "fire frigate" and "cyber incident response of last resort". However, cybersecurity would never be prevented if the criminals were left unaffected. It is required that every nation enact a comprehensive set of laws on cybersecurity to *Deter Cybercrimes*. The existence of relevant law and regulations can be explained as a major form of progress of the government in the prevention of cyber crimes (World Bank, 2004). The last integral element is making sure that everyone involved in cyber activities understands the risk of cyber vulnerability and takes appropriate action to prevent crimes from happening. Thus, the government must take a leadership role in bringing about a *Culture of Cybersecurity* and in supporting the efforts of other participants. The Organisation for Economic Co-operation and Development (OECD) study suggested that the key driver of a culture of cybersecurity at the national level is e-Government applications and services, and the protection of national CI and CII (ITU-D, 2008). It is a huge benefit for the government to implement e-Government services and applications to improve their internal operations and provide better services to the private sector and to citizens. As the citizen and private sector enjoy the services they will be more aware of cybersecurity issues and the way to deal with them.

4. Assessing Cambodia's Efforts on Cybersecurity and Policy Implications

Based on the assessment framework, it can be established that Cambodia has accomplished or is in an advantageous position for the implementation of some of the key elements including:

1) *1)Promoting Cybersecurity Culture:* Since the launch of the e-Government service and its application, government has set up several awareness seminars to provide training for civil servants and citizens in the basic knowledge of online services and transactions (Phu, 2003). These actions supported the argument of ITU's framework that cybersecurity culture could be effectively spread to the citizen and industry through e-Government services and applications.
2) *Establishing a national CSIRT:* The formation of a national working group on information security in 2004 was later converted into CamCERT in 2007. Handling Information Security is an important step towards the establishment of a national cybersecurity mechanism (Council of Ministers, 2007).
3) *Attracting the top leaders:* The chairmanship of the Prime Minister over the National Information Communication Technology Development Authority (NiDA, 2003) has implied that many of the top leaders could be easily persuaded. In the Cambodian context the support of the top leaders could easily bring the government agencies to work together and solve the differences among the policymakers. This support also provides another strong voice for promoting collaboration between public and private partnership.

As expected, the result showed that the government's efforts in cybersecurity have not been effective enough to combat the cyber threat, because there are several tasks that have been left behind. These "left over" tasks can be identified as *(1) a detailed national cybersecurity strategy, law and policy; (2) the scope of collaboration and trust between public and industry; (3) sources of financial support; (4) promoting a cybersecurity culture nationwide, and the most important and urgent task, (5) building the cyber incident response capability of CamCERT.*

These incomplete tasks are used as the basis to design a national development framework. Figure.1 presents an overview of the national framework toward cybersecurity that requires the participation of all individuals in society.

In the national cybersecurity framework, the first task is to define which of the government agencies should be given a leading role in designing and improving the cybersecurity policy. In Cambodia, there are two agencies dealing with the ICT sector: the Ministry of Posts and Telecommunications of Cambodia (MPTC) and the NiDA. MPTC is the regulator and policymaker of ICT industry. While working on drafting the Telecom Act, the ministry is responsible for licensing all the ICT businesses and solving the conflict of interest among the telecom operators (Moa, 2006).

For technical and strategic benefit, it is recommended that NiDA should take the leading role in national cybersecurity because of the characteristic of NiDA as a national promoter of ICT development, and having a board that comprised of senior officers from various ministries. These characteristics make it more convenient for NiDA to lead, coordinate, or call for the participation of interested government agencies of and other stakeholders. Moreover, the bureaucracy of NiDA over CamCERT has a technical advantage in drafting national cybersecurity strategy and policy.

A precise cybersecurity policy and strategy is required as a basic component of the national framework. It requires participation from various stakeholders such as ministries, law enforcement agencies, lawmakers, industry, academics and, to some extent, citizens, to assess what are the imminent vulnerabilities of the cyber community and what action should be prioritized.

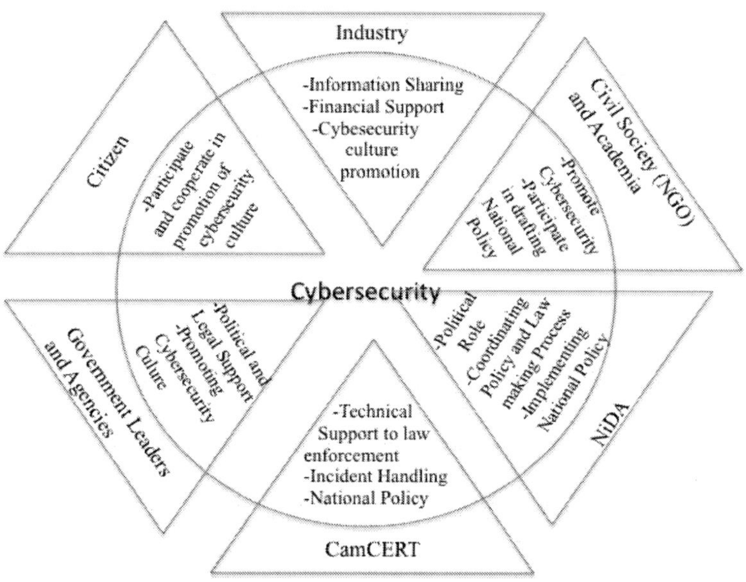

Figure 1. National framework for establishing cybersecurity.

Again, this strategic plan would have more weight, should there be strong support from the top leaders. Their support would also give another push for the promotion of cybersecurity culture to both the public and private sectors. Another integral part of this national framework is cyber law and regulations, which should be done in respect to the existing legal procedures and regulations in order to avoid conflict.

Nevertheless, only government's effort is not enough, because cybersecurity is not an individual but a nationwide issue. In a developing country, there is no doubt that the private sector can have the ability to handle the issue better than the public sector, due to its technical, financial, and infrastructure superiority. However, it does not posse the legal power to prosecute criminals or defining their misconduct. These mutual benefits motivate the government and the private sector to establish a partnership. In this partnership, private companies need to cooperate with government as a complementary role in information sharing and financial support. As the governing body, the government can take the leadership role and offer coordination and legal support.

In that case, trust is the key to this collaboration, because all the private sector's information related to CII and CI will be shared with the government. Therefore, it is suggested that both government and industry must show their confidence in handling the issues according to the regulations and memorandum of understanding. NiDA should play an active role in this process in terms of coordinating, drafting the national cybersecurity policy and strategy, and managing financial support. CamCERT should support NiDA on technical aspects of the draft and participate actively in every meeting and discussion.

International assistance could be another source of technical and financial support. MPTC should play an active role in calling for assistance from various sources such as the ITU, World Bank, or private companies, due to its closed cooperation with those sources. Civil society (Non Governmental Organizations) and academia could assist in promoting the cybersecurity culture by conducting a seminar or awareness program to provide basic knowledge on cybersecurity to citizens.

While dealing with the policy issues, government must improve the efficiency of CamCERT by building its cyber incident response capability both in the management and technical perspectives. The Incident Response Capability of a National CERT is an urgent task that needs to be prioritized.

However, since its formation, CamCERT has had very limited strength to work in its capacity as a national CERT/CSIRT. In other words, it possesses no technical strength even at the basic level to watch, warn, and recover the damage caused by cyber incidents. A limited human resource capacity and a small budget have been identified as the main constraints (Ou, 2008). The current status of CamCERT can be compared to a house that is short of furniture, electricity, running water, and food.

Killcrece (2004) designed a framework called *"Steps for Creating National CSIRTs"* to help the national CERT/CSIRTs in establishing an incident response capability. His five-step model is represented in Figure 2 and the detailed analysis of his step for CamCERT was conducted by Cheang and Sang (2009).

The first step concentrates on announcing a CamCERT constituency and defining the cybersecurity stakeholders, CI and CII, and laws/regulations that needed to be changed. The second step focuses on finding the sources of finance and designing the organizational structure. To ensure long term operation, CamCERT, even in its capacity as a government agency should not rely solely on a government budget, it should seek funding from other sources to cover its operation costs through an appropriate service charge to its subscribers for alerts, advice, training, and security assurance services.

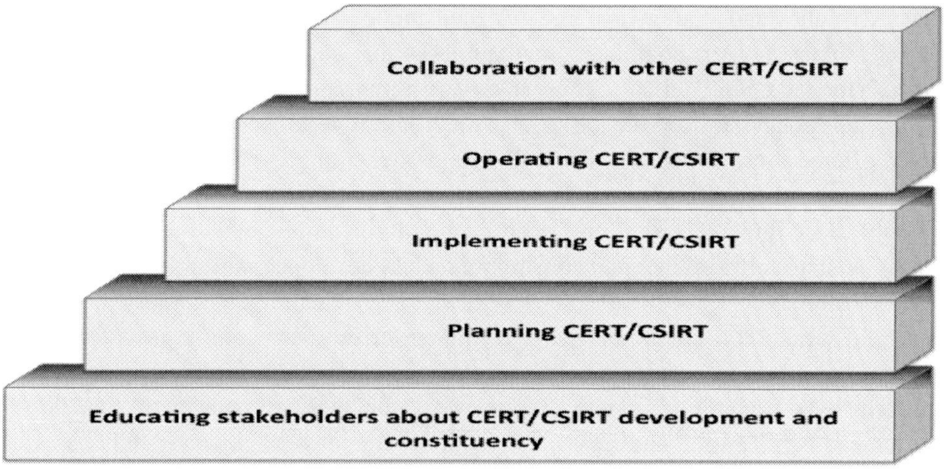

Figure 2. Killscrece's model to establish an incident response capability of a national CERT.

Moreover, an effective organization structure is the most important factor for ensuring the efficiency of an organization operation. Hence, CamCERT should be divided into four specific units that can operate with specific functions (Cheang and Sang, 2009). In addition to its incident response management capability, CamCERT has to improve its technical strength. Penedo (2006), West-Brown et al. (2003) outlined important factors that can improve the technical strength of national CERTs, and the details of a technical infrastructure that CamCERT should take into consideration.

The third step focuses on implementing the second stage plan, developing the operational and internal policy and procedures, and recruiting and training staff. By law, CamCERT will serve not only as the national CERT, but also as the national working group to handle the national information security affair, including strategy and policy (Council of Ministers, 2007). Hence, CamCERT should also recruit professional policy staff, due to its future capacity as cybersecurity policymaker and regulator.

The core task in the fourth step involves the development and implementation of a mechanism to evaluate the effectiveness of its operation. Should it complete the four steps successfully, CamCERT would have enough capacity to operate as a professional CERT/CSIRT. In the last stage, CamCERT should be able to participate in combating cyber incidents on the international stage by establishing cooperation with other CERTs/CSIRTs, and participating in international Cybersecurity agencies.

Conclusion

The progress of government efforts and the security status of the Internet community in Cambodia have been presented and analyzed. Results of the assessment show the tasks that the governing body has not achieved in order to catch up other countries in fighting the cyber threat. Hence, a unified national development framework is needed. This policy framework must be founded upon the participation of and collaboration between government agencies, industry, civil society, academia, citizens, and international partners, so that it can serve the best interests of not only individuals but society as a whole. While a bold national cybersecurity policy and strategy is being designed, an operational agency is also needed.

CamCERT has not yet completed strategic tasks that could give them the capacity of a functional national CSIRT/CERT. Thus, it is very important and urgent for CamCERT to review its actions and follow the tasks that they have overlooked. NiDA and CamCERT should be offered a crucial role in drafting and implementing cybersecurity policy with no need to create another agency to handle that issue. Having multiple agencies to handle one issue would cause the administration system to be more complicated and consume more of the budget, which is always the main constraint in a less developed nation like Cambodia.

In conclusion, before a national framework can be designed, it is necessary to identify the strengths and weaknesses of the current government efforts. This study provides first hand information and a broad overview of the progress of the Cambodian government's efforts in cybersecurity, by designing a simple framework for the assessment, in which policy implication can be identified and served as a national framework. However, this paper could not investigate the readiness of cybersecurity and the effectiveness or efficiency of government policy by using more sophisticated methodologies due to the shortage of data. These issues, including the identification of cybersecurity indicators and the design and computation of a cybersecurity readiness index, are the subjects of future study.

REFERENCES

British-North American Committee (2007), Cyber Attacks: A risk management Primer for CEOs and Directors.

Cheang, S., Sang, S. (2009), Establishing Cambodia's National Cybersecurity Incident Response Mechanism: Building the Cybersecurity Incident Response Capability of CamCERT, *International Conference on e-Commerce, e-Administration, e-Society, and e-Education (e-Case), Singapore.*

Council of Ministers (2004), Ministerial Declaration on Establishing National Working Group on Information Security, *Office of the Council of Ministers of Cambodia.*

Council of Ministers (2007), Ministerial Declaration on Establishing Cambodia Emergency Response Team, *Office of the Council of Ministers of Cambodia.*

Grønlund, A. (2002), Electronic Government - Design,. Applications and Management, *Hershey (PA): Idea Group Publishing, 2002, pp. 61-77.*

Gumansingh, J. (2003), Assessing the Progress Towards E Government: The Bahamas, Barbados, Guyana, Jamaica, Suriname and Trinidad and Tobago, *On Developmental Assignment RE3/OD6, Inter-American Development Bank.*

Hellstrom, T. (2007), Critical Infrastructure and Systematic Vulnerability: Toward a planning framework, *Safety Science, Vol. 45, No.3, 415-443.*

ITU-D (2008), Report on best practices for a national approach to cybersecurity: A management framework for organizing national cybersecurity efforts. *Study group Q.22/1, ITU-D secretariat draft.*

Keuk, M. (2008), Public Private Partnership in Information Security, *Global IT Policy and Technology Conference, Seoul, Republic of Korea.*

Killcrece, G. (2004), Steps for Creating National CSIRTs, *Carnegie Mellon Software Engineering Institute, Pittsburg, PA, USA.*

Kshetri, N. (2005), Pattern of global cyber war and crime: A conceptual framework, *Journal of International Management, Vol. 11, No. 4, December 2005.*

Lee, J.Y., Anderson, C. (2008), Policy Analysis, *Choon Hwan Lim Daeyoung Moonhwasa Publishing Co., ISBN 978-89-7644 287-1, Seoul, Republic of Korea.*

Mom, K. (2008), Cambodian virus maker fails to boot infamous rep, *Phnom Penh Post Newspaper, Phnom Penh, Cambodia.*

Moa, C. (2006), Internet Governance, *13th sub-regional telecommunication meeting for Cambodia, Laos P.D.R, and Myanmar, Yangon, Myanmar.*

National Information Communication Technology Development Authority (NiDA) (2003), Draft on National ICT policy.

Ou P. (2008), PPP on Information Security Initiative in Cambodia: Issues and Challenge, *Global IT Policy and Technology Conference, Seoul, Republic of Korea, September 2008.*

Pacific Council on International Policy (2002), Roadmap for e-government in the developing world, *Working Group on e-Government in the Developing World.*

Penedo, D. (2006), Technical Infrastructure of a CSIRT, *proceeding of International Conference on Internet Surveillance and Protection, ICISP '06.*

Phu, L. (2003), Cambodia: Road to e-Government, *National Information Communication Technology Development Authority, Cambodia.*

Pishva, D., Kitamura, N., Tsugawa, S., Takeda, K. (2007), An Initiative to Improve the State of Information Security at Local Governments in Japan, *Proceedings of 2007 41st Annual IEEE International Carnahan Conference on Security Technology, USA.*

Riggins, F.J. (1999), Riggins, F.J. A Framework for identifying Web-based electronic Commerce opportunities. *Journal of Organizational Computing and Electronic Commerce, Vol. 9, No. 4, 297–330.*

United Nation General Assembly (2002), Creation of a Global Culture of Cybersecurity, *UNGA resolution 57/239, New York, USA.*

West-Brown, M., Stikvoort, D., Kossakowski, K., Killcrece, G., Ruefle, R., Zajicek, M. (2003), Handbook for Computer Security Incident Response Teams (CSIRTs), *Carnegie Mellon Software Engineering Institute, Pittsburg, PA, USA. 2nd Edition, April, 2003.*

White House (2003), The National Strategy to Secure Cyberspace: Cyber Threats and Vulnerabilities, *Global Issues, United States of America.*

World Bank (2004), Assessing country readiness for results-based monitoring and evaluation systems, *Prime Note, Public Sector.*

In: Information and Communication Technologies… ISBN 978-1-60876-671-0
Ed: Almas Heshmati and Sun Peng

Chapter 4

HARNESSING ICTs FOR THE COMPETITIVENESS OF SMEs IN NEPAL: PROSPECTS AND CHALLENGES

Shisir P. Manandhar*
Kathmandu Metropolitan City, Nepal and
Seoul National University

ABSTRACT

Technology plays an increasingly important role in development, be it economic or social. In the prevailing world economic order the pervasive use of technologies has brought countries like Nepal to the crossroads between traditional approaches and a paradigm shift towards sustainable development by capitalizing innovations in information and communication technologies (ICT), particularly the Internet. It is imperative for Nepal to adopt an information technology-friendly business environment so that it can further boost domestic and international trade regime in the wake of its paramount willingness to be a competitive newest republic in the globe. This calls for coordinated efforts from both public and private sectors aimed at promoting e-commerce in Nepal. The contribution of small and medium-sized enterprises (SMEs) to the overall economic growth and the GDP is highly significant in Nepal, where SMEs constitute almost all establishments covered by censuses and contributes 63% of the value-added segment. SMEs are the major source of income, a breeding ground for entrepreneurs and a creator of jobs. Such SMEs' efficiency can be enhanced by ICTs which also reduce costs and broaden market reach, both locally and globally. Unfortunately, many such factors discourage SMEs from fully realizing the benefits of ICTs, including a lack of knowledge, resources and trust. This paper attempts to highlight how ICTs can enhance the export competitiveness of SMEs in Nepal, and thereby the prospects and challenges with policy implications in the changed context of building a 'new' Nepal.

Keywords: SMEs, ICT, e-commerce, e-business, competitiveness, knowledge economy, value chain, partnership.

* E-mail: spmanandhar@hotmail.com

1. INTRODUCTION

Nepal, situated between two economic powers, India and China, is one of the least developed countries in the world. It is a landlocked country with a diverse topography located on the southern slopes of the Himalayan range. The population of the country is 26.4 million[1] which is growing at a rate of 2.2% per annum. Its economy remains mostly traditional, underdeveloped and backward, largely dependent on agriculture which contributes 40.1% to GDP, while the manufacturing sector contributes about 10.0% to the Gross Domestic Product (GDP) of which SMEs contribute around 9.3%.[2] The GDP per capita of Nepal reached US$ 386 in 2007[3]. Nepal became the 147th member of World Trade Organization (WTO), being the first least developed country to complete the accession procedure of the organization (Paudel, 2006).

Given the lack of effective mechanisms for favorable enterprise development environment, a huge number of entrepreneurs have informal micro and small enterprises (SMEs).

The majority of them are of survival nature. A very few enterprises are successful in progressing to formal medium-sized or large enterprises. Large enterprises, on the other hand, are typically constrained by a small domestic market and high operating costs and are characterized by a chronic underutilization of capacity (UNCTAD, 2001).

Business development services are needed to transform those with potential into dynamic growth-oriented enterprises (Nepal and Karki, 2004). The eighth five-year plan (1992-1997) of Nepal aimed at promoting SMEs in order to substitute imports and improve them using locally available resources emphasizing the role of the private sector in industrialization[4]. However, a weak institutional base and the lack of a favorable environment made the efforts in planning not up to the mark despite some remarkable limited changes in technological advances in the enterprises through private sector boost up.

In the context of globalization coupled with an information technology boom, Nepal has also adopted an economic liberalization policy, resulting from the accession to WTO membership.

This has brought both prospects and challenges as Nepal needs to compete in the world market and to focus on the priorities appropriate to a less developed country. Technology, on the other hand, continues to revolutionize the industrial sector. Widespread use of ICT, particularly the Internet, has brought dynamism with both prospects and challenges for a country like Nepal. These technologies are increasingly changing the way business is performed, thus, signaling a fundamental paradigm shift in international trade and commerce (Bhattarai, 2000).

Figures indicate that private businesses, banks and financial institutions, Non-Governmental Organizations (NGOs), INGOs and international agencies operating within Nepal are on the forefront of using information and communication technology (ICT) resources compared to the government and small business sector.

---

[1] 2007 Projection with 23.15 million in 2001(Central Bureau of Statistics, Nepal)

[2] 2001 data in 'Promoting Business and Technology Incubation for Improved Competitiveness of Small and Medium-sized Industries through Application of Modern and Efficient Technologies in Nepal' pp. 289

[3] Ministry of Finance (2007) Nepal, Economic Survey

[4] http://www.npc.gov.np/

It is imperative on the part of the government to implement e-governance in its mechanism to foster transparency, rule of law, accountability and facilitate an ICT-induced business environment to SMEs and large enterprises, the backbone of the industrial base of the country. Nepal is expected to have peace, stability and a favorable climate for economic development as the new government has been in place declaring the newest republic after the election of the constitutional assembly which took place in May 2008.

In the prevailing world economic order, the pervasive use of technologies has brought countries like Nepal to the crossroads between traditional approaches and a paradigm shift towards sustainable development by capitalizing innovations in ICTs, particularly the Internet and its derivative, e-commerce (Bhattarai, 2000). A steady and continuous development in ICT use can be observed in Nepal, as a result of which many companies have been in the information technology (IT) outsourcing business, SMEs, particularly in the service sector, have been deploying ICT to the largest extent possible in terms of their capabilities, and more training and academic institutions have been in services. However, the concentration is in urban areas, depriving the majority of population who are out of reach of such technology and are away from reaping what the 'knowledge economy' has to offer.

Given this context, the paper develops an analytical framework that centers on the need of ICT-enabled SMEs for the economic development of a country and also explains how ICT adoption can bring competitiveness in SMEs. The framework has five distinct models: reinforcing dynamics and system dynamics view of firm response to competitive pressures (Kotelnikov, 2007), Porter's value chain proposition, Bass' diffusion model and Roger's innovation adoption curve. The argument is that as economies around the world, particularly the economies of neighboring countries India and China, continue to be driven by knowledge-based technologies, it is imperative for Nepal to create an enabling environment to benefit from competitive advantage offered by ICT in promoting export competitiveness and providing domestic demands for the substitution of increasing import trends.

The primary contribution of the paper is to shed light on the issues by proposing policy recommendations for smooth and efficient ICT-enabled cottage, small and medium enterprises.

The rest of the paper is structured as follows. The next section describes briefly the features of SMEs and their Nepalese context and is followed by the presentation of a basic analytical framework on how SMEs work to enhance national competitiveness together with innovations and how ICT can be adopted by Nepalese SMEs. The fourth section presents the steps or advances in ICT adoption in SMEs. The fifth section explains the institutional initiatives in Nepal by the government, the private sector and business associations in order to raise Nepalese SMEs' capabilities and efficiency and their ICT adoption. The sixth section deals with opportunities of ICT adoption and sees the role of research and development, technology transfer and FDI. Despite numerous advantages and prosperity opportunities, Nepalese SMEs have many challenges in ICT adoption, which will be reviewed in the seventh section. The eighth section, as mentioned before, identifies policy recommendations for harnessing ICTs in SMEs for enhancing productivity and competitiveness in order to raise national competitiveness in the global market. Concluding remarks will be made in the final section.

2. SMEs by Definition

The definition of SMEs varies by country and is usually based on the number of employees, assets, sales volume or a combination of them. The European Commission has categorized SMEs into three types, namely micro, small and medium-sized firms in terms of headcount and turnover rate or balance sheet. Japan has also classified SMEs in terms of employment and assets, and Korea in terms of employment, assets and sales revenue. Nepal has defined SMEs[5] in terms of assets and they are classified as cottage, small and medium-sized industries. Cottage industries are those that utilize specific skills or raw materials and resources, and are related to national tradition, art and culture with fixed assets up to two hundred thousand Nepalese rupees[6]. Industries with a fixed capital investment of up to thirty million Nepalese rupees are classified as small industries. Enterprises with a fixed capital investment of between thirty million and one hundred million Nepalese rupees are classified as medium-sized enterprises.[7] (See Annex 1 for the categories of industries in Nepal)

> "SMEs play a vital role in virtually all countries: they are the major source of income and a breeding ground for entrepreneurs. They drive economic growth, generate employment and thus help to achieve long-term sustainable poverty reduction. Access to information and support services and the use of ICTs are instrumental in helping SMEs to grow and become competitive." *World Summit on Information Society (WSIS) Report, 2003*

In Nepal, cottage, small and medium enterprises have played an important role in promoting growth and reducing poverty. As they are considered relatively more labor intensive, they help reduce poverty by employing the growing labor force. They are more flexible in terms of acquiring and adopting new technology. SMEs are the engine for balanced development of a country since they can be established at any part of the country according to the resources available there.

3. An Analytical Framework

Any analytical framework that deals with the issues of enhancing competitiveness of SMEs through ICTs in Nepal needs to tackle why SMEs are significant, how ICTs can be applied in both demand and supply schemes and how ICTs propagate value addition for fostering competitiveness to survive in the local as well as international markets.

In this paper, an analytical framework synthesizes five distinct models: reinforcing dynamics and system dynamics view of firm response to competitive pressures (Kotelnikov, 2007), value chain proposition (Porter, 1985), diffusion model (Bass, 1969) and innovation adoption curve (Roger, 1995).

---

[5] Cottage and Small Industries are referred to as SMEs in Nepalese context.
[6] 1 US$ = NRs. 79.14 (as of December 6, 2008)
[7] Industrial Enterprises Act 1992, Nepal

3.1. Reinforcing Dynamics

SMEs are the driver of economic growth and innovation (Kotelnikov, 2007). The total number of SMEs in the economy depends on the rate of SME creation and rate of SME destruction. This two way causal relationship or reinforcing dynamic generates economic growth. Profitable market opportunities increase the rate of firm creation. This increases job creation and income per capita.

Now people increase their consumption, which in turn opens up new market opportunities that attract more firms. Unlike multinational corporations, the SMEs directly benefit the country because most of the SMEs are domestic firms.

The reinforcing circle of innovation also drives economic growth. As the number of SMEs increases, their knowledge prompts those to innovate on the product or process. This competitive advantage attracts more people to establish more firms to capture the opportunity. Figure 1 illustrates the two way causal relationship or reinforcing dynamic of SMEs.

The development of SMEs, on the other hand, helps achieve other development goals by providing goods and services in such areas as health and education, or providing a source of income to disadvantaged and marginalized people. Efforts to develop women entrepreneurs, for instance, facilitate increased gender equality by providing women with a source of income. The Women Entrepreneurs Association of Nepal (WEAN), an active women entrepreneurs group, is a good example in this regard.

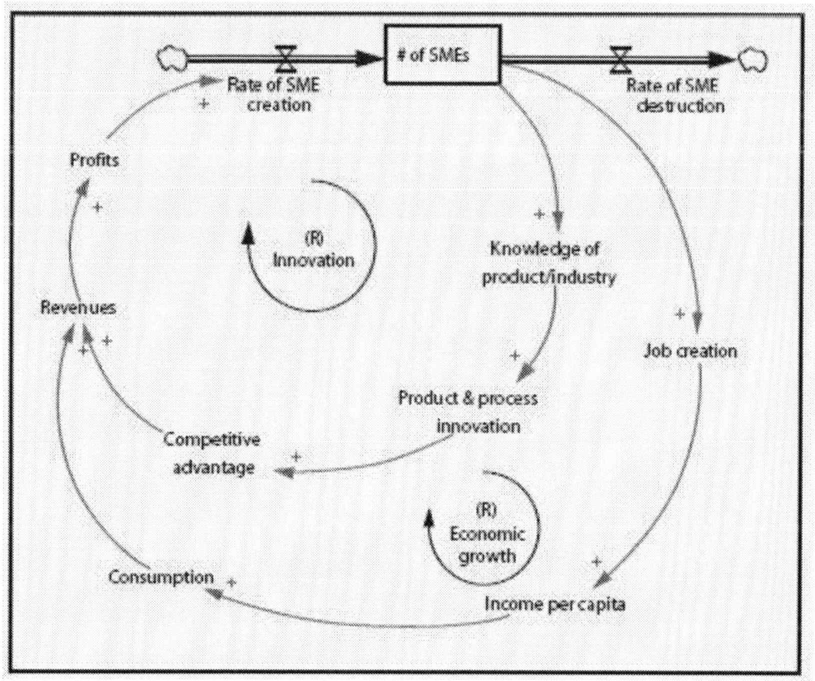

Source: Kotelnikov (2007).

Figure 1. Reinforcing dynamic of SMEs.

3.2. System Dynamics View of Firm Response to Competitive Pressures

ICT provides an enabling technological platform to create and launch new products. As ICT fundamentally improves the efficiency of data and information processing, its effective exploitation not only leads to an expansion of product possibilities but also creates new business formats and new industries. By providing a cost-effective, time-efficient, borderless medium to store, present, and transmit information, ICT networks enhance SME efficiency and productivity and expand market reach both locally and globally, thus, contributing to the national economic growth. If supported by trade liberalization efforts, the international market offers these IT-using firms new business opportunities and scope to reap economies of scale, which are unavailable to traditional services.

In today's globalized world, firms need to be familiar not only with their local environment but also with the developments happening around the world. Countries require a strong ICT-literate skills base which can innovate and adapt quickly to change to compete in the knowledge economy (Kotelnikov, 2007). Many industrialized and newly industrialized countries such as Korea, China and India have a strong firm base for SMEs to adopt emerging business opportunities through knowledge-based applications. Contrary to this, Nepalese firms are very slow in adopting ICTs in their production, business processes, operation and management simply because of the lack of infrastructure – physical and human resources, lack of incentives and appropriate policies.

ICT can play a significant role in helping SMEs create business opportunities and resist pressures from competition. The systems dynamics of firm's response to competitive pressure is illustrated in Figure 2. Competition among SMEs increases with the increase in their number, which results in a decrease in prices and customer base. As a result, profit also goes down and the growth rate of SMEs becomes slower.

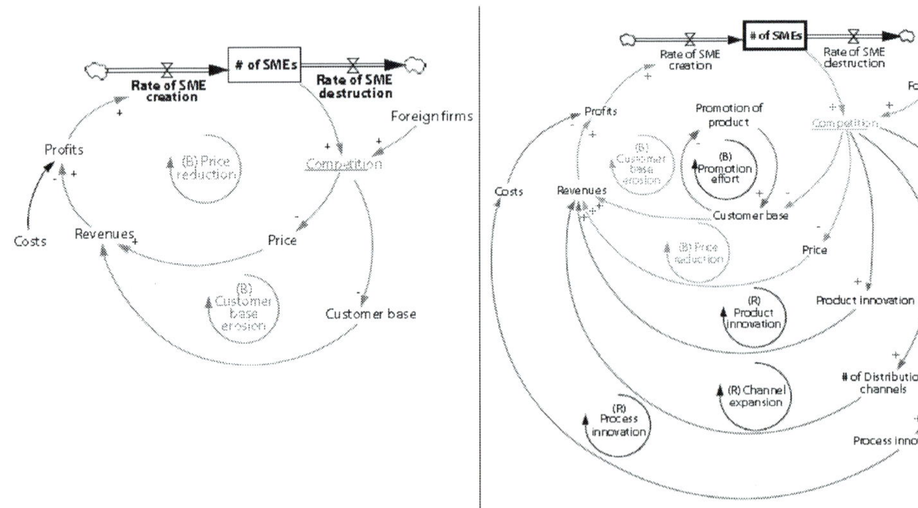

Competitive Pressures of SMEs

Ideal Firm Reaction to Competitive Pressures

Source: Kotelnikov (2007).

Figure 2. A System dynamics view of firm response to competitive pressures.

In order to compete in such a situation, firms lower prices, increase product innovation through product promotion, quality enhancement and RandD related functions, put in more distribution channels and improve internal processes through information and communications technologies.

Foreign firms, on the other hand, apply even more pressures particularly when they come up with innovation-oriented products and services. This is typically a deterrent factor for the promotion of SMEs in a country like Nepal. Knowledge-based technological intervention can be an effective measure for tackling the situation, which can be fostered through value propositions of the firms using information and communications strategies.

3.3. Value Chain Framework

The value chain framework of Michael Porter is a model that helps to analyze specific activities through which firms can generate value and competitive advantage (see Figure 3). The model sees a manufacturing or service firm as a system, comprising subsystems each with inputs, transformation processes and outputs which entail the acquisition and consumption of resources – man, money, materials, equipment, buildings, land, administration and management. Costs depend on value chain activities which affect profits.

Firms engage in numbers of activities in the process of converting inputs to outputs. These activities can be classified generally as either primary or support activities that all businesses must undertake in some form.

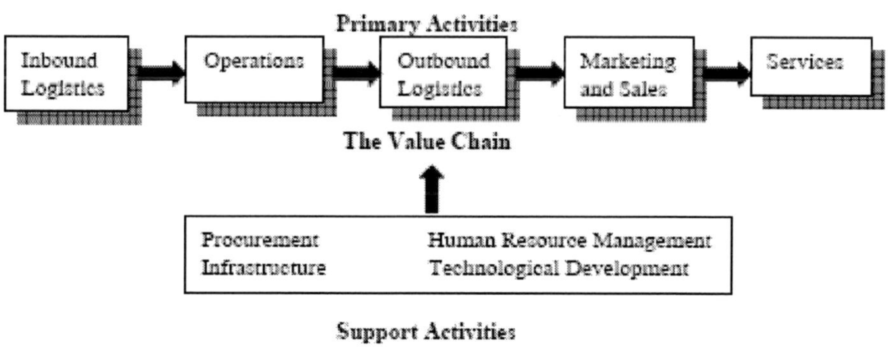

Figure 3. Porter's Value Chain Support Activities.

The benefits of ICT tools can be categorized according to the activities mentioned in Porter's Value Chain as follows. The primary activities are:

1. Inbound logistics – have cheaper and faster communication with suppliers through supply chain management to receive, store, and distribute incoming products and services to the business process.
2. Operations – are all the activities required to transform inputs into outputs, i.e., creating the final products and services, for example, machining, packaging, assembly, equipment maintenance etc, which can be better done through enterprise resource planning (ERP) software, rapid prototyping and manufacturing programs (Kotelnikov, 2007).

3. Outbound logistics – include all the activities required to collect, store, and distribute the output or the product to the customer, including warehousing, order fulfillment etc., which can be better dealt with by the use of ICTs to link to global supply chains and have outsourcing opportunities.
4. Marketing and sales – are those activities associated with getting buyers to purchase the products and services, now accessible with e-commerce provisions such as e-marketing through websites.
5. Service – activities are those that enhance and maintain the value of product or service including customer support, repair services etc. which can be efficiently handled with customer relationship management software.

Support activities that sustain primary activities are:

1. Procurement – is the acquisition of materials/inputs used in the organization's value chain that can be most effectively managed through an e-procurement system.
2. Human Resource management – comprises all activities involved in recruiting, hiring, training, developing, compensating and (if necessary) dismissing or laying off personnel. Recruitment of employees through web portals, personnel information systems (PIS) for general administration systems, e-learning for training employees can be much more effective for efficient human resource management.
3. Technological Development – is related to developing technologies such as equipment, hardware, software, procedures and technical knowledge to improve the transformation of inputs into outputs. Enterprise application integration enhances the integration of different software platforms resulting in better knowledge management within the firm.
4. Infrastructure – serves the company's needs and ties its various parts together with functions or departments such as accounting, legal, finance, planning, government relations, quality assurance and general management. Improved communication between different departments is obtained through the intranet. Software packages help in better accounting and financial management practices. Easier access to information facilitates a better business environment and market. Business planning capabilities are strengthened through models that are created from knowledge-based management.

3.4. Bass Diffusion Model

Wikipedia describes the Bass diffusion model as the process through which new products get adopted as an interaction between users and potential users. It is widely used in product forecasting and technology forecasting. The model serves as one of the tools to describe and predict the number of purchases for new consumer durable products

The following formula characterizes the spread of a new product/concept/method in a market.

$$N_t = N_{t-1} + p\,(m - N_{t-1}) + q(N_{t-1})*(m - N_{t-1}) / m$$

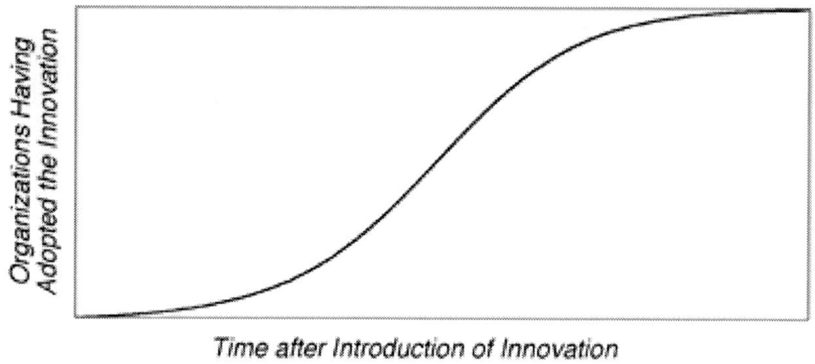

Figure 4. The Standard Bass curve (with the average values of *p* and *q* of 0.03 and 0.38 respectively).

In this formula, N_t indicates the number of adopters (companies/people) at time *t*. The 3 parameters of the model to predict N_t are:

- *m* = the market potential, the number of people who will eventually use the product
- *p* = the coefficient of innovation (external influence), the likelihood that somebody who is yet to use the product will start using it because of mass media coverage or other external factors
- *q* = the coefficient of imitation (internal influence), the likelihood that somebody who is yet to use the product will start it because of 'word-of-mouth' or other influence from those already using the product.

From the Nepalese perspective, ICT adoption seems to be at the beginning stage of the curve (see Figure 4).

3.5. Innovation Adoption Curve

Roger's Innovation Adoption Curve is a model that classifies adopters of innovations into different categories according to their adaptive culture (see Figure 5). It is based on the idea that certain people are inevitably more open for adaptation than others. The model has the following five categories.

1. Innovators – Brave people, pulling the change; very important communication mechanisms
2. Early Adaptors – Respectable people, opinion leaders, try out new things but in a careful way
3. Early majority – Thoughtful people, careful but accept change more quickly than average people do
4. Late majority – Skeptical people, will use new products only when the majority is using them
5. Laggards – Traditional people, conservative, critical about new ideas and will accept only when the new idea has become mainstream or even traditional

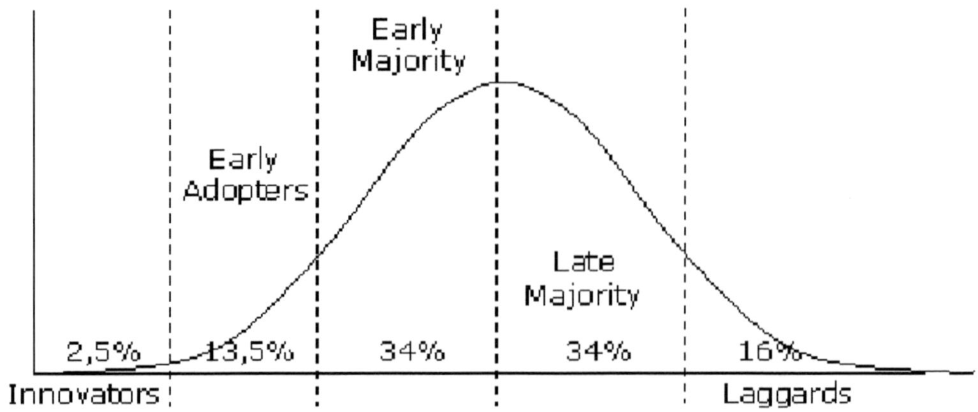

Source: http://www.12manage.com/methods_rogers_innovation_adoption_curve.html.

Figure 5. Roger's Adoption/Innovation Curve.

According to this model, in order to induce mass adoption of ICT, government efforts should target SMEs characterized as innovators and early adopters. The percentage given in the figure can be used as a first draft to estimate target groups for communication purposes. This strategy helps increase the total number of SMEs that use ICT, which further increase the overall awareness of the advantages of ICT and encourage adoption by other firms.

ICT adoption in such enterprises such as travel agencies, tour operators, trekking agencies and export-oriented manufacturing firms is seen as innovators and early adopters as their clients are international customers, affecting their entire supply chain. The government agencies such as the Tourism Board, the Export and Trade Promotion Center and business organizations such as the Chamber of Commerce and the Exporters' Association can also have their websites and can be developed into e-commerce portals, which help foster competitiveness and innovation.

The innovation adoption model explicitly indicates that the majority of the adopters are early majority and late majority who get conscious of the benefits of ICT through word-of-mouth, canvassing, mass media, seminars. For them, the cost benefit of ICT adoption should be clearly interpreted so that they consider using it after they are convinced that it is more beneficial in terms of cost, efficiency and ease and it is user-friendly, too. For advances in ICT adoption see Figure 6.

4. Advances in ICT Adoption

ICTs play a greater role in increasing the efficiency in internal business and in enhancing productivity. They reduce communication costs and link to local and global supply chains, and facilitate capacity building through e-learning and for many more reasons. In many developing countries, SMEs are poorly connected and initiatives to provide an environment of self-empowerment and sustainability have been slow because of inadequate information, high adoption costs and poor understanding of the dynamics of the knowledge economy. Hence, the enterprises should be well equipped with ICT infrastructure for fostering national competitiveness through knowledge-based changes and development.

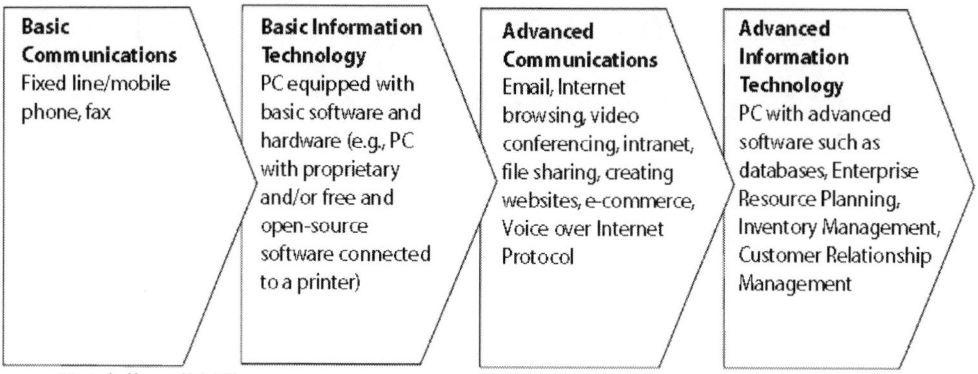

Source: Kotelnikov (2007).

Figure 6. Advances in ICT adoption.

The use of ICT in SMEs starts with basic communication technology such as radio and fixed line telephone to advanced information technology such as enterprise resource planning and customer relationship management as per their nature of business, affordability, convenience and capabilities.

> Nowadays the hardware products are so light-weighted that most of them are transportable by airplanes while the software products are weightless and can be transportable over satellite and other telecommunication links. For example, the Meiken Digital Technology office in Kathmandu, Nepal, which receives the original data on gas and water pipes deployed in various cities in Japan, produces digital maps of the cities containing information as to where the pipes are actually being laid, and sends the map data back to Japan via a satellite link. This is a very good example of what ICT can do to countries such as Nepal which is located at a great distance away from where customers are located and without a seaport.

Source: The Kathmandu Post, Sunday Edition, February 16, 2003

Figure 6 illustrates the ICT usage phases from basic communications, basic information technology, and advanced communications to advanced information technologies. Basic communications with a fixed line or mobile phone allow businesses to communicate with clients without the need to pay a visit. Then a PC with basic software helps in basic word processing and accounting. Internet connection further helps them in more advanced communications capabilities like e-mail, file sharing, website creation and e-commerce. This may be sufficient for service sector industries while manufacturing sector industries further need to acquire advanced information technology with databases, enterprise resource planning, inventory management, supply chain management and so on. The Internet and intranet system plays a crucial role in creating business opportunities and fostering competitiveness. Just as IP-based networks have revolutionized the computing landscape, Voice over Internet Protocol (VoIP) will have the same effect on the SMEs environment with the potential to lower costs, improve productivity, and consolidate management.

5. Nepalese Perspective of ICT-Enabled SMEs

The economic survey 2007 indicates that the number of industries registered under the 'cottage and small' category in FY 2005/06 as compared to the figure in FY 2004/05 increased by 2.49 percent. Neither the survey nor other available literature mentions about how many SMEs are ICT-related firms or ICT-enabled firms. Nevertheless, we can assume that such firms are growing at a substantial rate since service, including tourism sector, firms have grown massively. In this section, a brief analysis of the initiatives taken by the government and private sector will be discussed.

5.1. Government Initiatives

The government of Nepal has adopted an open and liberal policy for accelerating economic and social development of the country. The policy aims at providing the private sector with a dominant role, the government being the facilitator and regulator, with the ultimate goal of achieving efficiency and productivity. The Industrial Policy emphasizes simplification of procedures, transparency in implementation and improvement of productivity through upgrading technical know-how and efficiency of the industries in order to make them capable of competing in the competitive world market by utilizing comparative advantages of the country with minimum adverse effects on the environment (Industrial Policy 1992). The policy provides various concessions to those SMEs located in rural and remote areas.

There are several government organizations that regularly conduct enterprise development programs and provide necessary support. The Department of Cottage and Small Industry (DoCSI) works for entrepreneurship development and small enterprise promotion through training in business creation, business management, skill training programs and technical consulting services[8]. The National Productivity and Economic Development Center (NPEDC) and Industrial Enterprise Development Institute (IEDI) are responsible for the dissemination of information technology to SMEs, business management and consultancy services. The Trade and Export Promotion Center (TEPC) facilitate exports and support in identifying potential suppliers for SMEs. It organizes SME trade fairs, publishes a directory of SMEs and facilitates interactions between large and small enterprises. There are 10 industrial districts in different locations, which have been providing various kinds of support to SMEs.

In order to create employment and income opportunities in rural areas, the Government of Nepal and UNDP initiated the Micro-Enterprise Development Program (MEDEP)[9], whose goals were poverty reduction in low-income families by means of self-employed micro enterprises and capacity building and the development of a service delivery mechanism to promote micro-enterprise.

Realizing the problems associated with the ICT sector, the government has introduced various initiatives. The IT Policy was introduced in 2000. The Nepal Telecommunications Authority (NTA), established in 1998, served as the apex regulatory body to create a

[8] http://www.dcsi.gov.np/

[9] http://www.medep.org.np/

favorable and competitive environment for the development, expansion and operation of telecommunications services with private sector participation. The High Level Commission for Information Technology (HLCIT)[10] has been working on policy measures for e-commerce practice to make it sustainable and far reaching for the benefit of SMEs.

As far as technology transfer and innovation are concerned, there is no strong institutional mechanism developed solely for this in the SME sector (Dhungana, 2003). There is legal provision of technology transfer allowed even in projects where foreign investment is not allowed and those firms established with foreign participation are treated equally with 100 percent Nepalese-owned firms, but such provisions have not received wider attention. Various institutions are involved, in some way or the other, in the field of technology development and transfer in general (Paudel, 2006). Such organizations can be found in the government, non-government and private sectors, but the majority of them are involved basically in skill development training at cottage and micro-enterprise level, based on the human resources and physical infrastructures available. The science and technology related organizations are not in a position to contribute significantly even in areas indicated by state policies due to lack of adequate budgetary support from the Government (Paudel, 2006).

The above scenario shows that the government has indeed taken a very liberal policy for strengthening enterprise development but has not focused on knowledge-based industrial development. Most of the government institutions and agencies have their websites, but only a few sites such as http://www.tepc.gov.np/ are informative and updated. Online provision of government information and services is still not achievable. It is expected that the government portals will be available for an effective online registration system of firms and industries and other services which will complement the provisions made for both domestic and international investors and entrepreneurs to come into practice.

5.2. Private Sector Initiatives

Most of the private sector organizations, actively involved in enterprise developments are either federations or associations of entrepreneurs and businessmen. There appear to be very few other private organizations that specialize in the field of enterprise development.

Globalization, accelerated by innovations in ICT, has integrated markets and brought nations and people under one roof of the global economy (Dhungana, 2003). It is estimated that Internet traffic doubles every three months with e-commerce growing by 100 percent a year (Bhattarai, 2000). However, the case of Nepal is different. Despite an international and regional boom in ICT, the use of IT for promotion of exports of Nepalese products and its application for disseminating knowledge and information to the manufacturing sector is still in its infancy (Bhattarai, 2000).

With the early efforts to launch websites undertaken by a few *Pashmina*[11] traders, a numbers of exporting companies have their websites now. The creation and maintenance of a website is only a small beginning to an ICT-induced working culture. There are some isolated cases of dot.com and software businesses with no visible impact on the manufacturing sector. Therefore, concerted efforts from the government and the private sector to utilize IT for the

[10] http://www.hlcit.gov.np/

[11] very soft and warm textile used primarily in scarves and shawls

promotion of Nepalese exports as well as to vitalize the manufacturing industry as a tool to disseminating knowledge and information via rich user interface and complete information are an important requirement.

A small segment of the private sector is active in providing skill-oriented training in ICT and is engaged in the business of data transcription, software production and providing other IT services such as the establishment of cyber cafes around the country, particularly in urban areas.

The ICT sector has been steadily booming in Nepal with the enthusiastic initiatives taken by the private sector. The Computer Association of Nepal (CAN) has been very active in promoting an ICT environment and it has been organizing information technology exhibitions under the 'CAN INFO-TECH' banner since 1995 with overwhelming participation of companies and participants and viewers. Evidence of this is that 282,590 people saw the exhibition with 110 companies' participating in 2006, while the number of observers grew to 305,000 with 115 companies in 2007. The exponential growth of the participating companies and visitors is a good sign of ICT awareness and usage in Nepal. The comparative figures are attached in Annex 2.

The Federation of Nepalese Chamber of Commerce and Industries (FNCCI) could also create a dedicated e-commerce cell to coordinate all e-commerce related activities taking an initiative in forming an alliance with international Trusted Third Parties (TTP) and leading provider of trust services like VeriSign Inc. (www.verisign.com) (Bhattarai, 2000).

5.3. Possible Areas of ICT-Enabled SMEs in Nepal

Taking the resource constraints of Nepalese SMEs in mind, the SMEs involved in the following sectors can effectively apply ICT-enabled services to the extent of e-commerce realization.

1. Handicrafts, carpets, *pashmina* and readymade garments
2. Digital contents such as Nepalese music (audio, video)
3. Computer programming, software and other IT related services
4. Food products, spices and herbal products
5. Hotels, travel agencies, tour operators and tourism related services
6. Consultancy

5.4. Developing the ICT Workforce

Nepal is in need of skilled systems designers, software developers, systems engineers, communication and network engineers, data managers, data supervisors, computer instructors, skilled programmers, operators and managers with extensive knowledge of ICT. University graduates in IT and related fields are far fewer than the number that are required every year, although IT education and training are provided at formal academic and non-formal (for example, industrial qualifications and on-the-job-training) level, a gap which needs to be addressed by both public and private sector for solving the unemployment and under-employment problem. Besides, there is a lack of adequately trained manpower for the operation and maintenance of imported machinery. This problem can be resolved by ensuring training programs.

It is observed that the number of colleges offering IT courses and their capacity is growing every year. A number of colleges have been established with affiliation with foreign universities. Private training institutes are now offering long term professional training courses. The worst part of the story is that the country is not capable of retaining most of the IT graduates, who see the charm of migration to the US and other countries.

6. Opportunities of ICT Adoption

Developed countries have a very high level of ICT-related technological development. These countries have made significant investment in innovation and achieved success at par. Countries like Nepal have great opportunities to adopt the technologies with appropriate means of technology transfer.

Neighboring countries China and India have significantly leapfrogged in economic development through inducing foreign direct investment and technology transfer particularly in knowledge industries. India's Silicon Valley can be a good source of inspiration for Nepal as in the example presented in the box on page 13 about the success story of a firm serving clients overseas. E-business provides SMEs with the opportunity to access global markets, broadening their customer base and enhancing export prospects. ICT acquisition enables the prospects of extending the value chain as modeled by Porter. For example, in the travel business, an airline ticket becomes an entrée for a hotel booking, car rental, travel insurance, tour operation and so on. In this connection, much greater attention will need to be given to analyzing how firms relate to each other within global value chains and to the specific the types of transactions with which they are involved.

The sustained steady improvement in the telecommunications sector, mainly mobile communications and rural penetration, have offered opportunities for expanding the outreach of the industry and business sector to the wider market. However, the quality of infrastructure such as power, connectivity, bandwidth issue and others need to be improved.

7. Challenges in ICT Adoption

Despite the growing trend of SMEs and ICT awareness and its usage by them, Nepal is facing a strong challenge to meet sufficient capacity and technical know-how of SMEs. There are many obstacles to their sustainable growth. An absence of clear definition and appropriate institutional backup, poor access to credit and technology, lack of information, diseconomies of scale, unfair competition from imported inferior products, and vanishing skills are major impediments (UNCTAD, 2001). Under such circumstances ICT adoption in Nepalese SMEs is at a very slow pace. A number of factors hinder or discourage them from fully realizing the benefits of ICTs, including, among others, lack of knowledge, resources and trust (Alampay, 2007). The major problem of limited adoption of ICT by SMEs lies between the demand and supply mechanism of SMEs and ICT firms. As ICT products available in the market are too complex and expensive, SMEs are not capable of using them and naturally the demand for

ICT products is rather low and the supply of ICT products and services has naturally become limited. In this context, the following problems can be traced as the impediments for the slow adoption of ICT by SMEs in Nepal.

1. The basic infrastructure that enables the ICT-induced working environment, namely the telecommunications network, is still in short supply in Nepal. Most of the rural areas of the country have poor communication facilities, which is a major obstacle for SMEs located in remote areas even for using basic telecommunication services. Relatively high communication tariffs, bandwidth shortage together with difficulty in obtaining a telephone connection are disappointing scenarios. The numbers of ISP and VSAT service providers are also in short supply and the cost of Internet connection and usage is still beyond the reach of SMEs, particularly those located in rural and remote areas of the country. This can be summed up as a low level of e-readiness on the whole.
2. The problem lies more in the adaptive behavior of the SMEs rather than in the technical one. What the learning curve brings for technology adoption is not that easy in Nepalese SMEs as the owners are reluctant to apply innovative and technological inputs because of the high cost, lack of time, information and knowledge, on the other hand, employees, if given the opportunity, do not easily wish to adopt new technology.
3. Most advanced ICT products and services are designed to target larger firms, which discourage SMEs from adopting the software and services. High initial set up cost is a challenge in general.
4. Lack of IT skills in both owners and employees has prevented them from using appropriate technology. They do not understand how ICT can facilitate their business promotion.
5. Unclear legal and regulatory provisions have resulted in hesitation to practice online payment and other forms of e-commerce. The security issue is a great concern.
6. There is not a strong entrepreneurial culture in SMEs. Low technical capabilities, inadequate finance for entrepreneurial companies and weak international profiles of the Nepalese are the major obstacles to securing a supportive SME environment.

8. Strategies and Policy Framework for ICT-Enabled SMEs in Nepal

Any strategic and policy framework designed for ICT-enabled SMEs in Nepal should be premised around an internet-based business model comprising national and international dimensions and micro and macro economic implications (Bhattarai, 2000). Therefore, the strategies and policies should be addressed at three levels:

1. International level
2. National level
3. Business enterprise level

8.1. International Level

Since Nepalese SMEs need to build their business through ICTs across national boundaries and also to get foreign investment or technology and knowledge transfer from overseas, a number of issues come up with regard to commercial transactions. International practices should be taken into consideration and forums like WTO should be used effectively in favor of the country's SMEs so that they have enough space to play on the international market.

8.2. National Level

The following issues pertaining to SME and ICT use need to be addressed at a national level from a strategy and policy perspective.

1. National ICT policy and strategy
2. National SME policy
3. Infrastructure and technology
4. Government initiative for promotion of business enterprises

The national ICT policy should be directed towards building infrastructure, investing in research and development, facilitating technology transfers, creating science parks, creating legal and regulatory frameworks and so on. The national SME policy, on the other hand, should be oriented towards providing SME financing and business consulting services, simplifying registration procedures, providing tax breaks, creating incubation centers and so on.

The national ICT policy for SMEs needs to incorporate provisions such as providing tax incentives for investment in ICT, subsidizing ICT training for SMEs, creating incentives for e-procurement, creating awareness and providing exposure of ICT uses in SMEs.

8.3. Business Enterprises Level

From the perspective of SME firms and the business community at large, issues at this level are related to access, trust, fraud, digital contracts and guarantees (Singh, 1999). Even developed countries have found it a challenging task, and a country like Nepal must prepare for even more complicated challenges to address the issues. There are some fundamental questions involved as to how these issues should be tackled such as to what extent the government can intervene, what could be the trade off between individual versus collective efforts while trying to address the issues involved, given the technical feasibility of advertising and setting-up of data bases, virtual shopping malls, common platforms and supply chains (Bhattari, 2000).

SMEs in Nepal will find themselves confronting these issues, since it is expected that 80 percent of growth in e-commerce will come from business-to-business transactions (Singh, 1999).

9. Policy Recommendations

Nepal needs a coherent and comprehensive set of e-strategies which should be both practical and relevant. They should consist of actions, priorities, implementations and resources that operate on a cross-sectional basis. In line with this, the following recommendations should be taken into consideration while developing initiatives to encourage the adoption of ICT by SMEs.

1. Given that many SMEs are not aware of the benefits and the direct financial gains as a result of ICT adoption and have a poor understanding of potential integration of ICT solutions leading to a great degree of inefficiency, the government needs to assist in creating awareness and reducing psychological barriers to ICT adoption by showcasing SME success stories, best practices and benefits gained through ICT acquisition (Kotelnikov, 2007). The government support, both financial and non-financial, to acquire solutions such as software-as-a-service (SaaS) and access to latest software would enable a partnership environment to foster confidence for enterprise development.
2. Efforts should be made to strengthen ICT literacy to enable effective communication between business and ICT functions and ensure an ICT function playing role in creating value in business promotion with the provision of training and other related capacity-building measures.
3. The government needs to tackle issues of corruption and bureaucratic inertia by simplifying registration and other legal processes, creating locally relevant resources online and providing tax incentives to SMEs that buy ICT products and services from local firms.
4. In order to enhance the competitiveness of the SMEs, the government has to facilitate the provision of purchasing goods and services from domestic SMEs using an e-procurement system so that it can foster transparency and accountability, and attract SMEs with quality products and services. This leads to greater realization of e-commerce and can be an example of promoting e-culture among SMEs.
5. The government needs to create a transparent and competitive business environment with a clear cut regulatory regime to address security, privacy, intellectual property rights and consumer protection interests focused on the avoidance of cyber crimes and spam.
6. Measures should be adopted to encourage financial institutions to service the SME sector. Such measures should be complemented by strengthening business development training and services, including marketing and access to technology. One way in which to upgrade technology and spread its use by enterprises is to establish technology development and dissemination centers, technology parks, and research and development institutions.
7. ISPs should also consider playing the role of Commercial Service Providers for e-commerce solutions.

CONCLUSION

Overall Nepal's SMEs employ the biggest number of people in the country. They need technically-backed promising human resources and an ICT-induced business mechanism to innovate new products and services and market them into new destinations.

A 'modern' SME is technically competent, environmentally conscious, well connected to information networks and highly competitive. To compete efficiently, SMEs need to bring their production costs down by adopting suitable business technologies. Besides, capacity building development of necessary skills is also very crucial for SMEs. International best practices are to be incorporated for SME development. The government in collaboration with multinational organizations can support SME development.

The policies should encourage the progressive expansion of enterprises, and support services for entrepreneurship development and particularly technology capacity-building and innovation for enhancing the competitiveness of SMEs.

Despite the fact that Nepal is facing challenges associated with a poor economy, a low level of technology transfer, being in the infant stage of the business environment, learning from the developed countries Nepal can benefit in every sector.

Particularly, the knowledge of manufacturing and trade, capital market development, RandD, technology transfer and promotion of the private sector all need urgent attention and assistance with a view to develop conditions for long term development. One way of ensuring progress in technology building and innovation is partnership among all stakeholders.

In these respects, the entire stakeholders, private and public, should tackle the structural as well as micro level issues to enhance the competitiveness and capacity building of the SMEs in order to achieve socio-economic goals for the benefit of the wider population across the country.

ANNEX 1.

Classification of Industries as per Industrial Enterprise Act 1992	
Manufacturing industries	Industries that produce goods by utilizing or processing raw materials, semi-processed materials, by-products or waste products or any other goods
Energy-based industries	Industries which generate energy from water resources, wind, solar, coal, natural oil, gas, biogas or any other forms of such resources.
Agro and forest based industries	Enterprises mainly based on agriculture or forest products such as integrated sericulture and silk production, horticulture and fruit processing, animal husbandry, dairy industry, poultry farming, fishery, tea gardening and processing, coffee farming and processing, herbs processing, vegetable seed farming, mushroom farming, vegetable farming or processing, tissue culture, green house, bee keeping, honey production, floriculture, and forestry-related enterprises such as lease-hold forests, agro-forestry etc.

ANNEX 1. (CONTINUED)

Mineral industries	Mineral excavation or processing thereof
Tourism industries	Tourism, lodging, motel, hotel, restaurant, resort, travel agencies, skiing, gliding, water rafting, cable car complex, pony-trekking, trekking, hot air ballooning, paragliding, golf-course, polo, horse-riding, etc.
Service industries	Mechanical workshop, printing press, consultancy service, ginning and bailing business, cinematography, construction business, public transportation business, photography, hospital, nursing home, educational and training institution, laboratory, air services, cold storage, etc.
Construction industries	Industries such as road, bridge, ropeway, railway, trolley bus, tunnel, flying bridge, industrial/commercial and residential complex construction and operation

ANNEX 2. CAN-INFOTECH AT A GLANCE

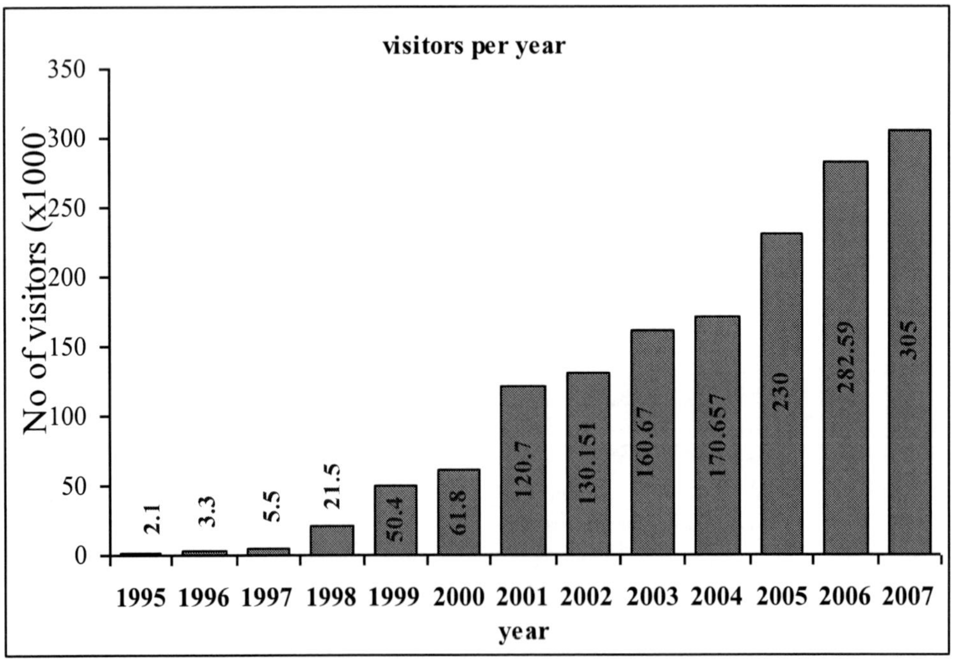

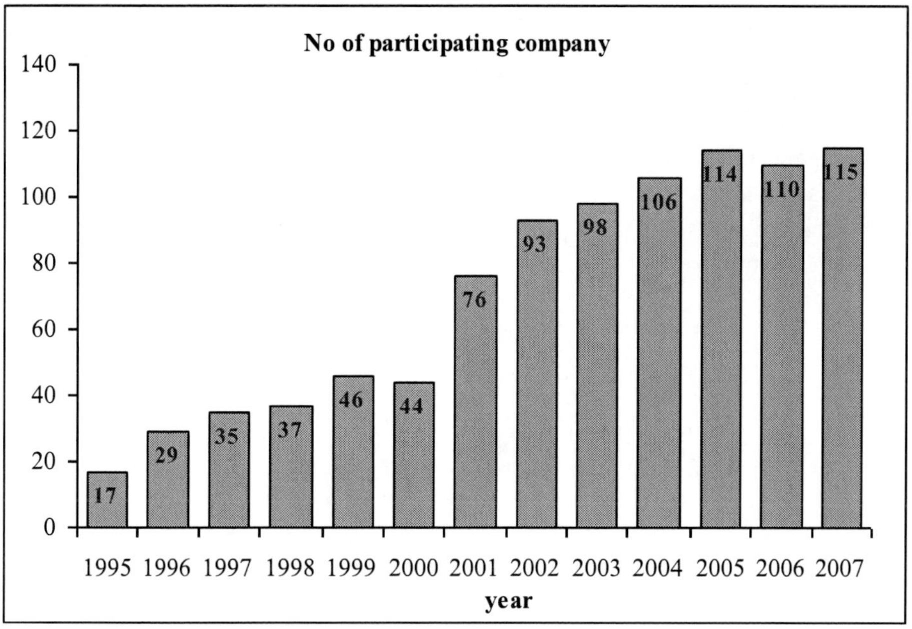

Source: CAN Newsletter Volume 3 Issue 20 January 2007.

REFERENCES

Alampay, G. (2007), The Role of Governments in Promoting ICT Access and Use by SMEs: Considerations for Public Policy, *ARDIP e-note 12/2007.*

Bhattarai, M.K. (2000), A Position Paper on E-commerce in Nepal, E-commerce Subcommittee, Formulation of Information and Communications Technology Policy and Strategy, Nepal, available at http://www.ict.mn/midas/section3/module.php?do=show_pageandlang=mglandpage=mpolicy.

Dhungana, B.P. (2003), Strengthening the Competitiveness of Small and Medium Enterprises in the Globalization Process: Prospects and Challenges.

Kotelnikov, V. (2007), Small and Medium Enterprises and ICT, United Nations Development Programme – Asia-Pacific Development Information Programme, e-Primers for the Information Economy, Society and Polity.

Nepal, C.and Karki, B.R. (2004), Promoting Business and Technology Incubation for Improved Competitiveness of Small and Medium-sized Industries through Application of Modern and Efficient Technologies in Nepal, paper compiled by Economic and Social Commission for Asia and the Pacific, United Nations.

Paudel, M. (2006), SMEs in Nepal, Their Innovation Strategies, paper presented at National Workshop on Sub-national Innovation Systems and Technology Capacity Building Policies to Enhance Competitiveness of SMEs.

Singh, D. (1999), Electronic Commerce: Issues for the South, Working Paper, South Centre, available at http://www.southcentre.org/index2.php?option=com_docmanandtask=doc_viewandgid=179andItemid=69.

UNCTAD (2001), Growing Micro and Small Enterprises in LDCs the "missing middle" in LDCs: why micro and small enterprises are not growing, UNCTAD/ITE/TEB/5.

Web sources

http://en.wikipedia.org
http://www.can.org.np/
http://www.nepalchamber.org/
http://www.dcsi.gov.np/
http://www.hlcit.gov.np/
http://www.npc.gov.np/

In: Information and Communication Technologies… ISBN 978-1-60876-671-0
Ed: Almas Heshmati and Sun Peng

Chapter 5

THE EFFECT OF MAIN TELECOMMUNICATION INDICATORS ON INFLOW OF FOREIGN DIRECT INVESTMENT

Zafar M. Mukhrumbaev*

ISTEDOD Foundation of the President of the Republic of Uzbekistan and Seoul National University

ABSTRACT

Since the telecommunications sector plays an important role in the overall development of a country, much foreign direct investment (FDI) has been attracted to information and communication technology (ICT) sectors in many developed and developing countries in the world. Taking the importance of the issue into account, the main purpose of this study is to analyze the effect of the main telecommunication indicators which have a significant influence on the inflow of FDI to the host countries' ICT sector. One of the most popular techniques, stochastic frontier analysis (SFA), has been applied to the data of 161 countries during 1997–2005, obtained from the International Telecommunications Union (ITU) and World Development Indicator (WDI) Databases. Empirical results of the present study demonstrate that revenue generated from mobile communication services and the overall economic development of the country have a significant positive influence on FDI inflow to target countries.

Keywords: FDI, telecommunication indicators, mobile penetration, fixed line penetration, SFA.

* E-mail: zafarmm1978@yahoo.com

1. INTRODUCTION

From the early stages of the development, the telecommunications sector has been estimated as one of the main and most important sectors in the overall economic development of many countries of the world. It has been found that the telecommunications sector has a significant positive influence on the overall development of a country. As one of the first researchers who observed this relationship, Hardy (1980) found that telephones contribute to the economic development of the country. Besides, it is also found that these technologies have a positive impact on a decrease of the transaction and information expenditures (Leff, 1984). It is obvious to predict that this decrease of expenditure will have a positive impact on economic development, especially in developing countries. Besides, the issue of the positive relationship between telecommunications and economic development is found in many other academic studies (Roller and Waverman 2001; Butler 1983; Cronin et al. 1993).

Basically, foreign direct investment (FDI) issues in telecommunications are quite an important issue among academic scholars. Development of this topic has taken into consideration the importance of the following topics such as economic stability and the political climate (Schneider and Frey, 1985; Nigh, 1985; Hein, 1992). Quite recent empirical studies demonstrate, in addition to economic stability and political climate, the importance of information and a telecommunications infrastructure as a source of FDI flow to target countries (Reynolds et al, 2004). The relationship between information and telecommunication infrastructure and FDI flow has become important, since a connection between these two indicators develops special ways to promote technology transfer in the country and develop high-tech infrastructure in the host country. As well, countries with high penetration cannot find additional room for further growth in terms of subscribers and users of telecommunication services. Thus, focus on telecommunication infrastructure development becomes quite obvious. Additionally, the importance of the telecommunication sector to the overall economic development of the country plays an important role to force and develop the sector to capture the benefits of the technology.

For the reasons mentioned above, most developed countries achieved a mature market in telecommunications relatively fast. Of course, it is also important to mention that this fast development of the telecommunications sector in developed countries was achieved by early introduction of liberalization, privatization and fair competition in the sector. As well strong regulatory framework played a crucial role in the fast development of the sector. In that sense, today, most developed countries have matured and highly developed markets with less and less opportunity to further extension in the local market. Less opportunity in local markets forces the telecommunications companies to expand further to less developed markets with better potential for growth. For example, Jakopin (2008) presents a brief review of 356 internalization cases in the telecommunications industry. The author explains that, nowadays, with a growing body of information and the importance of this topic becomes significant.

It is important to mention that foreign direct investment plays one of the strategic roles in successful international collaboration from the perspective of developing countries. Taking into consideration that most international collaboration cases occur between developed and developing countries, where companies from a developed country expand their business to a developing country, the role of foreign direct investment comes forward and determines whether the company should undertake such collaboration or not.

The level of the foreign direct investment also plays an important role from the perspective of expanding a company's activity. But, it is more important for them to focus on other key factors and indicators that may affect later the return of those initial investments in the telecommunications industry. Thus, first of all, international corporations expanding outward pay attention to the development level of the telecommunications sector and the overall economic development of target countries in their country level analysis. Then, as a second issue, they focus on a firm level analysis to choose the best firm in the country to collaborate with[1].

Taking the importance of a country level analysis into consideration, the main purpose of the present study is to investigate the importance of the main telecommunication indicators, as well as the main economic development indicators, of target countries which may have significant influence on the flow of foreign direct investment in host countries' information and communications technology (ICT) sector. To do so, one of the most popular techniques, a stochastic frontier analysis (SFA), has been applied to data of 161 countries during 1997–2005, obtained from the International Telecommunications Union (ITU) and World Development Indicators (WDI) Databases.

The present study shows the importance of key indicators which should be considered in depth by the telecom companies in their decision-making about whether to expand in the international market. Moreover, the present study is important not only from the perspective of internationally expanding companies, but also from the perspective of target or host countries in indentifying the factors that may affect foreign direct investment inflow to the country and promote investment in necessary infrastructure build up.

The rest of the paper is organized as follow. The next part of the paper reviews the literature related to the telecommunications industry and foreign direct investment. Based on those reviews a related hypothesis for the paper is derived. Section 3 presents the methodology, a stochastic frontier analysis, which is used in the analysis. Section 4 describes the dataset obtained from the International Telecommunications Union and World Development Indicators databases. This part mainly describes variables chosen for the analysis, descriptive statistics and presents a correlation matrix among all variables. Section 5 explains the main results obtained from the analysis. Part 6 provides a conclusion and discussion of the results. Finally, Section 6 provides possible future extension of the present research.

2. Literature Review and Hypothesis

During recent decades, international market expansion and foreign direct investment in the telecommunications sector have played one of the important roles in the academic research area. Moreover, global trends indicate that foreign direct investment is becoming an increasingly important consideration in telecommunications for many developing countries. There has been a large amount of research focusing on the impact of foreign direct investment and telecommunication services, such as mobile communication, fixed line phones and the internet. This part of the paper describes and reviews some of that research in the academic field to derive a related hypothesis for the present study.

[1] The second issue that focuses on firm level analysis is beyond of the scope of the present study.

The first issue among previous research that this paper is going to tackle is to discuss the role of overall economic development of the country on foreign direct investment inflow. In many papers the decision of foreign investor companies was focused on the overall economic development level of host countries. For example, Madden and Savage (1998) found a strong relationship between the economic development of the country and the telecommunications infrastructure investment in Central and Eastern Europe. The paper suggests that an upgrading and extension of the telecommunications network should be seen as a main and important objective for policy makers to facilitate growth in the telecommunications sector and this growth, on the other hand, will be important indicator to attract foreign direct investment in the country. Root and Ahmed (1979) took into account the importance of 38 variables that may affect foreign direct investment. The results of a discriminant analysis for 70 developing countries shows the importance of gross domestic product (GDP), GDP per capita, level of economic integration and other factors that affect foreign direct investment inflow. Reynolds et al (2004) analyzed the effect of the telecommunications industry on foreign direct investment inflows. They found that growth of GDP has a significant positive impact on foreign direct investment inflows.

Thus, it is expected that:

> H1: The level of economic development, estimated as the amount of gross domestic product, has a positive significant influence on foreign direct investment inflow to host countries.

Besides overall economic development indicators such as gross domestic product, other studies focused on main telecommunications indicators as long as telecommunications investment is considered. For example, Chang et al. (2005) analyzed China's telecommunications industry and its effect on foreign direct investment inflow. It is explained that during the last five years China has made considerable improvements to its telecommunications sector. The authors compare the Chinese telecommunications industry between 2000 and 2005 and explain that China improved its fixed line penetration, mobile penetration and mobile network infrastructure. It is also said that international telecommunications companies spent considerable time and money in defining the best way to estimate the Chinese telecommunications market conditions as well as how to enter the market. By providing important implications for foreign investors' willingness to enter the Chinese market, the authors show the importance of financial indicators that can be obtained as a return on investment. Besides, other relevant implications and suggestions are derived for foreign investors in the study.

Joseph (1995) indicates that there are several explanations for foreign direct investment ranging from macro level to micro level. Using a micro level approach (or firm level analysis), foreign direct investment focuses on how firms attempt to increase or maintain profits in an increasingly global business environment. It says that foreign direct investment can be seen to fall into two main and broad categories such as: market-oriented investments and cost oriented investments. Basically, market-oriented investment relates to a firm or company investing overseas to directly serve a market. In the case of cost-oriented investment, these types of investments have traditionally been located in resource-based industries where location close to a valuable asset is considered to be vital. Anyway, in either case the importance of financial indicators that generate a return on invested money plays an important role.

Thus, it is expected that:

H2: Revenue generated from mobile communication services and fixed line services have a significant positive influence on foreign direct investment inflow to target countries.

3. METHODOLOGY

As Coelli et al. (2005) indicated, a stochastic frontier analysis (SFA) was proposed by Aigner et al. (1977) and Meeusen and van den Broeck (1977), independently. Basically, SFA is the econometric methodology which is used to evaluate best performance and explain the benchmark gap between observed performance and best performance. SFA methodology takes the following form:

$$\ln Y_i = X_i^{'}\beta + v_i - u_i \qquad (1)$$

$$i = 1, 2, ..., I$$

where,

Y_i is the output of i-th decision making unit, (DMU) such as firms, countries and so on;

X_i is $K \times 1$ vector containing the logarithms of inputs;

β is a vector of unknown parameters which is going to be estimated;

v_i is the systematic random error;

u_i is non-negative random variable representing technical inefficiency of each DMU.

From equation (1), technical efficiency for the i-th unit at the t-th observation is defined by the following equation:

$$TE_{it} = \exp(-U_{it}) = \exp(-z_{it}\delta - W_{it}) \qquad (2)$$

Based on this methodology, our model specification in the context of country level analysis of the relationship between FDI and ICT takes the following form:

$$\ln FDI_{it} = \beta_0 + \beta_1 \ln(MREV_{it}) + \beta_2 \ln(FREV_{it}) + \beta_3 \ln(GDP_{it}) + v_{it} - u_{it} \qquad (3)$$

$$U_{it} = \delta_0 + \delta_1(MOBPEN_{it}) + \delta_2(FIXPEN_{it}) + \delta_3(INTPEN_{it}) + \delta_4(YEAR_{it}) + W_{it} \qquad (4)$$

where,

FDI_{it} - foreign direct investment to ICT sector of country i at time t;

$MREV_{it}$ - revenue generated from mobile communication services of country *i* at time *t*;

$FREV_{it}$ - revenue generated from fixed line services of country *i* at time *t*;

GDP_{it} - gross domestic product of country *i* at time *t*;

$MOBPEN_{it}$ - number of mobile subscribers per 100 inhabitants in country *i* at time *t*;

$FIXPEN_{it}$ - number of main lines per 100 inhabitants in country *i* at time *t*;

$INTPEN_{it}$ - number of internet users per 100 inhabitants in country *i* at time *t*;

It should be noted that the original SFA model was introduced and specified as a production function analyzing the relationship between inputs and outputs for firm level analysis. Here we use the model to specify the relationship between foreign direct investment and its determinants at the country level. In addition the model is used to estimate the country's effectiveness in attracting foreign direct investment and explain the level of efficiency by identifying and estimating the effects of its determinants.

4. Data

The main dataset used in the present analysis has been obtained from the International Telecommunications Union (ITU) and World Development Indicators (WDI) databases. Descriptive statistics for the variables used in the analysis are given in Table 1. The unbalanced dataset includes 157 countries that belong to the following group of countries classified by the World Bank: High income countries (40); Upper Middle income countries (28); Lower Middle income countries (47); and Low income countries (42). The numbers in parenthesis indicate the number of countries in each income group. The period of analysis covers 1997 to 2005. The total number of observations is 1100.

Table 1. Descriptive statistics of the data

#	Variables	Mean	Std. Dev.	Min	Max	Observations
1	LN_FDI	8.590	1.197	5.000	11.507	1100
2	LN_MREV	8.110	1.219	4.051	10.952	1100
3	LN_FREV	8.519	0.977	2.064	11.363	1100
4	LN_GDP	10.326	0.999	6.713	13.039	1100
5	MOBPEN	24.008	30.705	0.004	154.828	1100
6	FIXPEN	21.591	20.921	0.017	83.619	1100
7	INTPEN	10.682	15.498	0.000	87.755	1100
8	TIME	4.612	2.465	1.000	9.000	1100

This table exhibits basic descriptive statistics for all variables used in the analysis. The total number of observations is 1100. Note: FDI – Foreign Direct Investment spent on ICT sector, MREV – revenue generated from mobile communication services, FREV – revenue generated from fixed line services, GDP – gross domestic product, MOBPEN – number of mobile subscribers per 100 inhabitants in country, FIXPEN – number of main lines per 100 inhabitants in country, INTPEN – number of internet users per 100 inhabitants in country. LN indicates that the variable is transformed to logarithmic form.

The sample of countries is large and representative of the population of the countries. It covers the period when the telecommunications industry developed and was diffused across countries rapidly.

As the chosen methodology requires dependent, independent and additional characteristics variables, foreign direct investment inflow to target country was chosen as a dependent variable. Three main independent variables are chosen to include: revenue generated from mobile services, revenue generated from fixed line services and gross domestic product, representing the main telecommunications and economic indicators for the target countries. These explain the inflow of direct investment. As additional indicators that might have influence on foreign direct investment inflow, the following were chosen: number of mobile subscribers per 100 inhabitants, number of main lines per 100 inhabitants and number of internet users. These sets of indicators explain the variation in level and temporal variations in efficiency in attracting FDI. However, other related variables (for instance, revenue generated from internet services and so on) have not been chosen due to unavailability of data.

5. Empirical Results

This part of the paper presents the results obtained from a stochastic frontier analysis. The results of the present study consist of two kinds of results. Firstly, a stochastic frontier analysis was applied to the whole sample and secondly, the analysis is run to every group depending on their income level defined by the World Bank country group classification. The specification of the two aggregate pooled and separate income group models is similar. It should be possible to have a country group specific specification, whose choice is limited by the availability of the data. Discrimination of the model is statistically testable using a likelihood ration test.

Table 2 presents the results obtained from the analysis of the pooled sample. The estimation results of the analysis of the whole sample show that several indicators have a positive and significant influence on the level of foreign direct investment inflows to the ICT sector in the target countries.

As shown in Table 2, revenue generated from mobile communication services has a positive and significant influence on FDI flow to the ICT sector. The result suggests that a 1% increase of revenue from mobile communication services increases foreign direct investment inflow to 0.13%. It can be also interpreted, if companies in target countries make an effort to increase their mobile communication revenues by 1%, then the foreign investor's decision to invest in that target market will increase to 0.13%. Besides, it is found that the level of economic development of the target country plays a significant positive role on the investment decision of companies expanding internationally. Compared to revenue generated from the mobile communications sector, the level of economic development of target countries plays an even more important role. Because, as the results suggest, a 1% improvement in the level of the development of target countries increases 0.67% of foreign direct investment inflow in the ICT sector of the country. These results show that hypothesis 1 is fully confirmed and that hypothesis 2 is partially confirmed.

Table 2. Results of Stochastic Frontier Analysis

#	Variable	Coefficient	Standard Error	T-ratio	Cases
1	Intercept (β_0)	0.775***	0.228	3.394	1100
2	MREV (β_1)	0.131***	0.034	3.798	1100
3	FREV (β_2)	0.046	0.033	1.384	1100
4	GDP (β_3)	0.679***	0.047	14.332	1100
5	MOBPEN (δ_1)	-0.000	0.038	-0.002	1100
6	FIXPEN (δ_2)	-0.008	0.006	-1.290	1100
7	INTPEN (δ_3)	-0.018***	0.007	-2.454	1100
8	YEAR (δ_4)	-0.020	0.014	-1.376	1100
Sigma-squared		1.367***	0.145	9.386	1100
Gamma		0.880***	0.017	49.579	1100

This table exhibits the results of Stochastic Frontier Analysis. Note: MREV – revenue generated from mobile communication services, FREV – revenue generated from fixed line services, GDP – gross domestic product, MOBPEN – number of mobile subscribers per 100 inhabitants in country, FIXPEN – number of main lines per 100 inhabitants in country, INTPEN – number of internet users per 100 inhabitants in country.

*** - indicates significance level at 1%.

Except for the mobile communication revenue and economic development of the target country, the increase of penetration rate of internet users has a significant positive influence on foreign direct investment inflow. However, the revenue generated from fixed line services, mobile penetration rate, fixed line penetration rate and time are found to be insignificant. These results fully confirm hypothesis 1 derived earlier based on previous literature. With respect to hypothesis 2, it is also partially confirmed.

Additionally, a stochastic frontier analysis was applied to all different countries distinguished by income level following the definition employed by the World Bank. These results are presented in Table 3 and interpreted as the following.

First, the results for these four income level based country groups show that in all groups, economic development in the country has a significant positive impact on foreign direct investment inflow at a 1% level of significance. This can be explained in that a foreign investor who is trying to expand business to a target country, firstly and importantly will focus on the level of economic development in the country. Second, revenue obtained from the mobile communication sector has a positive significant influence on foreign direct investment in low income countries, while it has a negative significant influence in high income countries. Taking into consideration that most international outward market expansion cases occur from developed countries to developing countries, revenue obtained from the mobile communication sector plays a significant important role in the decision of foreign investors' to invest in low income countries. Third, revenue obtained from fixed line services has a positive significant influence on foreign direct investment in the ICT sector in lower income countries.

From the two results reported above it can be seen that revenue generated from the telecommunications sector plays an important role for low and lower middle income countries to attract foreign direct investment.

However, the results demonstrate that mobile service maturity in upper middle income and high income countries has a negative significant influence on foreign direct investment inflow to these countries.

Of course, it is obvious that a foreign investor deciding to invest to international markets will probably choose a low developed market with high potential for growth in order to gain from the market more highly compared to highly matured markets. However, on the other hand, the results shows that fixed line service penetration rate in upper middle and high income countries has a significant positive impact on foreign direct investment inflow. Thus, it is important to see that fixed line development in high income countries plays a better role to attract foreign direct investment.

In summary, if foreign direct investment in the ICT sector of high income countries plays an important role, then the decision-maker needs to take into account the importance of the development of fixed line services by some integrated converged services, because attention to developing fixed line services itself is not a beneficial decision as far as the development of mobile services is concerned in the market. Additionally, the results demonstrate that internet user penetration rate does not have influence on the decision of a foreign investor in any of the income groups.

Even the internet penetration rate is found positive for some groups and negative for others, however, it is not significant for any of the four different groups. Finally, the influence of the time has a significant positive impact in high income countries and low income countries. For the middle income countries, the impact of the time effect is found to be insignificant.

Finally, in concluding the overall results of the analysis it is important to mention that even an analysis for the whole sample of countries demonstrates that the level of economic development in the country represented as gross domestic product and revenue generated from the mobile communication industry has a positive and significant influence on foreign direct investment inflow. These results are found to be the same only for the group of low income countries while running the analysis for each income group separately.

The present analysis demonstrates an important implication for decision-makers who have decided to invest in international expansion of their market through foreign direct investment and also for policy makers in their attempts to attract foreign direct investment to their countries.

However, in order to clearly understand this relationship between foreign direct investment and the importance of telecommunications and economic development further extension of the research is needed.

Thus, suggestions on future research are discussed after having provided conclusions on the present results.

Table 3. Results of Stochastic Frontier Analysis by Groups

#	Variable	LINC	LMIC	UMIC	HINC
1	Intercept (β_0)	-1.703* (-1.548)	0.824** (2.177)	1.080*** (3.176)	1.043* (1.603)
2	MREV (β_1)	0.625*** (3.668)	0.027 (0.542)	0.040 (0.550)	-0.550*** (-3.384)
3	FREV (β_2)	0.354 (1.223)	0.211** (2.316)	0.012 (0.120)	0.019 (0.400)
4	GDP (β_3)	0.165*** (17.784)	0.613*** (7.470)	0.759*** (6.595)	1.249*** (7.543)
5	MOBPEN (δ_1)	-0.139 (-0.741)	-0.149 (-1.210)	0.150*** (3.989)	1.087*** (4.705)
6	FIXPEN (δ_2)	-0.043 (-0.144)	-0.032 (1.071)	-0.021*** (-2.855)	-0.115*** (-3.086)
7	INTPEN (δ_3)	0.065 (0.154)	-0.011 (-0.429)	0.000 (0.123)	-0.029 (-1.024)
8	YEAR (δ_4)	-0.082*** (-4.161)	-0.059 (-0.729)	-0.006 (-0.507)	-0.067*** (-3.458)
Sigma-squared		0.270** (2.091)	1.601*** (4.073)	0.430*** (4.618)	3.334*** (2.749)
Gamma		0.180 (0.104)	0.940*** (49.896)	0.957*** (53.656)	0.938*** (36.856)

This table exhibits the results of Stochastic Frontier Analysis for the 4 group divided by level of income. Note: LINC – Low Income Countries, LMIC – Lower Middle Income Countries, UMIC – Upper Middle Income Countries, HINC – High Income Countries, MREV – revenue generated from mobile communication services, FREV – revenue generated from fixed line services, GDP – gross domestic product, MOBPEN – number of mobile subscribers per 100 inhabitants in country, FIXPEN – number of main lines per 100 inhabitants in country, INTPEN – number of internet users per 100 inhabitants in country.

*, **, *** - indicates significance level at 10%, 5% and 1%., respectively

CONCLUSION

Since the telecommunications sector plays an important role in the overall development of countries, much foreign direct investment has been attracted to the ICT sector in many developed and developing countries of the world. Taking into consideration that from the early stages of the development, the telecommunications sector has been estimated as one of the main and most important sectors in the overall economic development of many countries of the world, the present study takes into account the importance of telecommunications and economic indicators to attract foreign direct investment as a measure for promoting their development.

Considering the importance of the issue, the main purpose of the present study is to analyze the importance of the main telecommunication indicators which are expected to have significant influence on the inflow of foreign direct investment in host countries' ICT sector. One of the most popular techniques, the stochastic frontier analysis has been applied to the data of 161 countries during 1997–2005, obtained from the International Telecommunications Union and World Development Indicators databases. Two stage analyses were conducted by analyzing a whole sample dataset as a first stage and by dividing the whole sample into four groups consisting of Low Income, Lower Middle Income, Upper Middle Income and High Income countries.

Empirical results of the present study demonstrate that there are several indicators which have positive and significant influence on foreign direct investment inflows to the ICT sector in target countries. First, revenue generated from mobile communication services has a positive significant influence on foreign direct investment to the ICT sector for the aggregate sample of countries in the dataset and especially for Low Income countries. Besides, it is found that the level of economic development of the target country plays a significant positive role on the investment decision of corporations expanding their market internationally in all income groups of countries.

FUTURE RESEARCH

The present study can be further extended at least in two ways. First, even though the results of the present study identify some important characteristics and indicators of the telecommunications market concerning foreign direct investment inflow, it will be clearer if additional telecommunication indicators are accounted for in future studies. Second, the present study demonstrates results at the country level analysis. As has been mentioned earlier, firstly, internationally investing companies pay attention to the development level of the telecommunications sector and overall economic development of target countries (country level analysis). However, as a second issue, they focus on a firm level analysis to choose the best or better market among possible target countries. Thus, the present study can be extended by taking into consideration firm level analysis which might be helpful for foreign investors to make a clearer decision to define where to invest. From the perspective of target countries, these two extensions of the present study will be important for target countries in order to clearly define how to attract foreign direct investment and what kind of country level and firm level indicators play the most prominent role in firms' investment decisions.

REFERENCES

Aigner, D.J., C.A.K Lovell and P. Schmidt (1977). “Formulation and Estimation of Stochastic Frontier Production Function Models”, *Journal of Econometrics* 6, 21–37.

Butler, R. E. (1983). “Everybody on the line: The telephone as a key to development”, *Media Asia* 103, 144–149.

Chang, J., X. Fang and D. C. Yen (2005). “China’s telecommunication market for international investors: opportunities, challenges, and strategies”, Technology in Society 27, 105–121.

Coelli, T.J., D.S.P. Rao, C.J. O’Donnel and G.E. Battese (2005). “*An Introduction to Efficiency and Productivity Analysis (2nd ed.)*”, Springer, New York.

Cronin, F.J, E.B. Parker, E.K. Colleran and M.A. Gold (1993). "Telecommunications infrastructure investment and economic development", *Telecommunications Policy* 17(7), 415–428.

Hardy, A. P. (1980). "The role of telephone in economic development", *Telecommunication Policy* 4, 278–286.

Hein, S. (1992). "Trade strategy and the dependency hypothesis: a comparison of policy, foreign investment, and economic growth in Latin America and East Asia", *Economic Development and Cultural Change* 40, 495–521.

Jakopin, N. M. (2008). "Internationalization in the telecommunications services industry: Literature review and research agenda", *Telecommunication Policy* 32, 531–544.

Joseph, R. A. (1995). "Direct foreign investment in telecommunications: A review of attitudes in Australia, New Zealand, France, Germany and the UK", *Telecommunications Policy* 19(5), 413–426.

Leff, N. H. (1984). "Externalities, information cost, and social benefit-cost analysis for economic development: an example of telecommunications", *Economic Development and cultural Change* 32, 255–276.

Madden, G. and S.J. Savage (1998). "CEE telecommunication investment and economic growth", *Information economics and Policy* 10, 173–195.

Meeusen, W. and J. van den Broeck (1977). "Efficiency Estimation from Cobb-Douglas Production Functions with Composed Error", *International Economic Review* 18, 435–444.

Nigh, D. (1985). "The effect of political events on United States direct foreign investment: a pooled time-series cross sectional analysis", *Journal of International Business Studies* 16, 1–15.

Reynolds, T., C., Kenny, J., Liu and C. Z. W. Qiang (2004). "Networking for foreign direct investment: the telecommunications industry and its effect on investment", *Information Economics and Policy* 16, 159–164.

Roller, H.L and L. Waverman (2001). "Telecommunication infrastructure and Economic Development: A Simultaneous Approach", *American Economic Review* 94, 909–923.

Root, F. R. and A. A. Ahmed (1979). "Empirical determinants of manufacturing direct foreign investment in developing countries", *Economic Development and Cultural Change* 27, 751–767.

Schneider, F. and B. S., Frey (1985). "Economic and political determinants of direct investment", *World Development* 13, 161–175.

In: Information and Communication Technologies… ISBN 978-1-60876-671-0
Ed: Almas Heshmati and Sun Peng

Chapter 6

EFFECTS OF INFORMATION TECHNOLOGY ON COST, QUALITY AND EFFICIENCY IN PROVISION OF PUBLIC SERVICES

*Nabaz T. Khayyat**
Ministry of Agricalture and Water Resources, Kurdistan Region, Iraq
and Seoul National University

ABSTRACT

Information and communications technology (ICT) has a great role in public sector operation, reform and governance. It can also help to improve the transparency and efficiency of the public sector, create network links across service delivery agencies, cut bureaucratic red tape and realize vast savings in the public budget which can be used in productive activities. ICT in the public sector can engage citizens as participants in the overall development for the future. The issues of cost, quality and efficiency are in general neglected due to the ineffectiveness of the organization, lack of experience and resources. IT is a new tool that can be used in the cost and quality control enhancement of efficiency. In Kurdistan Region of Iraq, most of the public services are provided publicly in a traditional way. This study demonstrates the possibility of providing these services in a separate or joint public-private partnership and by using ICT in their delivery. In particular, it proposes the use of ICT in the control of the cost, quality and efficiency of goods and services both in the public and private domains. Based on the current status concerning the privatization trend, quality and administration capacity, efficiency, the role of private sector, competition and regulations, we propose necessary policy measures to enhance the use of ICT to achieve these targets.

Keywords: information technology, e-government, quality, efficiency, costs, public services.

---

* E-mail: nabaz2009@temep.snu.ac.kr

1. Introduction

The public service provision has become globally a matter of concern for many governments and international development agencies (JMMS, 2001). Much research focuses on the effectiveness and efficiency of public service activities that will take us further to ask the question: should publicly funded services to consumers be provided by the government through the public sector, or should they be outsourced to the private sector? The economic discussion by the World Bank (1995) shows that privatization usually lowers the cost of providing public goods and services, but the question is whether the quality of the service will be controlled and improved or will be lowered as a result of lowering the price of the service.

Competitiveness among organizations in the new world of globalization is linked to the ability firms have to innovate and to how fast they can make this innovation real. The intensity of market demand and competition forces organizations to continually search for improvement and offer better services. Thus, the importance of information and communication technology ICT usability becomes a matter of concern for organizations to survive. ICT has contributed to the redesign, simplification and innovation in work processes, making organizations more responsive and active in the implementation of innovations and their insertion in the global market.

Outsourcing or contracting out services has become the main management philosophy in the search for production cost reduction and the consequent improvement of service and product quality. By adopting outsourcing, the company can concentrate on its end activities. The management of ICT has evolved into a mix of self management and outsourcing of technical tasks. This model has been consolidated in public administration mainly if we follow the concepts of outsourcing technical tasks and focus on the business itself. In the case of government, technology is definitely not its main business.

Outsourcing is used in systems development in order to reach the public faster and supply momentary demands. Given the difficulties in hiring personnel, it is more practical for public organizations to use already existing outsourcing contracts with labor or software companies whenever necessary. This way the number of employees may increase or decrease without creating any major problems. In the operational and infrastructure areas, public administration is st free from having to deal with large work teams without having any major impact on these areas.

This management approach, considered by many as a business philosophy, has been discussed, improved and broadened over the years. Allen et al. (2001) stated that, typically in the ICT sector, it is vital for managers to stay updated with the best market practices given the continuous and dynamic nature of the sector. This daily evolution has brought into the market new methodologies of IT management. Government administration finds itself within this context as well and, as a result, there is a constant need to adapt its heavy structure to this new world, searching for ways to implement new methodologies in technological management in an attempt to keep up with the modern techniques used by the market.

The use of information and Communication technology has revolutionized the structure of management and the nature of competition in a variety of industries. ICT is especially important in the service sector, which now accounts for about 74 percent of the value added in the U.S. gross domestic product (GDP) and enjoys a healthy $52 billion trade surplus (www.usa.gov). Estimates indicate that about 85 percent of all measured investments in ICT hardware are in services. Contrary to the widespread misconception of services as predominantly simple, labor-intensive activities, the service industries include many large, technology-intensive and technically sophisticated firms in transportation, financial services, banking, insurance, retail and wholesale trade, telecommunications, health care, and professional and personal services.

As ICT becomes less expensive, more portable, better integrated and interconnected, and embedded in a wider variety of devices, new applications in these fields and whole new industries such as interactive multimedia systems for business, home entertainment, and communications purposes are likely to evolve and to have profound effects on industry structures, employment, and economic growth.

The magnitude of the investment in ICT in the past decade has prompted questions about payoff for both the nation and individual enterprises. Because ICT is often used to automate processes (that is, to perform tasks that might otherwise require substantial human intervention), and because automation is popularly associated with efficiency and cost reduction, questions about payoff have usually centered on productivity, as the latter is a concept that relates the level of outputs to the level of inputs used in their production. In particular, some economic studies have suggested that the large investment in ICT by the service sector has not been associated with substantial gains in productivity as measured by national macroeconomic statistics.

While some studies indicate that U.S. productivity levels themselves compare quite favorably with those of international competitors in several important service industries, others suggest little correlation between investment in ICT and productivity, profitability, or returns on investment at the industry or enterprise level.

ITC has been associated with growing complexity and customization in each of these different industries. At the same time, growth in the volume of transactions, in the number, variety, and linkages among enterprises, and in the kinds of equipment available has led to demands for greater technical standardization. Across all industries studied, lags in the development of standards, software, and management systems rather than hardware limitations have been the main constraints to progress. Cycle times for the introduction of products in all major service industries have dropped, and greater control over the mix and size of inventories has become essential to success.

ICT cuts across all sectors to bring greater efficiency and opportunities to people from services such as education and health care to employment and trade, and from public participation to democracy. ICT is a powerful information processing tool which, when used appropriately as part of an overall development strategy, generates widespread benefits. The cornerstone of an ICT-led development strategy is the enabling environment, which allows for a rapid acquisition, application, and utilization of knowledge for economic and social development.

ICT also has a great role in public sector reform and governance.,it can help improve transparency and efficiency of the public sector, create network links across service delivery agencies, cut bureaucratic red tape and realize vast savings. ICT in the public sector can engage citizens as participants in the overall development for the future. The issues of cost, quality and efficiency are in general neglected due to ineffectiveness of the organization, lack of experience and resources. ICT is a new tool that can be used in cost and quality control enhancement of efficiency.

In the Kurdistan Region of Iraq, most of the public services are provided publicly by the Kurdistan Regional Government KRG, in a traditional way, in other words, the use of ICT is mostly absent in terms of public service provision. In this article we will demonstrate the possibility of transferring these services to the private sector or joint public and private sector in the region, and discuss the possibility of using ICT to contribute in service delivery and see how this will lower the price and keep the efficiency of the service. This paper proposes the use and usefulness of ICT in controlling for cost, quality and efficiency of goods and services both in the public and private domains.

The rest of the study is organized as follows. In Section 2 the use of ICT in public administration in the form of e-government and its domains is discussed. Section 3 is on public services provision at Kurdistan Region of Iraq including current status, privatization, quality and administration, efficiency, the role of the private sector, competition and regulations. Section 3 concludes.

2. Use of ICT in Public Administration

Several approaches to ICT management have been used by public administration over the past years. In Kurdistan Region of Iraq the model which prevailed for quite some years was centered in the Joint Humanitarian Information Center JHIC, a UN agency which held all the development of information systems and provided the government with the entire necessary technological infrastructure.

In Iraq (when the Kurdistan Region was administratively part of the Iraqi government) in the middle of the 1980s, main frame computers were brought into the country, they were mainly used to control banking processes (interest accounts, saving accounts, daily in and out cash records, etc.). At that time, providing ICT services was restricted to the government, after that, industries started to bring the new technology to their market use. This approach was valid at the time because of the size of the hardware and the concentrated capacity of processing data, not to mention its high cost. There were few computer technicians available in the market and users played only a timid role in the process of definition and project follow up. Technology was restricted to developing computer systems with limited applications aiming mainly at data input and report production. Thus, adopting such a model at the time seemed appropriate.

2.1. e-Government

e-Government can be defined as the use of information and communication technologies (ICT) to improve the activities of public sector organizations. Some definitions restrict e-Government to Internet-enabled applications only, or only to interactions between government and outside groups, or can be defined as the umbrella term that refers to the conduct of public sector processes, outputs and services through computer-mediated networks. In terms of service provision, -Government can refer to the transactions (both financial and non-financial) related to the role of Government in public administration and provide services to the community. This term includes e-business, e-commerce and e-procurement.Moreover, the World Bank has a different definition of e-Government: (http://go.worldbank.org/M1JHE0Z280):

> "e-Government refers to the use by government agencies of information technologies (such as Wide Area Networks, the Internet, and mobile computing) that have the ability to transform relations with citizens, businesses, and other arms of government. These technologies can serve a variety of different ends: better delivery of government services to citizens, improved interactions with business and industry, citizen empowerment through access to information, or more efficient government management. The resulting benefits can be less corruption, increased transparency, greater convenience, revenue growth, and/or cost reductions". It goes further to illustrate that:
>
> "Traditionally, the interaction between a citizen or business and a government agency took place in a government office. With emerging information and communication technologies it is possible to locate service centers closer to the clients. Such centers may consist of an unattended kiosk in the government agency, a service kiosk located close to the client, or the use of a personal computer in the home or office.
>
> Analogous to e-commerce, which allows businesses to transact with each other more efficiently (B2B) and brings customers closer to businesses (B2C), e-Government aims to make the interaction between government and citizens (G2C), government and business enterprises (G2B), and inter-agency relationships (G2G) more friendly, convenient, transparent, and inexpensive".

On general terms, "e-Government" was the concept used to describe the relationship between government and several social structures through Information and CommunicationTechnology intensive use. Although many authors adopt a different definition, in essence the meaning is the same. This interaction between the society and the Government can be classified in three different groups, depending on who is going to benefit:

- Government solutions for companies or to make business easier.
- Solutions designed to improve the relation between public administration and the general population.
- The applications to increase the relations between the Government agencies or between the levels of Government.

Nowadays, one of the most widely used typology was developed by The Gartner Group in 2000 and identifies four different levels of Electronic Government development on the Internet: presence, interaction, transaction and transformation:

- Presence: It is the initial level in which information about the departments and agencies of the Government are disclosed on the Internet. Usually the information is basic, such as the mission and address.
- Interaction: At this level there are some search services, downloadable forms, links for other government sites and contact by email with the staff personnel.
- Transaction: That is the level at which more complex services becomes available on-line, like self services that go all the way from the filling out of forms to receiving the answer, consulting and paying taxes, etc. The Internet becomes a service portal open 24 hours a day, seven days a week.

- Transformation: its characteristics are not only having the services and information on the World Wide Web, but rethinking the whole philosophy of public services. The ideal is to have just one door (portal) for the citizens to get into a government website, no matter the subject of interest. The portals are a big step in the improvement of public administration publicity. The governments do not have to go through all these levels of development. Although it is not very usual, it is possible to go directly from level 1 to 3 or from level 2 to 4.

With all those considerations, e-Government must be seen as a management policy centered on the citizens' needs, bringing together different Information Technology trends in the provision of services and public service information, raising the level of state government accountability.

There are three main domains of e-government, illustrated in Figure 1 (adapted from: Ntiro (2000)):

- Improving government processes: eAdministration
- Connecting citizens: eCitizens and eServices
- Building external interactions: eSociety

Respectively, these particularly address the problems that government is too costly, too inefficient and too ineffective (e-administration); too self-serving and too inconvenient (e-citizens and e-services); and too insular (e-society).

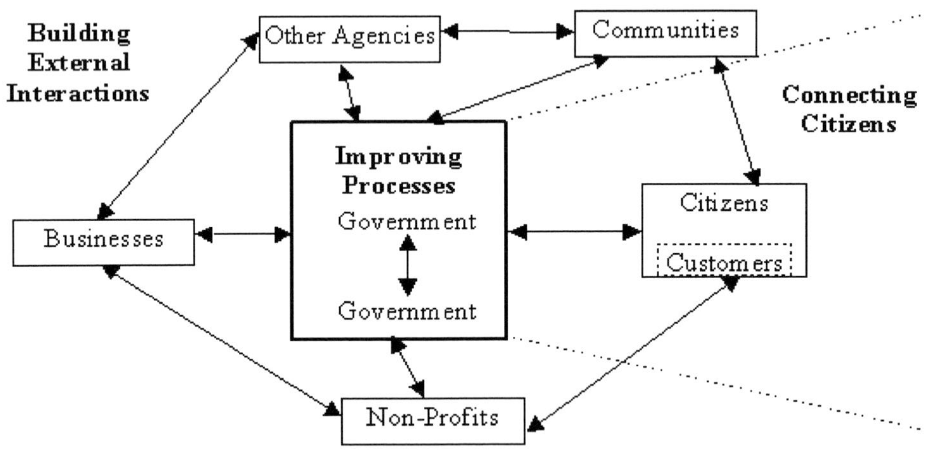

Source: Ntiro (2000) eGovernment in Eastern Africa, KPMG, Dar-es-Salaam.

Figure 1. Focal Domains for e-Government Initiatives.

In a little more detail, the domains of e-government are as follows.

B1. Improving Government Processes: e-Administration

e-Government initiatives within this domain deal particularly with improving the internal workings of the public sector. They include:

- *Cutting process costs*: improving the input: output ratio by cutting financial costs and/or time costs.
- *Managing process performance*: planning, monitoring and controlling the performance of process resources (human, financial and other).
- *Making strategic connections in government*: connecting arms, agencies, levels and data stores of government to strengthen capacity to investigate, develop and implement the strategy and policy that guides government processes.
- *Creating empowerment*: transferring power, authority and resources for processes from their existing locus to new locations.

B2. Connecting Citizens: e-Citizens and e-Services

Such initiatives deal particularly with the relationship between government and citizens: either as voters/stakeholders from whom the public sector should derive its legitimacy, or as customers who consume public services. These initiatives may well incorporate the process improvements identified in section B1. However, they also include a broader remit:

- *Talking to citizens*: providing citizens with details of public sector activities. This mainly relates to certain types of accountability: making public servants more accountable for their decisions and actions.
- *Listening to citizens*: increasing the input of citizens into public sector decisions and actions. This could be flagged as either democratisation or participation.
- *Improving public services*: improving the services delivered to members of the public along dimensions such as quality, convenience and cost.

B3. Building External Interactions: e-Society

Such initiatives deal particularly with the relationship between public agencies and other institutions – other public agencies, private sector companies, non-profit and community organisations. As with citizen connections, these initiatives may well incorporate the process improvements identified in section B1. However, they also include a broader remit:

- *Working better with business*: improving the interaction between government and business. This includes digitising regulation of, procurement from, and services to, business to improve quality, convenience and cost.
- *Developing communities*: building the social and economic capacities and capital of local communities.
- *Building partnerships*: creating organisational groupings to achieve economic and social objectives. The public sector is almost always one of the partners, though occasionally it acts only as a facilitator for others.

According to Ribeiro (2005), e-Government represents a new way to manage and to offer public services. He quotes Ferguson (2002), “the main target of e-Government is to transform government services and governing in benefit of consumers and citizens.” Vaz (2003) and Soares (2002) claim that the most relevant aspect of these necessary changes is the quality of the service offered with an eye on the user and a focus on the citizen. If an e-Government site is disconnected from the transformation process inside state organizations, it runs the risk of continuing bureaucratic practices with a new interface.

Given the lack of agility of the government, implanting e-Government in its broadest sense is a difficult task, leaving the government behind private organizations. Bahiense (2002) states that, most of the government sites are mainly for display of institutional information. They do not offer services and are not interactive, although there has been some effort to change them. Cunha et al. (2001), in a multiple case study of the three levels of government, concluded that, so far, the objective of government in creating Internet sites has been efficiency and not the main purposes the sites are meant for, which are actual democratic and citizenship practices.

It is not enough to build a site on the Internet. It is necessary to invest in the transformation of the information systems which will support the services offered. It is crucial that services are provided in real time, consulting data bases and adding or deleting the necessary information as a direct reflex of production banks. This new vision has forced the field of applications development to rethink the way projects are designed and solutions are implemented. The web systems must be light and have a user-friendly interface since their main target is now the client or citizen. In addition to simplicity, there is a need to invest in safer systems and environments since production banks are now being directly accessed by a web user.

2.2. Role of ICT in Controlling Cost, Quality and Efficiency

Public administrations everywhere are under considerable pressure to improve the quality and effectiveness of their services. Effectiveness from the perspective of consumers and businesses means that government is addressing the real needs of its citizens (consumers) in a satisfactory way. It has to be done by public administrations being responsive and transparent, imagining the position of the citizens, informing them about the rights they are entitled to, and the duties they have, while not bothering citizens (consumers) with redundant questions or helping them with only partial solutions, or even worse not helping them at all. Public administrations have to offer more personalized services, where possible in a proactive way, through multiple use of information and one-off (once-only) data provision, which help to reduce unnecessary administrative burdens (fewer information obligations) and deliver a better quality of services. This is of course with due respect to the privacy of citizens, mostly safeguarded by national legislation and data protection rules in force in Member States, and with respect to the different perceptions of data protection issues in Member States. At the same time, downward pressure on public sector spending is driving efficiency gains and doing more for less. Efficiency from a more internal view means that government is offering the best value for money. Standard ICT tasks also offer a potential for saving money or achieving higher productivity and quality. Thus, relieving administrative staff of routine tasks gives them more opportunity to dedicate time to individual non-routine cases and customer service and digitizing tasks can improve management information.

Since citizens and business should be at the centre of service delivery, the primary focus for them is an effective government. However, when reshaping processes, efficiency benefits should be delivered as well for citizens (and businesses), and to the administration itself. Collectively, these benefits should achieve a multiplier effect for society at large.

The multiple roles of government, at all levels, must be recognized and understood if it is to be effective in access to information and communications technology. In effect, government:

- Uses information and communication technology provided by the private sector for public administration;
- Produces public information to which citizens must have access;
- Has the authority to establish marketplace rules and establish regulatory structures that ensure that everyone participates and benefits from growth of the knowledge economy.

There is an inextricable relationship between the government role as a user of information and communication technology, and its capacity to formulated public policy for the knowledge economy. Governments that learn how to use these technologies in order to operate more efficiently and improve public services are more likely to effectively stimulate and contribute to the knowledge economy public policy debate. Online delivery of services benefits both government and its constituents as well as lowering costs and making services more accessible.

The horizontal and vertical interconnection of government bodies brings forth serious issues related to representation and responsibility. There are at least two questions that e-government raises in democratic societies: What are the risks involved in treating the citizen as a consumer and client of customized public services? What are the consequences that may result from this new form of mediation between the government and its citizens? The establishment of a peer-to-peer relationship between the government and the citizen or business when providing a public service by electronic means helps to improve accountability, transparency and trust. This is not only important at the national and regional level, but should also be used locally, in transactions related to permits, tax collection or receipt of benefits. Through its ability to spread accurate and comprehensive information, e-government can be a powerful tool for social control. Nothing is more powerful in combating corruption than conducting transactions openly and with public knowledge of the rules and criteria to be applied.

3. Public Services Provision in Kurdistan Region of Iraq

3.1. The Current Status

The public services provided by the Kurdistan Regional Government KRG are healthcare, education, electricity, the household water supply, roads, transportation and airlines, municipality services, security, law enforcement and recreation. These services are provided at a low quality and are out of coverage in some areas due to the low income budget of the KRG since its establishment in 1992. These services have obviously lowered in quality if evaluated according to the general principles of the public services that include: continuity, equality, adaptability, the need of a public authority to respond to consumers, and consumers' participation in achieving structural reform. The inexistence of a responsibility system, or even its low effectiveness, has, as a consequence, lowered the quality of the services that are rendered to the citizens. There is no transparency regarding who is responsible for what. Above all, the most serious problem is responsiveness to the population's needs.

The quality of public services provided by the private sector is generally better than that provided publicly, for instance, the telecommunications service in the region has relatively improved once it transferred to the private sector and the companies Eagle-Dalia, Newroz and Fanos took over the service in the three governorates.

In developed countries, telecommunication companies depend on ICT for operations management, billing and customer service, product differentiation, and new-product development. These companies further provide the infrastructures of telephone, cable television, satellite, microwave, and fiber-optic-cable connections that enable other industries to operate effectively. They provide the pathways over which a variety of new concepts and products have been introduced by the financial services, entertainment, data services, software, direct distribution, education, travel, and health care industries, among others. Deregulation in the 1980s increased the variety of services available and decreased their costs for most customers. Improved communications have allowed companies to manage materials and services purchased anywhere in the world, control inventories on a just-in-time basis, gather information, and manage diversified producing locations in ways that have changed basic premises about industry boundaries, the organization of enterprises, and many traditional management techniques. At the same time, the use of ICT has enabled telecommunications companies to shift to the consumer much of the labor of placing calls, although consumers themselves often find self-service dialing a convenience.

The airline service in the region is at the beginning of its development, as this sector only started its services in 2004 for civil people. In airlines, innovation through using ICT have been associated with competitive leadership and with survival as complexity has increased. Airlines depend heavily on ICT within aircraft and airports, in air traffic control systems, and for sales, marketing, maintenance, and safety systems, as well as for capacity, load management, and logistics planning. Computerized reservation systems have changed the entire pattern of competition and profit-making in the airline industry, although in the 1980s, airline profits were highly erratic in the shakeout that resulted from the deregulation of the industry. Competition has forced airlines to pass on to customers the savings gained through increased efficiency, but new route structures enabled by the use of ICT have also allowed airlines to pass certain costs (notably inconveniences caused by the "hub-and-spoke" system) on to customers.

The healthcare service in Kurdistan Region of Iraq is mainly publicly provided by the KRG to the people taking into consideration that advanced surgical operations are mostly done in private hospitals due to the lack of high technological resources in public hospitals. In health care, the use of ICT has become increasingly important in diagnosis and therapy. For business operations, ICT has generally been less well used in health care than in other industries, and there may be great untapped potential for its use in such operations as well as in new clinical applications, outpatient care, and the monitoring of outcomes. Measures of economic output in health care are extremely tenuous because of the presence of many non-market forces and problems in defining quality. Although numerous new and improved cures, therapies, and diagnostics have been introduced since 1970, there is wide consensus that measured productivity in health care has been dropping. Yet few would like to do without the potentially better diagnosis and treatment that electronic devices permit in health care today and the costs of dealing with today's complex reporting requirements would soar further without electronic systems.

Education is free of charge in the region. There are a few foreign private schools that cannot be considered as competitive assets. The quality of education and the resources used are at a relatively low level if it is compared with other countries.

Moreover, electricity is provided jointly by the public and private sectors at a very low quality of service; demand is simply growing much more rapidly than electricity can be generated due to the migration of Iraqi people from the south and the middle parts of Iraq to Kurdistan for better security, and the rapid development process that has taken place in the region.

It has become an established fact that the age we live in these days is the age of communication and information. Over the last decade or so, entire oceans of information have formed, and continue to expand every moment. Any piece of data has now become available and accessible to everyone – young and old – anywhere in the world, and time and distance are no longer considered barriers that impede the ongoing quest for knowledge.

Along with this enormous human contribution that has manifested itself with the rise of the Internet, have come new challenges and requirements that ultimately defined this era and its technology. As these endless oceans of information are continually nourished by the world's organizations, businesses, institutes, individuals and others, there has appeared the need for tools that share a unified goal: helping all knowledge-seekers effortlessly and swiftly sail these oceans and find their destinations, where they would then be rewarded by the availability and authenticity of the information they embarked on a search for, and would ultimately make a contribution by adding to and enriching this human experience further and further. Globally, measuring the progress and development of a nation or organization has become fundamentally associated with the amount of information and services they contribute to the Internet. Most organizations with an online presence have developed and utilized various tools through which relevant information and services are offered to their customers

Since 2003, after the general elections in Iraq, Kurdistan Region has been continuously receiving multinational help to begin an e-government program and set up an e-government intranet network to link the entire public sector establishment together as a first step. From the table below (see Table 1), it shows the actions taken towards achieving the first stage of connecting the facilities:

Table 1. Survey conducted by the Department of ICT, Council of Ministers in 2007

	Questions	Information and Telecommunication Resources									
No	Ministry/Public sector unit	Q1	Q2	Q3	Q4	Q5	Q6	Q7	Q8	Q9	Q10
1	Municipality of Ankawa	-	552	8	No	0	winxp	No	No	0	15
2	Mine Action Agency	-	397	95	Yes	1	winxp	Yes	-	2	-
3	Min. Agriculture	-	11485	261	Yes	3	winxp	No	No	0	18
4	Min. Communication	No	3166	358	No	0	winxp	Yes	Yes	-	14

Table 1. (Continued)

5	Min. Construction and housing	-	6755	403	Yes	6	winxp	No	No	-	18
6	Min. Education	No	113738	5078	Yes	6	winxp	Yes	Yes	-	37
7	Min. Culture	-	2024	116	No	0	winxp	No	No	0	6
8	Min. Endowments and Regions Affairs	No	799	109	Yes	1	winxp	No	No	-	25
9	Min. Electricity	-	11766	985	No	0	winxp	No	No	-	8
10	Min. Environment	-	71	44	Yes	1	winxp	No	No	-	24
11	Min. Extra Regional Affairs	-	87	51	Yes	2	winxp	No	No	-	5
12	Min. Higher Education	No	253 divan	75	Yes	11	winxp	Yes	No	-	22
13	Min. Health	-	26213	1833	Yes	1	winxp	Yes	Yes	4	17
14	Min. Finance, Sulimanya	-	4447	356	No	5	winxp	No	Yes	-	6
15	Min. Finance, Hawler	No	256 divan	34	-	-	winxp	Yes	-	-	-
16	Min. Industry	-	3454	185	Yes	5	winxp	No	No	-	17
17	Min. Human Rights	No	364	68	No	0	winxp	No	No	-	10
18	Min. Justice	No	4174	381	No	1	winxp	No	Yes	-	8
19	Min. Martial and Anfal Affairs	-	399	104	No	no	xp-me	Yes	No	-	21
20	Min. Tourism	-	726	130	Yes	3	winxp	No	No	-	16
21	Min. Natural Resources	-	2165	137	No	1	winxp	Yes	No	-	14
22	Min. Planning	No	206	176	Yes	5	winxp	Yes	No	-	4
23	Min. Water Resources	-	1588	116	No	1	xp-vista	No	No	-	22
24	Min. Trade	-	2075	259	No	1	winxp	No	No	-	34
25	Min. Transportation	-	1467	132	Yes	2	winxp	Yes	Yes	-	19
26	Min. Youth and Sport	-	-	-	-	-	-	-	-	-	-
27	Min. Labor and Social Affairs	-	2954	579	Yes	2	winxp	No	No	0	17

Source: General information on ICT for Kurdistan Regional Government ministers and other public sector units.

List of Questions:
Q1: IT Structure
Q2: Number of Employees
Q3: Number of Computers
Q4: Do you have an IT Department?
Q5: Number of IT Staff
Q6: Operating System
Q7: Network
Q8: Do you have Server?
Q9: Number of Servers
Q10: Number of Departments, General and Directorate.

3.2. Trends in Privatization of Public Services

The term 'Privatization' is associated with the process of transferring assets in terms of ownership from the public to the private sector. Privatization has been linked to a range of actions which include:

- Asset Sales: Government sells all or part of national property.
- Outsourcing Services: Public officials act as service managers.
- Internal Market Arrangements: The purchasing of services is separated from their provision.
- Consumer Fees: Government levy charges for services that are still provided publicly.
- Joint Private-Public Sectors: Government finances, manages and shares the risk with the private sector on a joint project.

The range of actions indicates that privatization is increasingly defined clearly to include all efforts to encourage private sector participation in the delivery of public services.

However, if the public services are provided by the public sector, there will be misuse for economies of scale, also the transaction costs will be minimized. If one provider for a good or a service was available, there will not be any competition and the cost will not be lowered (Abelson and Chung, 2005). An example can be cited from Kurdistan Region of Iraq, the telecommunication companies are examples of one supplier of the service of communication, Korek in Erbil and Duhok, AsiaCell in Sulaymaniah and some other cities outside the region.

In the context of public service reforms, privatization is regarded as an important means to achieve improved efficiency and quality of services and there is considerable evidence that the private sector generally supplies services at a lower cost than the public sector.

Borcherding et al. (1982) provided an intensive analysis of comparative studies of public and private costs in 52 studies of productive efficiency in 19 economic sectors in five OECD countries, mainly in Germany and the US. The authors concluded that in 40 of the studies, private supply was more efficient, only in three cases was public supply less costly than private. Lundsgaard (2002) and Bailey (2002) provided more recent case studies. Their results showed that competitive contracting of services traditionally supplied by the public sector, such as trash collection, office and street cleaning, water supply, and road and park maintenance, produced large savings, often of 20 per cent or more.

However, some cost savings may be achieved through reducing the quality of the services, if we take into consideration the fact that a private supplier of public services may have a stronger incentive to keep down costs, at least this may happen if quality is difficult to measure. This problem should be addressed by the government regulation of these services through establishing necessary institutions and work practices and methods to develop the market further and consumer satisfaction.

Outsourcing public service provision is emerging as a result of the need for solutions that can deliver cost savings, for instance many public service organizations are turning to private support and collaboration for healthcare services, waste management and road maintenance and public properties. These cost savings are delivered primarily by more flexible work practices and economies of scale.

With public service organizations faced with more bargaining, enforcing and monitoring costs associated with contract maintenance, outsourcing public services permits an influence on private sector efficiency. With the ability to set performance targets and provide necessary incentives that reward efficient service delivery, public organizations can outsource routine services where the key elements of the contract can be precisely specified and transaction and monitoring costs are low.

Economies of scale also contribute to the preference of public organizations to outsource public services. Areas such as waste management and the provision of road maintenance services have several supporting case studies which indicate that private sector organizations can deliver considerable cost savings.

The incapacity of the government authorities in unstable countries, especially at a municipal level has generated a gap between economic, social and environment needs on one side and service provision on the other, outsourcing of responsibility for service provision has been seen and noted as a way to close the gap (Martin, 2001).

It is recommended as a consequence to maintain a direct channel of communication among the services providers and users, aiming to assess the level of users' satisfaction and to stimulate the presentation of suggestions and allow users to follow and to supervise public services. This will be much more possible if the service provision has been transferred to the private sector or joint public-private sector facility (Jeger, 2000).

As indicated above, we can conclude that governments and organizations have to encourage the outsourcing of the public service provision, to achieve that in our case the KRG will face considerable control requirements through defining goals and specifying tasks, designing contracts, then coordinating and supervising service delivery, these processes will become increasingly complex and complicated.

3.3. Efficiency and Quality

Privatization of public services is often seen as guarantor of greater efficiency and quality. A number of studies on privatization have shown clear evidence that private firms in competitive markets do better than government provision of goods and services. In examining the experience of municipal contracting out in the United States, some researchers suggested that competently designed privatization leads to lower unit cost and improved service quality. This study is not borne out by a review of research findings (Martin, 2001). Some studies based on exhaustive international empirical research found that in the long run, in electricity generation better investment planning led to lower operating costs, while in transmission and distribution there was no evidence that privatization would bring lower costs in the short or long run. A consideration that is often overlooked is that efficiency in service management is also highly dependent on costs and risks other than direct financial costs.

3.4. The Role of the Private Sector

Where efficiency and improvement are central concerns and respond well to competitive pressures and where quality and price can be relatively regulated when necessary and consumers are able to meet directly most of the cost of delivery, then regulated private-sector delivery is appropriate. Hence privatization can be motivated, based on the fact that the ownership of a private service would increase efficiency.

In the years between 1979 and 1997, a large amount of assets were transferred from the public to the private sector in the UK. The main utilities: telecommunication, gas, electricity, water, bus, and rail were transferred to the private sector and with the exception of buses, specific regulatory institutions were set up to deal with newly privatized entities. Two lessons can be gained from the UK privatization (Grout, 2003):

- The impact on the privatized sectors has been larger than most observers and analysts expected.
- The regulatory instruments have proved more susceptible to the problem of information rent than anticipated (By information rent we mean the ability of regulated companies to use their informational superiority over the regulator to profitable effect).

Megginson and Netter (2001) provided another international survey of studies of privatization. They end up with the fact that divested firms always become more efficient, more profitable, and financially healthier, and increase their capital investment sending.

An extensive study for the UK, by Martin and Parker (1997), reports the most negative results: a comparison between the post-privatization and nationalization periods for 11 industries, they failed to identify any systematic improvement in performance, contrary to Newbery (1997) who says: 'privatization is necessary but not sufficient'. A problem in such studies is that welfare effects on consumers are rarely examined. The benefits of efficiency frequently go to shareholders or can even appear to have an extremely high quality of standards that may not reflect consumer preferences. We cannot conclude that private ownership unambiguously improves the welfare of consumers.

Privatization of public services cannot be assessed independently without a regulatory system. Part of the problem is political rather than economic. The stock markets, along with everyone else, failed to recognize the potential profitability of the companies. Even ignoring the specific gains to small shareholders, share prices at privatization typically did not reflect the potential for efficiency gains and information rent. If they had done so, regulators might have had greater flexibility. Instead, high returns for shareholders made regulators anxious to claw back where possible, making entry harder. Generally, regulation has not proved as light-handed or short-lived as expected at the start of the privatization program.

3.5. The Role of Competition

It is obvious that in the competitive market, goods and services will be lowered in price, if the service provision is opened to competition the service quality will improve consequently.

Three important roles for competition can be observed according to Knabe and Birch Sorensen:

- In the presence of doubt about costs and other conditions under outsourcing, competitive tendering ensures the efficiency of alternative organizational forms.
- Competition may ensure that the most cost effective producer will get the business.
- Competition may eliminate rents to service providers and consequently reduce the associated risk of corruption. However, transparency and fairness is required which may be difficult to achieve if corruption is a problem.

The competition argument assigns the higher productivity in private organizations to the higher degree of competition in the private sector (Boyne, 1998). According to this, private organizations are only expected to produce their services more efficiently when the competition is keener in this sector.

3.6. The Role of Regulation

The public authority seeks an improvement in public service quality, which will be achieved through building necessary institutions to monitor and supervise the performance of the private sector provision for public services by regulating the services.

The regulation may function on two levels: continuous technical supervision and, regulation achieved by a specialized authority. The role of regulation can be summarized as follows:

- Supervise the contractual commitments.
- Achieve the statistic comparisons.
- Provide assistance to the local public power partner in the contract.
- Offer support to the public power in adapting the rules and the institutional framework.
- Necessary for a good development of the public-private partnership.

However, some initial steps are required to implement the regulation process:

- Quality Control.
- Simplification of administrative procedures and regulatory reform.
- Transparency in delivery of services.
- Develop accountability, more effective financial management, and improved use of information technology to meet business and organizational needs (OECD, 2001).

The bottom line is that in-house public service provision is sufficient for improving service provision and cost efficiency. Public funding does not require service supply to public institutions. Instead, it gives incentives to the private sector to supply services more flexibly while shaping their incentives, which may be a better solution for government as a principal in terms of promoting efficiency with a range of different institutional approaches being used to that end.

CONCLUSION

In the context of public service transformation, privatization is regarded as an important means to achieve improved efficiency and quality of services. There is significant evidence that the private sector generally supplies services at a lower cost than the public sector. With public service organizations faced with more bargaining, enforcing and monitoring costs associated with contract maintenance, outsourcing public services permits leveraging private sector efficiency. Economies of scale also contribute to the preference of public organizations to outsource public services. Privatization of public services is often seen as guarantor of greater efficiency and quality.

In terms of service provision, e-Government can refer to the transactions (both financial and non-financial) related to the role of Government in public administration and providing services to the community. With all those considerations, e-Government must be seen as a management policy centered on the citizens' needs, bringing together different Information Technology trends in the provision of services and public services information, raising the level of state government accountability.

In this brief it has been suggested that information and communication technology will play a key role in enhancing service delivery by ensuring a better fit between information systems and strategic intent. Information management seeks to provide decision-makers with information systems that meet expectations. This it does by empowering business managers with analytical tools to evaluate information systems through definition, procurement and operation. These first measures may all be adopted within existing legal frameworks, and may then help to impel the much-needed transformation of government.

REFERENCES

Abelson P. and D. Chung (2005), The Real Story of Housing Prices in Australia from 1970 to 2003, *Australian Economic Review*, 38(3), pp 265–281.

Allen, B.A., Juillet, L., Paquet, G. and Roy, J. (2001), "E-Governance and Government Online in Canada: Partnerships, people and prospects", *Government Information Quarterly*, Vol. 18, 93-104.

Bahiense, G.C (2002). "Alinhamento estratégico de tecnologia da informação no setor público: a oferta de services eletrônicos em secretarias de fazenda no Brasi"l. Tese de Doutorado, FGV.

Bailey, S.J. (2002), Public Sector Economics: *Theory, Policy and Practice, MacMillan*, London.

Borcherding, T.E., Burnaby, B.C., Pommerehne, W.W., and F. Schneider (1982), "Comparing the efficiency of private and public production: the evidence from five countries", *Zeitschrift fur Nationalokonomie*, 89, 127-56.

Boyne, G.A. (1998), "Bureaucratic Theory Meets Reality: Public Choice and Service Contracting in U. S. Local Government", *Public Administration Review*, Vol. 58(6), 474-84.

Cunha, Maria Alexandra V.C., Reinhard, Nicholas. (2001), Portal of Public Services and Information Citizen: a survey of cases in Brazil. In: XXV Annual Meeting National Association of Programs Pósgraduação in Administration. September 2001.

Ferguson, M. (2002), "Estratégias de governo eletrônico: o cenário internacional em desenvolvimento. In:Eisenberger, José; Cepik, Marco". Internet e política:teoria e prática da democracia eletrônica. *Belo Horizonte*: Ed.UFMG.

Grout, P.A. (2003), "Financing and Managing Public Services", CMPO Working Paper Series No. 03/076, University of Bristol, Margaret Stevens, Lincoln College, Oxford.

Jeger, A. M. (2000), *Community Mental Health and Behavioural Ecology*, New York: Plenum Press.

JMMS (2001), "The Impact of Decentralization and Privatization on Municipal Services", International Labour Organization, Sectoral Activities Programme, Geneva, 15-19.

Lundsgaard, J. (2002), Competition and Efficiency in Publicly Provided Services, *Economics Department Working Papers*, No.331, OECD, Paris.

Martin, R. (2001): Central and Eastern Europe and the international economy: The limits to globalization, *Europe Asia Studies*, Vol. 70, No. 1.

Martin, S., and Parker, D. (1997), The Impact of Privatisation: Ownership and Corporate Performance in the UK, London, Routledge.

Megginson William L. and Netter Jeffry M. (2001), From State To Market: A Survey Of Empirical Studies On Privatization, *Journal of Economic Literature*, Vol. 39, No. 2 (June., 2001), pp. 321-389.

Newbery, D. (1997), Privatization and Liberalization of Network Utilities, *European Economic Review*, 41(3–5), 357–83.

Ntiro, S. (2000), "eGovernment in Eastern Africa", KPMG, Dar-es-Salaam.

OECD (2001), Regulation In Services: OECD Patterns And Economic Implications (2001), OECD Economics Department Working Paper No. 287.

Ribeiro, C.A (2005). "Governo Eletrônico na Reforma do Estado: inter-relações e Perspectivas", iP-Informática Pública,Vol. 7.

Soares, Ana Paula F. M (2002). "Instrumentos gerenciais utilizados na admnistração pública com foco no cidadão". *Dissertação de Mestrado*, FGV.

Vaz, J.C. (2003). "Limites e possibilidades do uso de portais municipais para a promoção da cidadania: construção de um modelo de análise e avaliação". Tese de Doutorado FGV.

World Bank (1995), Annual World Bank Conference on Development Economics 1995, World Bank ISBN: 0-8213-3280-5, Edited by Boris Pleskovic , Michael Bruno.

Online References

http://www.egov4dev.org/egovdefn.htm.

In: Information and Communication Technologies... ISBN 978-1-60876-671-0
Ed: Almas Heshmati and Sun Peng

Chapter 7

ANALYSIS OF PRODUCITVITY IN KOREAN ICT MANUFACTURING INDUSTRY

Yongil Kim*
Seoul National University

ABSTRACT

During the last 10 years, Korea has rapidly developed, particularly in the Information and Communications Technology (ICT) sector. This paper analyses the Total Factor Productivity (TFP) growth in Korea's ICT manufacturing industry. An econometric approach is employed to measure technical change in two different ways: using Time Trend (TT) and General Index (GI) models. The TT and GI models are estimated in form of both production and cost functions. The TT model captures technical change in terms of long term trend, but the trend hardly explains reality, especially when unexpected fluctuations like economic crisis take place. According to previous research, it has been proved that GI model performs better than the TT model. Twenty four Korean telecommunications equipment manufacture plants data from 1993 to 2003 is used in this paper. The results suggest that GI cost function model fits well to measure the rate of technical change. We observe both positive technical change and TFP growth rates in Korean ICT manufacturing industry. There might have been structural change and changes in return to scale in the industry through the Asian financial crisis.

1. INTRODUCTION

In Korea, like many other countries, people tend to prefer to own brand-new mobile phones. It is common in Korea to replace old phone after two years' usage. The frequency might be even higher among the young generation. Thanks to such tendency and other successful factors, the Korean ICT manufacturing industry developed more rapidly than other sectors. Korea is known to have suffered severe financial crisis resulting from dollar

* E-mail: npacificy@temep.snu.ac.kr

depletion in the mid 1990s, and the ICT sector is generally credited for making a significant contribution to the recovery of the economy.

In this paper, technical change in the ICT manufacturing industry is analyzed. The main interest is the sign of technical change, the magnitude of rate of technical change and the determinants of technical change. For this purpose, panel data on 24 plants of Korean Standard Industrial Classification (KISC) dataset at the 5-digit level was collected; 32201 and 32202 over the period 1993-2003. For the estimation, a translog production function and cost function was specified and estimated. The rate of technical change and total factor productivity was calculated by the TT model and GI model introduced by Baltagi and Griffin (1988).

The results show that TFP and technical change decreased during the crisis but soon recovered. Most of the rate of technical change was explained by the pure technical change. The average rate of pure or neutral technical change was 10.7% and non-neutral component was -1.7% according to the TT model using a production function approach. The results of TT and GI models were compared with that of divisia index as a benchmark. There was no significant difference between mean values based production function approach and cost function approaches.

The rest of the paper is organized as follows. The econometrics models with time trend and general index of technical change are outlined in section 2. Section 3 describes the data. Empirical results are reported in Section 4. Section 5 contains summary and conclusion of this study.

2. METHODOLOGY

Diwert (1979) classified four approaches to measuring technical change; econometric estimation of cost and production functions, divisia indexes, exact index numbers, and nonparametric methods using linear programming. In this study the methods of econometric estimation; TT model and GI model (Kumbhakar, Nakamura and Heshmati, 2000) is used. A second approach, the divisia index is used as a non-parametric benchmark model. For various comparisons, both production function and cost function are estimated at the same time. For the specification of functional form, instead of a simple Cobb-Douglas function, a flexible functional form, the transcendental logarithmic function is used (Christensen and Jorgenson, 1973).

A. Time Trend Model

First of all, translog production function specification is defined as follows:

$$\ln y = \alpha_0 + \sum \beta_i \ln X_i + \frac{1}{2}\sum\sum \gamma_{ij} \ln X_i \ln X_j + \frac{1}{2}\phi t^2 + \sum \theta_i \ln X_i t + \varphi t + v \quad (1)$$

where, y is output, X_i is vector of input quantity (i=1 for capital, i=2 for labor, i=3 for material), t is time and v is a random error term.

For the purpose of estimation and interpretation, the data are transformed to logarithmic form. Different input elasticities and the rate of technical change can be calculated based on the estimated coefficients. Elasticities of inputs are obtained by the derivative of production function with respective production inputs. The sum of input elasticities is a measure of returns to scale expressed as below.

$$\varepsilon_i = \frac{\partial \ln y}{\partial \ln X_i} = \beta_i + \sum \gamma_{ij} \ln X_j + \theta_i t, \quad RTS = \varepsilon_1 + \varepsilon_2 + \varepsilon_3 \tag{2}$$

where, ε_i: is input elasticity (i=1 for capital, i=2 for labor, i=3 for material), RTS is Return to scale. In similar way the rate of technical change is computed as the derivative of production function with respect to time:

$$\dot{T} = \frac{\partial \ln y}{\partial t} = \phi t + \varphi + \sum \theta_i \ln X_i$$

$$\widetilde{TFP} = \dot{T} + (RTS - 1) * \dot{y}, \ \dot{y} = \frac{(y - y_{-1})}{y_{-1}} \tag{3}$$

where, $\dot{y}$ is growth rate of output. TFP is the sum of technical change ($\dot{T}$) and scale economy ($(RTS - 1) * \dot{y}$). Technical change also can be decomposed into two components; (i) pure technical change ($\phi t + \varphi$), and (ii) non-neutral technical change ($\sum \theta_i \ln X_i$). As a benchmark of TFP, the divisia index can be calculated by subtracting weighted average of input growth rate from output growth rate.

$$Divisia = \dot{y} - (\varepsilon_1 * \dot{k} + \varepsilon_2 * \dot{l} + \varepsilon_3 * \dot{m}) \tag{4}$$

where, $\dot{k}$: growth rate of capital $\dot{l}$ is growth rate of capital labor and $\dot{m}$ is growth rate of material.

In terms of cost function, the estimation could be specified similarly using a translog cost function:

$$\ln(TC) = \alpha_0 + \sum \beta_i \ln P_i + \rho \ln y + \frac{1}{2} \sum \sum \gamma_{ij} \ln P_i \ln P_j + \frac{1}{2} \mu (\ln y)^2 + \frac{1}{2} \phi t^2$$

$$+ \sum \lambda_i \ln P_i \ln y + \sum \theta_i \ln P_i t + \omega \ln y t + \varphi t + v \tag{5}$$

where, TC is total cost, P_i is input price (i=1 for capital, i=2 for labor), and t is time. Using the Shepherd's lemma, cost share can be obtained. Owing to the characteristics of the system equations, the third input, i.e. material is omitted.

$$S_i = \frac{\partial \ln TC}{\partial \ln P_i} = \beta_i + \sum \gamma_{ij} \ln P_j + \theta_i t + \lambda_i \ln y, \ i = 1, 2$$

$$S_3 = 1 - (S_1 + S_2) \tag{6}$$

where, S_i is cost share input i (i=1 for capital, i=2 for labor, i=3 for material). Given estimation of the parameters in equations (5) and (6), the rate of technical change can be computed as the derivative of cost function with respect to time:

$$\dot{T} = \frac{\partial \ln TC}{\partial t} = \phi t + \varphi + \sum \theta_i \ln P_i + \omega \ln y \quad (7)$$

The technical change can be decomposed into the following three components: (i) pure technical change ($\phi t + \varphi$), (ii) non-neutral technical change ($\sum \theta_i \ln P_i$), and (iii) scale-augmenting technical change ($\omega \ln y$). Furthermore total factor productivity can be estimated as:

$$\dot{TFP} = -\dot{T} + (1 - \varepsilon_{CY}) * \dot{y}, \; \dot{y} = \frac{(y - y_{-1})}{y_{-1}}$$

$$\varepsilon_{CY} = \frac{\partial \ln TC}{\partial \ln y} = \rho + \mu \ln y + \sum \lambda_i \ln P_i + \omega t \quad (8)$$

where, $\dot{y}$ is growth rate of output, ε_{CY} is output elasticity of total cost, same as the inverse of return to scale

B. General Index Model

General index model differs from the time trend model in the sense that time trend cannot fully represent the characteristics of technical change as time elapses. In addition, general index can provide richer information for analysis. For example, we can find out determinants of technical change using the model. In particular the model assumes that there is unique technical change in every year. The yearly rate of technical change can be captured by the regression using dummy variables. In the production function, “firm” and “year” dummy variables were created to calculate the general index. The translog production function specification is defined as follows:

$$\ln y = \alpha_0 + \sum \xi_k D_k + A(t) + \sum \beta_i \ln X_i + \frac{1}{2} \sum \sum \gamma_{ij} \ln X_i \ln X_j + \sum \theta_i \ln X_i A(t) + v \quad (9)$$

where, y is output, X_i is a vector of inputs (i=1 for capital, i=2 for labor, i=3 for material), D_k is firm specific dummy variables. The rate of technical change is derived as:

$$\dot{T} = \frac{\partial \ln y}{\partial A(t)} = A(t) - A(t-1) + \sum \theta_i [A(t) - A(t-1)] \ln X_i \quad (10)$$

The specification in practice is as follows where A(t) is replaced by yearly time-dummy variables.

$$\ln y = \alpha_0 + \sum \xi_k D_k + \sum \delta_t F_t + \sum \beta_i \ln X_i + \frac{1}{2} \sum \sum \gamma_{ij} \ln X_i \ln X_j + \sum \theta_{it} \ln X_i F_t + v \quad (11)$$

where, F_t is time specific dummy. The overall rate of technical change is the sum of pure technical change (A(t)–A(t-1)) and non-neutral technical change $(\sum \theta_i [A(t) - A(t-1)] \ln X_i)$ components. The above equation (9) is called purely general index of technical change (Baltagi and Griffin, 1988) because of A(t). But the drawback lies in the fact that A(t) is not observable. Therefore instead of A(t), time-specific dummy variables are introduced in the model estimation. So the revised specification (11) was used in the analysis. Input elasticity and return to scale can be calculated in the same way as in the time trend model case. Divisia index, as a benchmark for TFP, is also calculated similarly.

As for the cost function approach, a general index model of technical change in translog form is as follows:

$$\ln(TC) = \alpha_0 + \sum \xi_k D_K + A(t) + \sum \beta_i \ln P_i + \rho \ln y + \frac{1}{2} \sum \sum \gamma_{ij} \ln P_i \ln P_j$$

$$+ \frac{1}{2} \mu (\ln y)^2 + \sum \lambda_i \ln P_i \ln y + \sum \theta_i \ln P_i A(t) + \omega A(t) \ln y_i \tag{12}$$

where, TC is total cost, P_i is a vector of input prices (i=1 for capital, i=2 for labor), t is time representing technology. Using the Shepherd's lemma, cost share can be obtained as:

$$S_i = \frac{\partial \ln TC}{\partial \ln P_i} = \beta_i + \sum \gamma_{ij} \ln P_j + \lambda_i \ln y + \theta_i A(t), \text{ i=1, 2} \tag{13}$$

The rate of technical change in the general index cost model is obtained from:

$$\dot{T} = \frac{\partial \ln TC}{\partial A(t)} = A(t) - A(t-1) + \sum \theta_i [A(t) - A(t-1)] \ln P_i + \omega [A(t) - A(t-1)] \ln y \tag{14}$$

In this model A(t) is not observable either, so time specific dummy variable will be used instead of A(t). Also, technical change can be decomposed into 3 underlying components; (i) pure technical change (A(t)-A(t-1)), (ii) non-neutral technical change $(\sum \theta_i [A(t) - A(t-1)] \ln P_i)$, and (iii) scale-augmenting technical change $(\omega [A(t) - A(t-1)] \ln y)$. For empirical estimation, a vector of time dummies instead of the unknown A(t) is used.

2. DATA

The data used in this paper are the plant-level panel data assembled from the Annual Report on Mining and Manufacturing Survey in Korea. The data include information on 24 plants which belong to the Korean Standard Industrial Classification (KSIC) at the 5-digit level; 32201 and 32202. The first category (KISC 32201) is manufacturing of wire-line telecommunication equipment; the latter one is manufacturing of radio communication broadcasting and related equipment without any line connection. The analysis period is from 1993 to 2003.

Table 1. Descriptive statistics of the data

Variable	N	Mean	Standard deviation	Minimum	Maximum
Year of observation	264	1998	3	1993	2003
Output	264	129866	418294	46	3075314
Total cost	264	172912	486234	95	3004632
Capital	264	18244	38134	33	270821
Labor	264	311	554	7	4009
Material	264	266268	814490	18	5980542
Price of capital	264	1.001	0.078	0.868	1.112
Price of labor	264	1.055	0.075	0.573	1.215
Price of material	264	0.580	0.136	0.154	0.990

Among population of plants, 24 plants, which have complete information of the related items, were selected. Small firms with less than 10 employees are excluded and the plants with missing observations were also omitted. Some large plants were also excluded because of restructuring or mergers and acquisitions (M&A) which occurred during the Asian financial crisis of 1997-1998.

Four kinds of data were used in the analysis. For simplicity, one output and 3 input variables were selected. The gross production of each plant was used as a measure of output, while capital, labor and materials were used as input variables. Output is measured as real production value deflated by the producer price index at the 3-digit industry level (namely, 322). As is shown in Table 1, output varies in the interval 46 million to 3 trillion Korean Won (KW).

Regarding capital input, the average book value of capital stock at the beginning and end of the year was used, but first deflated by the capital goods price index deflator. The number of workers was used as a measure of labor input. Workers include paid employees and working proprietors. In calculating material input, the sum of direct and indirect material costs was used.

4. Empirical Results

A. Time Trend Model

Table 2 and 3 show the TFP, elasticity, rate of technical change and its decomposition into two components based on the TT production function model. According to Table 2, during the period, the average of annual rate of technical change was 9.1% and consequently TFP mean was 10.1%. The TFP shows that the sector had relatively higher productivity growth than expected, considering the recession after financial crisis. The returns to scale is approximately 1, which is shown in Table 2. The annual scale effect is calculated and reported in Table 3. Except for the year 1998 and 2001, the scale effect as difference between

TFP and Technical Change(TC) was positive. In 1998, it was negative due to decreasing returns to scale reducing TFP growth rate by 0.5%.

Table 2. TT production model results (sample mean)

Variable	N	Mean	StdDev	Minimum	Maximum
Capital elasticity	264	0.131	0.127	-0.225	0.478
Labor elasticity	264	0.253	0.217	-0.318	0.899
Material elasticity	264	0.666	0.260	-0.138	1.411
Return to scale	264	1.050	0.056	0.906	1.185
Technical change	264	0.091	0.104	-0.106	0.300
Pure TC	264	0.107	0.107	-0.061	0.276
Non-neutral TC	264	-0.016	0.020	-0.066	0.034
Total factor productivity	264	0.101	0.113	-0.171	0.343
Divisia index	264	0.003	0.683	-5.495	3.626

Table 3. TT production model results (yearly mean)

year	Capital elasticity	Labor elasticity	Material elasticity	RTS	TC	Pure TC	Non- neutral TC	TFP	Divisia
1993	0.251	0.283	0.522	1.055	-0.074	0.061	-0.013	-0.074	0.000
1994	0.233	0.278	0.541	1.052	-0.040	-0.027	-0.012	0.006	0.060
1995	0.198	0.252	0.596	1.046	-0.006	0.006	-0.012	0.006	-0.154
1996	0.161	0.231	0.646	1.038	0.030	0.040	-0.010	0.035	-0.243
1997	0.129	0.208	0.697	1.034	0.063	0.074	-0.011	0.080	0.148
1998	0.098	0.201	0.736	1.035	0.095	0.107	-0.013	0.090	-0.150
1999	0.111	0.244	0.696	1.051	0.122	0.141	-0.019	0.124	-0.041
2000	0.088	0.223	0.742	1.053	0.152	0.175	-0.023	0.170	-0.320
2001	0.076	0.263	0.722	1.060	0.185	0.208	-0.024	0.183	0.113
2002	0.042	0.259	0.754	1.055	0.220	0.242	-0.022	0.233	0.213
2003	0.053	0.342	0.675	1.070	0.253	0.276	-0.023	0.254	0.405

The positive rate of technical change was mainly influenced by the positive pure technical change (i.e., +10.7%). The non-neutral technical change was negative (i.e., - 1.6%), which means that the industry experienced input mix changes during the period. From Table 3, we can tell that average TFP was consistently positive and increasing except for the year 1993. The pattern is partially a natural outcome when time trend model is adopted. However divisia index fluctuated during the entire period. Such fluctuation contradicts the increasing trend of technical change for the entire period suggested by the time trend model, but might correspond to real technical change better. Divisia shows that the industry recovers in terms of productivity from year 2001 in the aftermath of the financial crisis. It can be noted that divisia index is lower in 2001, but higher in 2003, compared with the TFP growth rate based on the parametric TT production model.

Table 4. TT cost model results (yearly mean)

year	Capital elasticity	Labor elasticity	Material elasticity	RTS	TC	Pure TC	Non-neutral TC	TFP	Divisia
1993	0.286	0.014	0.700	0.974	0.069	0.058	0.011	-0.069	0.000
1994	0.284	0.017	0.698	0.981	0.041	0.030	0.011	-0.071	-0.006
1995	0.297	0.020	0.683	0.986	0.014	0.002	0.012	-0.018	-0.204
1996	0.310	0.023	0.668	0.990	-0.014	-0.027	0.013	0.016	-0.245
1997	0.310	0.028	0.662	0.996	-0.042	-0.055	0.013	0.048	0.045
1998	0.314	0.024	0.663	0.998	-0.068	-0.083	0.015	0.056	-0.068
1999	0.325	0.034	0.640	0.997	-0.098	-0.111	0.014	0.105	-0.242
2000	0.338	0.036	0.626	1.005	-0.124	-0.140	0.016	0.130	-0.978
2001	0.356	0.041	0.603	1.006	-0.152	-0.168	0.016	0.154	0.132
2002	0.361	0.052	0.588	1.007	-0.181	-0.196	0.015	0.183	0.179
2003	0.335	0.088	0.577	0.990	-0.219	-0.224	0.006	0.221	0.313

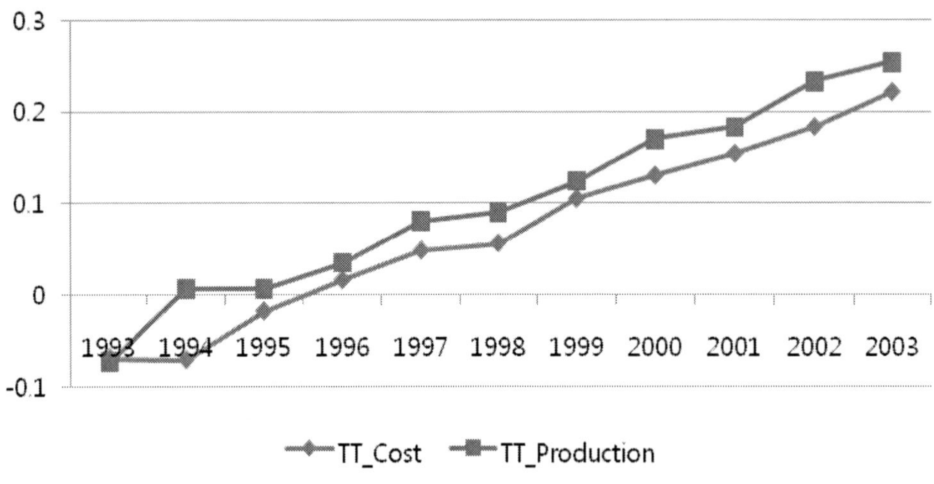

Figure 1. TFP comparison based on TT production and TT cost models.

Table 4 represents results from the time trend cost function model. Compared with production model, TC and TFP are somewhat smaller. Owing to the characteristics of cost function, returns to scale is less than one, decreasing returns to scale, compared to increasing RTS in the production function model. As is shown in Table 4, RTSs are less than one except for year 2000-2002. In analyzing the decomposition of TC into pure TC and non-neutral TC, we can find that TC mainly consists of a pure component and the non-neutral component , which is same as in the production model. The size of non-neutral technical change is increasing over time, which means that negative effect from input change increases through the period. The scale augmenting technical change is nearly zero. However the overall direction and trend of TFP are similar to those in the TT production model case.

Figure 1 represents the TFP comparison between time trend cost function and production function approaches. TFP of TT cost model is always smaller than that of TT production model. Definitely the trend is increasing during the whole period because they are based on time trend technical change model.

B. General Index Model

The results from GI production model were different from the corresponding TT production model. First of all scale economy is opposite. Table 5 shows that sample mean RTS is less than one, which is contrary to RTS in TT production model which was suggesting increasing returns to scale.

From Table 5, we can see the sample mean scale effect is –1.5%. As is shown in the RTS column of Table 6, the yearly RTS is less than one. It means that returns to scale is decreasing and that the scale is too large for an optimal size. The scale effect is almost negative with the exception of year 1994 and 1998, as is shown in Table 6. The non-neutral component of technical change was positive (i.e., +1.1% in Table 5), which is contrary to TT model. It was also found that TFP was negative in 2000 when IT bubble burst. According to Table 6, TFP trend can be divided into several sub periods; negative in 1995 and 1996, positive in 1997-1999, negative in 2000, and recovery period 2001-2003.

In comparing the parametric TFP with the non-parametric divisia index, the size and the signs are similar with the exception of year 1998, when divisia index was negative but TFP was positive.

This difference might have occurred owing to the structural change of Korean economy through financial crisis. As a result it can be said that GI model can explain the technical change more accurately than TT model on the whole.

Table 5. GI production model results (sample mean)

Variable	N	Mean	StdDev	Minimum	Maximum
Capital elasticity	264	0.047	0.074	-0.170	0.259
Labor elasticity	264	0.254	0.211	-0.310	0.829
Material elasticity	264	0.673	0.207	0.021	1.258
Return to scale	264	0.973	0.088	0.783	1.171
Technical change	264	0.119	0.154	-0.056	0.625
Pure TC	264	0.108	0.141	-0.042	0.487
Non-neutral TC	264	0.011	0.022	-0.048	0.138
Total factor productivity	264	0.104	0.173	-0.385	0.611
Divisia index	264	0.050	0.580	-3.189	3.603

Table 6. GI production model results (yearly mean)

year	Capital elasticity	Labor elasticity	Material elasticity	RTS	TC	Pure TC	Non-neutral TC	TFP	Divisia
1993	0.099	0.331	0.566	0.996	0.000	0.000	0.000	0.000	0.000
1994	0.084	0.317	0.584	0.985	0.169	0.152	0.017	0.183	0.115
1995	0.076	0.281	0.619	0.976	-0.047	-0.042	-0.005	-0.065	-0.122
1996	0.065	0.253	0.649	0.967	-0.002	-0.002	0.000	-0.027	-0.225
1997	0.044	0.223	0.692	0.959	0.146	0.128	0.018	0.086	0.237
1998	0.034	0.207	0.720	0.961	0.051	0.044	0.006	0.060	-0.082
1999	0.044	0.231	0.691	0.966	0.065	0.058	0.007	0.034	0.014
2000	0.034	0.198	0.725	0.958	0.011	0.010	0.001	-0.020	-0.174
2001	0.030	0.229	0.711	0.971	0.175	0.159	0.016	0.174	0.131
2002	0.009	0.222	0.740	0.971	0.211	0.191	0.020	0.200	0.221
2003	-0.004	0.298	0.701	0.994	0.528	0.487	0.041	0.519	0.430

Table 7. GI cost model results (yearly mean)

year	Capital elasticity	Labor elasticity	Material elasticity	RTS	TC	Pure TC	Non-neutral TC	Scale Augmenting TC	TFP	Divisia
1993	0.33	0.031	0.639	1.264	0.000	0.000	0.000	0.000	0.000	0.000
1994	0.326	0.033	0.641	1.263	-0.040	-0.048	0.008	0.000	0.243	-0.006
1995	0.306	0.026	0.668	1.266	0.114	0.140	-0.025	0.000	-0.018	-0.204
1996	0.302	0.023	0.675	1.269	0.052	0.065	-0.013	-0.001	0.006	-0.245
1997	0.292	0.024	0.684	1.268	-0.022	-0.027	0.005	-0.001	0.204	0.045
1998	0.323	0.017	0.66	1.268	-0.044	-0.055	0.012	0.000	0.150	-0.068
1999	0.301	0.014	0.685	1.266	0.032	0.041	-0.008	-0.001	0.025	-0.242
2000	0.271	0.006	0.723	1.272	0.162	0.210	-0.046	-0.002	-0.056	-0.978
2001	0.334	0.028	0.638	1.271	-0.243	-0.314	0.071	0.000	0.250	0.132
2002	0.356	0.044	0.599	1.266	-0.193	-0.248	0.054	0.001	0.262	0.179
2003	0.335	0.055	0.610	1.236	-0.473	-0.538	0.061	0.004	0.499	0.313

Table 7 shows the results from estimation of the GI cost function model. Compared with production function model, RTS is more than one indicating increasing returns to scale. We can see that TFP reflects the divisia index with regard to overall direction, but not with regard to signs. When it comes to the decomposition of TC, TC mainly consists of pure technical change and non-neutral technical change components. The scale augmenting technical change is extremely small. In this case, non-neutral technical change has negative effect excluding 4 years. However the overall direction and trend of TFP are similar to those of GI production case.

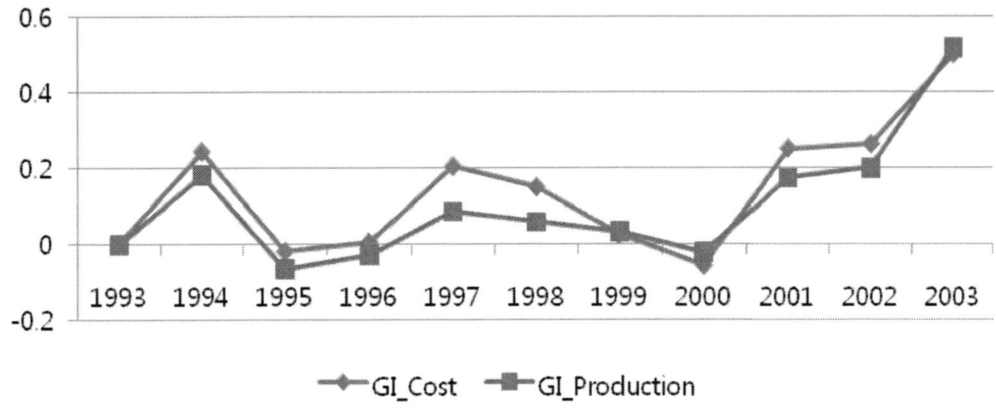

Figure 2. TFP comparison GI production and GI cost function models.

In comparison with the TFP of GI production model, TFP of GI cost model is larger except for year 2000. That is shown in Figure 2. It is contrary to the TT model where the TFP of production function was larger than that of cost function.

C. Major Findings

First, from the viewpoint of technical change there was an increase in the rate of technical progress during the study period in the industry. This increasing trend of technical progress is expressed as TT_Prod and TT_Cost line in the Figure 3. But GI_Prod and GI_Cost can provide more detailed information about technical change. The period can be divided into 3 sub-periods – pre-financial crisis period (1993-1996), IT bubble period (1997-2000) and recovery period (2001-2003). When compared with TC in cost model, TC in production model is generally larger.. This characteristic is common both in TT model and in GI model.

Second, the non-neutral component of technical change was negative through the study period except for GI cost model. It means that productivity decreased due to change of input factors mix. We can observe that there was structural change in the capital/labor ratio in the ICT industry after financial crisis emerged.

Third, when it comes to TFP, GI cost model captures well the pattern of the non-parametric divisia index more accurately. According to Figure 4, in general the TFP growth rate based on GI cost model corresponds to divisia index better than that of the TT cost model. In 2000, the gap between divisia index and TFP is ? large. This might result from the ICT bubble burst in that year.

Fourth, with regard to return to scale, there exist differences between TT model and GI model specifications. For example, increasing RTS appeared in TT production but decreasing RTS appeared in the GI production model. It seems that there was a significant change in scale economy during the study period. We can presume that RTS decreased after the Asian financial crisis period.

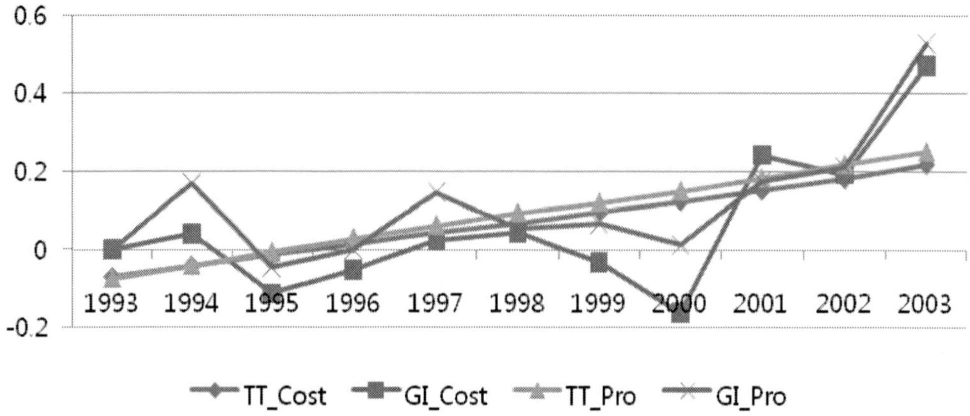

Figure 3. Comparison of TC among the 4 parametric model specifications.

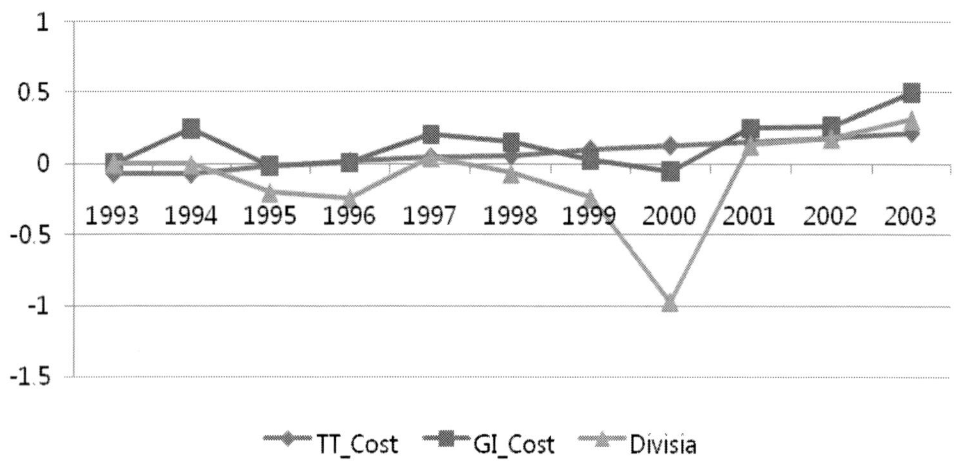

Figure 4. Comparison between TFP and divisia index of productivity growth.

SUMMARY

This paper focused on the parametric measurement of the rate of technical change in Korean ICT manufacturing industry over year 1993-2003. As for the methodology, estimation of production function and cost function based on time trend model and general index model are used. The estimation results show that, the TFP growth rate of Korean ICT industry increased so fast over the period of Asian financial crisis. Namely the sector contributed to the recovery of the whole economy. And the main factor of the technical change was pure technical change component. The non-neutral component of technical change was negative except for GI production model.

GI models perform better than TT models. GI models capture similar patterns as that of the non-parametric divisia index better, which is asserted by many previous researchers. But the general index of technical change is not observable, so it is represented by other variables, e.g. time-specific yearly dummy variables. The main difference between TT model and GI with time-dummy is the square term of time variable. To develop GI model further, more efforts should be made to specify relevant indexes.

Regarding return to scale, it was increasing in the TT model but showing a decreasing pattern in the GI model. Accordingly, the scale effect was positive in the TT model but was negative in the GI model. So it can be said that the scale effect was not deterministic in the sector. To understand the scale effect more accurately, we need more extended or advanced research.

REFERENCES

Baltagi B.H. and J.M. Griffin (1988), A General Index of Technical Change, *Journal of Political Economy* 96, 20-41.

Christensen, L., D. Jorgenson, et al. (1973). Transcendental logarithmic production frontiers, *The Review of Economics and Statistics*, 28-45.

Diewert, W. (1979). The theory of total factor productivity measurement in regulated industries, University of British Columbia, Dept. of Economics.

Kumbhakar S.C., Nakamura S. and A. Heshmati (2000), Estimation of Firm-Specific Technological Bias, Technical Change and Total Factor Productivity Growth: A Dual Approach, *Econometric Reviews* 19(4), 493-515.

In: Information and Communication Technologies… ISBN 978-1-60876-671-0
Ed: Almas Heshmati and Sun Peng

Chapter 8

NETWORK NEUTRALITY AND THE EFFICIENCY OF INTERNET APPLICATION SERVICE PROVIDERS: A META-FRONTIER ANALYSIS

Daeho Lee*
Seoul National University

ABSTRACT

As applications require a wider and more stable bandwidth, Internet service providers (ISPs) try to control application services, and it has caused the network neutrality debate. This paper categorizes application services into four groups according to the attributes of bandwidth-usage and latency-sensitivity. By estimating the efficiency of four groups, whether there is difference in efficiency among those four groups is tested so as to see the discrimination of ISP under the circumstance in which network neutrality is not kept. Efficiency which is comparable among companies with different production functions can be calculated using a meta-frontier production function. Based on the estimated result, when the degree of freedom changes under network neutrality regulations, we forecast the effect of the development of the application service area and evaluate the network neutrality regulation.

Keywords: network neutrality, Internet application, Internet service providers, efficiency, meta-frontier.

1. INTRODUCTION

Network neutrality means the maintaining of Internet openness that makes anyone access freely every application through the network without any discrimination that gives preference

* E-mail: deafish@temep.snu.ac.kr

to a network provider's own application service and degrades the service application of others (Ford et al., 2006).

In the initial stages, the development of the Internet was based on the fundamental principles of openness and nondiscrimination. However, since this early dynamic was established, various applications have been developed and the role of Internet service providers (ISPs) has expanded. Applications require different amounts and stability of bandwidth determined by the characteristic of the application. As applications require a wider and more stable bandwidth, ISPs try to control application services to maximize their profit, and thereby this has caused an intensive neutrality debate about the network.

In this situation, network neutrality proponents and opponents make opposing assertions. The proponents of the network neutrality principle say that network neutrality can prevent ISPs abusing their market power and promote the innovation of application service providers (ASPs) so as to increase consumers' welfare. The opponents of the network neutrality principle, on the other hand, assert that network neutrality delays the innovation of application services because it hampers the development of the network itself.

Therefore this paper categorizes application services into four groups according to the attributes of bandwidth-usage and latency-sensitivity. By estimating the efficiency of the four groups, whether there is difference of efficiency among those four groups is tested, so as to see the discrimination of ISP under the circumstance in which network neutrality is not kept.

The rest of this paper is organized as follows. Section 2 shows previous studies. Section 3 explains the reason of the network neutrality debate and the motivation of this paper again. Section 4 describes meta-frontier methodologies, and section 5 explains the data. Section 6 shows the estimation equation, and section 7 is the result of estimation. Section 8 summarizes this paper and concludes.

2. Literature Review

Discussion of the network neutrality started in the United States. In the U.S. in 2004 a small North Carolina telecom company, Madison River Communications, blocked their DSL customers from using the Vonage VoIP service. Since this, several researchers have offered law and economics information on network neutrality. In particular a conflict of opinions has arisen over network and Internet innovation.

Network neutrality opponents say that network neutrality harms the entire society because it reduces the supply of network infra and delays network innovation. In his paper Yoo (2005) asserts there is no evidence that 'innovations operating at the network's edge must be preferred to 'innovations in the network's core', and also insists in his other paper that the assertion that network neutrality regulation promotes innovation is wrong from the view point of the Internet. Yoo (2006) and Hahn and Wallsten (2006) also opposed network neutrality and worried that network neutrality regulation would decrease investment incentives, distort innovation, and finally harm consumers. Sidak (2006) is also an opponent of network neutrality, and say that non-regulation induces investment in the network and promotes network innovation. Moreover, he argues that a non-regulation circumstance induces innovation at the edges of the network.

Contrarily, network neutrality proponents say the monopolistic conduct of network operators can be prevented by keeping the network neutrality principle. Barbara (2007) analyzes the network neutrality problem with an economic approach and asserts that network neutrality eliminates ISP's threat of discrimination but it does not mean that there is no cost. However, Barbara says that network neutrality is beneficial because, potentially, the benefit of economic growth from application innovation is much bigger than the cost of network neutrality even though network neutrality makes the conflict of application innovation and the decrement of network infra supply. Wu (2005) also asserts that the end-to-end design principle advances the Internet. He says that it promotes the innovation from the network edge. Additionally, regarding the difference between himself and Christopher Yoo, who is the representative of the network neutrality opponents, Wu (2006) says that Yoo thinks that ISPs like ATandT never deter innovation, but rather are the driving force of future innovation. However Wu is skeptical about Yoo's opinion and he insists that ISPs threaten the current business model of ASPs by blocking the entry with innovative technology.

On the other side, while expressing the network neutrality proponents as 'Openists' and the opponents as 'Deregulationists', Wu (2004) says that the former is mainly interested in a general end to innovation whereas the latter is mainly interested in a means, and the conflict can be reconciled because the means that 'Deregulationists' want is sustainable non-regulation by government. Additionally, Wu mentions that both proponents and opponents agree with the fact that innovation is the source of economic growth. With a similar viewpoint, Peha (2006) insists the need for a 'balanced policy' that does not limit constructive innovation and prevents the abuse of the monopolistic market power of network operators.

3. Innovation, Spillover and Efficiency

What causes the network neutrality debate primarily, and why cannot this debate lead to a decision? It is because both proponents and opponents assert the opinion of their own side and both assertions are right from the viewpoint of their own side. When ASPs innovate, this innovation spills over into the ISP area in various ways. For instance, when the streaming service of YouTube wins popular favor, to show a YouTube filmstably becomes a primary function of ISP. Accordingly, ISPs try to improve the quality of network so as to broaden the bandwidth and provide Quality of Service (QoS). Contrarily, when ISPs innovate, this innovation also spills over into the ASP area. For example, if ISPs did not provide a broad and stable network service using QoS, the Voice over Internet Protocol (VoIP) service could not even be developed. Figure 1 shows the spillover of innovation that circulates among ASP and ISP.

If the amount of spillover of innovation could be estimated and all the innovation from ASP spilled over into ISP, so the innovation from ASP induced the same amount of innovation of ISP, and vice versa, then the debate of network neutrality would be meaningless, because whether the innovation of ASP area is activated under network neutrality principle or the innovation of ISP area is activated without the network neutrality principle, the effect will be exactly equal.

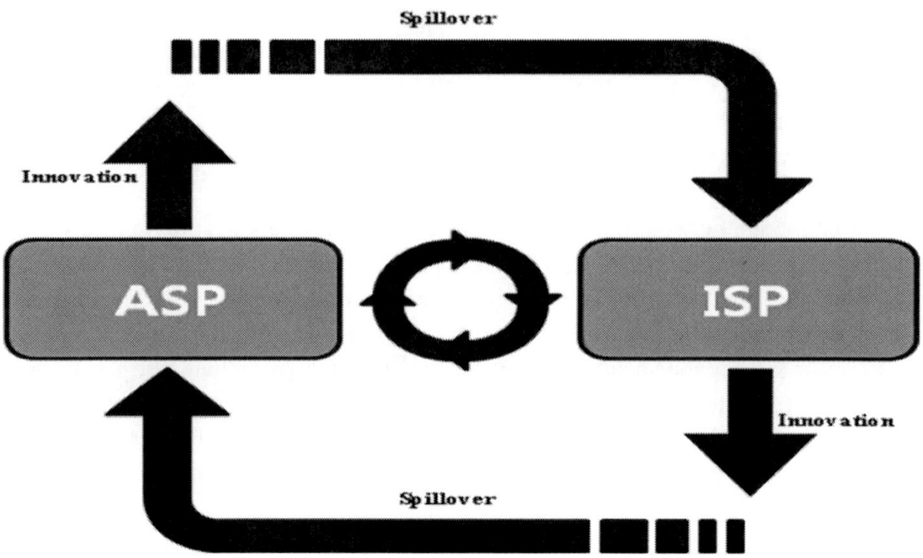

Figure 1. Innovation Spillover between ISP and ASP.

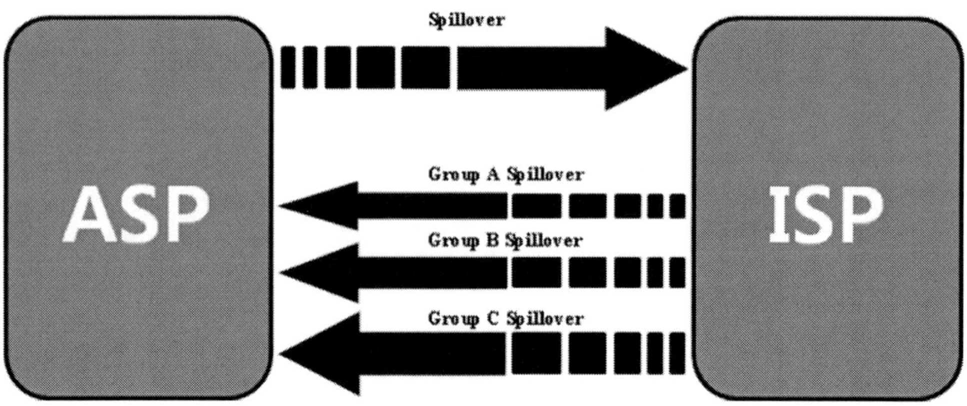

Figure 2. The amount of spillover among the categorized groups.

However, it is impossible that the innovation of one field spills over into another field perfectly and, moreover, without the network neutrality principle, the amount of spillover of innovation can be different depending on the bandwidth-usage or latency-sensitivity of the application service even if all the application services use the same ISP to provide their application services. According to Wu (2005), it does not matter when it is delayed by a couple of seconds in the case of latency-insensitive services like E-mail, but in the case of the real time streaming service of movies, it matters substantially. Therefore network neutrality proponents say that, as the service uses more bandwidth and is more sensitive to latency, ISP has more incentives to discriminate in the application service. It is supported by the fact that the discussion of network neutrality started with the occurrence of VoIP, whereas there was none when there existed http and E-mail services only. That is, the amount of spillover of innovation from ISP can be different depending on the attributes of the application service, even though the innovation of the network circulates by spillover effects.

Therefore this paper categorizes application services into four groups according to the attributes of bandwidth-usage and latency-sensitivity. By estimating the efficiency of four groups, whether there exists any difference in efficiency level among those four groups is tested so as to see the discrimination of ISP under the circumstance in which network neutrality is not kept.

4. Econometric Methodology

The original parametric frontier model was developed by Aigner, Lovell and Schmidt (1977) and Meeusen and van den Broeck (1977), and has since then been extended by Battese and Coelli (1992), Kumbhakar (2002), and others. In this study, the meta-frontier analysis proposed in Battese et al. (2004), which is based on meta-frontier production function approach, is used to accommodate the group variation of application service production frontiers and obtain comparable technical efficiencies. Recently, Chen et al. (2008) calculate the efficiency and technology gap in China's agriculture using a regional meta-frontier analysis, and Hossain et al. (2007) analyze the technical efficiency and varietal differences in pistachio production in Iran using the same methodology.

Using a standard stochastic frontier analysis, it was impossible to estimate technical efficiency when firms are using different technologies. However, efficiency which is comparable among companies with different production functions can be calculated using a meta-frontier production function. Suppose that there are *R* different groups within the Internet application industry. The stochastic *j*-th group frontier is defined by:

$$Y_{it}(j) = f(x_{it(j)}, \beta_{(j)})e^{V_{it(j)} - U_{it(j)}}$$

where i = 1, 2, … , N_j, t = 1,2, … , T, j = 1, 2, … , R. N_j is the number of firms in *j*-th group. The model for the j-th group is assumed for simplicity by:

$$Y_{it} = e^{x_{it(j)}\beta_{(j)} + V_{it(j)} - U_{it(j)}}$$

In Table 1 we explain the definition of variables used in equations (1) and (2) and the subsequent estimation procedure.

From Battese, Rao and O'Donnell (2004), and by using their notations, the meta-frontier production function model is defined as:

$$Y_{it}^* \equiv f(x_{it}, \beta^*) = e^{x_{it}\beta^*}$$

where *i* = 1, … , N, $N = \sum_{j=1}^{R} N_j$, t = 1, … , T. β^* is the vector of meta-frontier parameters satisfying the condition:

$$x_{it}\beta^* \geq x_{it}\beta_{(j)}$$

for all j = 1, … , N_j. According to equation (4), the meta-frontier production function graph is always above all the frontier production function graphs of each group and each period. That is, the meta-frontier production function envelopes production group frontier production function.

Table 1. Variables used in the Meta-Frontier Analysis

Variable	Meaning of variable	Remarks
$Y_{it(j)}$	the output for the *i*-th firm in the *t*-th time period for the *j*-th group	one output
$x_{it(j)}$	a vector of values of functions of the inputs used by the *i*-th firm in the *t*-th time period for the *j*-th group	three inputs
$\beta_{(j)}$	the parameter vector associated with the x-variables for the stochastic frontier for the *j*-th group	
$V_{it(j)}$	identically and independently distributed as $N(0, \sigma^2_{v(j)})$-random variables	independent of the $U_{it(j)}$s
$U_{it(j)}$	the truncation (at zero) of the $N(\mu_{it(j)}, \sigma^2_{(j)})$-distributions	

Equation (2) can be expressed as equation (5).

$$Y_{it} = e^{-U_{it(j)}} \times \frac{e^{x_{it}\beta_{(j)}}}{e^{x_{it}\beta^*}} \times e^{x_{it}\beta^* + V_{it(j)}}$$

Table 2 analyzes equation (5). The equation is divided into three parts: the technical efficiency of the stochastic frontier, the technology gap ratio and the technical efficiency of the meta-frontier function.

Table 2. Technical Efficiency and Technology Gap Ratio

Sequence	Term	Meaning of term	Remarks
the first term on the right-hand side of equation (5)	$TE_{it} = \frac{Y_{it}}{e^{x_{it}\beta_{(j)} + V_{it(j)}}} = e^{-U_{it(j)}}$	technical efficiency of the stochastic frontier for the *j*-th group	
the second term on the right-hand side of equation (5)	$TGR_{it} = \frac{e^{x_{it}\beta_{(j)}}}{e^{x_{it}\beta^*}}$	technology gap ratio (TGR) for sample firm	ratio of frontier of *j*-th group over meta-frontier production function
the third term on the right-hand side of equation (5)	$TGRE^* = \frac{Y_{it}}{e^{x_{it}\beta^* + V_{it(j)}}}$	technical efficiency of the meta-frontier function	

Accordingly, from the equations above, the technical efficiency of the stochastic frontier, TE_{it}^{*} is given by the following two components:

$$TE_{it}^{*} = TE_{it} \times TGR_{it}$$

Battese et al. (2004) estimates the parameters of the meta-frontier function in two different ways. One is by minimizing the sum of absolute deviation which is named the linear programming (LP) problem, and the other is by minimizing the sum of squared deviation which is named the quadratic programming (QP) problem.

The LP problem approach is defined by:

$$\min_{\beta^*} L^* = \sum_{t=1}^{T}\sum_{i=1}^{N} |x_{it}\beta^* - x_{it}\hat{\beta}_{(j)}| \quad s.t.\, x_{it}\beta^* \geq x_{it}\hat{\beta}_{(j)}$$

and the QP problem approach is expressed as follows:

$$\min_{\beta^*} L^* = \sum_{t=1}^{T}\sum_{i=1}^{N} (x_{it}\beta^* - x_{it}\hat{\beta}_{(j)})^2 \quad s.t.\, x_{it}\beta^* \geq x_{it}\hat{\beta}_{(j)}$$

5. DATA

This paper shows the four groups according to the bandwidth-usage and latency-sensitivity of the ASP service which are: (1) UCC, (2) Online Game, (3) Online Music, (4) Weblog, Community, Web Portal as in Figure 3. Group 1 is the UCC group which stands for "user created contents." This is also well known as user generated contents (UGC) in the States. Pandora TV, Afreeca which is serviced in Korea is similar to the State's YouTube which specializes in video streaming services. This group has the largest bandwidth-usage and latency-sensitivity. Group 2 is the Online Game group which has the most diversified elements within the group and has a fairly high bandwidth-usage and latency-sensitivity. Group 3 is the Online Music group where the user of a firm, that is a member of this group, can listen to the music in real time. Group 4 is a group that consists of Weblog, Community, Web Portal, etc. The services of Weblog, Community and Web Portal are grouped into a single group due to the fact that, although they have a minor difference in their types of service, their bandwidth-usage and latency-sensitivity are very similar. This group shows the lowest bandwidth-usage and latency-sensitivity.

This study uses the unpublished plant-level data assembled from the Annual Report on Mining and Manufacturing Survey. The data covers Internet companies with more than five employees in the Republic of Korea. The data set used in this study is unbalanced panel data from 2000 to 2007.[1] In order to maintain the homogeneity of the data sample, only firms without any offline shops are selected. Firms such as the learning company and online shopping mall are eliminated because the efficiency of the firm is heavily dependent on the lecturer's ability or the quality of products, respectively.

[1] The data before 2000 is excluded because the Internet services were not broadband, so the application services were totally different from now.

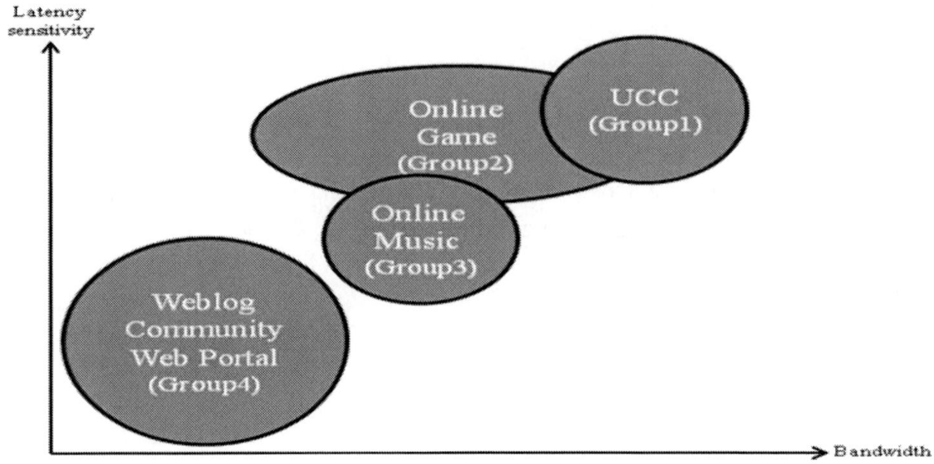

Figure 3. Attributes of four different groups with respect to bandwidth and latency.

A number of variables are used in the estimation of the production function and the measure of efficiency. Before analyzing the variables, the previous studies from Chen et al. (2004) show that the financial performance of an e-business market was measured by using the number of employees, inventory cost, total asset and cost of goods sold as the input variable and used sales and net income as the output variable. Barua et al. (2004) used the Mann-Whitney examination to measure the performance of efficiency between the groups and used IT capital, NIT capital, number of employee and establishment year as the input variable and used sales and gross profit as the output variable. Lastly, Serrano-Chica et al. (2005) used 40 Internet firms to measure the efficiency and proposed different DEA models for each different group and used the number of employees and total operating costs as an input variable and used sales and the number of visitors as the output variables.

This paper uses the sales as an output variable and asset, the number of employees and the cost of goods sold as the input capital, labor and sale costs variables. It is common to use either sales or net income as the output variable of a firm. Internet firms' output is similar to standard firms for its business transactions such as selling products and services results in sales and net income, which is a portion of the sales. Net income does not fully reflect the output of a firm, because it not only includes an intermediary step such as the COGS (cost of goods sold) and sales, it also includes the cost and profits aspects (Donthu and Yoo, 1998). Sales can also raise questions in measuring the output of a firm's operational efficiency, depending on the price of the product, the number of products sold could affect the total sales. However, normally firms attempt to increase their profits by increasing their sales in many different ways and this is no exception to the Internet firms which will not be able to survive without high profits through increasing sales. Thus our study uses sales as our output variable that reflects the operational activities of a firm, because sales include the intermediary processes in order to reach the net income.

The sample statistics for the input and output variables distinguished by the four groups and used for estimation are reported in Table 3.

Table 3. Summary statistics for data on Internet firms from year 2000 to 2007

Variable	Symbol	Unit	Group1	Group2	Group3	Group4
Output	Y	10^6won	8,240.9 (6066.0)	29,947.0 (51,987.5)	19,888.0 (19,971.0)	63,177.9 (61,009.1)
Capital	x_1	10^6won	1,902.3 (1,665.2)	3,645.9 (2,571.2)	3,847.6 (2765.4)	10,259.0 (13,097.0)
Labor	x_2	person	63 (56)	181 (266)	75 (42.6)	213 (170)
Material	x_3	10^6won	4,573.9 (5,197.7)	10,348.2 (11,902.8)	13,087.2 (15,511.0)	40,362.0 (44,832.6)
Observations		# of firms	5	18	5	6

6. Estimation

We estimated the technical efficiency using a translog functional form based on equation (1) and (3). It can be specified by:

$$Y_{it} = \beta_0 + \sum_{m=1}^{3} \beta_m x_{mit} + \sum_{m=1}^{3} \sum_{k=1}^{3} \beta_{mk} x_{mit} x_{kit} + \beta_{00} D_{it} + V_{it} - U_{it}$$

where *m* denotes the *m*-th input (m=1, 2, 3) of the *i*-th firm in the *t*-th time period; Y_{it} denotes the total value of output for the *i*-th firm in the *t*-th year (in one million Korean won); x_1 denotes the total value of capital (in one million Korean won); x_2 denotes the total number of paid laborers; x_3 denotes the total value of costs (including expenditure on electricity, rent of buildings, machinery, and bandwidth) in one million Korean won; and *D* is a dummy variable for year of observation. The model is estimated using a combination of maximum likelihood method and linear programming procedure in MALAB programming code.

7. Results

The maximum-likelihood estimates of the parameters in the frontiers of each group were obtained using the FRONTIER 4.1 program (Coelli (1996)) while the meta-frontier was estimated using MATLAB 7.1 program.[2] Table 4 shows the result of estimation. The last column shows the Meta-frontier coefficient by solving the linear programming problem.[3]

Estimates of technical efficiencies and *TGR*s are presented in Table 5. On average across 2000 to 2007, UCC group achieved the highest mean technical efficiency (0.9890) with the lowest standard variation (0.0287) and Online Game group has the lowest mean technical efficiency (0.3886). Also, the technical efficiency with respect to the group frontiers of group 1 and group 3 is very high, whereas that of group 2 and group 4 is low relatively.

[2] Hossain et al. (2007) used SHAZAM and Battese et al. (2004) used GAUSS to estimate Meta-Frontier.

[3] MATLAB 7.1 uses 'Large-Scale Optimization' algorithm for the LP problem. See Zhang (1995) for details.

Table 4. Parameter estimates for the stochastic frontier models and meta-frontier

	Group1		Group2		Group3		Group4		Meta-Frontier Coefficient
	Coeffi-cient	S.E.	Coeffi-cient	S.E.	Coeffi-cient	S.E.	Coeffi-cient	S.E.	
Constant	204.4060	0.9980	-12.2441	0.9981	18.1005	16.9631	25.2575	0.9998	446.4828
$\ln x_1$	-9.4045	0.7378	-1.2850	0.7635	-1.6018	0.9007	2.0904	0.8004	-12.7528
$\ln x_2$	6.9359	1.0000	4.9101	1.0992	9.7406	2.8325	8.2325	1.4529	56.7084
$\ln x_3$	-9.2120	0.7552	2.7207	0.7901	-0.6061	1.1619	-4.3841	0.6659	-23.8918
$(\ln x_1)^2$	-0.2664	0.0576	0.0684	0.0320	0.0003	0.0006	-0.0545	0.0417	-0.0694
$(\ln x_2)^2$	0.0044	0.0341	0.1852	0.0706	-0.0318	0.1567	0.2864	0.0588	2.5439
$(\ln x_3)^2$	-0.1951	0.0471	0.0145	0.1234	-0.0621	0.0315	0.1209	0.0410	0.3539
$\ln x_1 \cdot \ln x_2$	0.0201	0.0898	-0.0116	0.0578	-0.5489	0.1324	-0.1285	0.0868	-1.4999
$\ln x_1 \cdot \ln x_3$	0.9297	0.0905	-0.0698	0.0334	0.1697	0.0563	0.0387	0.0785	1.0294
$\ln x_2 \cdot \ln x_3$	-0.3252	0.0809	-0.2660	0.0445	0.1236	0.1481	-0.3225	0.0757	-1.9419
sigma-squared	0.0377	0.0097	0.3842	0.1182	0.0778	0.1707	0.1420	0.0818	
Gamma	0.0003	0.0004	0.6321	0.0902	0.8172	0.4231	0.8118	0.0790	
Mu	-0.0071	0.2715	0.9856	0.2746	-0.5045	1.4365	0.6792	0.2533	

Table 5. Estimates of technical efficiencies and meta-technology ratios

Group	Mean	St. Dev.	Minimum	Maximum
Technical efficiency with respect to the group frontiers(TE)				
UCC	0.9890	0.0287	0.9368	0.9987
Online Game	0.3886	0.1913	0.2007	0.8843
Online Music	0.9138	0.0773	0.8005	0.9746
ETC	0.5055	0.1967	0.3203	0.8652
Technology Gap Ratio				
UCC	0.9431	0.0275	0.8490	0.9595
Online Game	0.9893	0.0138	0.9497	1.0000
Online Music	0.9647	0.0273	0.8520	1.0000
ETC	0.9835	0.0141	0.9476	1.0000
Technical efficiency with respect to the meta-frontier				
UCC	0.9173	0.0437	0.8781	0.9839
Online Game	0.3233	0.1873	0.1982	0.8696
Online Music	0.8980	0.0760	0.7626	0.9335
ETC	0.4188	0.1975	0.3150	0.8596

It is not because group 1 and group 3 are efficient but because there are few differences of digital contents in the case of UCC and online music services. In other words, both groups do not produce the contents by themselves, but just distribute the contents that are produced by professionals or end users. Therefore, all the firms distribute almost the same contents and efficiency should be high. In this case, *TGR* is more important because *TGR* will be different depending on whether there exists ISP discrimination against ASPs or not. If TGR gets lower as the bandwidth-usage and latency-sensitivity of the service gets higher, then one can say that there is discrimination without network neutrality regulation.

Table 5 shows the estimated value of *TE, TGR,* TE^* which was described in Table 2. One can see that the mean *TE* values of the UCC group and the Online Music group are larger than that of the Online Game group and the ETC group, whereas the mean *TGR* values of the UCC (0.9431) and Online Music group (0.9647) are relatively low compared with that of the Online Game group (0.9893) and the ETC group (0.9835). It can be analyzed in three ways. First, group 1 and 3 have a smaller value of labor and capital than group 2 and 4 as seen at Table 3. That is, group 1 and 3 include smaller size firms on average, and the groups consisting of small size firms show higher efficiency. Second, the value of *TGR* gets lower as bandwidth usage and latency sensitivity gets higher except for the Online Game group. This implies that ISPs could discriminate between ASPs without keeping the network neutrality principle. When there is no network neutrality regulation, ISPs can increase their profit by discriminating between ASPs, and the increment of profit is higher when ASPs use more bandwidth and are more sensitive to the latency. It is because the higher the bandwidth-usage and latency-sensitivity is, the more the quality of the ASP service depends on the quality of the ISP service. Third, the Online Game group shows a high *TGR* value even though its bandwidth usage and latency sensitivity are high. It is because this group includes many more firms than other groups. That is, this group is more competitive than other groups. Therefore, online game firms must have tried to innovate for survival and it shows a relatively high value of *TGR*.

8. Discussion and Summary

In the initial stages, the development of the Internet was based on the fundamental principle of openness and nondiscrimination. However, since this early dynamic was established, various applications have been developed and the role of ISPs has expanded and the importance of the network neutrality principle has become a sensitive issue. This paper categorized Internet firms into four groups according to the bandwidth-usage and latency-sensitivity of the ASP service which are (1) UCC, (2) Online Game, (3) Online Music, (4) Weblog, Community, Web Portal, and estimated the efficiency of those four groups using Meta-Frontier analysis. As a result, 4 groups showed a different value of TE^*, and it can be analyzed by being separated into *TE* and *TGR*. On average across 2000 to 2007, UCC group achieved the highest mean technical efficiency (0.9890) with the lowest standard variation (0.0287) and Online Game group has the lowest mean technical efficiency (0.3886). Also, the technical efficiency with respect to the group frontiers of group 1 and group 3 is very high, whereas that of group 2 and group 4 is low relatively. Additionally, the mean *TE* values of the UCC group and the Online Music group are larger than that of the Online Game group and the ETC group, whereas the mean *TGR* values of the UCC (0.9431) and Online Music group (0.9647) are relatively low compared with that of the Online Game group (0.9893) and the ETC group (0.9835).

This field still needs further studies. The number of firms that we could get the data for was small because most Internet firms are still venture companies. Additionally, it should be analyzed precisely that the existence of network neutrality, competitiveness, and the size of the firm can make the difference in efficiency. However, it gives some implications. First, except for the Online Game group, the value of *TGR* increases as the latency-sensitivity and bandwidth usage decreases. It could be possible under the current regulation that ISPs can be discriminated from ASPs. Government needs to consider the introduction of the network neutrality principle. Second, government needs to encourage competition. The Online Game group could achieve a high value of *TGR* in spite of high latency-sensitivity and bandwidth usage because this group was more competitive than other groups.

REFERENCES

Aigner, D., C.A.K. Lovell, and P. Schmidt. (1977). “Formulation and estimation of stochastic frontier production function models.” *Journal of Econometrics*, Vol. 6. 21-37.

Barbara, V. S. (2007), “Towards an Economic Framework for Network Neutrality Regulation,” *Telecommunications and High Technology Law*, Vol. 5. 329-391.

Barua, A., P.L. Brockett, W. W. Cooper, H. Deng, B.R. Parker, T.W. Ruefli and A. Whinston. (2004), "DEA evaluations of long- and short-run efficiencies of digital vs. physical product "dot com" companies," *Socio-Economic Planning Sciences*, Vol. 38, No. 4. 233-253.

Battese, G. E., D.S.P. Rao, and C.J. O'Donnell. (2004). “A metafrontier production function for estimation of technical efficiencies and technology gaps for firms operating under different technologies.” *Journal of Productivity Analysis*, Vol. 21, No. 1. 91−103.

Battese, G.E. and T.J. Coelli. (1992). “Frontier production functions, technical efficiency and panel data: with application to paddy farmers in India.” *Journal of Productivity Analysis*, Vol. 3. 153-169.

Chen, T.Y., L. Motiwalla and M.R. Khan. (2004), "Using super-efficiency DEA to evaluate financial performance of e-business initiative in the retail industry," *International Journal of Information Technology and Decision Making*, Vol. 3, No. 2. 337-351.

Chen, Z. and S. Song. (2008). “Efficiency and technology gap in China’s agriculture: A regional meta-frontier analysis.” *China Economic Review,* Vol. 19. 287-296.

Coelli, T. (1996). “A guide to Frontier version 4.1: a computer program for stochastic frontier production and cost function estimation.” CEPA Working Paper 96/07, Centre for Efficiency and Productivity Analysis, University of New England, Armidale.

Donthu, N. and B. H. Yoo. (1998), "Retail productivity assessment using data envelopment analysis," *Journal of Retailing*, Vol. 74, No. 1. 89-105.

Ford, G. S., T. M. Koutsky, and L. J. Spiwak, (2006). “Net Neutrality and Industry Structure.” Phoenix Center Policy Paper No. 24, *Phoenix Center for advanced Legal and Economic Public Policy.*

Hahn, R. W. and S. Wallsten. (2006) "The Economics of Net Neutrality," *The Economists' Voice*: Vol. 3, No. 6. Article 8.

Hossain, M. B., R. A. Villano and E. Fleming. (2007). “Analysis of Technical Efficiency and Varietal differences in Pistachio Production in Iran Using a Meta-Frontier Analysis.” *The 51th Annual conference of the Australian Agricultural and Resource Economics Society.* Queenstown New Zealand.

Kumbhakar, S.C. (2002). “Specification and estimation of production risk, risk preferences and technical efficiency.” *American Journal of Agricultural Economics*, Vol. 84. 8-22.

Meeusen, W. and J. van den Broeck. (1997). “Efficiency estimation from Cobb-Douglas production functions with composed error.” *International Economic Review*, Vol. 18. 435-444.

Peha J. M. (2006). “The Benefits and Risks of Mandating Network Neutrality, and the Quest for a Balanced Policy.” *34th Telecommunications Policy Research Conference*.

Serrano-Cinca, C., Y. Fuertes-Callen and C. Mar-Molinero. (2005), "Measuring DEA efficiency in Internet companies," *Decision Support Systems,* Vol. 38, No. 4. 557-573.

Sidak, J. G. (2006). “A Consumer-Welfare Approach to Network Neutrality Regulation of the Internet. ” *Journal of Competition Law and Economics*. Vol. 2, No. 3. 349-474.

Wu, T. (2004). “The Broadband Debate: A User's Guide.” *Journal of Telecommunications and High Technology Law*, Vol. 3, No. 69. 69-95.

Wu, T. (2005). “Network Neutrality, Broadband Discrimination,” *Journal of Telecommunications and High Technology Law*, Vol. 2. 141-78.

Wu, T. (2006). “Network Newtrality redux,” *Lessig Blog*, http://www.lessig.org/blog/ rchives/003391.shtml.

Yoo, C. S. (2005). “BEYOND NETWORK NEUTRALITY,” *Harvard Journal of Law and Technology*. Vol. 19, No. 1. 1-77.

Yoo, C. S. (2006). “Network Neutrality and the Economics of Congestion.” *Georgetown Law Journal*, Vol. 94, Vanderbilt Law and Economics Research Paper No. 05-28; Vanderbilt Public Law Research Paper No. 05-33.

Zhang, Y. (1995). "Solving Large-Scale Linear Programs by Interior-Point Methods Under the MATLAB Environment," Technical Report TR96-01, Department of Mathematics and Statistics, University of Maryland, Baltimore County, Baltimore, MD.

In: Information and Communication Technologies… ISBN 978-1-60876-671-0
Ed: Almas Heshmati and Sun Peng

Chapter 9

THE RELATIONSHIP BETWEEN EFFICIENCY AND OWNERSHIP STRUCTURE: THE CASE OF CHINA'S LISTED ICT COMPANIES

Shaofei Wang[1] and Almas Heshmati*[2]

[1]State-owned Assets Supervision and Administration Commission of the State Council of China

[2]Seoul National University

ABSRACT

If we take an overview of enterprise reform in China during the last 30 years, we will find that this process has always been accompanied by the debate of ownership identity and ownership structure. Numerous pieces of research on the relationship between the efficiency and ownership structure in China have been undertaken, but the conclusions vary and even contradict each other. This dissertation will explore the unique characteristics of the ownership structure of Chinese companies, and illustrate the effects of ownership structure on the efficiency of companies and finally discuss how to adjust the ownership structure to improve their efficiency. Unbalance panel data for listed ICT companies from 2003 to 2007 are collected to conduct an empirical analysis of the relationship between performance and the ownership structure of firms. A two-step procedure is used. In the first step, data envelopment analysis (DEA) Window model is applied to measure the efficiencies of these companies. In the second step, the Tobit regression model is used to establish the relationship between efficiency and the ownership structure, to identify the determinants of efficiency and to estimate their impacts. A sensitivity analysis with respect to model specification is conducted. In addition, this dissertation attempts to provide an explanation for the conclusions drawn, and provides policy guidelines for future adjustments in the ownership structure. In conclusion, the results suggest that the proportions of state-owned and private corporate shares do not affect the efficiency of companies significantly. However, the ownership concentration exhibits a positive impact on the efficiency level of the sample ICT firms.

---

* Corresponding author Email: heshmati@snu.ac.kr

Keywords: Efficiency, Ownership Structure, Data Envelopment Analysis, Tobit Model, China's Listed Companies.

1. INTRODUCTION

The development of the commodity economy, technology and the production levels of society has promoted the expansion of the production scale and increased the complexity of management activities. In order to meet the requirements of large-scale specialized production and financing, joint-stock companies were started. The diversity and decentralization of ownership made it possible to finance large-scale production, which also led to the separation of ownership and management, and stimulated the emergence of professional managers. However, the separation of ownership and management has also resulted in the principal-agent problem, insider control problems, incentive and monitoring problems, problems regarding the interests of minority shareholders who have been deprived and a series of other corporate governance issues. The ownership structure is an essential element of the economic system and the base of corporate governance. Domestic and foreign research shows that the ownership structure is very important for securities markets, corporate governance, and corporate behavior and performance.

To emphasize the importance of ownership and ownership structure, it is important to review the ups and downs of China's enterprise reform during the last 30 years. Before 1979, the right of residual claim and control was entirely held by the government. That is, the state owned all the enterprises. In 1979, China's state-owned enterprise reform was launched. The main feature was that the rights of decision-making and residual claim gradually shifted from government to enterprises. In the early phase of the reform, the basic policy was to grant autonomy and to share profits. From 1986 to the early 1990s, the specific model named as "manager's contracted responsibility system" came into being. The basic content of the "manager's contracted responsibility system" was that managers signed a contract with government representatives. Under this system, the manager became a natural owner who controlled part of the corporation, while the enterprise could retain a large share of the profits, which encouraged managers to seek short-term profits. Managers could hide profits and misappropriate assets which could be more than the actual contracted residual claim. This phenomenon can be thought as a disguised form of privatization (Zhang, 2006). Until the late 1980s, most of the state-owned enterprises were suffering from heavy losses, which promoted the growth of the capital market. In the following few years, private sectors of the economy grew rapidly, which made the market more competitive. Under these circumstances, more and more state-owned enterprises were "incorporated" by selling shares to their own employees or other companies. The State Council decided to establish two national stock exchanges in 1989. According to this regulation, the Shanghai Stock Exchange (SHSE) opened in December, 1990, and the Shenzhen Stock Exchange (SZSE) opened in April, 1991. As the real listed companies emerged, the discussion around the ownership structure of companies has never stopped.

Tthe association between ownership and efficiency is the question being researched in this chapter. The objective of this research is to analyze the effects of different ownership identities and ownership concentration on the efficiency of listed ICT companies in China.

The aim is to find the relationship between efficiency and the ownership structure, and illustrate how to improve the efficiency of the sampled companies through adjustment of the ownership structure and related policies.

In this research, an unbalanced panel data including 77 ICT listed companies in 2003, 82 in 2004, 85 in 2005, 89 in 2006 and 98 in 2007 (supported by WIND Database[1]) is applied. At the First step, a Data Envelopment Analysis (DEA) Window variable returns to scale (VRS) output-oriented model[2] is used to estimate the efficiency scores of companies. In the second step, the Tobit model regression analysis is employed so as to determine the relationship between the ownership structure and the efficiency of firms. Afterwards, for the purposes of sensitivity analysis, unrestricted and restricted nested models are specified and estimated. A log-likelihood ratio test is used to compare different alternative models performance with a different subset of independent variables to determine the most proper model specification.

2. ICT Industry In China

Since the late 1990s, the world has experienced a dramatic revolution in information and communications technology. China's ICT industry has taken off because of the country's strong manufacturing performance. In the mid-1990s, foreign ICT enterprises treated China as a low-cost assembly factory. Chinese ICT industry just relied on the imports of key components from the United States, Japan, and China Taiwan to survive. In the late 1990s, foreign multinational companies established components factories, employed Chinese managers, and launched science and technology RandD projects in China. During this period, the local Chinese ICT companies were fast emerging. Lenovo, Bird, Haier and Huawei, and other companies joined the competition in the market.

Nowadays, Chinese ICT companies are playing a more and more important role in the world market. According to a report by the Organization for Economic Cooperation and Development (OECD), the proportion of "Made in China" was only 10% in the US total imports of ICT products in 2000. In 2004, this proportion rocketed to 27%. From 1996 to 2004, the value of United States ICT trade grew by over 50% and reached 375 billion U.S. dollars. Moreover, with in the same period, the total value of Chinese ICT trade climbed from 35 billion U.S. dollars to 329 billion U.S. dollars, and the growth rate was as high as 1000 percent. In 2004, Chinese ICT product exports such as laptop computers, mobile phones and digital cameras, grew by 46% to 180 billion U.S. dollars. It was the first time for China to surpass the United States, whose exports of ICT products were 149 billion U.S. dollars. In 2005, ICT products took 30% of China's total export trade, and became the world's largest supplier of ICT products (Steinbock, 2007).

Chinese ICT companies still have the potential to develop. For instance, in 2005 the domestic consumption of Chinese ICT products accounted for only 4.5% of GDP, which was far lower than the distribution of the ICT industry of the OECD (9% of GDP) (Steinbock,

---

[1] WIND database is a database collected and processed by Shanghai Wind Information Co.,Ltd., the website is www.wind.com.cn.

[2] DEA window variable returns to scale output-oriented model is a statistical package operated by the software named DEA solver Pro version 5.0.

2007). This means that there is a huge space left for the consumption of ICT products in the future development. According to forecasts and statistics from McKinsey and Company Inc.(2006), the annual growth rate of China's top 100 high-tech enterprises was 26% from 2004 to 2006, which was more than twice the overall market growth rate of 12% and nearly four times the annual global rate of 7%. It is expected that China will generate a significant portion of the future growth in the global high-tech industry (Von Morgenstern, 2006).

In the 11th "Five-Year Plan" published by the Chinese Government, one strategy was announced, which is increasing input to encourage innovation in high-tech industries to increase domestic self-patented technology in order to reduce dependence on foreign technology and intellectual property rights. This will open a new chapter for Chinese ICT industry and ICT enterprises.

In this chapter, the ICT listed companies in China are selected to explain the relationship between ownership structure and efficiency. Undoubtedly, the ICT industry has been the fastest-growing industrial sector in recent years, and is playing a significant role in China's economic growth. More importantly, it is considered as the key driving force for the future development of China. The competition between ICT enterprises in the industry is relatively transparent. Moreover, ICT enterprises perform much better in establishing a modern enterprise system, corporate governance and management than enterprises in other sectors. In addition, ICT listed companies' financial statements are more reliable, which would reduce the error of the study.

3. Literature Review

3.1. Core Concept

The concept of ownership evolves from legal and jurisdictional issues of title over land and related resources, and is explored to be a more conceptual notion that the public are interested in. In joint-stock companies, ownership is the right for owner to share the economy profit of companies, to participate the operation management and decision making of companies, which is based on the proportion of shareholding in companies' capital.

Jensen and Meckling (1976) first tried to develop a theory of the ownership structure of the firm by integrating elements from the theory of agency, the theory of property rights and the theory of finance. According to Gürsoy and Aydoğan (1998), ownership structure includes two dimensions: ownership concentration and ownership identity. Generally, the ownership structure could be described by Figure 1 below.

"Ownership concentration is defined by both the number of large-block shareholders and the total percentage of what they own" (Hitt, Ireland and Hoskisson, 2001). From the perspective of the basic principle, all the methods can be classified into two measures. One is to calculate the sum of proportions of top N shareholders' shareholding. The other is to calculate HHI (Herfindahl-Hirschman Index) of proportions of top N shareholders' shareholding. It is defined as the sum of the squares of proportions of N top shareholders' shares (S) in the whole shareholding in a given time t. The formula is give as (Allen et al., 2005):

$$HHI = \sum_{i=1}^{n} S_i^2 \qquad (1)$$

The ownership structure of companies in China is different from other countries because of the special ownership mechanism and state regulations. Before the non-tradable share reform in 2005, a unique phenomenon in China's capital market was the coexistence of tradable shares and non-tradable shares.

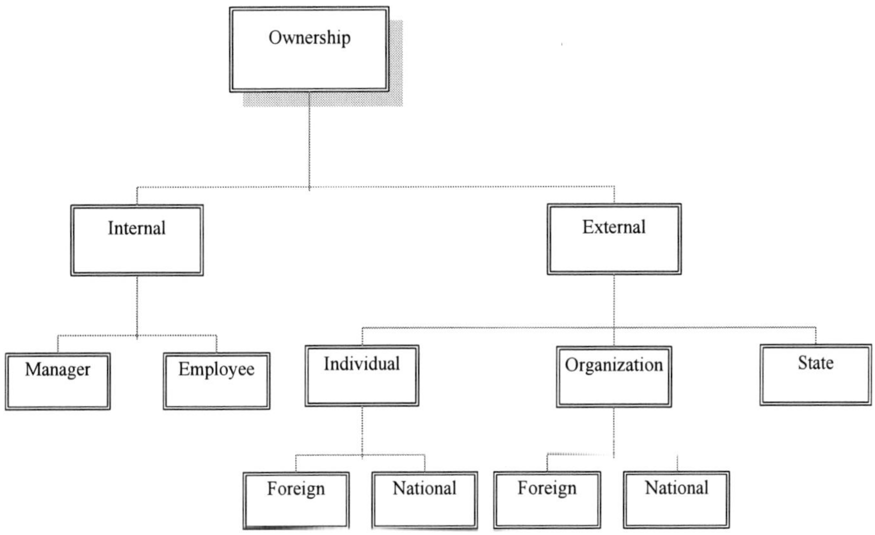

Figure 1. Ownership Structure of firms.

Briefly, the most fundamental reason for the invalidity of the capital market was the irrational ownership structure. Figure 2 illustrates the ownership structure of Chinese companies before the non-tradable share reform.

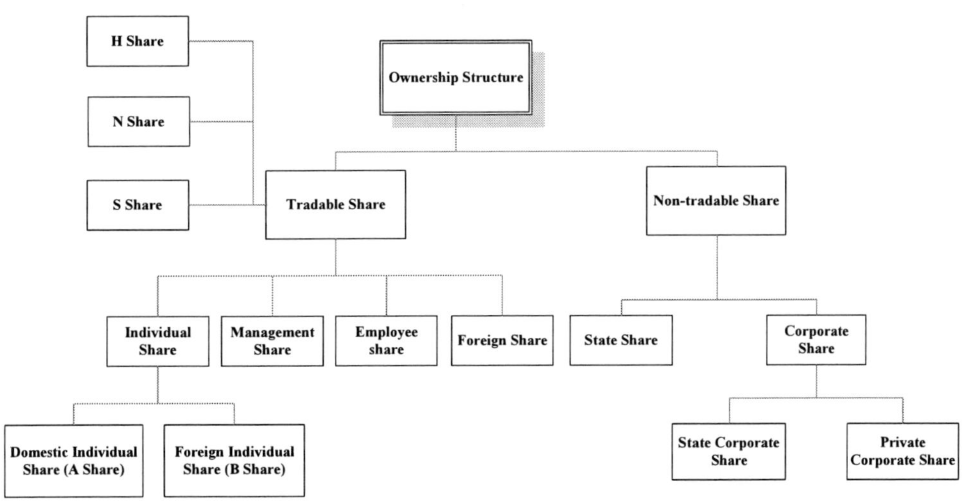

Figure 2. Ownership Structure in China before 2005.

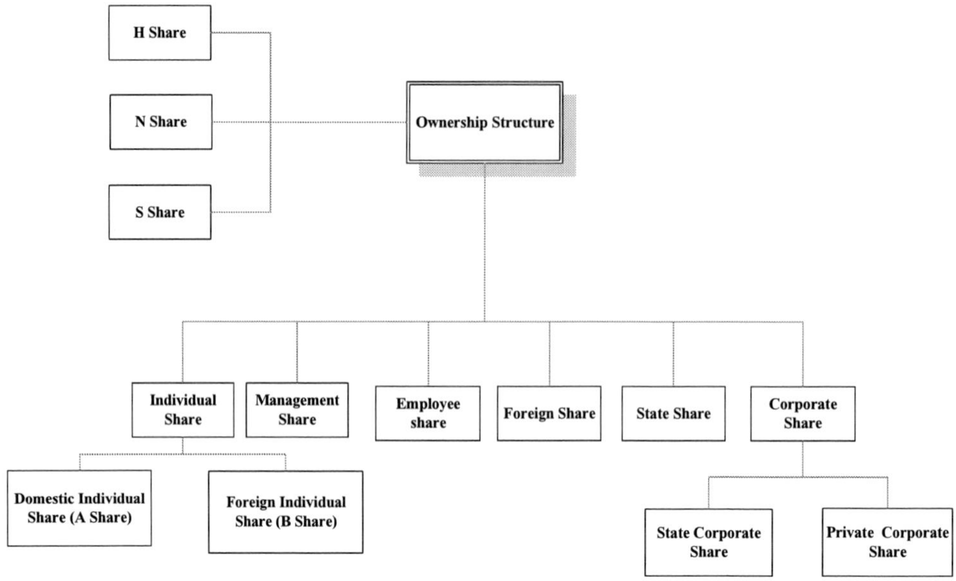

Figure 3. Ownership Structure in China after 2005.

On May 8th 2005, the China Securities Regulation Commission issued a notice on the pilot reform of non-tradable shares of listed corporations, which announced the reform of Chinese non-tradable shares. According to the notice, the shares of most listed companies could already be traded on the stock market, which has brought tremendous changes to companies' ownership structure (Figure 3).

However, this Chinese official categorization does not point out who is the ultimate owner in certain listed companies. According to the insight of ownership, whether the owner is government or government-dominant enterprises, there is no differentiation on the motivation and behaviors of owners. Hence, in this research, the state corporate shares are treated as part of state-owned shares and private corporate shares considered as non-state corporate shares.

3.2. Previous Research

The research on the relationship between ownership structure and performance of corporations could be traced back to the 1930s. In subsequent decades, the bulk of research on ownership structure demonstrated their suggestions continuously.

McConnell and Servaes (1990) did empirical research based on 1173 companies in 1976 and 1093 companies in 1986. According to the findings, there was a significant nonmonotonic correlation between Tobin's Q and the proportion of inside owner's shareholding. When the proportion of inside owner's shareholding increased, Tobin's Q increased, but when the proportion reached 40%-50%, Tobin's Q decreased. Five years later, based on the previous research, McConnell and Servaes (1995) investigated 990 firms in

1976, 876 firms in 1986 and 780 firms in 1988, and divided the firms to two different groups which were High-growth firms and Low-growth firms. The comparison revealed that the proportion of inside shareholding was obviously higher for high-growth firms than that for low-growth firms.

Demsetz and Villalonga (2001) investigated 223 samples from 1976 to 1980 to analyze the relationship between the ownership structure and the performance of corporations. In their research, ownership was made multi-dimensional and treated as an endogenous variable. They found that there was no statistically significant relation between ownership structure and the performance of firms.

In a related study, Kapopoulos and Lazaretou (2007) did an empirical analysis using the data of 175 Greek listed companies. They first treated the ownership structure as an endogenous variable, and then considered two different measures of ownership structure which reflected different shareholders with conflicting interests. They suggested that the larger the ownership concentration was, the higher the profitability for the firms were.

McConnell, Servaes and Lins (2008) found a curvilinear relation between firm value and insider ownership. The value of the firm first increased, and then decreased, as insider share ownership increased.

McKnight and Weir (2007) examined the impact of governance and ownership variables on agency costs for a panel of large UK quoted companies. They found that increasing board ownership reduced agency costs.

King and Santor (2008) investigated 613 Canadian firms from 1998 to 2005 to analyze how family ownership affected the performance and capital structure. They found that freestanding family-owned firms had a similar market value which was Tobin's Q as other firms, but a superior return of assets, and higher debt of total assets.

Sun and Huang (1999) analyzed the relationship between Tobin's Q and the proportion of largest shareholder's shareholding based on 503 firms in 1998. They found that as the largest shareholder, corporate share did a better job on performance of firms than state share. There was an inverted U-shape relation between Tobin's Q and the proportion of largest shareholder's shareholding.

Zhang (2000) did empirical research on the relation between Tobin's Q and the proportion of the top five shareholder's shareholding. He found there was an inverted U-shape relation between Tobin's Q and the proportion of corporate share.

Wu (2002) investigated 1555 firms from 1997 to 2000. He concluded that there was an inverted U shape relationship between ownership concentration and performance, as well as between insider shareholding and performance. There was a U-shape relation between the proportion of tradable shares, state shares, domestic corporate shares and the performance of firms.

Chen, Firth and Xu (2007) analyzed the relationship between different types of ownership and the performance of China's listed companies. They found that the performance of the firms controlled by central government was the best, and that of the firms controlled by state assets management bureau and privately was the worst. Firms controlled by local government were in the middle.

In summation, most scholars hold the view that the ownership structure indeed affects the efficiency of firms, but the impacts of ownership structure are thought to be different, which means that the shareholding with the same identity might be thought to have contradicted the impacts on the efficiency of companies. For example, through the overview of previous research in China, some researchers believed that the proportion of state-owned shares positively affects the performance of a company, however, other scholars argued that it negatively affects the performance. Furthermore, someone concluded that it does not affect the performance of a company. Meanwhile, other scholars such as Demsetz insist that there is no significant relationship between ownership structure and the efficiency of firms since the ownership sturcture is endogeneous and consistent with the value maximization of a company. Obviously, the research on the relationship between efficiency and ownership structure does not suggest a single conclusion based on the theory. Even with a large amount of empirical analysis, it still does not achieve a unanimous result.

3.3. Hypothesis

Based on theory and previous research, it is assumed that in China the state-owned shareholding may negatively affect the efficiency of a company. However, according to the literature review, the private corporate shareholding is expected to positively affect the efficiency of the company. The other types of shares such as management share, individual share and institutioanl share may perform better on the efficiency of a company.

In this paper, it is assumed that ownership concentration may positively affect the efficiency of a company because the concentrated ownership in the case of private-owned firms makes the objectives of majority shareholders consistent with the objectives of profit maximization. Despite the differences in objective in the case of state owned enterprises the ownership concentration is expected to affect positively the operation of firms and it may not be in conflict with the maximization of the welfare of citizens.

4. METHODOLOGY

4.1. Method Framework

In this research, a two-stage analysis method is proposed in order to explore the relationship between ownership structure and the efficiency of companies.

At first, Data Envelopment Analysis (DEA) is applied using the Window variable returns to scale (VRS) output-oriented model to yield the efficiencies of companies. DEA could produce a frontier which is optimal and represents the maximum output (minimum input) available for any DMU in a certain study, for its given input (output). Hence, the DEA technique was applied in the analysis. In this research, the DEA window model is considered as the best tool to evaluate the efficiency of the observations across 5 years, based on the assumption of "variable return to scale" and "output-oriented". Three input variables and two output variables are introduced for the anlysis. The input variables include the number of employees, the total assets and the main business costs. The output variables include the main business income and net profit. In this process, an unbalanced panel data is applied, which includes respectively 77 companies in 2003, 82 companies in 2004, 85 companies in 2005, 89 companies in 2006 and 98 companies in 2007.

Considering the effects of inflation, the monetarily measured variables including the value of the total assets, the main business cost, the main business income and the net profit are transformed to fixed prices by using a producer price index (PPI).

After the computation by DEA window VRS output-oriented model, the efficiency noted by score located in [0,1] interval is achieved for every company in every year.

Secondly, the Tobit model is used to conduct a regression analysis. The efficiency scores obtained by the DEA model are transferred to inefficiency scores which are used as the dependent variable to suit to the Tobit model. Following this data transformation the fully effective firms are assigned a zero inefficiency level making the Tobit model a suitable method of regression analysis. The proportion of state-owned shares, the proportion of private corporate shares and ownership concentration are selected as independent variables. The company size and the year are used as dummy variables. The software Limdep 2.0 is used for analysis.

In order to find the best model to explain the relationship between dependent variables and independent ownership variables, a Log-likelihood ratio test is used to compare the performance of alternative models with a different subset of independent ownership-related variables.

4.2. Specification of Model of Determinants of Efficiency

In this research, in order to analyze the relationship between efficiency and the ownership structure, the Tobit model is chosen to do the regression analysis according to the characters of the data set which is censored.

Consequently, the regression models between inefficiency and different subsets of independent variables are established. This will help to identify the model best fitting the data and its selection, based on statistical tests. The models are nested and can easily identify the model with best performance in explaining the degree of inefficiency. The general and unrestricted model is written as:

$$INEFF_{it} = \alpha_0 + \alpha_1 POS_{it} + \alpha_2 POPC_{it} + \alpha_3 OCON_{it} + \alpha_4 S_{M\,it} + \alpha_5 S_{L\,it} + \alpha_6 Y_{4\,it} + \alpha_7 Y_{5\,it} + \alpha_8 Y_{6\,it} + \alpha_9 Y_{7\,it} + \mu_{it} \tag{1}$$

If RHS>0

=0, otherwise (2)

where *INEFF* is inefficiency, *POS* is the proportion of state-owned shares, *POPC* is the proportion of private corporate shares, *OCON* is the ownership concentration, S_M is medium size, S_L is Large size, Y_4, Y_5, Y_6, Y_7 in turn means the year of observation from 2004 to 2007, RHS means the right-hand side. The restrcited models are nested in the general model above by equating some explanatory variables to zero.

4.3. Testing Model Specification and Selection

The Likelihood ratio test is a method to test nested model assumptions. The Likelihood ratio test compares the goodness of fit of the unrestricted and restricted models using the log likelihood function. In this study, the Log-likelihood ratio test is employed to determine the best model which should be applied.

The procedure of Log-likelihood ratio test can be stated as below (Ruud, 2000).

1. Compute the value of the log-likelihood function for the restricted model $\hat{\theta}$ which can be noted as $\log L_{\hat{\theta}}$, and note that the restricted model should be nested in the unrestricted model Θ;
2. Compute the value of the log-likelihood function for the unrestricted model Θ which can be noted as $\log L_{\theta}$;
3. Compute

$$LogLR_{\hat{\theta}-\theta} = -2(LogL_{\hat{\theta}} - LogL_{\theta}) \tag{3}$$

This statistic is always positive because the restricted maximum value always is smaller than unrestricted one.

4. Compare $LogLR_{\hat{\theta}-\theta}$ with the critical value of a chi-square χ^2 distribution with *K*-*M* degrees of freedom, or restrictions, here *K* is the number of parameters in unrestricted model, *M* is the number of parameters in restricted model.

$$LogLRT_{\hat{\theta}-\theta} = -2(LogL_{\hat{\theta}} - LogL_{\theta}) > \chi^2_{(K-M)}, \tag{4}$$

accept the unrestricted model Θ, otherwise accept the restricted model $\hat{\theta}$.

In this research, there are eight nested and unrestricted models, therefore, the procedure of Log-likelihood ratio test is carried out for different restrictions imposed on the unrestricted model specification. After the likelihood ratio test procedure is completed, the most appropriate model should be determined and used in the analysis.

5. Data and Variables

5.1. Variable Description

A. DEA Model

In DEA model, below variables are selected as input:

Employee contributes labor and expertise to the production of enterprises. Among the three factors of production, employees usually provide the labour. The number of employees is used as the labour input indicator which includes the number of directors, managers and workers.

Total assets are all assets owned or controlled by the enterprises, including current assets, fixed assets, intangible assets and other long-term assets, such as defered taxes. They are listed in the corporate balance sheet. More specifically, current assets refer to the assets that are realized or consumed within production cycle in a year or more than one year, such as a variety of cash deposits, short-term investments, accounts receivable and prepayments, inventory and so on.

Main business costs are the profit and loss account category, accounting for the cost took place in the normal activities for sales of goods, products, services and transfer of assets, such as materials, wages, manufacturing costs (depreciation of equipment, water, electricity, and accessories). Main Business is the main content of project listed on the business license of company.

And the output in DEA model is listed as below.

Main business income like "Main business costs", is in profit and loss account category. It presents the income that the enterprises achieve by engaging in production and business activities, and indicates the level of the production and operation.

Net Profit is defined as the enterprises' retained profits after deducting income taxes from total profits. It is also refered to as an after-tax profit or net income. At the same time, net profit is also a basic tool used to evaluate the profitability, performance and the solvency of enterprises. It is a comprehensive indicator to measure enterprises' efficiency on the main targets.

B. Regression Analysis Model

The proportion of the state-owned shares indicates how many shares the government (central government and local government) or state-owned enterprises hold. In most formulas and tables of this research, the proportion of the state-owned shares is presented as POS.

The proportion of private corporate shares implies that the percentage shares is held by non-state-owned corporate enterprises. In China's official catalogue, the private corporate share is refered to as the domestic corporate share. In all tables and formulas of this study, the proportion of private corporate shares is noted as POPC for convenience.

Ownership concentration was explained in the section of the literature review. In this research, the proportions of the top three shareholders' shareholding for each companies are chosen to calculate transferred *HHI* which is log*HHI* to illustrate the ownership concentration for those listed companies.

$$OCON = \log HHI = \log(s_1^2 + s_2^2 + s_3^2) \quad (5)$$

where the *OCON* represents the ownership structure, S_1 represents the proportion of shares controlled by the largest shareholder, S_2 represents to the second largest shareholder, and S_3 represents to the third largest shareholder.

In this research, size and year are considered as dummy variables. The effects of size are captured by creating dummy variables of different numbers of employees. When the number of employees is less than or equal to 1000, the enterprise is regarded as small-sized. When the number of employee is more than 1000 but less than or equal to 3000, the enterprise is considered as middle-sized, otherwise the enterprise is thought of as large-sized. The small-size category is used as a reference. In the same way, the effects of years are captured by creating dummy variables from 2003 to 2007 with 2003 considered as reference. Table 1 illustrates the abbreviations appearing in the research.

Table 1. List of Abbreviations

Abbreviation	Origin
EFF	Efficiency
INEFF	Inefficiency
POS	Proportion of the state-owned shares
POPC	Proportion of the private corporate shares
OCON	Ownership structure
SL	Large size
SM	Medium size
SS	Small size
Y3	2003
Y4	2004
Y5	2005
Y6	2006
Y7	2007

5.2. Descriptive Analysis of the Data

The dataset used in this study includes all the ICT companies without H, N or S shares listed on the Shanghai stock exchange and the Shenzhen stock exchange, observed for a period of 5 years from 2003 until 2007.

On the Chinese stock market, there have been 103 ICT companies until now according to the classification standard published by China Securities Regulation Commission. 4 companies which issued B shares are excluded because of a different trade system. China Unicom is also excluded since it is one of the monopoly companies in the Chinese telecommunications market. China Unicom is controlled by the State-owned Assets Supervision and Administration Commission, and is therefore strongly supported by central government. Hence, it is not meaningful to compare the efficiency of China Unicom with other ICT-listed companies. After the exclusion, the 77 companies listed in 2003, 82 companies in 2004, 85 companies in 2005, 89 companies in 2006 and 98 companies in 2007 left are chosen as the analysis samples. To consider the effects of free-entrance and free-exit, the final dataset used in the empirical analysis of this study is an unbalanced panel data containing companies observed for 5 years consecutively with a total of 431 firm-year observations. Total assets, main business costs, main business income and net profit are transformed by producer price index as shown in Table 2.

Table 2. Producer price index (PPI) and PPI (transformed)

Year	PPI	PPI*
2003	103.00	100.00
2004	107.10	103.98
2005	103.20	100.19
2006	103.10	100.10
2007	105.43	102.36

Table 3 provides a brief description of the main variables used in the DEA Window Analysis. The mean values of employee and total assets of these companies kept increasing from 2003 to 2007. The mean values of main business cost decreased from 2003 to 2004, increased through the following years, and changed significantly in 2006 and 2007. The mean values of main business income also increased from year to year, but the mean values of net profit continuously decreased from 2004 to 2005, and increased from 2006 to 2007. Compared with other years, the mean value of net profit in 2007 was outstanding since China's stock market dramatically expanded. There are numerous complex reasons to explain the expansion which are beyond the scope of this research.

Table 4 provides the descriptive statistics of ownership structure from 2003 to 2007. The mean values of proportion of state-owned shares kept declining from 2003 till 2007 which revealed the state-owned enterprises reform policy of the Chinese government. Meanwhile, the mean values of proportion of private corporate shares also decreased through the 5 years. This phenomena implied that the proportion of other types of shares such as managerial shares, foreign shares, individual shares began to rise, and the ownership diversification has been on the way.

But the degree of decreasing is different for these two types of shares. From 2003 to 2007, the proportion of state-owned shares decreased to around 9%, while the proportion of private corporate shares only shrank to around 5%. That could be attributed to the different attitude shown by the government to these types of shares. The mean values of ownership concentration increased from 2003 to 2004, after which it declined up to 2007.

Table 5 provides the descriptive statistics of ownership structure by size. The mean value of proportion of the state-owned shares is around 17.10% for small size companies; less than that of the other groups. In the group of medium size companies, the mean value is the highest at 31.5%.

For the large size companies, the mean value is 21.64%. However, the mean value of proportion of private corporate shares is high for the group of small size companies which is around 27.90%, and more than 22.14% of large size companies and 16.91% of medium size companies. From the insight of ownership concentration, the mean value for medium size companies is highest which is 3.1519, in turn 3.0936 of large size companies and 3.0716 of small size companies.

Table 3. Summary statistics of data used in DEA Window Model (Fixed value)

Year	Variable	Observa-tion	MEAN	Standard Deviation	Minimum	Maximum
2003	Employee	77	1408.57	2070.00	22.00	16609.00
	Total assets	77	171545.63	213151.07	6045.52	1576695.49
	Main business cost	77	118999.95	189958.70	315.03	1011538.02
	Main business income	77	146893.85	247159.75	401.11	1603603.49
	Net profit	77	1948.19	18248.48	-116058.11	75249.85
2004	Employee	82	1549.10	2934.86	26.00	25515.00
	Total assets	82	177871.01	252867.88	8732.23	2005192.25
	Main business cost	82	118747.65	208747.93	614.98	1381910.56
	Main business income	82	147564.92	285943.10	606.29	2182934.51
	Net profit	82	-221.60	23714.88	-148821.66	97025.39
2005	Employee	85	1640.58	3476.04	11.00	30811.00
	Total assets	85	181119.93	273749.13	9046.75	2173782.91
	Main business cost	85	126010.03	229033.15	146.99	1391835.21
	Main business income	85	153339.76	295111.49	164.65	2153500.35
	Net profit	85	-2624.06	26946.13	-153282.76	119207.81
2006	Employee	89	1758.01	4279.29	18.00	39266.00
	Total assets	89	184251.09	316650.30	7676.13	2589105.79
	Main business cost	89	147753.42	304230.46	67.55	1906140.91
	Main business income	89	177745.55	361501.72	252.29	2300867.53
	Net profit	89	2182.18	18314.94	-77082.92	80654.65
2007	Employee	98	1915.78	5034.96	6.00	48261.00
	Total assets	98	205547.45	428654.67	137.61	3826992.58
	Main business cost	98	150092.86	318040.98	129.55	2247415.10
	Main business income	98	184644.07	414813.80	174.05	3397536.25
	Net profit	98	8285.93	20125.73	-57995.33	122328.84

Table 4. Summary statistics of the data on Ownership structure over time

Year	Variable	Observations	Mean	Standard Deviation	Min	Max
2003	POS	77	0.26	0.25	0.00	0.75
	POPC	77	0.25	0.24	0.00	0.75
	OCON	77	3.14	0.33	1.74	3.70
2004	POS	82	0.26	0.25	0.00	0.75
	POPC	82	0.25	0.25	0.00	0.79
	OCON	82	3.16	0.33	1.75	3.70
2005	POS	85	0.23	0.26	0.00	0.75
	POPC	85	0.25	0.24	0.00	0.79
	OCON	85	3.13	0.34	1.77	3.70
2006	POS	89	0.20	0.23	0.00	0.67
	POPC	89	0.22	0.23	0.00	0.75
	OCON	89	3.05	0.35	1.79	3.60
2007	POS	98	0.17	0.22	0.00	0.74
	POPC	98	0.20	0.21	0.00	0.79
	OCON	98	3.02	0.35	1.96	3.60

Table 5. Summary statistics of Ownership structure by size of firms

Size	Variable	Observations	Mean	Standard Deviation	Min	Max
SS	POS	244	0.17	0.23	0.00	0.74
	POPC	244	0.28	0.24	0.00	0.79
	OCON	244	3.07	0.30	2.17	3.68
SM	POS	140	0.30	0.24	0.00	0.75
	POPC	140	0.17	0.21	0.00	0.64
	OCON	140	3.15	0.39	1.74	3.70
SL	POS	47	0.22	0.23	0.00	0.58
	POPC	47	0.22	0.26	0.00	0.75
	OCON	47	3.09	0.39	1.79	3.56

6. EMPIRICAL RESULTS

6.1. Empirical Results of Efficiency

Table 6 provides a breakdown of the samples efficiencies into various categories according to size and year. The 244 small companies' share is 56.61% of the whole sample, that of the 140 medium companies is 32.48%, and of the 47 large companies it is 10.90%. The mean efficiency of large firms is the highest, followed by the medium firms and the small firms respectively, implying that efficiency is closely correlated to the size of companies in China. The mean value of efficiency decreased slightly from 2003 to 2005, then increased in 2006, and declined slightly again in 2007. The increase in 2006 could be due to the "non-tradable share reform" which promoted the liquidity of the stock market. The decrease in 2007 could be explained by the stock market bubble which burst after September 2007.

Table 7 provides the frequency distribution of samples efficiencies from 2003 to 2007. The proportion of companies with efficiencies below 0.5 was the highest in 2005, decreasing yearly, with efficiencies between 0.5 and 0.8. The efficiencies above 0.8 decreased from 2003 to 2005, then increased after 2005.

Table 8 provides the frequency distribution of samples efficiencies by size. At the efficiency level below 0.6, there are 33.61% small size companies, as well as 17.14 medium size companies, but no large size companies. At the efficiency level between 0.6 and 0.8, there are 43.03% small size companies, 47.85% medium size companies, and 57.45% large size companies. However, at the efficiency level above 0.8, there are 23.36% small size companies, around 35% medium size companies, and 42.55% large size companies.

Table 9 shows the correlation matrix between variables in the DEA window analysis over 5 years. In the matrix, efficiency was found to be positively correlated with other variables at the 0.01 significant level. The correlations among employees, total assets, main business costs and main business income are relatively high at the 0.01 level of significance, since all those variables are related to the scale of companies in China. However, the net profit and other variables are moderately correlated at the 0.01 level of significance.

Table 6. Efficiency Estimation by DEA Window VRTS and Output-oriented model

	Observations	Mean	Standard Deviation	Min	Max
SS	244	0.66	0.19	0.12	1.00
SM	140	0.74	0.15	0.37	1.00
SL	47	0.79	0.14	0.61	1.00
2003	77	0.70	0.19	0.15	1.00
2004	82	0.68	0.17	0.22	1.00
2005	85	0.68	0.18	0.21	1.00
2006	89	0.72	0.18	0.20	1.00
2007	98	0.71	0.17	0.12	1.00

Table 7. Frequency distribution of efficiency over time

EFF	2003		2004		2005		2006		2007	
	Freq.	%	Freq.	%	Freq.	%	Freq.	%	Freq.	%
0.0-0.5	8	10.39	8	9.76	12	14.12	9	10.11	8	8.16
0.5-0.6	14	18.189	15	18.29	12	14.12	8	8.99	12	12.24
0.6-0.7	16	20.78	21	25.61	23	27.06	26	29.21	29	29.59
0.7-0.8	16	20.78	18	21.95	16	18.82	17	19.10	17	17.35
0.8-0.9	12	15.58	8	9.76	12	14.12	15	16.85	20	20.41
0.9-1.0	11	14.29	12	14.63	10	11.76	14	15.73	12	12.24

Table 8. Frequency distribution of efficiency by size of firms

EFF	Small Size		Middle Size		Large Size	
	Freq.	%	Freq.	%	Freq.	%
0-0.5	41	16.80	4	2.86	0	0.00
0.5-0.6	41	16.80	20	14.29	0	0.00
0.6-0.7	65	26.64	35	25.00	15	31.91
0.7-0.8	40	16.39	32	22.86	12	25.53
0.8-0.9	34	13.93	25	17.86	8	17.02
0.9-1	23	9.43	24	17.14	12	25.53

Table 9. Pearson Correlation matrix based on data used in the DEA Window Model

	Efficiency	Employee	Total assets	Main Business cost	Main Business Income	Net Profit
Efficiency	1.000					
Employee	0.246**	1.000				
Total assets	0.311**	0.888**	1.000			
Main Business cost	0.426**	0.711**	0.805**	1.000		
Main Business Income	0.418**	0.818**	0.884**	0.981**	1.000	
Net Profit	0.318**	0.500**	0.485**	0.413**	0.475**	1.000

Note:**.Correlation is significant at the 0.01 level(2-tailed).

6.2. Empirical Results from Regression Analysis

Table 10 displays the correlation matrix which reveals that there are no multicollinearity problems between the main variables. The most absolute values of correlation coefficient $r <$ 0.5, implies that the variables are correlated at a low degree, the only exception is the correlation coefficient of POS and POPC, which is smaller than 0.8, showing moderate correlation.

The proportion of state-owned shares and the proportion of private corporate shares were found to be negatively correlated with inefficiency, but not statistically significant, the ownership concentration was negatively correlated with inefficiency and was significant at the 0.01 level. Size was also found to be negatively correlated with inefficiency and the correlation was significant at the 0.05 level.

The proportion of state-owned shares was found to be negatively correlated with the proportion of private corporate shares, yet positively correlated with the ownership concentration at the 0.01 significant level. The correlation between ownership concentration and the proportion of state-owned shares is much closer than between ownership concentration and the proportion of private corporate shares.

Table 11 provides a comparison of empirical results estimated by nine different Tobit regression equations which respectively includes a different independent variables subset. The different values of the coefficient of independent variables were given out, as well as the likelihood function of each model.

In order to determine the best model among these nine, a log-likelihood ratio test at a 5% level of significance was applied. Table 12 provides the procedure and results of the test. Since Models 2-9 are all nested in Model 1, the log-likelihood ratio tests between Model 1 and Models 2-9 are respectively implemented, and then Models 6-9 were proved to be much better and acceptable.

Since Model 2 and Model 6 are also nested in Model 8, the test also shows that Model 6 is preferred to Model 8. More over, Model 7 was proved to be better than Model 9. Eventually, Model 6 and Model 7 were left to be the final models to explain the relationship between inefficiency and ownership structure.

From Table 11, model 6 the coefficient of the proportion of state-owned shares is -0.0625 which means that the effect on efficiency is positive, but it is not statistically significant (b/St.Er = -1.423).

The coefficient of the proportion of private corporate shares is -0.0665, and is not statistically significant (b/St.Er. = -1.425). In model 7 the coefficient of the ownership concentration is -0.0469, and it is statistically significant at 5 and 10%, which means the ownership concentration positively affects the efficiency of the company, but is very weak statistically.

In both models, the coefficient of "Large size" is around -0.13, and is statistically significant at less than the 1% level, the coefficient of "Medium size" is around -0.09, and is statistically significant at the less than 1% level. This implies that the size of a company positively affects its efficiency.

Table 10. Pearson Correlation Matrix based on data used in the Tobit model analysis

	INEFF	POS	POPC	OCON	SL	SM	Y4	Y5	Y6	Y7
INEFF	1.000									
POS	-0.092	1.000								
POPC	-0.024	-0.643**	1.000							
OCON	-0.112*	0.472**	-0.077	1.000						
SL	-0.176**	-0.003	-0.023	-0.007	1.000					
SM	-0.176**	0.261**	-0.199**	0.105*	-0.243**	1.000				
Y4	0.039	0.080	0.023	0.086	-0.018	0.005	1.000			
Y5	0.048	0.016	0.022	0.047	0.014	-0.020	-0.240**	1.000		
Y6	-0.052	-0.052	-0.032	-0.078	0.024	-0.023	-0.247**	-0.253**	1.000	
Y7	-0.024	-0.117*	-0.081	-0.125**	0.006	0.014	-0.263**	-0.269**	-0.277**	1.000

note: **.Correlation is significant at the 0.01 level(2-tailed).
*.Correlation is significant at the 0.05 level(2-tailed).

Table 11. Parameter estimated from maximum likelihood estimation Tobit models

variable	Model 1	Model 2	Model 3	Model 4	Model 5	Model 6	Model 7	Model 8	Model 9
	Coef.	Coef.	Coef.	Coef.	Coef.	Coef.	Coef.	Coef.	Coef.
Constant	0.4991a	0.3330a	0.4806a	0.3433a	0.2915a	0.3730a	0.4874a	0.3786a	0.5001a
POS	-0.0377.	-0.0981b	-	-	-	-0.0652.	-	-0.0815c	-
POPC	-0.0572.	-0.0495.	-	-	-	-0.0665.	-	-0.0812c	-
OCON	-0.0439.	-	-0.0585b		-	-	-0.0469c	-	-0.0526b
SL	-0.1337a	-	-	-0.1341a	-	-0.1348a	-0.13314a	-0.1339a	-0.1323a
SM	-0.0873a	-	-	-0.0902a	-	-0.0881a	-0.0863a	-0.0872a	-0.0857a
Y4	0.0189.	-	-	-	0.0221.	-	-	0.0181.	0.0206.
Y5	0.0228.	-	-	-	0.0276.	-	-	0.0218.	0.0255.
Y6	-0.0215.	-	-	-	-0.0110.	-	-	-0.0208.	-0.0168.
Y7	-0.0106.	-	-	-	0.0019.	-	-	-0.0105.	-0.0040.
N Observation	431	431	431	431	431	431	431	431	431
Log likelihood function	119.5572	99.69121	100.0256	115.3671	98.77907	116.6132	117.1581	118.4503	118.9103
Sigma	0.1733	0.1817	0.18155	0.17504	0.18217	0.17455	0.17428	0.1738	0.1736

Notes: 1.Model 1 is general and unrestricted model, Model 2-9 are restricted models nested in Model 1.
2.Significant at less than 1%(a),1-5%(b),5-10%(c), not significant( ).

Table 12. Log-likelihood ratio test results

	Log Likelihood ratio	χ^2	Result
M1-M2	39.73	14.07	accept M1
M1-M3	39.06	15.51	accept M1
M1-M4	8.38	14.07	accept M1
M1-M5	41.56	11.07	accept M1
M1-M6	5.89	11.07	accept M6
M1-M7	4.80	12.59	accept M7
M1-M8	2.21	3.84	accept M8
M1-M9	1.29	5.99	accept M9
M2-M6	33.84	5.99	accept M6
M2-M8	37.52	12.59	accept M8
M3-M7	34.27	5.99	accept M7
M3-M9	37.77	12.59	accept M9
M6-M8	3.67	9.49	accept M6
M7-M9	3.50	9.49	accept M7

6.3. Analysis of the Results

A. The Effects of State-Owned Shares

From the review of regression results, the proportion of state-owned shares positively affects the efficiency of companies, but the t-ratio test shows that it is statistically insignificant. This implies that the number of state-owned shares in the company does not improve or pull down the efficiency of company. This result contradicts the hypothesis in the literature review. Although nominally state-owned shares are held by the state, the state is actually a vacant owner. In fact, a small number of government officials or departments become agents of the state-owned shareholding, but they do not have the final residual claim and do not concern themselves about the performance of company which results in serious principal-agent problems. In contrast, government officials and the managers appointed by government officials may collude with each other, which leads to serious "insider control" problems. In theory, the problems mentioned above may potentially damage the company's efficiency.

On the other hand, the efforts and wisdom shown by the Chinese government in the state-owned enterprise reform should also have an impact. For example, the launch of the non-tradable share reform allows the state-owned shares to flow freely in the stock market, which ultimately increases the liquidity of companies' shareholding. The establisment of a board of directors in the state-owned enterprises and the introduction of outside directors that account for more than half of the number of board of directors constrain the decision-making of managers. Moreover, in the past the managers were directly appointed by the government, but nowadays they are independently recruited by companies, which is a great transition.

Meanwhile, for the companies with state-owned shares, the government kindly gives them financial and policy support. Because China's banking sector has not carried out privatization, the companies can more easily get access to credit with the government's security, which enables companies to invest in R and D to gain a competitive advantage. Also, central government sets up the threshold in some areas of the market so as to make these companies enjoy monopolistic privileges.

In summation, the positive effects and the negative effects of state-owned shares are offset to some extent, and therefore the impact on efficiency of a company is not very clear. This is consistent with the empirical findings in this study.

B. The Effects of Private Corporate Shares

The empirical results also show that the proportion of the private corporate shares positively affects the efficiency of companies, but is not statistically significant. It is also not consistent with the hypothesis. Compared with the state-owned shares, private corporate shares would solve the problem of "absent owner". The corporate shareholders have the rights of residual claim, which motivate them to participate actively in the supervision and administration of managers. The "insider control" problem can also be confined. Without the intervention by government, they are concerned about profit maximization more than others. In comparison with individual shares, private corporate shares are more stable. And the private corporate shareholders have more professional management knowledge and market experience to supervise managers, to give advice on production, to avoid risks and to establish a successful strategy. Furthermore, the private corporate shareholders focus on long-term performance improvements, so as to avoid short-term behaviors. In this case, RandD and innovation in management could be increased without worrying about short-term profits.

However, private corporate shareholders are often treated as "second-class citizens", compared with state-owned shareholders. In the competitive market, they are subject to many restrictions, such as capital, loans and RandD resources. In addition, due to the lack of a mechanism for companies to exit from the stock market and imperfect legal system, corporate shareholders find it easy to violate the rights and interests of small shareholders. Compared with the international private corporate shareholders, China's private corporate shareholders not only lack advanced knowledge and management experience, but also have to carefully maintain a special relationship with the government, which makes them sometimes deviate from the purpose of operating profit maximization.

In summation, the effects of private corporate shares are also not significant.

C. The Effects of Ownership Concentration

According to empirical results, it can be concluded that the ownership concentration positively affects the efficiency of a company at the 5% and 10% significant levels. This result supports the hypothesis given before. In theory, the use of a business model characterized by the separation of ownership and management is widespread in modern corporations, and managers and shareholders have different interests and objectives. As a result opportunistic behaviors and moral hazard emerge, the principal-agent problem appears and decision-making by managers usually undermines the interests of shareholders. Within the highly dispersed ownership structure, the proportion of shares held by any single shareholder is very low, shareholders are very scattered, and no single shareholder can occupy the leading position. Therefore, shareholders do not have the capacity to participate in corporate governance and lack the initiative of supervision because they are not willing to bear the cost of supervision. This may result in the inefficient management of the company. With the dispersion of ownership "manager control", also known as "insider control", becomes a serious problem that would lead to higher agency costs in the absence of other governance mechanisms. Additionally, most of the dispersed shareholders would behave as a "free-rider". However, if some shareholders can hold more shares, they would have the motivation and the ability to supervise operators and to monitor its receipt, which often brings back greater profits than the cost of supervision. The performance of the company will increase with the rise of concentration.

D. The Effects of Firm Size

The empirical results demonstate that the size of a company affects its efficiency, and it is statistically significant at the less than 1% level. This conclusion happens to coincide with the reality in China. In China large-scale companies usually benefit from the resources of the monopoly and government support. With increasingly fierce international competition, the Chinese government is anxious to foster international competitiveness in some companies and push these companies to compete in the international market. In addition, larger companies usually pay a large amount of tax to local governments. It is the reason that the larger the enterprise is, the more the government supports it. In particular, in the ICT industry selected in this study, technology and capital are very critical for the companies, and large-scale enterprises are usually able to use certain technology and investment, which the small-scale enterprises cannot employ. In a non-fully-competitive market like China, the size of q company means market power, market share, and no suspense, and generous loans from banks.

7. CONCLUSION

7.1. Summary

In this research, listed ICT companies are observed from 2003 to 2007 as research samples. The DEA window model is applied to evaluate the efficiencies of the companies. Moreover, the Tobit model is applied after transforming the efficiency scores to inefficiency scores, to conduct the regression analysis. Meanwhile, log likelihood ratio test is employed to test the best suited regression model. Eventually, the models specified by testing explain the relationship between efficiency and ownership structure.

The proportion of state-owned and private corporate shares positively affects the efficiency of a company, but is not statistically significant. However, the empirical analysis of different ownership identities implies that other types of shares such as institutional shares, management shares, foreign shares and individual shares might perform better than state-owned shares and private corporate shares. Meanwhile, the ownership concentration is proved to positively affect the efficiency and the result is statistically significant. In addition, the scale of a company has a positive impact on its efficiency.

Compared with previous research which has already been stated in the chapter on the literature review, most conclusions of this study are acceptable. The differences in conclusions might come from the different evaluation of efficiency of companies (DEA efficiency, SFA efficiency, Profitability, Return on the current assets or Tobin's Q), the different indicators of ownership structure or the different industry considered.

7.2. Policy Implications

Any research about China is complex and systemic. Its huge territory area, enormous population and collision between the political structure and the economic system, turn some simple questions into very complicated issues. Nowadays, economic competition under globalization has evolved into the competition among enterprises of different countries. The key to continuous improvement in the Chinese economy is the continuous reform of China's enterprises. At present there are more than a thousand listed companies in China. However, with the deepening of enterprise reform and the changes of the ownership structure, a number of issues also emerge.

In recent years, it has been proved by research and practice that the irrational ownership structure could be the deeply-rooted cause of those problems, and that optimizing the ownership structure is the key to ameliorating corporate governance and improving the efficiency of companies. Due to the difference of historical experience, cultural traditions, policies, laws and political systems, the ownership structures for enterprises significantly differ acoss the countries. How to combine the reality of China and international experiences in order to change the situation where the proportion of state-owned shares is too large and liquidity is limited has been a tough and controversial issue. It may depend on establishing a reasonable ownership structure, improving the efficiency of corporate governance, enhancing the performance of enterprises, and making the securities market healthy and continuously developing.

From the perspective of public policy making, for the companies to be fully competitive and profitable, state-owned shareholders should gradually evacuate and give up their status as controller. For the companies in such industries as national defense, which are the lifeblood of the national economy, they should be under the control of the government, and state-owned shareholders could consider making a moderate reduction in shareholding, while the state remains the controlling shareholder.

Government should break the restrictions of identity and region and encourage non-state-owned capital, especially financial institutionals, managers, individuals and foreign corporations to hold the shares of these companies. A fair environment for market competition, multi-channel financing environment, and the liberal policy environment must be created so that the non-state-owned economy can increase not only in quantity but also in quality, which can supply large numbers of corporate and individuals as investors. Moreover, the guidance for investors to obtain state-owned shares of the companies through corporate mergers, acquisitions and takeover should be provided. These measures may not only optimize the ownership structure, which enables enterprises to obtain economies of scale and thus to advance in market competition, but also to improve the industrial structure.

The mechanism for "the survival of the fittest" should be set up in the stock market in China. In practice, the threshold for one company to be listed on the stock market is very high in China. However, because listed companies do not face the risk of being eliminated from the stock market, the companies will lose the external pressure of market competition. Therefore, the stock market will lose its management functions, and the risks and resources cannot be optimally allocated, and further encourage the deprivation on the interests of the minority shareholders. When the mechanism of "the survival of the fittest" is established, "vote-by-feet" will be seen as more mandatory, and thus force companies to improve their efficiency. Additionally, many scholars believe that the shares of companies held by banks could improve the ownership structure of companies, and thus promote the efficiency of companies (Zhou et al, 1994). In fact in China, the problem of state-owned banks is the same as that of state-owned enterprises, implying that there is no real owner of state-owned banks to respond to operational risk (Zhang, 2006). Private capital should be allowed to participate in the banking sector so that banks can make their own decision to hold shares in enterprises. In this case, the banks would care about the actual value of their assets and use their natural advantages of capital and information to promote the efficiency of companies.

From the perspective of companies, the state-owned shares could be transferred by auction, sale, or by some mechanism, such as mergers and acquisitions. The transfer of state-owned shares based on agreement, should be open and transparent in order to reduce insider trading, to avoid excessive administrative action by government, and to allow the market mechanisms to play their rolefully. What is more, in the process of selling state-owned shares through the bidding auction, the initial price should be set not less than a benchmark price which is the evaluated price of the net assets. In some companies with a low asset-liability ratio and sufficient cash flow, the state-owned shares could be transferred to debts. The shareholders of state-owned shares thereby transfer their roles to creditors. The debts can be amortized, and also be traded in the market as convertible bonds. The specific way to determine the proportion of convertible bonds and repayment could be decided according to the specific conditions of companies. (Zhang, 2006)

Appropriate ownership concentration should be kept in Chinese companies, which is critical for improving the companies' performance. The ownership structure should not be highly dispersed. The checks and balances should be established among majority shareholders. The existence of a few major shareholders makes it possible to form a structure of checks and balances, which might be helpful to avoid "insider control" and "one shareholder being overwhelming" problems and build up a scientific corporate governance structure, and thus to reduce the agent cost.

7.3. Limitations and Further Research

Due to the limitations of data collection, only data covering five years was used. To analyze the relationship between the ownership structure and efficiency, it is better to include a longer time series, and more firm level observations. In fact, before 2002, the ownership structure had already been changed significantly. Therefore, without the data before 2002, a more obviously changing tendency might be ignored, which may influence the result of the empirical analysis.

ICT listed companies are selected as research samples. The empirical analysis was limited in one industry. Without the comparison among different industries, the effects of different industries on the relationship between the ownership structure and efficiency are not fully exhibited. As an emerging industry the ICT industry is more dynamic compared with other industries. Furthermore, ICT listed companies are more advanced in corporate governance and business management than companies in other industries, and gain more concern and support from the government. Therefore, it needs to be proved further whether the conclusion of this study could be generalized and made widely applicable to other industries as well.

In the further research a database including more time series should be applied. With the further development of ownership diversification, the data, such as the proportion of individual shares, foreign corporate shares, management shares and bank shares, could be collected as the indicators of ownership structure so as to accurately specify the effects of different types of ownership on efficiency.

In addition, this research only focuses on one industry - theICT industry. In order to prove whether the conclusion made in this research is widely acceptable and applicable, more industries should be considered.

Moreover, different econometric techniques could show different results. To evaluate the efficiency or inefficiency of companies, other methods such as a Stochastic Frontier Analysis (SFA) could also be applied in further research. SFA has the advantage that it conducts the measurement, identification of determinants and estimation of their effects on firm level inefficiency in a one-step procedure.

REFERENCES

Allen, W.B. et al, (2005). *Managerial Economics: Theory, Applications, and Cases*. 6th Ed, W.W.Norton and Company, Inc., New York.

Chen, G.M., Firth, M. and Xu, L.P., (2007). “Does the Type of Ownership Control Matter? Evidence from China’s Listed Companies”. *Journal of Banking and Finance*, doi:10.1016/j.jbankfin.2007.12.023.

Demsetz, H. and Villalonga, B., (2001). “Ownership Structure and Corporate Performance”. *Journal of Corporate Finance*, 7, 209–233.

Gürsoy, G. and Aydoğan, K., (1998). “Equity Ownership Structure, Risk-Taking and Performance: An Empirical Investigation in Turkish Companies”, prepared for *the International Global Finance Conference in Istanbul, Turkey*. available at http://www.bilkent.edu.tr/~aydogan /OwnershipStructure.pdf, [assessed: 14/11/2008].

Hitt, M.A., Ireland, R.D. and Hoskisson, R.E., (2001).*Strategic Management: Competitiveness and Globalization. 4th Ed.* South-Western College Publishing, Cincinnati.

Jensen, M.C. and Meckling, W.H., (1976). “Theory of the Firm: Managerial Behavior, Agency Costs and Ownership Structure”. *Journal of Financial Economics*, 3, 305-360.

Kapopoulos, P. and Lazaretou, S., (2007). “Corporate Ownership Structure and Firm Performance: evidence from Greek firms”. *Corporate Governance*, 15(2), 144-158.

King, M.R. and Santor, E., (2008). "Family Values: Ownership Structure, Performance and Capital Structure of Canadian Firms". *Journal of Banking and Finance*, 32, 2423-2432.

McConnell, J.J. and Servaes,H., (1990). "Additional Evidence on Equity Ownership and Corporate Value". *Journal of Financial Economics*, 27, 595-612.

McConnell, J.J. and Servaes, H., (1995). "Equity Ownership and the Two Faces of Debt". *Journal of Financial Economics*, 39, 131-157.

McConnell, J.J., Servaes, H. and Lins, K.V., (2008). "Changes in Insider Ownership and Changes in the Market Value of the Firm". *Journal of Corporate Finance*, 14, 92-106.

McKnight, P. J. and Weir, C., (2007). "Agency Costs, Corporate Governance Mechanisms and Ownership Structure in Large UK Publicly Quoted Companies: A Panel Data Analysis". *The Quarterly Review of Economics and Finance*, doi:10.1016/ j.qref.2007.09.008.

Ruud, P.A., (2000). *An Introduction To Classical Econometric Theory*, Oxford University Press, Inc., New York.

Steinbock, D., (2007). "Climbing the ICT Ladder". *China Business Review*, 34(2), 54-57.

Sun, Y.X. and Huang, Z.H., (1999). "Equity Ownership Structure and Performance of Corporations". *Economic Research Journal*, 12, 23-30.

Von Morgenstern, I.B., (2006). "How Foreign Companies Can Compete in China's High-tech Market". *The McKinsey Quarterly, Web exclusive,* January 2006, available at http://www.mckinseyquarterly.com /High_Tech/Strategy_Analysis/How_foreign_companies_can_compete_in_Chinas_high-tech_market_1736?gp=1, [accessed 24/11/2008]. The report named "How foreign companies can compete in China's high-tech market" was originally published as "High-tech groups seek a new mindset" in the *Financial Times* on January 11, 2006.

Wu, S.K., (2002). "Ownership Structure and Firm Performance: An Empirical Research on Chinese Public Companies". *China Industrial Economy*, 1, 80-87.

Zhang, H.J., (2000). "The Theoretical and Empirical analysis on Ownership Structure and Performance of China's Listed Companies". *Economic Science*, 4, 34-44.

Zhang, W.Y., (2006). The Theory of the Firm and the Reform of Chinese Enterprises, PeKing University Press, Beijing.

Zhou, X.C., et al, (1994). *Enterprise Rform: Model Choice and Matching Design*, China Economic Publishing House, Beijing.

In: Information and Communication Technologies… ISBN 978-1-60876-671-0
Ed: Almas Heshmati and Sun Peng

Chapter 10

A COMPARISON OF EFFICIENCY OF MOBILE OPERATORS IN SOUTH AMERICA

Sergio M. Borja-Barrera[1] and Almas Heshmati*[2]

[1]Presidency of the Republic of Colombia
and Seoul National University
[2]Seoul National University

ABSTRACT

Telecommunications plays a major role worldwide with the aim of achieving a better social life for citizens and is one of the major factors contributing to economic growth. This study provides an efficiency analysis of mobile operators in Colombia, Venezuela, Chile and Brazil.

For the empirical analysis, the stochastic frontier functions approach is employed to analyze data from 10 mobile operators from the sample countries. Mobile operators in Colombia are compared with others from Venezuela, Chile, and Brazil. Panel data from 2005 to 2007 is used in the analysis.

The efficiency estimation for each operator over time shows that the level is affected by some firms and market characteristics such as: type of ownership, market share, type of technology and firm level wages. One of the main findings of this research is that smaller operators work at the same level of efficiency compared with their larger counterparts.

Keywords: Stochastic frontier functions, mobile operators, efficiency, panel data, South America.

* Corresponding author E-mail: heshmati@snu.ac.kr

1. INTRODUCTION

The telecommunications sector plays an important role in terms of economic growth, development, and integration among the nations. In fact Telecommunication industry shows a continued rate of growth. Its influence is vital for the integration of most industries.

Amongst telecom industries, the mobile industry is the most significant. Gerpott et al. (2001) stated that "In terms of sales revenues and number of customers involved, the mobile cellular telephony market is by far the most important sub-market for mobile communications". Communication by mobile phone has entered the world markets giving benefits for citizens, corporations and improving the quality of life for people around the world. It is well known that the mobile phones follow the tendency of: "The mobile communication goes where the users go", as a result, people around the world can communicate anytime and anywhere.

According to Acosta (2004), at the end of 2003 the number of mobile subscribers was greater than the number of fixed line subscribers, showing the mobile industry to be the most dynamic sector in telecommunications. In all the countries in South America, the mobile industry is the most dynamic sector and the International Telecommunication Union (ITU) says that nowadays the percentage of mobile penetration is almost 65% in the region, and by the end of 2012, a 100% level of mobile penetration rate will be reached.

The mobile telephony in South America is now providing services to part of the population who live in areas difficult to reach. In this way it helps to reduce the digital divide, in order to give welfare to people in urban and rural areas. In terms of mobile subscribers the countries with most relevance are: Brazil, Colombia, Venezuela and Chile. For Brazil we have the limitation of only one operator, but, on the other hand for the other three countries the whole mobile industry is tackled in this study. Even though the sample is small, it includes the most important mobile telecommunications markets in South America.

This study provides an analysis of the mobile operators from the countries mentioned in the previous paragraph. For the empirical analysis the stochastic frontier function is employed using data from 10 mobile operators in the sample countries. This study will estimate the efficiency of mobile operators in Colombia, and compare them with mobile operators from Venezuela, Chile, and one mobile operator from Brazil. The data is a small panel data of mobile operators observed during the period from 2005 to 2007.

At the beginning of operation of mobile telecommunications in Colombia, the service was characterized by high cost for the user; only citizens with good income could pay for it. It was the same trend over the world. Nevertheless, the fast development of new technology brought a reduction in cost. As a result, mobile phones became more popular. Heshmati (2003) stated that new technology improved the efficiency and at the same time brought a reduction in prices. Pohjola (2002) mentioned that the fast growth of technology development growth is the cause of a decrease in the cost of devices and services, and Colombia is not an exception to this tendency and nowadays mobile phone are widely used across the country.

This study is the first work in this field that makes a stochastic frontier analysis for mobile operators only in South America. Previous work was focused especially on a performance analysis in manufacturing industries and other services in the Telecommunication industry as a whole, but not individually and specifically for mobile operators. This comparison of international mobile operators may give a basic understanding for regulators, owners and researchers about how the conditions are in the mobile operator industry in Colombia and in the countries compared.

In addition to a measurement of technical efficiency, this study shows how the efficiency of mobile operators is influenced by some characteristics of the market, such as ownership, market share, type of technology and operators' level of wages. Even though the sample data is small, we find that smaller operators are working at the same level of efficiency compared with the other larger competitors in the market in each of the country studies.

The rest of the study is organized as follows. Section 2 presents an overview of the literature at both aggregate national level and disaggregate firm level studies. In Section 3 we outline the methodology of frontier production functions to measure the performance of service firms. Section 4 describes the data and variables. Section 5 discusses the empirical results. The final Section 6 contains a summary of this study and policy implications.

2. Literature Review

The topic of efficiency has been widely studied around the world. It is related to competitiveness, productivity and performance. Nowadays, it is a very sensitive issue in which, many researchers have conducted many studies, analyzing the performance of the companies.

Talking about the Telecom Industry, we can see that it has become one of the most critical sectors not only for developed nations, but also for developing countries. Nowadays, most of the countries are improving their ICT infrastructure in order to maintain continued participation in the globalized world.

Since our study topic is related to the efficiency of mobile operators, this work will emphasize the previous literature written about the IT and Telecommunications industry. Nowadays, there is a strong relationship between efficiency, IT and the performance of the companies. In terms of IT, Shao et al. (2001) measured the influence of IT and they found that IT, as a production factor, had positive and significant impacts on the technical efficiency of the companies studied.

In the recent years in South America, the telecommunications market has been growing fast and in some ways companies depend on the efficiency of the telecommunications industry in order to achieve their goals. Taking into account that most of the telecommunications market is under the control of foreign enterprises that enter the market with their experience, investment and the latest technology, we can say that South American countries are not far behind developed countries in terms of the basic universal service provided by telecommunications.

Some research about the efficiency of the telecommunications sector investigates the industry as a whole, while other investigates firm level data. Considering the entry of foreign firms, the competition among them and taking into account that all of these topics have a relationship with this work, we classified the previous research about efficiency in the telecommunication sectors as follows: at the national and at the firm levels.

2.1. National industry Level Studies

Yang et al. (2007) conducted a study about the development of the Asian telecommunications sector. They analyzed 28 Asian countries and they found that among all of them, the income per country played an important role in the efficiency of the industry of the country. On average, countries like Japan with the highest income per country, showed a good level of efficiency, compared with countries with a low income.

Erber et al. (2005), used benchmarking about the efficiency of the telecommunications industries in U.S compared with the major European Countries, and they found that the first mover in terms of the adoption of new technology, gave a little improvement in its efficiency. Hence, they explained it as a normal result of innovation. However, they emphasized that this innovation in the adoption of new technology must be applied fast, because in the long run it could be a disadvantage because the process of switching customers from one technology to another carried the cost of attending a parallel networks infrastructure. They also remarked that those countries that failed in the adoption of new technology in the past must adopt new technology quickly. In terms of competition among firms, Gort et al. (1999), found positive effects of competition on efficiency in the U.S. telephone industry after the 1990s, compared with the earlier results, in which the market did not allow competition. In a related study, Oum et al. (1995) studied the effects of competition in the U.S. telephone industry and concluded that the telecom industry in U.S improved its allocative efficiency after the liberalization process in the Telecom Industry.

Rozo (2004) used SFA with a technical efficiency model. He applied the approach of Battese et al. (1995), in order to measure the productivity change and efficiency of the telecommunications sector in Colombia, compared with countries ranked as medium revenues incomes. He measured the efficiency of the sector before and after privatization. He used panel data of 28 countries, during the period 1983 to 1998, and he concluded that the telecommunications sector in Colombia was more efficient under monopolistic competition, where the state had the control of the whole telecommunications sector in the country.

In the case of competition and ownership, Ros (1999), found that countries, where at least 50% of their telecommunications infrastructure was under the control of the private sector and the market allowed competition, the services offered to customers were more efficient than the services offered in countries where the competition was not allowed and the ownership was under the control of the state. In terms of foreign direct investment (FDI) and its relationship with efficiency, Lin (2008) investigated the correlation between economic development and investment in telecommunications. The author concludes that the investments made by FDI bring technology transfer and increase competition. As a result, it will improve the efficiency of the telecommunications industry. The author observes that insufficient telecom infrastructure contributes to increased inefficiency and puts of investment by foreign enterprises. One study, with similar results was presented by Gholami et al. (2006), in which, they studied the relationship between ICT and FDI. They found that a good infrastructure in ICT attracts more inflow of FDI.

In a related study Thompson et al. (2007) concluded that the development and expansion of communication networks in developing countries contribute to economic growth and they emphasized that ICT is the engine to manage in an efficient way the use of the resources. In terms of cellular technology, Raghbendra et al. (1999) analyzed the impact of mobiles in the telecommunications sector among 23 OECD countries. They found that the diffusion of mobiles had positive effects on the productivity efficiency of the telecommunications sector.

2.2. Firm Level Studies

Tsai et al. (2006) measured the efficiency of Telecom operators. They took into account the services that companies gave to their customers and they found that full service telecom operators got better measurements of efficiency compared with operators that only gave one service. However, they found that the differences were not significant. The study preferred full service telecom operators to operators that gave not only fixed line services, but also mobile and internet connections.

In terms of competition among firms, Kang et al. (2005), analyzed the efficiency of "Chunghwa Telecom Company (CHT Co.), with other private-public telecom companies like Korea Telecom (KT) and NTT in Japan. They found, that CHT has limitations that avoid getting significant improvements in efficiency, even, after privatization. They suggest that the 50% ownership which is in the hands of government must be sold to complete the full privatization of the company, because there are regulations that limit the management efficiency of the company.

Another study about the case of CHT in Taiwan was made by Yang et al. (2008), in their work about the efficiency of integrated telecommunication firms in Taiwan. They found, that firms have to look for increasing market share in order to improve efficiency. They suggest that firms must combine the strategies to get more market share, with the improvements of services portfolios that they give to their users. Besides, they found that the only state-owned company CHT Co., was the firm with the lowest score for efficiency, and they justified the reason of the Taiwan Government to liberalize the market and privatize companies.

Resende et al. (2002), evaluated the efficiency of the telecommunications sector in Brazil, and did not find significant differences in the levels of efficiency between both periods. In a related study Resende et al. (2004) made the evaluation of price cap regulation and its incidences in quality efficiency among firms, and noted that the performance in quality was low in Brazilian telecommunications.

Lee et al. (2000), evaluated the impact of competition on Korea Telecom KT, and found that, in the short run, KT faced a competitive environment thereby reducing prices, but in terms of technical efficiency there were no significant improvements. They observed improvements in overall efficiency, as a result of a better management of resources and consequently improvement in allocative efficiency.

Following the competition, Picazo et al. (2002) compared the efficiency of telecommunications companies with 13 operators from OECD countries. They mention that operators from countries that allow free competition got better levels of efficiency compared with operators that worked in a monopolistic structure. In another study Bortolotti et al. (2002), found that after privatization, the operational efficiency and the flow of capital investment increased, but, at the same time the level of profitability decreased, as a result, they found a decreased level in the workforce used for local firms.

Mohamad (2004) wrote another study in which he studied the Malaysian mobile telecommunication firms. The results suggest that within the telecommunication industry, firms have great potential to improve their efficiency by adopting digital technology, because it gave the operators a comparative advantage over the other firms that delay the adoption of digital technology.

They concluded that first moving to adopt new technology gives an advantage in terms of improving efficiency, compared with firms that delay the adoption of new technologies. This result was consistent with Erber et al. (2005)

A recent study about the performance of mobile operators was conducted by Lee et al. (2008). It is one of the few studies about the efficiency of mobile operators, and they classified their analysis in two different periods of time.

In the first, the efficiency of foreign operators was better than their domestic counterparts, but in the second period the performance of domestic operators improved and started to show higher levels of efficiency in comparison with the first period.

3. METHODOLOGY

3.1. Research Outline

In this study the stochastic frontier function is used to measure the efficiency of mobile operators. One stochastic frontier model, namely the efficiency effect is used. In this model, in addition to an estimation of technical efficiency for each observation, the degree of efficiency is explained by its determinants. The variable returns to scale (VRS) is assumed for the model specification. The model is introduced in the following discussion.

As we mentioned in the previous paragraph, the technical efficiency effect model specification is applied. One output variable, two input variables and a set of five regressors are used for the analysis. Input variables are the number of employees and number of base stations.

The set of regressors is composed by: % of foreign ownership, % of market share, type of technology, average salary per employee and a time trend. They are among market and firm characteristics that influence the efficiency of mobile operators. Output variable is measured as total revenue.

3.2. Production Frontiers and Technical Efficiency

The production frontiers can be defined as the association between inputs and outputs. The frontier production provides the limit of the possible combination of production between outputs and inputs for each firm. Firms can be located on the frontier or below it, and the level of inefficiency is the ratio of comparing the existing output with the maximum possible output that can be obtained for given inputs. Therefore production frontier shows the state of technology in the industry. If firms are operating on the frontier, they are called technically fully efficient firms, on the contrary if firms operate below the frontier; they are not technically fully efficient firms. To clarify these concepts more deeply, we introduce Figure 1. The horizontal axis in Figure 1 represents the inputs, and the vertical axe represents the outputs; the line between the points 0 and F' is the production frontier. To make clear the definition of technical efficiency, we can see that firm A produces fewer outputs with the same amount of inputs, and by comparing firm A with B, it is clear that firm C produces the same amount of outputs as firm A, using a lower quantity of inputs. Hence, it is clear that firms B and C are operating on the frontier, as a result, they are technically fully efficient firms, and firm A is not a technically fully efficient firm.

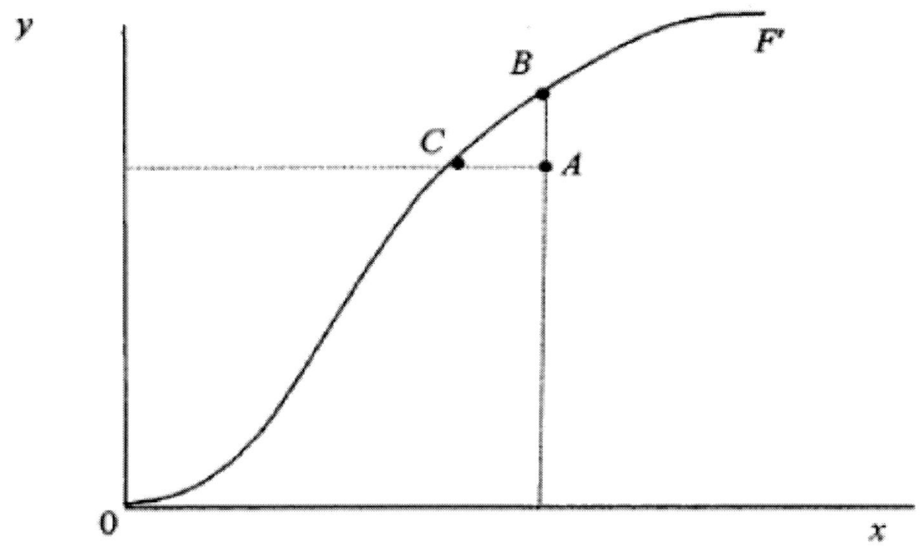

Figure 1. Production frontier and technical efficiency Source: Coelli et al. (2005: p.4).

According to Kumbhakar and Lovell (2000), technical efficiency (TE) has 5 properties which include:

1. TE(y, x) ≤ 1. Technical efficiency is limited to 1.
2. TE (y, x) = 1 $\Leftrightarrow$ $y \in IsoqP\ (x)$
3. TE (y, x) is non-decreasing in y
4. TE (y, x) = is homogeneous of degree +1 in y
5. TE (y, x) = is invariant with respect to the units in which x and y are measured.

Taking into consideration that this study only uses a stochastic frontier analysis (SFA), other production frontiers approaches are beyond the scope of this paper.

3.3. Stochastic Frontier Production – Overview

The Cobb-Douglas production function is written as:

$$Ln\ (Y_i) = f(x_i \beta) + V_i - U_i;\ i = 1, 2, \ldots\ldots, N \qquad (1)$$

where Y_i, is the output of the firm i, x is a vector of inputs used by firm i; and β is the vector of unknown parameters which are to be estimated. Vi is statistical noise, assumed to be independently and identically distributed with a mean of zero and constant variance and represents the effect that firms cannot take into its control such as luck, earthquakes, weather, and so on. *Ui* represents technical inefficiency and is assumed to be independent of *Vi*. Its value must satisfied $Ui \leq 0$.

Equation 1 could be rewritten as:

$$Y_i = \exp(\beta_0 + \beta_1 \ln x_i) * \exp(v_i) * \exp(-u_i) \quad (2)$$

The first component on the right hand side represents the production frontier, the second represents noise, and the last represents technical inefficiency.

To explain graphically these concepts, we introduce Figure 2 below, showing the noise and inefficiency effects for firm A. It uses one input and one output model. Firm A uses xA inputs to produce YA. If there were inefficiency effects, the value of UA must be greater than 0. The frontier outputs for company A are located beneath the production frontier, and as a result we can conclude that the noise effect is lower than 0.

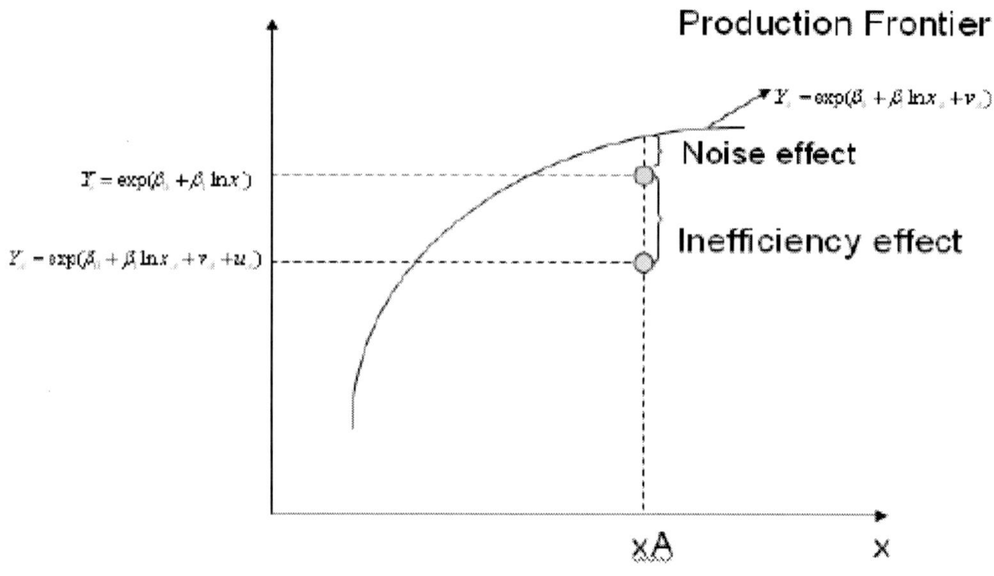

Figure 2. The stochastic production frontier.

As noted earlier, the ratio of output observed, compared to the maximum possible output (Frontier), is the measure of technical efficiency. Taking this into account, the equation to calculate technical efficiency can be written as:

$$TE_i = \frac{Y_i}{\exp(\beta x_i + v_i)} = \frac{\exp(\beta x_i + v_i - u_i)}{\exp(\beta x_i + v_i)} = \exp(-U_i) \quad (3)$$

Kumbhakar et al. (1991) introduced a similar model including in the expression U_i a set of regressors characteristics that explains inefficiency. The variable U_i takes the form:

$$|U_i| = \delta_0 + \sum_{j=1}^{n} \delta_j Z_j \tag{4}$$

where δ 's represents vector of parameters to be estimated and Z represent the set of market's and firm's determinants of inefficiency.

A similar model has been applied and mentioned in the literature (Battese et al. 1992; Tijani 2006, and Adeleke et al. 2008), and it will be used in the model specification of this work. Heshmati (2003) provides a review of the literature with applications to manufacturing and service sectors.

3.4. Model Specification

The Cobb-Douglas production function is written as:

$$Log\ (y_{it}) = \beta_0 + \beta_1 Log\ (L_{it}) + \beta 2 Log\ (K_{it}) + \varepsilon_{it} \tag{5}$$

where $Log\ (y_{it})$ is the logarithm of the output (total revenue) of the i-mobile-operator, i = 1, 2, ……, N; N=10 and t shows the year of observation, for t = 1, 2, 3 years. L_{it}, and K_{it}, represent Labor and Infrastructures. They correspond to the values of Number of employees and Number of base stations. The β's is the vector of unknown parameters to be estimated and ε_{it} is the residual or unobservable features set that influence the market and affect the output, and it is defined as:

$$\varepsilon_{it} = -U_{it} + V_{it};\ V_{it} \sim NCO\ , \sigma_v^2;\ U_{it} \sim (\mu_{it,} \sigma_u^2) \tag{6}$$

Following Battese and Coelli (1995) Where V_{it} is the measurement of statistical error assumed to be independently and identically distributed normal random variables with a mean of zero and constant variance $N(0, \sigma_v^2)$. The U which captures inefficiency in the production is defined as:

$$U_{it} = \delta_0 + \delta_1 + \delta_2 + \delta_3 + \delta_4 Log\ (W_{it}) + \delta_{it} \tag{7}$$

where U_{it} is a function of the set of Z variables that are inherent to the markets function and can influence the final output production (1) or they are determinants of inefficiency in production.

The set of Z variables includes different features of the market like: percentage of foreign ownership, percentage of market share, type of technology, average salary per employee, and time.

U_{it} represents the technical inefficiencies and its assumed to be non-negative with normal distribution like $U_{it} \sim N(\mu_{it}, \sigma^2)$, so Technical efficiency will be:

$$TE_{it} = \exp(-U_{it}) \quad (8)$$

4. Variables and Data

4.1. Variables Description

Table 1, shows the dependent, independents and set of regressor variables used in our analysis.

The dependent variable total revenues (TRV), is one of the most common output variables used to measure the efficiency in the telecommunications sector. Some advantages of using TRV are described by Mohamad (2004) as the primary source to measure growth in telecommunication industries. Pentzaropoulos et al. (2002) noted that it is the main indicator to rank telecommunications firms, because it is used to measure the performance of the sector, and Rozo (2004) said that the aim of any company is to generate revenues, for instance at least to measure technical efficiency is considered an ideal output variable.

Quintero (2006) indicated that firms in the service sector can take better control of their inputs than their outputs; as a result it is more relevant and significant to evaluate their capacity to generate revenues.

Table 1. Output, inputs and characteristic variables

Output	Description
TRV (Total Revenues)	Revenues corresponding to one year for the service provided by the mobile operator. It is measured in millions.
Input	Description
NOE (Number of employees)	It includes full-time staff used by operators of mobile telephony in each country. It is measured in units
NBS (Number of Base Station)	Access point to cover the geographic area and provide the communication service for users and it is measured in units of base stations.
Set of Z Characteristics	Description
FOP (Foreign ownership)	Percentage of foreign shareholder participation in the company.
MSH (Market Share)	Percentage of market shares of the operator at the end of the year.
TOT (Type of Technology)	Technology used by operators to provide the service, e.g. CDMA, TDMA or GSM. It is measured as a dummy variable taking the value of 1 if the operator used only GSM, and 0 for the combinations of technologies used by mobile operators.
AWG (Average Salary)	It is total average income received by employees in the mobile operator company. It is measured in millions.
Year (t)	It is measured as 1, 2, and 3 for the years 2005, 2006, 2007 respectively, and it is expressed as a dummy variable.

Concerning its disadvantages, Raghbendra et al. (1999) observed that sometimes it can show companies as efficient firms, especially in comparisons among international firms, because of some external issues like price regulation in the country or the differences in tax rates among countries. He noted that simple differences in economic growth among countries can show the firms in the country as efficient firms.

In the inputs variables, we used the most common variables. Labor is represented by number of employees (NOE) and Capital is represented by number of base stations. Most of the studies in the telecommunications sector work with capital expenditure, but in our case, the number of base stations is considered as a second alternative definition of capital. This means the access point to cover the geographic area and provide the communications service to users and it is measured in units of base stations. We include NBS, since it is one of the main components of the technological infrastructure of any mobile operator in the world. There are other components like MSC (Mobile Switching Center) and HLR / VLR (Home Visitor Location Register), but NBS is essential for determining the coverage of the mobile operator. The geographical coverage of the operator is directly related to the number and distribution of base stations in the service area. In the countries in this study mobile operators are competing to give the service to whole countries where they are operating. They should cover the same geographical area in each country. So, we considered the use of NBS as an important factor to analyze the level of coverage of the operator compared to its competitors.

It is important to note the affirmation made by Pentzaropoulos et al. (2002), who observed that revenues in Telecommunication sectors are primarily influenced by the physical telecom infrastructure, and currently we have NBS as the main indicator of technological infrastructure. The set of variables inherent to the markets function, that they are determinants of inefficiency in production are: FOP, MSH, TOT AWG and t.

It should be noted that all monetary values are expressed in fixed 2005 prices using consumer price indices accounting for purchasing power parity. Therefore, it eliminates the potential inflation effects and the discrepancies of purchasing power among countries.

4.2. Descriptive Analysis of the Data

The data used for this study include a small balanced panel data for 10 mobile operators observed from 2005 to 2007. It was collected from the annual and financial reports of the mobile operators, and different kinds of reports from the regulators and research conducted by some non-governmental institutions in each of the sample countries. A summary of the variables used in this study is given in Table 2.

Table 2. Summary Statistic of the variables

Variable	N	Mean	Standard Deviation	Min	Max
TRV	30	2,788.13	2,938.83	173.36	12,657.32
NOE	30	2,061.30	1,572.84	597.00	6,084.00
NBS	30	1,591.37	1,841.12	238.00	7,442.00
AWG	30	824.57	180.79	527.38	1,405.56

Notes: Dummy variables t refers to the year of observations, and type of technology (TOT) (1. just for GSM, 0. The mix among GSM, CDMA, WCDMA etc) are not included).

Table 3. Output and Inputs variables and their values for the mobile operators

Ope	Country	TRV	NOE	NBS	FOP	MSH	TOT	AWG
Comcel	Col	3,916	2,899	1,101	99.4	65.0	0	719
Movistar	Col	1,698	1,778	1,530	100.0	26.0	0	746
Tigo	Col	598	669	376	51.0	9.0	1	722
Movistar	Ven	4,181	1,638	890	93.0	42.0	0	798
Digicel	Ven	1,017	653	588	0.0	17.6	1	715
Movilnet	Ven	2,303	3,381	1,076	0.0	41.0	0	956
Claro	Chil	470	1,030	558	100.0	18.0	0	1,015
Movistar	Chil	1,564	949	1,410	100.0	43.0	0	1,069
Entel	Chil	1,649	1,747	1,523	0.0	39.0	0	636
Vivo	Bra	10,485	5,860	6,862	100.0	36.7	0	867

Table 4. Summary of variables per country

Country	TRV	NOE	NBS	AWG
Colombia	2,071	1,782	1,002	729
Venezuela	2,500	1,891	851	823
Chile	1,228	1,242	1,164	907
Brazil	10,485	5,860	6,862	867

TRV is expressed in thousands of dollars, NOE and NBS in units and AWG in Dollars.

Table 3 shows the values associated with outputs and input variables. For TRV, NOE, NBS, and AWG, the values correspond to the average of these variables during the study period. For FOP and MSH, their values are the corresponding percentages at the end of 2007.

By looking at tables 2, 3 and 4, we can easily note that there are huge variations in all variables. In table 2, there are great differences between the minimum and maximum values compared with the average values. The main inferences from these tables are:

(i) The most profitable companies are: Vivo, Movistar and Comcel, from Brazil, Venezuela and Colombia respectively. They have in common that they have the biggest market share in each country. Claro from Chile is the least profitable company.

(ii) Movistar and Tigo from Colombia, Digicel and Movilnet from Venezuela, and all Chilean operators have revenues lower than the mean of revenues in their respective countries.

(iii) Vivo, in comparison with all operators is the largest company. It has nearly the same amount of subscribers than Comcel from Colombia, but it has to give the service to its subscribers in a geographic area almost five times bigger than Colombia. That is why its values are much higher than the others operators.
(iv) In terms of base station that refers to infrastructure technology, Tigo has the smallest amount of base station, and in terms of countries, Chile has the best technology infrastructure. It is important to note that among all countries in this study Chile has the highest penetration rate with almost 80%.
(v) Operators Tigo from Colombia and Digicel from Venezuela, are the only operators that use only GSM technology as their unique and standard technology infrastructure.
(vi) Chile is the country where operators use the least number of employees on average, but at the same time the country that pays a higher salary.

Table 5 shows a simple correlation analysis for the all the variables used by our study. The input variables are highly correlated with the output variable, with the exceptions of foreign ownership, average salary and time showing relatively low among them.

Taking into account that there are only 3 operators by country, we saw in Table 3 that there are large differences among them, especially in terms of the size. Before starting with the next section, it is important to make a brief analysis in order to get a better picture in terms of differences about the size of the firms.

Table 5. Correlation matrix among variables

	TRV	NOE	NBS	FOP	MSH	TOT	AWG	T
TRV	1.000							
NOE	.863**	1.000						
NBS	.900**	.848**	1.000					
FOP	0.355	0.281	0.287	1.000				
MSH	.422*	.497**	0.241	.391*	1.000			
TOT	-0.338	-.453*	-0.306	-.589**	-.690**	1.000		
AWG	0.007	0.052	0.078	.421*	0.048	-0.298	1.000	
T	0.168	0.063	0.088	-0.015	-0.019	0.000	0.235	1.000

**. Correlation is significant at the 0.01 level (2-tailed). *. Correlation is significant at the 0.05 level (2-tailed).

4.3. Size of the Mobile Operator in Each Country

In this study, all mobile operators were classified as large companies in their respective country. The national statistical bureau in each country classified firms based on several independent criteria, such as number of employees, total revenues, total assets etc. Nevertheless in this study, our approach tried to get a closer inference about the size of the company in order to get the most feasible information to infer which of the three operators in each country is the smallest or the largest.

From Table 3, a huge difference among operators within the same country can be observed. Therefore, in each country we analyzed which operator had the least number of employees, the lowest amount of total revenue, the lowest investment in capital expenditure and the weakest technology infrastructure in terms of base stations installed across the country. We found that in Colombia the smallest mobile operator is Tigo, in Venezuela it is Digicel and in Chile it is Claro. All of them are notably smaller in their respective countries, compared with their larger counterparts. We assumed that all criteria mentioned before were important to classify whether the operator was small or large compared with the other operators in its respective country. It is important to note that the differences across countries prevent a comparison of all of them using the term small companies. For example; there was no way to compare Vivo from Brazil versus the others, because all operators are small companies compared with Vivo. The term small operator in this study only refers to companies within the same country.

5. Empirical Results and Analysis

5.1. Results

In order to explain the estimation results, it is important to note that we are working with logarithmic values. Since the relationship among the variables is measured in percentages terms, it means that if the number of employees increases by 1% and the number of base stations remains constant, total revenues would increase by 0.73%. Table 6 shows the summary of the maximum likelihood estimation results using FRONT41 statistical package.

Table 6. Frontier production function parameters estimated

		Coefficient	Standard-Error	T-Ratio
Stochastic Production Frontier				
Constant	β_0	-0.0895	-0.3923	0.2283
Log(NOE)	β_1	0.7336	0.1721	4.2623 ***
Log(NBS)	β_2	0.3815	0.1810	2.1073 **
Set of Z Characteristics				
FOP	δ_1	-0.2597	0.1406	-1.8471 *
MSH	δ_2	-1.5533	0.4475	-3.4711 ***
TOT	δ_3	-1.3238	0.4371	-3.0284 ***
Log(AWG)	δ_4	0.4778	0.0871	5.4845 ***
T	δ_5	-0.2004	0.0785	-2.5544 **
Variance Parameters				
sigma-squared	$\sigma2$	0.0215	0.0112	1.9235 *
gamma	γ	0.4700	0.2038	2.3066 **

*** Significance level at 1%; ** at 5%; * at 10%.

In this model, the value of the β_1 parameter (number of employees), is significant and helps to explain the variations in total revenue at the 1% level of significance. The t-value of β_1 is 4.2624 and it is statistically significant. The value of the variable β_2 (number of base stations) is also statistically significant at the 5% level. This means that if the number of base stations increases by 1%, (and the number of employees remains constant), the total revenue will increase by 0.38%.

The value of $\gamma = 0.47$ implies that there is inefficiency in operators' production, as indeed is found in the coefficients of δ_1, δ_2, δ_3, δ_5, which are statistically different from zero. The negative sign implies that inefficiencies in the total revenue from mobile operators decreased by increasing foreign ownership, the market share that the operator has in the country where it operates, technology and seniority. Again the estimation of δ_4 has a positive sign, indicating that there is a direct relationship between inefficiency and the average wage, thus an increase in the average salary increases inefficiency, since it generates expenditure.

5.2. Analysis

Table 7 shows the summary of efficiencies obtained by operators during the time period of this study.

We observed that all operators improved their efficiency during the study period; as a result, all of them, year by year installed more base stations to provide a larger and sufficient coverage and provide better services to their customers. It should be noted that all countries have not reached the 100% mobile coverage rate and they need to install more telecommunications infrastructure to build up a higher service capacity.

The most efficient operators were Digicel and Tigo, from Venezuela and Colombia respectively working at 98% levels of efficiency. Similarly, operators MoviStar from Venezuela and Chile, and Vivo Brazil show high levels of efficiency ranging between 94% and 97%.

Table 7. Efficiencies per operators, 2005 – 2007

Firm	Eff.2005	Eff.2006	Eff.2007
Digicel_Ven	0.9788	0.9840	0.9882
Tigo_Col	0.9665	0.9806	0.9861
Comcel_Col	0.9455	0.9735	0.9827
Movis_Ven	0.9205	0.9637	0.9758
Movis_Chile	0.8326	0.8920	0.9420
Vivo_Brazil	0.7675	0.8876	0.9438
Movnet_Ven	0.6841	0.7928	0.8013
Movis_Col	0.6748	0.7608	0.8378
Entel_Chile	0.6601	0.7268	0.8030
Claro_Chile	0.4826	0.6251	0.6934
Mean	0.7913	0.8587	0.8954
Min	0.4826	0.6251	0.6934
Max	0.9788	0.9840	0.9882

The remaining operators present a ranking of efficiency between 69% and 83%. Notably, the operator with the lowest level of efficiency is Claro from Chile, but, it improved its efficiency by almost 21% during the study period.

In analyzing the operators Tigo and Digicel, we found that they are the only operators that are working with only GSM technology, and also the only operators working exclusively in the band 1900 MHz. The other operators work in 850 MHz and 1900 MHz and they use different kinds of technologies to provide services. As a consequence TIGO and DIGICEL are the youngest operators in Venezuela and Colombia. They started operations adopting GSM technology as standard. They are the smallest operators in Venezuela and Colombia. This result is in accordance with the result found by Pentzaropoulus et al. (2002). They mentioned that high levels of efficiency can be achieved even for companies with medium or small revenues. In addition, this result also supports the affirmation of Erber (2005) who suggests that the cost of attending parallel networks infrastructure means a higher cost and obviously a decrease in the efficiency levels. Here we can see how the smallest companies in the sample are in the top 2 efficiency levels among the operators (Tigo and Digicel do not have parallel networks infrastructure) and explain in a few words why the other operators are in the process of migrating their networks in order that they can work only with GSM technology as a unique standard technology.

Besides the concepts explained above; we found that among the four first operators with a mean efficiency over 0.95, all of them reduced the average salary for the previous year in the study period. Comcel reduced its average salaries, by at least 20% from year 1 to year 2. Firms that had a mean efficiency between 0.72 and 0.76 are firms with similar or better infrastructure in terms of coverage and management but their comparative revenues with the leaders of the market in each country are different in favor of the leaders.

For Chilean companies, we found that two of them are the operators with the least efficiency among all firms. As noted before, the negative influence of average salaries in the production function is difficult to measure, because Chile has the highest minimum salary in South America, and of course their average salary will be higher if we compare with the other employees from the same sector in other countries. In the case of Movistar and Entel, the remarkable issue is that Movistar has a little bit more market share than Entel and it receives significantly more revenues with a clearly similar infrastructure. It is clear that Chile is the country with best technology infrastructure in terms of coverage, but these results show us that Chilean operators are not getting good levels of efficiency. They could improve their performances because we can see that the value of the average mean efficiency for the study period was 0.8485, meaning that total revenues could increase by 15% in the short run just if the operators use the same technology as that of the operators with best practice production technology used by the frontier firm.

6. Conclusion and Policy Implications

6.1. Conclusion

Technical efficiency using Total Revenue (TRV) as a dependent variable in the production function shows that operators with the highest market share in each country have better conditions for improving their efficiency. The adoption of only GSM technology as a standard network platform for Tigo and Digicel gives them a notable privilege compared with the other competitors. We found significant influence of the determinant variables used to measure the inefficiency. We saw that the percentage of foreign ownership, technology, market share and wages are significant in improving the efficiency of the operators. We can see that at the country level Colombia is the only country where all operators are foreigners. Venezuela has two state-owned operators and Chile has one. It means that there is a good opportunity for establishing joint ventures between state and foreign multinationals. At least in Venezuela and Chile there are three companies that could make this kind of alliance.

The operators from Colombia are working at the same or even better levels of performance compared with their international counterparts. Operators from Chile show the lowest level of efficiency. They have in common the highest mean average salary per employee. We mentioned that salaries negatively influence the efficiency of the operators.

Finally, our main conclusion, taking the results from our analysis, is that smaller operators are working at the same levels of efficiency compared with their counterparts. Digicel in Venezuela as well as Tigo in Colombia showed good results and, comparing these two firms with all operators in the sample, we can say that they are working at similar or even better levels of efficiency; remarkable given that Tigo is the smallest operator among our sample. Digicel from Venezuela and Claro from Chile the smaller operators in their respective countries work with a similar performance to their counterparts in each country.

Based on the results, we saw that there is no implication about the size of the company in getting similar levels of efficiency, and our results are similar to the results of Sueyoshi (1994), Lien et al. (2001) and Pentzaropoulos et al. (2002). They suggested that size was not a determinant of level of efficiency.

6.2. Policy Implications

It is quite obvious that the markets of mobile operators in the countries included in this study are being dominated by foreign enterprises. As a result, governments should adopt policies that must focus on the way to stimulate these companies to encourage them to continue to invest and feel confident that their businesses will be profitable for all of the actors in the market.

The mobile penetration rate in each country is more than 60%, indicating that, compared with the fixed line penetration rate, the number of mobile subscribers is more than four times that of the subscribers of fixed telephone lines. The advent of technologies like 3.5G in mobile phones will boost the expansion of the internet in each country. As a result, even though the financial electronic-commerce is not well developed, the uses of mobile phones go beyond just the simple use of making calls. Currently, for all countries, the mobile operator market is the main contributor to connectivity and seems the perfect engine to generate spillover effects in other fields, like device manufacturers, e-commerce, e-government, e-health and so on. Ahn et al. (2006) said that the immense economic impact is not only for the mobile sector, but also for related industries like component parts and device manufacturers.

One of the biggest obstacles that mobile communication is facing now, is the high taxes that subscribers have to pay for the services. In the sample countries, mobile communication is classified as a luxury good. As a result, the use of the service is taxed heavily, which prevents the massive use of these devices. Taking into account that communication is a universal right for people, and based on the fact that mobile communication is nowadays the principal inter-communicator system, regulators must reduce the taxes charged on it, and set them at the same levels of other basic goods in order to stimulate the demand for this service.

The governments must boost the mass use of mobile phones by, for instance, reducing the tax charges to increase the demand of the services generated by mobile devices. For instance, in Colombia, the highest tax charged on the services generated by mobile devices is 20%. New laws related to mobile communications as a public service for all citizens must be adopted, because the luxury concept that is now employed for cellular phones and its services must disappear. Currently, the mobile phone is used by most people and the high taxes on the use of the services must be eliminated. Regulators must work on new rules that allow an increase in the demand for this sector, working on policies to encourage the companies to reduce prices without a reduction of profits. Also for the markets with a small oligopoly in each country, the government must be creative to promote competition among the few operators in the market.

Another topic that should be under consideration is the experience of most developing countries where the Mobile Number Portability (MNP) enables mobile telephone users to retain their mobile telephone numbers when changing from one mobile network operator to another. Up to now Brazil is the only country that adopts the Mobile Number Portability (MNP), a system where the users can change the operator while retaining their same mobile number. This system is at the first testing stage in Brazil and, according to ANATEL, will be fully available in the second half of 2009. Just for the testing stage there are 18,773 subscribers that are waiting to change their mobile operator.

In Colombia, this policy was approved by Congress, and it is to start operations in February 2010. The policy will give more tools to the users to choose or to change their current operator, but special attention must be paid to prevent the biggest companies from absorbing the small operators, because this law has been created in order to promote fair competition among operators and give social welfare services to subscribers. One of the most helpful steps for these countries consists of the allowance of the entrance of the third operator, although one must be careful to avoid the possible return to a duopolistic structure as before.

Even though the market is open to the fourth new operator in each country, it would be quite difficult to get into it. The market is almost consolidated and entry for new firms is quite difficult, in particular to be able to compete with 2 big multinationals like America Movil and Telefónica.

For operators, it would be very important to take advantage of their position in the telecommunications market. Most of them are multinational enterprises that are competing in the market around the world. They have enough experience acquired in other developed countries to transfer this experience to South American mobile markets. It is well-known that the latest technologies used in developed countries delay their arrival in developing countries. As a result, even though they were not the pioneers in this new technology, they already know the costs and benefits that this new technology will bring. Hence, they should take advantage of this situation to implement it in our countries.

For the case of Colombia, the operator Movistar seems not to have had the best performance amongst its competitors, and lost market share in the study period and, as we explained before, just 1% of increasing in market share could get unbelievable increasing in outputs. However, this operator is always the last operator to adopt new technologies. Comcel started operations of 3G at the end of last year, Tigo started them at the beginning of the second half of this year, and Movistar continue to delay its operations over this platform. Besides, Movistar Chile was the first operator to start the use of 3G as the first mover advantage in Chile. It is difficult to understand why, even though they are the same operator and have not started to use this technology in Colombia. Erber (2005) suggests that countries that in the past did not move fast and quickly in adopting new technologies that makes possible the convergence between Internet and the other communications tools, do not have time to lose in the adoption of new technologies, and even though this statement was formulated for countries, the same implications could be applied at the firm level in our case.

In the case of state-owned enterprises the results show that foreign ownership improves efficiency. As a result there is a good opportunity to enhance efficiency through mixed ownership in the telecom sector.

6.3. Possible Directions of Future Research

It could be very interesting to evaluate the performance among mobile operators, using both production function and cost function approaches. It will be helpful to get information about the operators' various marketing expenditures. We have to note that the sample data must include a longer period and more operators.

Moreover, variables like the number of subscribers, categorized by the kind of subscribers (Postpaid or Prepaid) should be considered in order to analyze their effects on the efficiency of operators. The variable NBS must be classified by the frequency that they are operating on. Namely 1900 MHz needs more RBS, but at the same time the QoS is much better.

Taking into consideration that in each country in this study the taxes on mobile services are at least 20%, further research must consider the use of this variable. In a case where total revenue is used as a dependent variable, one should adjust revenue for tariff or taxes to obtain an unbiased measure of revenue and performance.

As a result of the fact that the mobile operator industry in South America is dominated by America Movil and Telefónica, new research taking into account the suggestions mentioned above should focus on the measure of efficiency among operators by ownership. This will help to get valuable information about the performance of the same mobile operators who are operating in different countries.

REFERENCES

Acosta, Z. (2004). "Liberalizacion de los Servicios de Telecomunicaciones en Colombia". *Archivos de Economia*, Vol 262.

Adeleke, O.A., Fabiyi, Y.L., Ajiboye, A., and Matanmi, H.M. (2008). "Application of Stochastic Production Frontier in the Estimation of Technical efficiency of Cassava Farmers in Oluyole and Akinyele Local Government Areas of Oyo State". *Research Journal of Agronomy*, Vol 2, pp. 71 - 77.

Ahn, J., Lee, J.S., Lee, J.D., and Kim. T. (2006), "An Analysis of Consumer Preferences among Wireless Lan and Mobile Internet Services". *ETRI Journal*, Vol 28(2), pp. 205-215.

Battese, G., and Coelli, T.J. (1992). "Frontier Production Functions, Technical Efficiency and Panel Data: With Application to Paddy Farmers in India". *The Journal of Productivity Analysis*, Vol 3, pp. 153 - 169.

Battese, G., and Coelli, T.J. (1995). "A Model for Technical Inefficiency Effects in a Stochastic Frontier Production Function for Panel Data". *Empirical Economics*, Vol 20, pp. 325-332.

Bortolotti, B., Souza, J., Fantini, M., and Megginson, W. (2002). "Privatization and the sources of performance improvement in the global telecommunication industry", *Telecommunications Policy*, Vol. 26, pp. 243-268.

Erber, G., and Berlin, D. (2005). "Benchmarking efficiency of Telecommunication Industries in the U.S. and Major European Countries". *Communications and Strategies*, Vol 60, pp. 157-179.

Gerpott, T., Rams, W., and Schindler, A. (2001). "Customer retention, loyalty, and satisfaction in the German mobile cellular telecommunications market", *Telecommunications Policy*, Vol. 25, pp. 249-269.

Gholami, R., Lee, S., and Heshmati, A. (2006). "The Causal Relationship Between Information and Communication Technology and Foreign Direct Investment", *World Economy*, Vol. 29, pp. 43-62.

Gort, M., and Sung, N. (1999), "Competition and Productivity Growth: The case of the U.S. Telephone Industry", *Economic Inquiry*, Vol. 37. pp. 678-691.

Heshmati, A. (2003). "Productivity Growth, Efficiency and Outsourcing in Manufacturing and Service Industries", *Journal of Economics Surveys*, Vol. 17, pp. 79-112.

Kang, C., and Chung, R. (2005). "Privatization, Production, and Cost Efficiency in the Taiwan's Telecommunications Industry", Providence University, Taiwan.

Kumbhakar et al. (1991). "A generalized production frontier approach for estimating determinants of inefficiency in US dairy farms", *Journal of Business and Economic Statistics*, 9, 279-286.

Kumbhakar, S, and Lovell, C.A.K. (2000). "Stochastic Frontier Analysis". Cambridge University Press.

Lee, J., and Mukhrumbaev, R. (2008). "Performance of Communication Operators: A Cross Country Analysis", Technology Management, Economics and Policy Program, Seoul National University.

Lee, Y., Park, Y., and Oh, H. (2000). "The impact of competition on the efficiency of public enterprise: The case of Korea Telecom", *Asia Pacific Journal of Management*, Vol. 17, pp. 423-442.

Lien, D., and Peng, Y. (2001). "Competition and production efficiency Telecommunications in OECD countries", *Information Economics and Policy,* Vol. 13, pp. 51-76.

Lin, C. (2008). "Role of Foreign Direct Investment in Telecommunication Industries: A Developing Countries' Perspective", *Contemporary Management Research*, Vol. 4. pp. 29-42

Mohamad, N. (2004). "Productivity Growth in the Malaysian Mobile telecommunication industry", *Journal of Economic and Management*, Vol. 12, pp. 1-27.

Oum, T., and Zhang, Y. (1995). "Competition and Allocative Efficiency: The Case of the U.S. Telephone Industry", *The review of economics and Statistics*, Vol. 77, pp. 82-96.

Pentzaropoulos, G., and Giokas, D. (2002). "Comparing the operational efficiency of the main European telecommunications: A quantitative analysis", *Telecommunications Policy*, Vol. 26. pp. 595-606

Picazo, A., and Quirós, C. (2002). "Eficiencia y Liberalización en las telecomunicaciones, Programa de Investigaciones Económicas", *Discussion Paper* 0202, Madrid - España.

Pohjola, M. (2002), "The New Economy: facts, impacts and policies", *Information Economics and Policy*, Vol 14, pp. 133-144.

Quintero, J. (2006), "Eficiencia técnica y cambio en la productividad en las empresas turísticas de Cartagena, 2001-2004: ¿Qué tan competitivos son los hoteles y las agencias de viajes locales?", Serie de Estudios sobre la competitividad de Cartagena, Discussion Paper.

Raghbendra, J., and Majumdar, S. (1999). "A matter of connections: OECD telecommunications sector productivity and the role of cellular technology diffusion", *Information Economies and Policy*, Vol. 11, pp. 243-269.

Resende, M., and Facana, L. (2002). "Privatization and efficiency in Brazilian telecommunications: an empirical study", Applied Economic letters, Vol. 9, pp. 823-826.

Resende, M., and Facana, L. (2004). "Price cap regulation, incentives and quality: The case of Brazilian telecommunications", *International Journal of Production Economics*, Vol. 92, pp. 133-144.

Ros, A. (1999). "Does ownership or competition Matter? The Effects of Telecommunications Reform on Network Expansion and Efficiency", *Journal of Regulatory Economics*, Vol. 15, pp. 65-92.

Rozo, F. (2004). "Cambio productivo y eficiencia en telecomunicaciones: Colombia frente a una frontera de países de mediano ingreso", *Universidad de los Andes*, Bogota, Colombia.

Shao, B., and Lin, W. (2001). "Measuring the value of information technology in technical efficiency with stochastic production frontiers", *Information and Software Technology*, Vol. 43, pp. 447-456.

Sueyoshi, T. (1994), "Stochastic frontier production analysis: Measuring performance of public telecommunication in 24 OECD countries". *European Journal of Operational Research,* Vol 74, pp. 466-478.

Tijani, A. (2006). "Analysis of the technical efficiency of rice farms in Ijesha Land of Osun State", Nigeria. *Agrekon*, Vol 45, pp. 126-135.

Thompson, H., and Garbacz, C. (2007). "Mobile, fixed line and Internet service effects on global productivity efficiency". *Information Economics and Policy*, Vol 19, pp. 189-214

Tsai, H., Chen, C., and Tzeng, G. (2006). "The comparative productivity efficiency for global telecoms. *International Journal of production economics*", Vol 103, pp. 509-526

Yang, H., and Chang, C. (2008). "Using DEA window analysis to measure efficiencies of Taiwan's integrated telecommunication firm. Telecommunication Policy", doi:10.16/j.telpol.2008.11.001

Yang, Y., and Jia, H. (2007). "Estimation of the Asian telecommunication technical efficiencies with panel data", *The Journal of China Universities of Posts and Telecommunications*, Vol. 14, pp. 111-114.

In: Information and Communication Technologies… ISBN 978-1-60876-671-0
Ed: Almas Heshmati and Sun Peng

Chapter 11

MOBILE OPERATORS IN MENA REGION: IMPACT OF FOREIGN OWNERSHIP AND MARKET SHARE ON FINANCIAL PERFORMANCE AND TRAFFIC

***Rachid El-Rhinaoui*[1] *and Almas Heshmati**[*2]

[1]Ministry of Industry, Commerce and New Technologies of Morocco
[2]Seoul National University

ABSTRACT

As the process of telecommunication liberalization and increased competition evolves, the situation of market competition and the structure of mobile operators differs considerably across the Middle East and North African (MENA) countries. This study attempts to analyze the effects of foreign ownership and the market share on the traffic and financial performance of mobile operators in MENA region. To achieve these objectives, we use panel data estimation methods to assess MENA mobile industry performances using an unbalanced panel data of 13 mobile operators observed over the period 2002-2007. The empirical analysis results, using fixed and random effect models, showed that both foreign ownership and a higher market share have a significant positive impact on traffic, revenues, returns on sales and returns on investment of mobile operators in the MENA region.

Keywords: MENA, mobile operator, foreign ownership, market share, profitability, unbalanced panel data, individual effect.

1. INTRODUCTION

Historically, most telecommunication operators were state-owned companies with a natural monopolistic market structure. This was essentially due to the high level of initial

* Corresponding author E-mail: heshmati@snu.ac.kr

investment costs necessary to build up a telecom infrastructure. However, due to the technology revolution, new transmission systems were generated and the cost of establishing a network was continuously reduced.

Moreover, many people including policy makers, corporate managers and economists have long believed that private enterprises are performing much more efficiently and profitably than public enterprises (Sueyoshi, 1998). As a consequence, many countries have started to deregulate and liberalize some economic sectors gradually, especially in telecommunications, during the last two decades. MENA countries, as with many other developing countries, started reforming their telecommunications sector through liberalization and privatization.

With the rapid revolution of mobile technology and the opening of the telecommunications sector to foreign investments, telecommunications in MENA countries witnessed notable competition from a larger share of foreign investment by multinational corporations. This competition increased the number of mobile operators from 12 in 1999 to about 42 in 2007. Therefore, mobile communications has exploded creating a rapid penetration rate and even achieving a national penetration of more than 100% in some countries (such as Bahrain and Kuwait).

In fact, currently almost all countries in the MENA region have at least one mobile operator that is owned, partially or totally, by one or more foreign telecommunications operators.

However, the impact of these foreign investments and ownership gave mixed results as it had a positive impact on economic growth and job creation in some cases, while in others it showed no direct impact.

In this study, we seek to investigate empirically the possible links between the share of foreign ownership in a mobile operator (MO) and the MO financial performance measured as profitability (profitability here is measured as revenue, return on sales and investment intensity).

Moreover,, we study the impact of the share of foreign ownership on the total minutes of use as a measure of the traffic service produced. This paper contributes to the literature by studying the impact of the MO market share on a firm's financial performance, as well as the effect of MO market share on total minutes of use.

The novelty of this study comes from investigating and studying empirically the effect of foreign ownership and market share in the mobile telecommunications sector from the perspective of a developing economy (especially in the MENA region). The data used in this study is an unbalanced panel data from 13 mobile operators in 10 countries of MENA region over the period 2002 to 2007.

We adopt panel data methodology to estimate three models including revenue, return on sales and traffic in addition to a sub model of investment intensity taking account of temporal and individual effects.

This study is an important evaluation of the evolving liberalization process in MENA's mobile markets. It will be useful to consultants who want to have a clear understanding of thc evolution of MENA mobile activities and benchmarks of operator performances, as well as policymakers responsible for the telecommunication deregulation aspects.

It is also useful in the assessment of policies and their effects as well as in providing feedback effects on policy actions and establishing new operators to enhance the competitiveness of the market.

This paper is organized as follows. In chapters two and three we provide a background on mobile telecommunications globally and in the MENA region, followed by a literature review with a focus on "foreign ownership – profitability relationship" and "market share – profitability relationship".

In chapter four we introduce research methodology where we discuss the econometric models used, followed by model specifications. Chapters five and six present and describe the data sample used and the empirical results obtained. A discussion of the results is found in chapter seven.

Based on our empirical results we follow our line of argument by policy implications in chapter eight.

Finally, in chapter, nine, we conclude our work by more compact and summarized findings that answer our research questions, list the limitations of our research and suggest future directions.

2. Mobile Telecommunications Industry

2.1. Mobile Industry: Background Globally

The industry of mobile telecommunications is considered one of the fastest growing sectors in the world. The rapid diffusion of mobile technology was mostly due to technological progress and regulation.

Many detailed studies at the country level show empirical support for the development of the diffusion of mobile telecommunications services, the pricing policies in telecommunications industries and the role of entry barriers.

The mobile technological revolutions have increased the number of mobile subscribers worldwide. According to the ITU world telecommunication, 125 years were needed to reach one billion fixed lines, but the first billion mobile subscribers was achieved within just 21 years (2002).

After that, the boom in mobile telephony was sustained, and by mid-2007, there were as many as 3 billion mobile subscribers.

In fact, almost one out of two people had a mobile phone, and in Europe, penetration has surpassed 100%. More than one out of 4 Africans and one out of 3 Asians have a mobile phone.

A strong competition leading to a decrease in price has been able to shrink substantially the digital divide in mobile telephones. Figure 1 shows the evolution of mobile penetration in developed and developing countries and worldwide.

Telecommunications market reforms such as liberalization and the introduction of competition increase access to ICTs and revenues from telecommunications services and permit governments to meet their social and economic goals. These reforms have positively improved productivity and profitability, encouraged investment, enhanced the performance of the telecommunications and ICT sectors and created greater benefits for consumers and businesses.

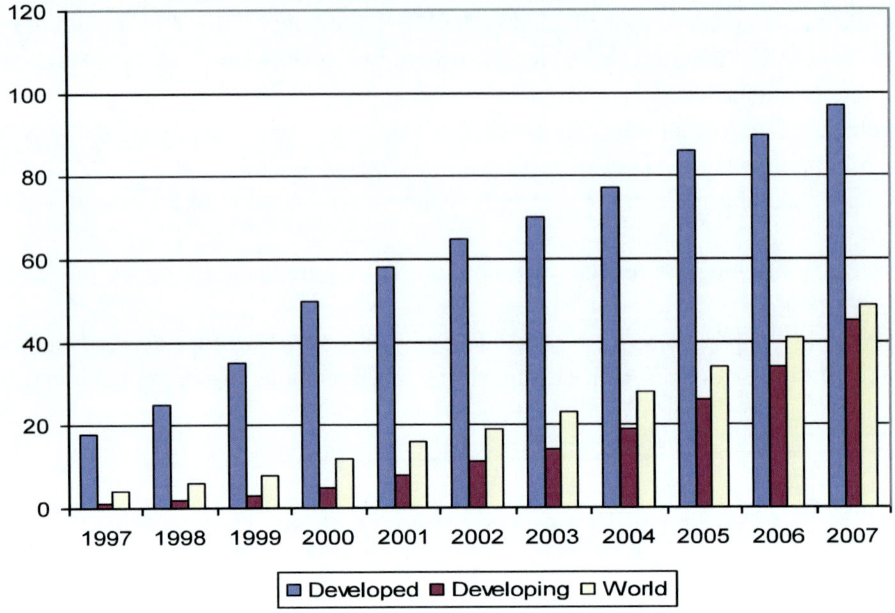

Source: ITU World Telecommunication.

Figure 1. Mobile subscribers (per 100 persons) in the world.

2.2. Mobile Industry in MENA Region: State-of-the-Art

In recent years many countries in the MENA region have started restructuring their domestic telecommunications market by adopting market liberalization policies. These reforms have made clear the separation between the role of the public and the role of the private sectors, and have created separate regulatory entities to put into effect service obligations, control anti-competitive practices and protect consumers. During this wave of telecommunications market liberalization many incumbents were privatized (partially) and new operators emerged via the issuance of new licenses to foreign telecom players. But, the degree of liberalization in the MENA region differs from one country to another. For instance, Jordan and Bahrain are the most liberalized and UAE and Qatar are considered to be the least liberalized.

a) Telecommunication market liberalization

Traditionally, in the MENA region, the ministry in charge of telecommunications played the roles of policy-maker, regulator and operator at the same time. In the process of liberalization and the introduction of competition, many MENA countries, therefore, established an independent regulatory authority to ensure fair competition and avoid discrimination; although this happened at different times in each country. However, some MENA countries still do not have a separate telecommunications regulatory body (e.g., Kuwait and Syria).

In the MENA region, only a few countries have totally liberalized their telecommunications sector. The process of liberalization is still evolving and concerns all telecommunications segments. Jordan's telecom sector is considered as the most liberalized in the MENA region; and for the mobile sector, a duopoly is the dominant mobile market structure. In addition, the level of government ownership in the telecommunications incumbents is still considered high compared to their contemporaries. The examples of the extent to which some MENA countries lag behind their contemporaries regarding the government telecom ownership are Algeria with 100% and Oman and Saudia Arabia with 70% whereas it is 0% in Italy and Spain and 14% in the Netherlands (according to Booz Allen Hamilton's web site).This situation is different for the case of non-incumbent mobile operators where private and foreign ownership are dominant. High levels of foreign ownership are found in Algeria (Djezzy and Wataniya), Jordan (Fastlink) and Tunisia (Tunisiana).

b) Growth in mobile operators and subscribers

The mobile sector was the first to profit from the reform of telecommunications in the MENA region. Many new mobile operators have emerged in their telecommunications market and some of them such as Orascom (Egypt), Zain (Kuwait), Etisalat (UAE) and Q-Tel (Qatar), often called the Big Four, have expanded their activities beyond the MENA region and have become regional major players in the mobile sector. The number of mobile operators in the MENA region grew from 13 in 1999 to 42 in 2007. Consequently, the number of mobile subscribers in the whole MENA region increased significantly from 2.5 million (1998) to 125 million subscribers (2007). This high growth and rapid penetration are not the same among all countries. Countries like Qatar, United Arab Emirates and Kuwait register higher penetration than the rest. Although the region does hold the promise of continual and sustained growth for the coming years, other countries like Egypt with a high population still register low penetration rates due to the low per capita GDP.

c) Economical and social impact of mobile telecommunications

The telecommunication reforms implemented by MENA countries have resulted in the growth and development of their overall economies. The introduction of competition in mobile markets has reduced the service prices, and thus encouraged the accessibility of these services and narrowed the barriers to information flow. Price reductions together with the resulting mobile service improvements have reduced the cost of doing business in the MENA countries, and thus promoted more investment, which has a positive impact on economic growth in the MENA region. In addition, mobile market liberalization has contributed indirectly to GDP growth through the creation of new jobs, and the revenues of mobile services have contributed directly to economic growth in MENA countries by increasing their GDP.

Another economic area that mobile telecommunications, after liberalization, affected positively is rural economies. The introduction of competition into MENA mobile markets alongside the relatively cheap first investment of mobile networks, in contrast to fixed networks, has resulted in the coverage of mobile networks of some rural areas not covered by fixed networks.

In conclusion, liberalizing mobile telecommunications sector has had an apparent positive impact on the economies of the MENA region, which can be measured in many ways including higher penetration rates, lower prices, and the higher share of mobile telecommunications in the country's GDP, in addition to greater investments, more new jobs created, and greater integration into the global economy. However, the mobile industry is in its infant stage and its effect on economic development has not completely matured yet.

From the social perspective, the mobile telephone has become a fundamental device of everyday life and a manifestation of individual freedom. It participates in reinforcing a system of society that is open and communicative, and acts as a solution to closed societies. Mobile telephones allow people to be in continuous contact, and deepen the quality of the contact by offering multiple services and effects which make interpersonal communication wider and more versatile.

Finally, in rural areas, far from the city center, mobile telephones help, in terms of quality, improved essential services which in many cases the state finds difficult to provide, such as urgent medical alerts, reliable transport and road safety, and information regarding specific issues.

3. Literature Review and Theory

3.1. Introduction

Telecommunications is generally considered the most essential infrastructure of any modern economy. Where it represents an imperative intermediate input for many outputs or final goods, telecommunications services have always had a considerable impact on efficiency, growth and development in all industries (Deardorff, 2001; Dvornik and Sabolić, 2007). By the time countries underwent telecommunications market liberalization processes, business and industries came to realize more efficient telecommunication services. With telecommunications liberalization, local market doors opened for foreign direct investment (FDI).

Generally, FDI is considered to be an important channel for knowledge and technology transfer. It promotes competition in the local market, generates new jobs and contributes to the development of human capital in host countries in all economic sectors. Earlier and recent empirical research has showed that foreign firms are more productive, efficient and profitable than domestic ones, and that the entrance of foreign firms stimulates the productivity performance in local firms operating in the same industry (spillover effect). For instance, Yudaeva et al. (2003) and Wang et al. (2002) found that foreign firms are more productive in manufacturing industry than locally owned firms and were able to have a positive effect on local firms. The positive effect from FDI was also clear in increasing efficiency and competitiveness (Bonin et al., 2005), increasing firm value, (Manoj and Manoranjan, 2007); and promoting exports and economic growth (Li and Liu, 2005).

The telecommunications sector was not different where FDI in the telecommunications market was repeatedly reported to play an influential role in the development of the telecommunications market (see for example Lin, 2008). However, the effect of foreign ownership and market share on financial performances in the telecommunications sector was overlooked especially in mobile telecommunications research literature. In this study, we shed light on these relations and ground the theory to be further investigated.

3.2. Foreign Ownership – Profitability Relationship

Different studies have analyzed efficiency, productivity and performance differences between private and public firms on one hand and between foreign-owned firms and locally-owned firms on the other hand. According to Banker et al., (1995) and Bitros, (2003), private enterprises perform more efficiently and more profitably than public enterprises. In fact, as the pressure of the market persisted, the threat of losing jobs and the resultant adverse reputation which does not exist in the case of public enterprises made private firms perform and produce in a more efficient way (Sarkar, 1998).

On other side, Ros (1999) argued that the type of ownership and market structure of an industry are important determinants for key firm survival variables such as output, price and technical efficiency. In fact the multinational corporations (MNCs) have a competitive advantage over domestic firms, realizing cost advantages by both economy of scale and economy of scope. In addition, MNCs possess insubstantial specific assets that generally local firms do not have, such as "knowledge capital" (production technique, intensive marketing, human resources and management skills), reputation, brand name, and market networks (Ge and Chen, 2008). With the internationalization of business, the MNC may transfer its knowledge and techniques to its overseas subsidiaries and thus perform and generate values better than local firms. In fact, Dimelis and Louri, (2002) argue that the higher the level of foreign ownership, the more intangible assets are accumulated through technology and management skills transfer and therefore more production efficiency is achieved.

Many empirical studies addressed the differences in terms of profitability, between foreign-owned enterprises and their local counterparts. For instance, in the banking sector both Claessens (2001) and Kim (2005) stressed that the entrance of a foreign bank leads to a more competitive banking market, affects the profitability and overall expenses of domestic banks and forces them to operate more efficiently. However, the results of Claessens (2001) showed that foreign banks have a higher profitability than domestic ones in developing countries; whereas Kim (2005) found a negative impact of foreign ownership on banking sector profitability in Korea. A similar finding was also reported by Naaborg and Lensink (2008) for "Central and Eastern Europe and Central Asia". However, Košak and Mitja (2008) could not find a statistically significant effect of foreign ownership on banks' profitability in South-Eastern Europe. The same was found by Oetzel and Banerjee (2008) in the insurance sector.

In manufacturing industries, foreign owned Brazilian firms showed higher ratios of value-added to output than domestically-owned firms of the same size and same industry (Willmore, 1986). Chhibber and Majumdar (1999) found that only firms with more than 51% foreign ownership showed better performances in their return on sales and return on assets. Moreover, while analyzing the performances of firms operating in Turkey, Aydin et al. (2007) found that foreign ownership participation level impacts positively the return on assets of firms achieved by savings in operating expenses generated from technology transfer and management models.

Other studies such as Newfarmer and Marsh (1981) found that the effect of foreign ownership on industrial performance is not always supportive in terms of earnings. They however emphasized that transnational companies create positive spillovers and generally make use of more capital-intensive technology and concluded that foreign ownership is an important parameter of market structure.

3.3. Market Share – Profitability Relationship

The relationship between market share and profitability has been recognized where numerous studies have generally confirmed a positive relationship between market share and business profitability. The important work of Buzzell et al. (1975) on PIMS[1] database showed that market share is a key to profitability, and is positively correlated with a return on investment. In explaining this positive effect Buzzell and his colleagues used well-grounded economic theories: economies of scale where increasing market share reduces the cost of production and distribution, market power where higher market share creates greater power market to the firm and management quality where highly skilled managers are successful in achieving high market share and generating maximum productivity from their employees to support these findings. Another notable study by Szymanski et al. (1993), analyzed 48 studies on the relationship between market share and profitability in which they found on average a positive impact of market share on business.

The market share – profitability relationship continued to be investigated by many scholars for different sectors. For instance, Kasuga and Shishikura (2006), in their study on the determinants of profit in the Japanese broadcasting industry, found a positive effect of market share on profit and revenue. In the banking sector, Smirlock (1985), Frame and Kamerschen (1997) found a strong and positively significant impact of market share on profit rates and on return on assets. Moreover, Chu et al. (2008) analyzed firms from security industries in Taiwan and had the same conclusions.

Nonetheless, Markell et al. (1988) could only find one industry (plastic industry) with a positive relationship between market share and profitability while studying three different manufacturing industries. A different result was reported by Feeny and Rogers (2000), where they examined 722 Australian firms and found the relationship between market share and profitability is U-shaped.

On the other hand, other studies refuted the positive causality between market share and business profitability. For instance, Bourantas and Mandes (1987), found that the relationship between market share and profitability is not causative and that the lower market share businesses may be more profitable than the higher market share ones arguing that firms must focus on management rather than on pursuit of market share for an increasing return on assets; the same result was reported by Schwalbach (1991). Ailawadi et al. (1999), examined the PIMS annual database, and found that although market share effect was not observable, firms with high market share were able to adopt certain profitable actions that may not be possible or profitable for firms with low market share. Another study by Laverty (2001)

[1] The PIMS (profit impact of marketing strategies) data base comprised financial and other information on 620 individual businesses supplied by 57 major North American corporations initially for the 3-year period 1970-1972.

confirmed the correlation between the market share and profitability, but found no evidence that an increase in profitability comes from an increase in market share (no direct association). In conclusion, although some studies found a weak relationship between market share and profitability, the majority of the literature confirmed the existence of this relationship.

3.4. Hypothesis Formulations

Despite the contradictory results reported in some of the previous literature on the effect of foreign ownership and market share on profitability, all studies point to the existence of such a relationship. This study contributes to the previous literature by investigating these effects in the mobile telecommunication sector. Consequently, by utilizing experience gained from the rich previous literature and theoretical studies we examine the following hypothesis in our mobile operator sample:

H1: An increase in the share of foreign ownership raises the profitability of the mobile operator (MO).
H2: An increase in the share of foreign ownership raises the traffic generated by the MO network.
H3: An increase in market share raises the profitability of the MO.
H4: An increase in market share raises the traffic generated by the MO network.

Improvement in profitability as a result of increased share of ownership arises from spillover and transfer management, skill and technology from multinational corporations to national telecommunications operators. The increase of traffic is a result of increased network capacity resulting from increased investment and technology capability of foreign firms with capital and experience from other markets. The positive effect of market share on traffic and profitability is due to scale effects and diffusion of technology reaching a critical mass point.

4. Research Methodology

4.1. Introduction

In the telecommunications sector, both parametric and non parametric methods were used to assess the performances of telecommunications firms depending on the data availability, the objectives and especially the preferences and knowledge of the researcher. In the case of non-parametric methods, Data Envelopment Analysis (DEA) was widely used to compute the relative efficiencies of a set of decision-making units (See Yilmaz and Dinc, 2002). In Parametric estimation methods, Stochastic Frontier Analysis (SFA) was widely used to estimate production function, cost function of a firm as well as measuring the technical efficiencies of a set of firms in an industry. Other studies used both DEA and SFA to assess and measure the performances of telecommunications firms (See for example Sueyoshi, 1994).

Due to data limitations and structure, this study uses a parametric method to estimate three models of revenue, return on sales and traffic in addition to a sub model of investment intensity taking account of temporal and individual effects. The following sub-section gives an overview of the econometric models used in this study; and the application of the econometric models is presented in the empirical results chapter.

4.2. Panel Data Model

There exist two kinds of panel data: balanced and unbalanced panel data sets. The balanced or complete panels data consider entities (individuals, enterprises, regions, countries, etc) which are surveyed periodically over a given timespan (Yafee, 2003). On the other hand, the unbalanced panel data consider entities which are not observed during the same period, and they are more likely to be the norm in typical economical empirical setting (Baltagi, 2005).

Panel data have many advantages including:

1. Controlling and capturing unobservable heterogeneity, due to omitted variables and/or specification problems, this can be observed neither in a cross section nor in a time series analysis. There are two types of non-observed heterogeneity:
   - Individual effects which affect in different ways each entity of the sample and its results, but which do not change over time like management and initial conditions.
   - Temporal effects (ut) represent effects that all entities in the same way are subjected to, but which change over time like policy and exchange rates.
2. And giving more informative data, more degree of freedom, and more efficiency (Baltagi, 2005).

Therefore, if the unobserved heterogeneity is not corrected, it will be in the error term and the estimated parameters will be biased. For a survey of performance analysis in manufacturing and service industries using cross section and panel data approaches (see Heshmati, 2003).

The core difference between fixed and random effect models lies in the role of dummies. If dummies are considered as a part of the intercept, this is a fixed effect model. In a random effect model, the dummies act as an error term.

4.3. Model Specifications

In the following, we establish three models; each one of them shows how foreign ownership percentage (fop) and market share (msh) affect the profitability measured in terms of revenue, return on sales and investment intensity, and the traffic of a mobile operator i in time t (year).

a) Model 1-Total revenue

To produce goods or services and generate revenue, an enterprise needs to spend money in the form of investments: capital expenditure (CAPEX) to build and extend its infrastructure and operating expenses (OEX) to pay its employees and to cover the costs of its daily activities.

Letting trv_{it} denote the output corresponding to the total revenue (in million of ppp $) of a mobile operator i in year t. The production function of the output trv can be written as follows:

$$Ln(trv_{it}) = \beta_0 + \beta_{opex} * Ln(opex_{it}) + \beta_{capex} * Ln(capex_{it}) + \beta_{fop} * fop_{it} + \beta_{msh} * msh_{it} + \beta_{som} * som_{it} + \beta_{time} * time \quad (1)$$

where, opex and capex denote operating expenses and capital expenditures, respectively, and are the inputs. Foreign ownership percentage (fop) is a characteristic that reflects the ownership structure of the mobile operator (MO). fop variable depends on the decision of the government (policy makers) to privatize, partly or fully, the incumbent or issue a new mobile license to a foreign operator. The fop value can change positively if the government or the domestic private firm decides to sell more to a foreign operator and negatively if the opposite occurs.

The market share characteristic (msh) reveals the power of the MO in the market. The msh variable depends on the number of subscribers of the mobile operator relative to the total subscribers of all mobile operators in the same market.

The situation of the market (som) shows whether the market of the MO is competitive or not. It is equal to 1 if the number of competitors is greater than 2 and 0 otherwise. Time is measured by year and is used to catch the temporal effect and reflects technology change.

b) Model 2-Return on sales

Return on investment (roi) and return on sales (ros) are commonly used as financial measures of a firm's strategic performance.

The variables roi and ros are related by the algebraic identity: (*) $roi = ros * Investment\ Turnover$. The return on sales is defined as follow: (**) $ros = \frac{profit}{revenues} = \frac{ebitda - capex}{trv} = 1 - \frac{1}{\pi}$. Where ebitda is earning before interest, tax, depreciation and amortization, and related to total revenue as follow: $revenues = trv = ebitda + opex$ and $\pi = \frac{revenues}{\exp enses} = \frac{trv}{opex + capex}$ is the profitability ratio.

And the investment turnover is defined as: $Investment\ Turnover = \frac{revenues}{Investment} = \frac{trv}{capex}$

The inverse of the Investment Turnover is: ($\frac{investment}{revenues} = \frac{capex}{trv}$) and it is called capital expenditure margin (capexmar) or investment intensity.

Instead of checking the effect of fop and msh on roi, we will do it for the component: return on sales (ros) and check after, based on the predicted values of ros, what level (percentage) of investments (capexmar), the shareholders decide to invest as a consequence.

The following equation permits an estimate of the effects of fop, msh, som and time on the ratio return on sales:

$$ros_{it} = \beta_0 + \beta_{fop} * fop_{it} + \beta_{msh} * msh_{it} + \beta_{som} * som_{it} + \beta_{time} * time \tag{2}$$

From the equation (**) and (2), we can deduce that any positive (negative) effect of any explanatory variable on return on sales implies a positive (negative) effect on the profitability ratio.

Letting prosit denote the predicted value of return on sales (ros) for mobile operator i at time t (year).

The following equation tells us how the investment intensity (capexmar) is decided, based on the values of predicted return on sales.

$$capexmar_{it} = \gamma_0 + \gamma_{pros} * \hat{pros}_{it} + \gamma_t * time \tag{2~}$$

where $pros_{it} = \hat{\beta}_0 + \hat{\beta}_{fop} * fop_{it} + \hat{\beta}_{msh} * msh_{it} + \hat{\beta}_{som} * som_{it} + \hat{\beta}_{time} * time$

β_x is the estimated coefficient of the independent variable X in the equation (2).

Using the equation (2), if, in the equation (2~), there is negative effect of pros on the capexmar we can conclude that any positive (negative) effect of any explanatory variable on return on sales implies negative (positive) effect on the ratio investment intensity; therefore positive (negative) impact on return on investment (by using (*)).

c) Model 3-Traffic of mobile network

The amount of traffic generated by a mobile network depends first on the capacity of the network itself characterized by the number of base stations (nbs) and the capacity of each base station, second, on the number of the mobile operator employees (noe), since they are responsible for serving their customers, maintaining the network and so on.

Let moupyit denote the output corresponding to the traffic (minutes of use of all subscribers) of a mobile operator i in time t.

Also in thc last few year, in the MENA region the rapid growth of mobile subscribers as a consequence of liberalization and the entrance of new operators has been related with increasing price competition and pricing innovations by cellular operators. By the entrance of the second mobile operator, the price of communication decreased, which pushed the incumbent to reduce its prices and then started a series of price competitions supported by frequent and intensive advertisements in the mass media. This price competition was called in some countries a price war.

The production function of the output moupy can be written as follows:

$$Ln(moupy_{it}) = \beta_0 + \beta_{nbs} * Ln(nbs_{it}) + \beta_{noe} * Ln(noe_{it}) + \beta_{price} * Ln(price) + \beta_{fop} * fop_{it} + \beta_{msh} * msh_{it} + \beta_{som} * som_{it} + \beta_{time} * time \quad (3)$$

In this model, we assume that the same quality of service is provided by each mobile operator in the sample.

Note that since the price information is not available, we assimilate the price with the average revenue per minute (ARPM), (See Sung, 2007). The model (3) is an ad hoc model which has no theoretical base, but is informative empirically.

5. Data

In this study, we take account of the experiences of a number of mobile operators from countries in the MENA region. The experience of each country with respect to the mobile market is unique due to a diversity of factors including regulatory environment, level of unmet demand, tariff strategies, geography, coverage, promotional approaches, etc. For the purposes of this empirical study, most of the data were gathered from annual and financial reports of the mobile operators; while some data were collected from the web sites, news articles and some papers.

5.1. Data Description

The sample of this study covers 13 mobile operators from 10 countries in the MENA region. The choice of these mobile operators was due to data availability. All mobile data used in this study, concern GSM mobile business and constitute an unbalanced panel data with data time of some mobile operators being slightly different from the data time of the others.

5.2. Summary Statistics

Data collected showed that all countries in our sample experienced an increasing mobile penetration rate; the number of subscribers grew by more than three times, on average, from 2002 to 2007. However, this increasing rate of subscribers is different from one country to another, since they do not have the same population. Less populated and high income countries such as Kuwait and Bahrain exceeds 100% penetration rate. Consequently, financial indicators which include ebitda, revenue, and capex averages increased for all mobile operators in the sample, the traffic volume shifted up and the expenses per subscriber sharply decreased to new low levels; see figures 2and3 (based on Table 1 of data summary in the appendix).

Table 1. Summary by mobile operator and year (Mean)

	Fop	msh	trv in m ppp $	ebitda in m ppp $	opex in m ppp $	capex in m ppp $	nos (000)	appm in ppp $	traffic per year in m of mn	nmo	prt	noe	nbs
Djezzy	0.80	0.70	2159.79	1286.45	873.35	803.67	6003.84	0.24	1118.26	2.67	0.32	2803.33	3687.33
MTC Vodafone	0.56	0.25	93.57	38.63	54.93	33.59	192.76	0.51	54.16	2.00	0.94	436.8	238.80
Mobinil	0.36	0.52	2999.96	1497.39	1502.57	895.60	6728.35	0.25	1372.76	2.17	0.18	2135	2296
Vodafone Egypt	0.64	0.48	2446.13	1294.41	1151.72	668.462	4724.17	0.41	660.13	2.17	0.18	2782	2148.33
Atheer	0.3	1	261.48	86.56	174.93	74.83	2950.59	0.04	830.04	1.00	0.22	1575	2064.25
Iraqna	0.88	1	331	185.25	146.75	99.44	1775.90	0.07	480.33	1.00	0.17	1686.67	1774
Zain Jodan	0.97	0.57	989.42	470.70	518.72	136.96	1529.80	0.29	362.06	3.00	0.52	1042	1243
Zain Kowait	0	0.58	624.28	359.06	265.22	98.56	1320.60	0.13	495.47	2.00	0.87	1249	1130.4
MTC Touch	1	0.50	48.73	7.44	41.29	0.38	535.05	0.08	63.73	2.00	0.28	668	682.5
MAT	0.47	0.68	3420.69	1645	1775.71	571.16	8074	0.86	551.17	2.17	0.39	3354.33	4142.33
Meditel	0.64	0.32	1144.50	460.08	666.91	620.36	3822.83	0.73	203.40	2.17	0.39	4163.17	1949.67
Tunisiana	0.95	0.39	968.042	431.70	536.35	292.94	2104.82	0.28	353.32	2.00	0.50	2268.6	1179.6
Etislat	0	1	2027.23	1228.78	798.45	259.37	4251.50	0.13	1590.80	1.00	0.97	5090	5067.5
2002	0.43	0.62	1229.51	563.30	666.21	384.10	2156.92	0.60	378.97	1.83	0.19	2346	2330.17
2003	0.47	0.53	1126.57	576.96	548.16	444.66	1927.65	0.63	359.38	1.90	0.26	1890	1774
2004	0.59	0.61	1139.43	597.35	539.85	269.32	2222.46	0.31	415.19	1.85	0.35	1861.15	1574.77
2005	0.60	0.62	1406.75	709.87	692.12	377.99	3436.42	0.24	617.31	1.92	0.48	2484.54	2045
2006	0.61	0.62	1753.99	921.46	832.53	396.53	4700.24	0.23	825.75	2.00	0.58	2688.92	2530.69
2007	0.58	0.59	2188.19	1148.52	1039.67	487.72	6645.97	0.20	1191.27	2.42	0.76	3046.25	3278.17

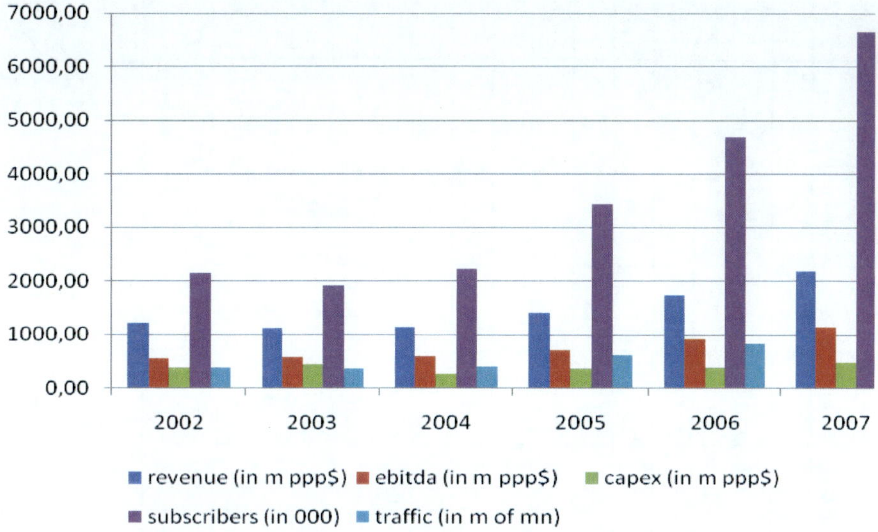

Figure 2. Evolution of revenue, ebitda, capex, subscribers and traffic per year (in average).

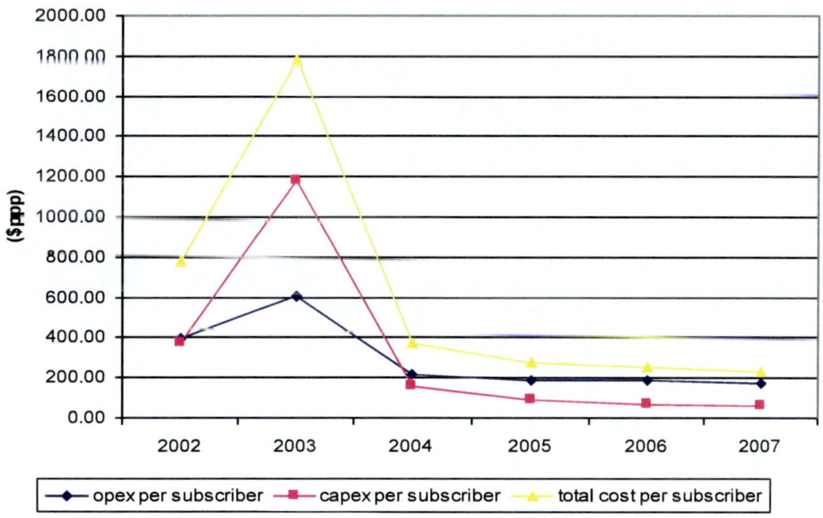

Figure 3. Evolution of expenses per subscriber per year (in average).

The data correlation matrix (Table 2) shows a strong significant correlation between the number of subscribers on one hand and revenue, ebitda and traffic on the other. Moreover, there is a significant correlation between traffic on one side, and the number of base stations, number of employees and price on the other side, in addition to the negative correlation between revenue and operating expenses as well as between revenue and capital expenditure.

Table 2. Correlation matrix

(Pearson Correlation)															
	trv_m	ebitda_...	opex_...	capex_...	nos_00...	moupy	noe	nbs	fop	msh	som	prt	appm	ros	year
trv_m	1.000														
ebitda_m	0.982**	1.000													
opex	0.977**	0.918**	1.000												
capex_m	0.675**	0.638**	0.687**	1.000											
nos_000	0.903**	0.885**	0.882**	0.644**	1.000										
moupy	0.667**	0.713**	0.588**	0.457**	0.768**	1.000									
noe	0.607**	0.616**	0.566**	0.360**	0.627**	0.586**	1.000								
nbs	0.711**	0.746**	0.641**	0.361**	0.741**	0.768**	0.813**	1.000							
fop	-0.126	-0.144	-0.101	0.036	-0.067	-0.311*	-.257*	-0.294*	1.000						
msh	0.091	0.148	0.026	-0.113	0.123	0.415**	0.258*	0.514**	-	1.000					
som	0.422**	0.450**	0.372**	0.371**	0.509**	0.386**	0.165	0.271*	0.319**	-0.063	1.000				
prt	-0.012	0.046	-0.076	-0.249*	0.036	0.240	0.215	0.219	-	-0.020	0.093	1.000			
appm	0.120	0.042	0.201	0.196	0.037	-0.318**	0.086	-0.009	0.026	-	-0.107	-0.209	1.000		
ros	0.303*	0.350**	0.237	-0.281*	0.253*	0.334**	0.241*	0.320**	-0.144	0.356**	0.143	0.269*	-	1.000	
year	0.271*	0.283*	0.246*	0.067	0.452**	0.427**	0.233	0.264*	0.133	0.033	0.393**	0.491**	-	0.337**	1.000
Number of observations	67	67	67	67	67	67	67	67	67	67	67	67	67	67	67

*. Correlation is significant at the 0.05 level (2-tailed).

**. Correlation is significant at the 0.01 level (2-tailed).

Table 3. Regression results of revenue, return on sales, investment intensity and traffic using individual fixed and random effects models

	Model 1: Revenue (Independent variable: ltrv)				Model 2: Return on sales (Independent variable: ros)				Sub model 2~: Investment intensity (Independent variable: capexmar)			
Parameter	Fixed Effect		Random Effect		Fixed Effect		Random Effect		Fixed Effect		Random Effect	
	Coeff estimate	Stdr error	Coeff estimate	Stdr error	Coeff estimate	Stdr error	Coeff estimate	Stdr error	Coeff estimate	Stdr error	Coeff estimate	Stdr error
Intercept	-107.4138^{b}	45.5665	-25.0691^{d}	38.6840	-145.7447^{b}	69.0381	-185.5327^{a}	65.2666	0.4053^{a}	0.0414	0.3651^{a}	0.0691
Lopex	0.7451^{a}	0.0684	0.9234^{a}	0.0480								
Lcapex	0.0391^{d}	0.0413	0.0778^{b}	0.0322								
Fop	0.7422^{a}	0.2368	0.0297^{d}	0.1470	1.2569^{a}	0.4692	0.0862^{d}	0.2222				
Msh	0.7027^{c}	0.3741	0.3515^{c}	0.2031	1.9757^{b}	0.7645	0.7100^{b}	0.3047				
Som	0.0575^{d}	0.0879	0.1266^{d}	0.0871	0.0156^{d}	0.1830	0.0305^{d}	0.1592				
Time	0.0556^{b}	0.0231	0.0127^{d}	0.0194	0.0718^{b}	0.0345	0.0924^{a}	0.0325				
Pros									-0.8751^{a}	0.1780	-0.3345^{a}	0.1093
F-test	F(6,48)=107.93 F(12,48)=5.29		--		F(4,50)=6.83 F(12,50)=3.03		--		F(1,53)=24.16 F(12,53)=3.78		--	
Breusch and Pagan	--		Chi2(1)=3.92		--		Chi2(1)=1.67		--		Chi2(1)=3.50	
Hausman test	Chi2(6)=18.99				--				--			
R^2 adjusted	0.9006		0.9756		0.3533		0.2543		0.3132		0.3130	
	Model 3: Traffic (Independent variable: lmoupy)											
	Fixed Effect		Random Effect									
	Coeff estimate	Stdr error	Coeff estimate	Stdr error								
Lntercept	-245.2854^{a}	69.7486	-185.4503^{b}	73.3510								
Lnbs	0.4255^{b}	0.1786	0.4343^{b}	0.1920								
Lnoe	0.1459^{d}	0.2571	0.4294^{c}	0.2598								
Lprice	-1.0426^{a}	0.1177	-0.8726^{a}	0.1183								
Fop	0.9630^{b}	0.3700	0.5273^{d}	0.3529								
Msh	1.0276^{c}	0.6127	0.7921^{d}	0.5904								
Som	0.0032^{d}	0.1412	0.1269^{d}	0.1484								
Time	0.1287^{a}	0.0351	0.09801^{a}	0.0368								
F-test	F(7,47)= 90.45 F(12,47)=26.68		--									
Breusch and Pagan	--		Chi2(1)=49.79									
Hausman test	Chi2(7)=34.11											
R^2 adjusted	0.3826		0.5937									
Nbr of obs	67											

Note: less than 1% (a), 1-5% (b), 5-10% (c), more than 10% (d).

6. EMPIRICAL RESULTS

In this section we explain the regression results of individual fixed and random effects models. Using the software STATA 9.2, we report the results of the three models in Table 3 (Appendix). For all our models, we used "F-test" and "Breush and Pagan test" to check the existence of individual fixed and random effects and the "Hausman" test to choose between fixed and random effect models. The results are highlighted in Table 3.

6.1. Model 1-Total Revenue (Fixed Effect Model Is the Most Appropriate)

The results show that all coefficients are positive, those of fop and opex being the most significant at the 1% level. The coefficient of msh and time are significant at the 6% and 2% level respectively, while those of som and capex are not significant. The positive effect of capex on trv implies that by investing more, the mobile operator generates more money; but still this effect is not significant.

Foreign ownership – revenues relationship: For foreign ownership– revenue relationship, the impact of fop on revenue, holding the other variables constant, is positive in the case of all mobile operators as a group and also in the case of each mobile operator for which the fop varies. In conclusion, our findings revealed a constant percentage effect of fop on total revenues. Thus, the percentage change in total revenues is the same for each additional 1% of fop, and equals to 0.74%, holding constant the other factors. The change in total revenues for an extra 1% of fop increases as fop increases; in other words, (1) implies an increasing return to fop.

Market share – revenues relationship: For market share – revenue relationship, the impact of market share on revenue, holding the other variables constants, is positive in the case of all mobile operators and also in the case of each individual mobile operator. In conclusion there is a constant percentage effect of msh on total revenues. The percentage change in total revenues is the same for each additional 1% of market share, and equals 0.70%, holding constant the other factors. The change in total revenues for an extra 1% of msh increases as msh increases; in other words, (1) implies an increasing return to msh.

6.2. Model 2-Return on Sales (Fixed Effect Model Is the Most Appropriate)

The results show that the coefficient of fop is the most significant at 1% level, while those of msh and time are significant at 5% level. The coefficient of som is not significant.

Foreign ownership – return on sales relationship: For foreign ownership– return on sales relationship, the impact of fop on ros, holding the other variables constant, is positive in the case of all mobile operators as a group and also in the case of each mobile operator for which the fop varies. In conclusion, our findings revealed a constant percentage effect of fop on ros. The percentage change in ros is the same for each additional 1% of fop, and equals 1.26%, holding constant the other factors. The change in ros for an extra 1% of fop increases as fop increases; in other words, (2) implies an increasing return to fop.

Note that by using equation (**), there is also a positive impact of fop on profitability ratio.

Market share – return on sales relationship: For market share – return on sales relationship, the impact of msh on ros, holding the other variables constant, is positive in the case of all mobile operators and also in the case of each individual mobile. In conclusion, there is a constant percentage effect of msh on ros. The percentage change in ros is the same for each additional 1% of msh, and equals to 1.98%, holding constant the other factors. The change in ros for an extra 1% of msh increases as msh increases; in other words, (2) implies an increasing return to msh.

Note that by using equation (**), there is also positive impact of msh on profitability ratio.

Model 2~: Investment intensity and predicted return on sales: (The fixed effect model is the most appropriate)

The results show that the intercept and the coefficient of the predicted return on sales (pros) are strongly significant and that an increase (decrease) in pros decreases (increases) the investment intensity (capexmar).

The negative effect of ros on the capexmar could be wrongly interpreted as that when a mobile operator earns more it invests less (See Figure 2). The explanation of the negative impact of ros ratio on capexmar is that the mobile operator generates increasing revenue higher than the increase in investments.

6.3. Model 3 Traffic Per Year (Including Price as Independent Variable): Fixed Effect Model Is the Most Appropriate

The results show that all coefficients are positives. Price and time are the most significant at 1% level; followed by nbs, and fop at 2 % level, and the msh at 10% level. The coefficient of noe and som are not significant.

Foreign ownership – traffic relationship: For Foreign ownership– traffic relationship, the impact of fop on traffic, holding the other variables constant, is positive in the case of all mobile operators as a group and also in the case of each mobile operator for which the fop varies. In conclusion, the foreign ownership – traffic relationship shows a constant percentage effect of fop on traffic. The percentage change in traffic is the same for each additional 1% of fop, and equals 0.96%, holding constant the other factors. The change in traffic for an extra 1% of fop increases as fop increases; in other words, (3) implies an increasing return to fop.

Market share – traffic relationship: For market share – traffic relationship, the impact of msh on traffic, holding the other variables constant, is positive in the case of all mobiles and also in the case of each individual mobile operator. In conclusion, the market share – traffic relationship shows a constant percentage effect of msh on traffic. The percentage change in traffic is the same for each additional 1% of msh, and equals 1.03%, holding constant the other factors. The change in traffic for an extra 1% of msh increases as msh increases; in other words, (3~) implies an increasing return to msh.

Discussion Of Resultes

The entrance of international mobile operators and the worldwide revolution of the mobile industry have increased considerably the number of mobile subscribers in MENA countries and because of that the mobile operators have generated increasing traffic, revenue, return on sales and return on investment.

- The results showing a positive effect of market share on revenues and traffic per year are not surprising, because an increase in market share percentage is mainly attributed to the subscription of new customers. The absence of a highly competitive mobile market and mobile number portability (in general), the increase in market share due to new mobile subscribers affects positively revenue and traffic. Also, and even with a successive decrease in mobile communication prices, the added-value as a result of added subscribers is much more important than the value equivalent to the cut in prices. This is because of the big number of new mobile customers (these results are supported by Figure 2). Additionally, the positive impact of market share on return on sales shows that the mobile operators are realizing some economies of scale (a drastic decrease in the per subscriber costs of mobile services, Figure 3), and growing efficiency.
- The positive impact of foreign ownership on traffic can be explained by the fact that the entrance of a foreign mobile operator or the increase in the share of fop stimulates mobile market competition which results in reducing mobile service prices, and then, encourages the actual subscribers to consume more minutes than before, in addition to the consumption of new subscribers.
- The mobile operators, Zain of Kuwait and Etisalat of UAE, which are locally owned companies, showed relatively high values of profitability in terms of return on sales compared with the other mobile players. This could be attributed to the expansion of the 2 players' mobile business in many countries abroad, especially in Africa and Asia, which allow them to acquire international experience and realize economies of scale. Yet these two rare cases cannot reject the findings of this study and suggest a negative or neutral impact of foreign ownership on profitability in terms of revenues and return on sales.
- The rapid increase of mobile subscribers in the countries of our sample means that there was a big unmet demand due to the high prices of mobile communication services introduced by the incumbent. Through the deregulation of the mobile sector, markets experienced the entrance of foreign mobile operators which changed the mobile industry landscape. As a consequence, foreign operators and increased foreign ownership created an increasing in traffic, revenues and profitability.

Policy Implications

Based on our findings, the market share is a driver for mobile operators to increase profitability in the MENA mobile markets. Given that many of the lower income countries have low penetration rates, some of them with a high population such as Egypt, and given that actual mobile subscribers may have more than one mobile phone number (GSM technology), mobile players can decrease their prices still further. This will lead to allowing their subscribers to consume more, and attract more and more other customers through network effects. As a result, mobile operators can generate more revenue and more profitability in terms of return on sales and return on investment, which leads to more benefits for business and consumers.

Our results show that the MENA region is a profitable area for foreign mobile investors. The governments of MENA countries have to use this advantage to attract more foreign investment in telecommunications and also in the other sectors. Thus deregulation and expansive investment in the telecommunications area is promoting direct investment in related services in the MENA region.

It is also shown in our results that mobile operators with high foreign ownership are generating increasing benefits for themselves in the form of revenues and profitability and for consumers in the form of more services and more consumed minutes. Governments should provide foreign investors with the proper incentives to invest more in the mobile sector in particular and in the telecommunications sector in general.

The results are interesting and motivating, since they support the fact that efforts provided to reform the telecommunications sector are, in general, on the right path and impacts are as expected. However, reformers still have to enhance competition more and more by deregulating and facilitating the entrance or the threat of entrance to reach 3 or more mobile operators in each MENA country market. By this we guarantee a continuous decrease in the prices, an increase in the quality of mobile services and an increase in national mobile penetration.

There is need for a new phase of telecommunications reforms in the MENA region, because full liberalization in MENA mobile markets has not yet been reached in many markets of the region. Still many MENA countries are experiencing duopoly and the MO's are enjoying its benefits while the country is struggling to increase its telecommunications penetration rates. With the introduction of a third operator, the competitive scene of MENA mobile markets will change rapidly, the operators will develop more services and provide new ones; subscribers will benefit from the fully liberalized mobile market and penetration will rise more, and create a positive impact on the whole social and economical aspect of the country. We believe that this new phase of telecommunications reform is needed more for low income countries in MENA than for those with a high income.

Finally, because the rapid growth in ICT access has been driven by mobile telephony and mobile business is the fastest and most profitable telecommunications sector in terms of growth, the governments of MENA countries have to use this positive advantage to pave the way to the development of the other telecommunications segments in particular and the ICT sector in general.

Conclusions, Limitations and Further Research

In a region that is still in an ongoing process of telecommunications market reform, this research studied two chief aspects of this reform in which we analyzed the effects of foreign ownership and the market share on financial performances and the traffic of mobile operators.

Using parametric estimation and an unbalanced panel data of 13 mobile operators over the period 2002-2007, this study empirically showed that foreign ownership and market share have a positive effect on revenues, return on sales (therefore on "profitability ratio" and "return on investment"), and traffic generated.

These results show that MENA is still an attractive and profitable region from the perspectives of foreign telecommunications investors. Yet, the flow of such investments needs to be coupled with proper public support to be able to attract more and more foreign investment to the mobile telecommunications service sector.

Moreover, the results illustrate that if MOs seek to increase their profitability in MENA mobile markets, they have to create new ways of increasing their market share such as price cuts, improved marketing strategies, and by the introduction of new mobile telecommunication services.

Despite its significant contribution, however, this study has experienced some limitations. First, the small data set size and lack of incumbent's data may create some bias in the results of this study. In fact, as much more data on mobile operators, mobile markets and countries become accessible for conducting an econometric analysis, we might get greater insights into the market, and develop new research directions, such as checking for some special effects like spillover effects, technology transfer effects, crowding out fixed line effects, e-government effects, etc. Secondly, the lack of some data variables that can be used as a control in specification and estimation of the models can create limitations on the degrees of freedom and therefore reveal more statistically definitive and significant results. Finally, this study needs to employ and use comparative analysis methodologies and study their effect on our models and results.

For further study, extending this research to include more developing countries outside the MENA region, comparing the results with other advanced countries and examining sectors other than the mobile telecommunications sector would reveal more insights about this research area. This will offer us a much more exhaustive and accurate view of the effects of the reforms and the impacts of foreign ownership, in particular on the provision of services in developing countries.

REFERENCES

Ailawadi, K. L., Farris, P. W. and Parry, M. E., (1999), "Market share and ROI: Observing the effect of unobserved variables", *International Journal of Research in Marketing*, 16, 17-33.

Aydin, N., Sayim, M. and Yalama, A., (2007), "Foreign Ownership and Firm Performance: Evidence from Turkey", *International Research Journal of Finance and Economics*, ISSN 1450-2887.

Baltagi, B. H., (2005), "*Econometric analysis of panel data*", 3rd ed, Chichester ; Hoboken, NJ : J. Wiley and Sons.

Banker, R. D., Chang, H. and Majumdar, S. K., (1995), "The consequences of evolving competition on the components of firms' profits: Recent evidence from the U.S. telecommunications industry", *Information Economics and Policy*, 7, 37-56.

Bitros, G. C., (2003), " Firm Ownership and Economic Efficiency", *The ICFSI Journal of Managerial Economics*.

Bonin, J. P., Hasan, I. and Wachtel, P., (2005), "Bank performance, efficiency and ownership in transition countries", *Journal of Banking and Finance*, 29, 31–53.

Bourantas, D. and Mandes, Y., (1987), "Does Market Share Lead to Profitability?", *Long Range Planning*, 20, 102–108.

Buzzel, R.D., Gale, B.T. and. Sultan, R.G.M., (1975), "Market share—a key to profitability", *Harvard Business Review*, 97–106.

Chhibber, P. K. and Majumdar, S. K., (1999), "Foreign Ownership and Profitability: Property Rights, Control, and the Performance of Firms in Indian Industry", *Journal of Law and Economics*, 42, 209-238.

Chu, W., Chen, C. N. and Wang, C. H., (2008), "The market share–profitability relationships in the securities industry", *The Service Industries Journal*, 28, 813–826.

Claessens, S., Kunt, A. D. and Huizinga, H., (2001), "How Does Foreign Entry Affect the Domestic Banking Market?", *Journal of Banking and Finance*, 25, 891-911.

Deardorff, A., (2001),"International Provision of Trade Services, Trade, and Fragmentation", *World Bank.*

Dimelis, S. and H. Louri (2002). "Foreign ownership and production efficiency: a quantile regression analysis", *Oxford Economic Papers*, 54, 449-469.

Dvornik, D. and Sabolić, D., (2007), "Telecommunication liberalization and economic development in European countries in transition", *Technology in Society*, 29, 378-387.

Feeny, S. and Rogers, M., (2000), "The role of market share and concentration in firm profitability: implication for competition policy", *Economic Analysis and Policy*, 30, 115-132.

Frame, W. S. and Kamerschen, D. R., (1997), "The Profit-Structure Relationship in Legally Protected Banking Markets Using Efficiency Measures", *Review of Industrial Organization*, 12, 9–22.

Ge, Y. and Chen, Y., (2008), "Foreign Ownership and Productivity of Joint Ventures", *Economic Development and Cultural Change*, 56, 895-920.

Heshmati A. (2003), "Productivity Growth, Efficiency and Outsourcing in Manufacturing and Services", *Journal of Economic Surveys* 17(1), 79-112.

Kasuga, N. and Shishikura, M., (2006), "Determinants of profit in the broadcasting industry: Evidence from Japanese micro data", *Information Economics and Policy*, 18, 216–228.

Kim, Y. S., (2005), "Foreign Ownership of Banks and Its Effect on Bank Performance: The Case of Korea", *Korea Observer*, 36, 229-263.

Košak, M. and Čok, M., (2008), "Ownership structure and profitability of the banking sector: The evidence from the SEE region", *Zb. rad. Ekon. fak. Rij*, 26, 93-122.

Laverty, K. J., (2001), "Market share, profits and business strategy", *Management Decision*, 39/8, 607-617.

Li, X. and Liu, X., (2005), "Foreign Direct Investment and Economic Growth: An Increasingly Endogenous Relationship", *World Development*, 33, 393-407.

Lin, C. H., (2008), "Role of Foreign Direct Investment in Telecommunication Industries: A Developing Countries' Perspective", *Contemporary Management Research*, 4, 29-42.

Manoj, P. and Manoranjan, P., (2007), "*Insider Ownership and Firm value: Evidence from Indian Corporate Sector*", MPRA Paper No. 6335.

Markell, S. J., Strickland, T. H. and Neeley, S. E., (1988), "Explaining Profitability: Dispelling the Market Share Fog", *Journal of Business Research*, 16, 189-196.

Naaborg, I. and Lensink, R., (2008), "Banking in transition economies: does foreign ownership enhance profitability?", *The European Journal of Finance*,14, 545-562.

Newfarmer, R.S. and Marsh, L. C., (1981), "Foreign ownership, market structure and industrial performance - Brazil's Electrical Industry", *Journal of Development Economics*, 8, 47-75.

Oetzela, J. M and Banerjee, S. G., (2008), "A case of the tortoise versus the hare? Deregulation process, timing, and firm performance in emerging markets", International Business Review, 17, 54-77.

Ros, A.J. (1999), "Does Ownership or Competition Matter?: The effect of Telecommunication Reform on Network Expansion and Efficiency", *Journal of Regulatory Economics*, 15, 65-92.

Sarkar, J., Sarkar, S. and Bhaumik, S.K., (1998), "Does Ownership Always Matter?—Evidence from the Indian Banking Industry", *JOURNAL OF COMPARATIVE ECONOMICS*, 26, 262–281.

Schwalbach, J., (1991), "Profitability and Market Share: a Reflection on the Functional Relationship", Strategic Management, Journal, 12, 299-306.

Smirlock, M., (1985), "Evidence of the (Non) Relationship between Concentration and Profitability in Banking", *Journal of Money, Credit, and Banking*, 17, 69-83.

Sueyoshi, T. (1998), "Privatization of Nippon Telegraph and Telephone: Was it a good policy decision?", *European Journal of Operational Research*, 107, 45-61.

Sueyoshi, T. (1994), "Stochastic frontier production analysis: Measuring performance of public telecommunications in 24 OECD countries", *European Journal of Operational Research*, 74, 466-478.

Sung, N., (2007), "Information Technology, Efficiency and Productivity: Evidence from Korean Local Governments", *Applied Economics*, 39, 1691-1703.

Szymanski, D. M., Bharadwaj, S. G. and Varadarajan, P. R. (1993), "An Analysis of the Market Share-Profitability Relationship", *The Journal of Marketing*, 57, 1-18.

Wang, C.,_Siler, P. and Liu,_X., (2002), "The relative economic performance of foreign subsidiaries in UK manufacturing", *Applied Economics*, 34, 1885-1892.

Willmore, L., (1986), "The Comparative Performance of Foreign and Domestic Firms in Brazil", *World Development*, 14, 489-502.

Yafee, Robert (2003), A Primer for Panel Data Analysis, *Connect Information Technology,* New York University.

Yilmaz, S. and Dinc, M., (2002), "Telecommunications and Regional Development: Evidence from the U.S. States", *Economic Development Quarterly*, 16, 211-228.

Yudaeva, K., Kozlov, K., Melentieva, N. and Ponomareva, N., (2003), "Does Foreign Ownership Matter? Russian Experience", *Economics of Transition*, 11, 383-409.

In: Information and Communication Technologies… ISBN 978-1-60876-671-0
Ed: Almas Heshmati and Sun Peng

Chapter 12

THE IMPACT OF IT ON EFFICIENCY OF POSTAL SERVICES IN INDONESIA

***Hertadi Iman-Santoso*[1] *and Almas Heshmati*[*2]**

[1]E-business Project, PT. POS, Indonesia

[2]Seoul National University

ABSTRACT

Information technology (IT) is a factor that has led to an improvement in the productivity and efficiency of the postal services organizations. This study aims to explain the degree of efficiency gained by the use technology of ICT and government support programs. These are used to test the hypothesis about the effect of technology and government support programs. The study is divided into two steps: the first step is an analysis of efficiency by using DEA, while the second step is a "Tobit Model" analysis used to estimate the influence of the determinant factors on the efficiency of postal offices. The empirical results show that IT capital investment has a positive impact on the efficiency of the service organization. The efficiency of postal services over time has been decreasing. The government and top management should be concerned about the necessary improvement in postal services management.

Keywords: Postal Service, Efficiency, DEA-window analysis, Tobit model, Indonesia.

1. INTRODUCTION

The public sector as a production unit ought to use their resources for producing output that is related to the objectives specified by the government. Measurement of performance of the public sector can be conducted in terms of productive efficiency. In addition "equity" is

[*] Corresponding author E-mail: heshmati@snu.ac.kr

another factor to be considered in measuring the performance of public sector (Boyne, 2003; and Pestieau, 2007).

Since increasing responsibilities and the value of public services has evoked awareness in technology utilization, IT usage in the organization has had a positive effect on their productivity and efficiency. Compared to the private sector, in general, the public sector has been lagging behind in terms of technology use (Ahmad and Zink, 1998).

In Indonesia, the public sector organization consists of two sub-sectors, namely (i) State owned enterprises, which are owned by the central government (BUMN), which is the sole or the majority shareholder, and (ii) Commercial enterprises owned by the provincial and local governments (BUMD) such as water utilities and regional development banks. Furthermore, some of the aims and objectives of the state companies or State Owned Enterprises include making a contribution to national economic growth in general and the state profits in particular, providing high quality goods and services to the public, and perform business activities that the private sector cannot provide (Fitriningrum, 2006).

Pos Indonesia is the name of the postal service in Indonesia, founded on September 27th 1945. Since 1995, it has been a State Owned Company, managed by the Ministry of Information and Communication (MIC). The Government under Law No. 37, 1985 assigned the Postal Service not only the responsibility of making profits as a business entity, but also a function concerning social obligation. With the recent expansion and changes in the postal industry and modern businesses in general, Pos Indonesia has transformed its business into Financial, Logistic and Communication services divisions.

The purpose of the utilization of advanced technology in the postal service is to maintain the organization in order to achieve express, exact and safe postal services, also to raise the innovation of new services in the postal business. Moreover Information Technology improves the productive and efficient process of service organization. Although there is a big development gap among regions in Indonesia, the postal service has to serve the public equally as stipulated by law. Later in 2003, in order to provide an equal service for the public in rural or remote areas (named Public Service Obligation - PSO), the government allocated some funds to support the postal services. Furthermore, the difference of geographic and demographic factors in each economic zone will, to a greater or lesser degree, influence postal operations and business.

The rest of this study is organized as follows. Section 2 contains a review of the literature. Section 3 outlines the theory, methodology and models estimated. Section 4 presents the characteristics of the postal service industry. Section 5 presents the empirical results and the final section presents the conclusions and policy suggestions.

Literature Review

Generally assessing performance of the public sector is more sophisticated compared with the private sector, because public sector organization has many objectives which are different from those of government. Some research found that the determinants of public service performance are quantity of output, efficiency, outcomes and quality of outputs, which have a direct or indirect influence on the aspects of management and organization (Boyne, 2004). Another recent study mentioned that the performance of the public sector can be classified in its quantitative and qualitative aspects, in terms of public sector efficiency (Sanches et al., 2007), and also observed that efficiency could have an impact on innovation systems, productivity and economic growth.

There are two methodologies which measure efficiency, namely parametric and nonparametric methods. One of the best-known non-parametric methods is Data Envelopment Analysis (DEA). Many researchers have used DEA methodology in public sector organization (Abbot and Doucouliagos, 2003). Some researchers used both technical and scale efficiency to analyze the efficiency in education, public health and tourism services (Abbot and Doucouliagos, 2003; Barros, 2004; Kirigia et al., 2004). Analyzing efficiency can also be approached through slack analysis (Akdede and Kazancouglu, 2006; Boyne, 2003). Some other studies applied a DEA window analysis due to a small number of decision making units (DMU), as well as changes in technology and the economic situation during the study analysis. Asmild et al. (2004) mentions that window analysis will minimize the unfairness condition when compared to other units.

Regarding the determinant factors of efficiency, some researchers mentioned that inefficiency of the firm could be subject to ownership, competition, and market structure as well as government autonomy (Borenstein and Becker, 2004). Environmental factors should be taken into account when measuring the performance of the public sector, such as the characteristics of the citizens being served, geography and culture, to explain the efficiency scores only in the second stages analysis (Smith and Street, 2005).

In the education sector, some variables such as state grants, private/public dichotomy and the student body of a school might be related to the efficiency score. Another study in health institutions showed that there are some variables, such as ownership and the operating environment; in addition those variables can be categorized as controllable and uncontrollable variables (Kirjavainen and Loikkanen, 1998; Rosko et al., 1995). At the country and provincial levels, Shiu and Heshmati (2006) studied applied dummy variables to account for skills, management differences and development at the provincial level.

Many studies show a positive and significant effect of IT on firm performance (Baily, 1986; Brynjolfsson and Hitt, 2000; Gholami et al., 2004). Moreover technology nowadays has become one of the critical issues that affects firms. Consequently the manager of the firm should pay attention to the development of technology because Information Technology (IT) would make the market more competitive. Besides, IT will make the firm more productive and efficient, as mentioned by Shao and Lin (2002).

The dynamics of the postal market and the role of ICT capability would offer many opportunities such as increasing efficiency in processing, developing new products, innovation and be fast to adjust to market changes. Consequently, the role of ICT is one of the key success factors. IT is also a factor in the company increasing its profits and surviving in business (Finger et al., 2005; Stratoplous and Dehning, 2000).

So far, there has not been much research on measuring the effect of government support on public sector organizations. This study tries to show the effect of government support on the efficiency of the postal service. Moreover, as a reference, this study approaches the effect of Research and Development (RandD) in the public sector organization or industrial area compared with the effect of government support. Some researchers have studied RandD and found a positive and significant effect from RandD on the firm's productivity growth (Lee et al., 2003; Matteuci and Sterlacchini, 2005). Both researchers focused on the effect in productivity growth, and for this study, we focus on the effects on the efficiency of the organization.

In terms of productivity growth, ICT is one factor which has a positive impact on productivity growth. However, another cause for an increase in productivity growth is the influence of changes in environmental factors, such as infrastructure, education and human capital. Thus the impact of ICT investment not only contributes to the organization, but also to country development (Heshmati and Yang, 2008; Shiu and Heshmati, 2006). Many studies about the impact of IT on productivity growth in the public sector have found a positive correlation between them and an increase not only in efficiency but also on the quality of service by applying IT (Micheli et al., 2005; Sung Nakil, 2007).

2. METHODOLOGY

A. Data Envelopment Analysis Model

Data envelopment analysis (DEA) was developed to assess input and output variables of the same weight (Borenstein and Becker, 2004; Charnes et al., 1978). DEA does not require price information of input to estimate efficiency (Maruyama and Nakajima, 2002). So far, in this study, the price data of postal service input and output variables are not available. By using DEA in the postal service, it will allow managers to identify each variable that contributes to efficiency in their service production unit. The DEA model is defined as follows:

$$\max_{uv}(u'q_j / v'x_j), \tag{1}$$

subject to $u'q_j / v'x_j \leq 1, \quad j = 1,2,...I, \quad u,v \geq 0.$

when the firm has many constraints such as government regulations, imperfect competition, it cannot be operated in an optimal scale, and hence variable return to scale (VRS) is considered, as mentioned by Coelli et al. (2005). This study will apply DEA under an input-oriented approach since the management has relatively more control over its input utilization compared to production of output. Another explanation is that the postal business right now could not expand their output due to tight competition with telecommunications businesses, such as mobile phones. Thus input-oriented approach suggests how much input quantities could be proportionally reduced without changing the output quantities, referring to Coelli et al. (2005).

The basic model of VRS input-oriented is as follows:

$$\min_{\theta\lambda} \theta, \tag{2}$$

subject to $-qi + Q\lambda \geq 0$, $\theta xi - X\lambda \geq 0$, $I1'\lambda = 1$, and $\lambda \geq 0$

The original DEA compares input and output only once, but in reality the usage of resources seems to move dynamically. This was the reason why a DEA model known as 'window analysis', was introduced, which was first developed by Klopp in 1985. DEA window analysis, by using panel data with several time periods, allows identification of the efficiency changes and the movements of DMUs over time. A DEA window analysis will have the possibility of recognizing the performance through a series of windows (Chung et al., 2008). The formulas of window analysis mention by Cooper et al. (2007) can be explained as:

Tobit Regression Model

Formula	Description
$W = k - p + 1$	Number of windows
$np/2$	Number of DMU in each window
npw	Number of "different" DMU
$n(p-1)(k-p)$	Number of increase of DMU
n = number of DMU	
k = number of periods	
p = length of windows, where $p \leq k$	
w = numbers of windows	

The Tobit model is used in the second step after obtaining efficiency scores by DEA. In the second step, the efficiency scores from DEA are transformed into inefficiency scores, which are censored at zero from the left. It means an inefficiency score is used as a dependent variable. This model has been used to test whether some characteristic, factors that are related to the postal service environment, have influence on the inefficiency level.

The Tobit model is defined as follows:

$$Y^* = \beta_i X_i + \mu_i \tag{3}$$

$$Y_i = Y_i^* \text{ if } Y_i^* > 0$$

$$Y_i = 0 \text{ if } Y_i^* \leq 0$$

where $\mu_i \sim N(0, \sigma^2)$, and Y_i^* is an unobserved latent variable representing inefficiency, Y_i is the observant inefficiency score, β_i is a k x 1 vector of unknown parameters and X_i is a kx1 vector of explanatory variables.

In relation with a panel data analysis, both fixed effects and random effects models are applied. In doing so, the focus has been concentrated on fixed effects model (Greene, 2005). The fixed effects model for our study is defined as follows:

$$y = \alpha_i + \lambda_i + \beta_1 X_{it}^1 + \beta_2 X_{it}^2 + \varepsilon_{it} \tag{4}$$

Since this study is investigating some characteristic factors, such as government support programs, ICT technology intensity, population, minimum regional wage and geographical coverage, that have a possible influence on inefficiency, as a result we adapt the fixed affect model to our variables.

$$Ineff = \alpha_0 + aSize + bZone + cGovsp + \beta_1 Pop + \beta_2 Gvprev + \beta_3 Techinst + \beta_4 Techinstsq + \beta_5 MinRW + \beta_5 GeoCov + \lambda T + \varepsilon_{it} \quad (5)$$

$$\varepsilon_{it} = \mu_i + \upsilon_{it} \text{ and } \mu_i = N(0, \sigma_{it}^2)$$

In this study, the slope coefficients are constant, but the intercept varies over post office size, zone as well as time (Yafee, 2003). In this model it is specified with *i-1*Size dummies, *i-1*Zone dummies, *i-1* Govsp dummies and *t-1* time trend dummies. The possibility that population, geographical coverage and a minimum regional wage influence inefficiency is still a question to be answered. However these variables are factors that must be incorporated in the analysis of the postal industry.

3. Characteristic of Postal Services

A. Data Description

The panel data used in this study included 206 post offices as a DMU providing services in 30 provinces in Indonesia and during the time period 2002-2007. The descriptive definition of inputs and outputs is given in table 1.

Several other factors, such as population, social class diversity and parent households should be taken into account in order to assess the performance of the public sector (Andrews et al., 2006). Those factors are relevant to policy makers for the design of systems of reward and punishment for public services. In order to discover factors that influence the efficiency score in this study some characteristic factors are collected as determinants of efficiency, which are Population, Geographical Coverage, Minimum Regional Wage, Technology Intensity, and Government support per total revenue.

Table 1. Inputs and output variables

Input	Description
Assets	Number of Branch, Counter, Mailbox
Technology (IT Capital)	Number of Computer, Weight Scales, Stamp Machine, Packing Machine, Barcode reader, Computer Support, Modem, Printer
Vehicle	Number of Car, Motorcycle, Truck
Number of employee	Number of Employee class I, II, III
Government support	Amount of Public Service Obligation fund
Total Expense	Amount of expense exclude Salary
Output	**Description**
Total Revenue	Amount of revenue

B. Summary Statistics of the Data

Table 2 summarizes the descriptive statistics of the data set. From the summary statistics, we observe a gradual decrease of the number of employees and the assets. Between 2004 and 2007 the numbers of technology and vehicles are relatively constant. Given a decreasing number of employees and constant technology input, there might be a slight increase in technology intensity. By contrast, government support increases gradually over the years.

Table 2. Summary Statistic Summary of the data, 2002-2007

	Min	Max	Mean	Std Dev
Tot_rev	178.317	87516.202	3910.406	7541.043
Gov_sup	0.000	1770.638	415.053	360.080
Assets	42.000	1827.000	359.088	312.938
Tech	8.000	331.000	55.370	51.762
Vech	1.000	113.000	17.413	19.982
Empl	12.000	801.000	91.294	111.008
Expense	71.747	20587.208	801.077	1285.877
Population	53327	7104572	1028114.937	777627.457
Govsp_rcv	0.000	2.527	0.286	0.298
Techsq_int	2.012	841.000	46.261	62.667
Tech_Int	0.096	5.800	0.786	0.530
Trend	1.000	6.000	3.500	1.709

3. Characteristics of Regions in Indonesia

In this section we explain some characteristics of the regions in Indonesia and find out more about the capacity of the postal service in each region. The purpose of this section is to establish the systematic differences between economic zones and size class of the postal service. Indonesia administratively consists of 30 provinces and each province has its own political legislature and governor. The provinces are subdivided into regencies (*kabupaten)* and sub districts (*kecamatan)*.

Indonesia consists of more than 17,000 islands and the five largest islands are Java, Sumatra, Kalimantan, Sulawesi and Papua. Thus, there are many different characteristics among the regions.

As we have already explained previously, we divided the region into 3 zones, Zone 1 is Java and Sumatra Island, Zone 2 is Kalimantan and Sulawesi Island, Zone 3 is Papua and East Indonesia Islands. In this section, we will give a brief description of some characteristics and the differences of each region.

Figure 1 shows the number of provinces and the postal service capacity in each zone. We can see here that the Indonesian postal service is more significant in Zone 1, which could be attributed to:

- The Indonesian population being mostly concentrated in Java and on Sumatra Island. Hence, the postal service has to concentrate on these zones to provide necessary services to the public,
- Dutch colonialists set up the first postal service in Java and on Sumatra Island. Up to now the number of post offices in Zone 1 is the highest among the 3 zones. Consequently, the capacity is the highest (assets, IT capital and employees), apart from the number of vehicles (see Figure 2). In Zone 1, the postal service has to outsource to some transportation companies the delivery of mail or parcels between post offices, so the number of vehicle in Zone 1 is lower.

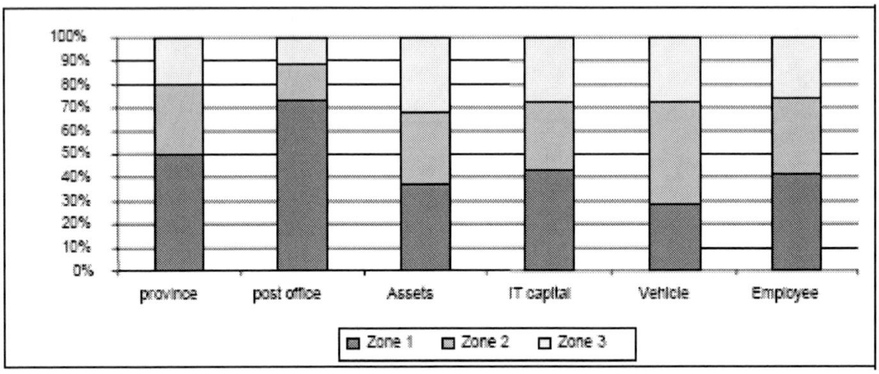

Figure 1. Characteristics of postal services by economic zone.

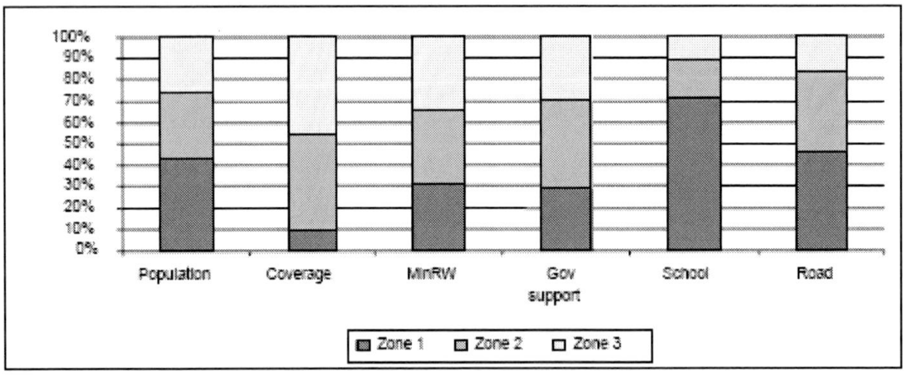

Figure 2. Characteristic variables by economic zone (mean of 2002-2007).

Figure 2 shows that Zone 1 is the most populated region in Indonesia, with the highest number of schools, more kilometers of roads and a lower minimum regional wage (the standard of living is the lowest). Regarding different gaps among zones, the Indonesian postal service has to sustain equitable services with a desirable level of performance and quality to all regions or zones. As a SOE, this condition is quite difficult to maintain, so as a consequence, government allocates the budget such as to promote equal service delivery to the public. Figure 2 shows that government support in Zone 2 is the highest compared to the others.

The number of schools and infrastructure (length of road) represent the development of regions. From Figure 2, the number of schools and kilometers of road is the highest, are more intensive and more highly concentrated in Zone 1 (Java and Sumatra Island). This implies that Zone 1 is more developed compared to other zones. The data was obtained from the Department of National Education (*Departemen Pendidikan Nasional)* and Department of Public Works (*Departemen Pekerjaan Umum).*

4. Empirical Results

A. Efficiency Scores

Here we present measures of efficiency in the public postal sector. Note that the main purpose of the public sector is to enhance public welfare. It can be seen from the data, that more than 60% of the 206 post offices in Indonesia made a loss. This means that socially-oriented responsibility is higher than profit-oriented objectives. Most postal offices, which are located in Java and on Sumatra Island, make a profit in their business services.

From Table 3 we conclude that, on average, postal service efficiency over the 6 years from 2002 to 2007 decreased slightly. In 2002 it was 0.7286, while in 2007 it decreased to 0.6313. By siz, the Size 4 post offices (with more than 400 employees) have the highest efficiency, at 0.753. This is not surprising, because all Size 4 post offices are located in large cities in the most populated areas, like Jakarta City, where post offices can utilize economies of scale better or generate higher revenues compared with other post offices located in smaller cities. By zones, post offices locate in Zone 1 (Sumatra and Java Island), which are the most developed regions/island achieved the highest efficiency, at 0.6613. Zone 3, as a less developed zone, was expected to have the lowest rate of efficiency, but surprisingly Zone 2 gets the lowest score, at 0.5838. The reason for this is that the postal service located in Zone 3 has higher revenue compared to Zone 2.

Table 3. Summary Statistics of Efficiency, 2002-2007

Yesr/Size/Zone	Minimum	Maximum	Mean	Std Dev
2002	0.3471	1.0000	0.7286	0.1845
2003	0.2816	1.0000	0.6571	0.1770
2004	0.2492	1.0000	0.6381	0.1840
2005	0.2483	1.0000	0.6615	0.1804
2006	0.2243	1.0000	0.5624	0.1849
2007	0.2467	1.0000	0.6313	0.1829
Size1	0.2662	1.0000	0.6716	0.1763
Size 2	0.2243	1.0000	0.5106	0.1788
Size 3	0.2414	1.0000	0.6074	0.1927
Size 4	0.2833	1.0000	0.7530	0.2208
Zone 1	0.2443	1.0000	0.6612	0.1877
Zone 2	0.2243	0.9900	0.5837	0.1807
Zone 3	0.3132	0.9900	0.6351	0.1869

Table 4. Frequency Distribution of Efficiency

Efficiency interval	2002	2003	2004	2005	2006	2007
≤ 0.4999	23	35	46	32	75	50
0.5000-0.5999	35	48	48	46	60	54
0.6000-0.6999	37	49	41	50	34	34
0.7000-0.7999	38	33	31	32	13	31
0.8000-0.8999	29	17	16	16	8	11
0.9000-0.9999	26	20	19	27	15	24
1.000	18	4	5	3	1	2

Table 4 shows that the efficiency interval of less than 0.4999 increased dramatically from 23 units in 2002 to 75 units in 2006. It is significant, with a mean efficiency score of 0.5624 in 2006 as the lowest (see also Table 3). The observed interval 0.50-0.59 also shows the increasing tendency from 35 units to 60 units in 2006. With increasing efficiency in 2007, the number of DMU in the interval of ≤ 0.49 and 0.5-0.59 is decreasing, but increasing in the interval of more than 0.70.

Overall, in terms of years of observation, sizes and zones, the results of the efficiency of postal services during the study period show a gradually decreasing efficiency level. As shown in Table 3, efficiency decreased in each year, because the percentage growth of total expenses each year is higher than the percentage growth in total revenue (measured as output) except in 2005. Total expenses decreased by 11% in 2004 and total revenue decreased by only 8% in 2004. The same tendency is observed in 2007. In sum there was an increase of total revenue during the 6 year study period. About 16% in 2006 followed by a decrease of total expense by 3.4% produced a high level of efficiency. In 2006, the revenue decreased by 15% from 2005 but on the other hand expenses increased by 14%. This showed the reasons for the lowest efficiency score during our study period.

Figure 3 shows the revenue and expense growth between 2002 and 2007. It shows the revenue in 2004 as the highest in our study period and revenue in 2006 as the lowest.

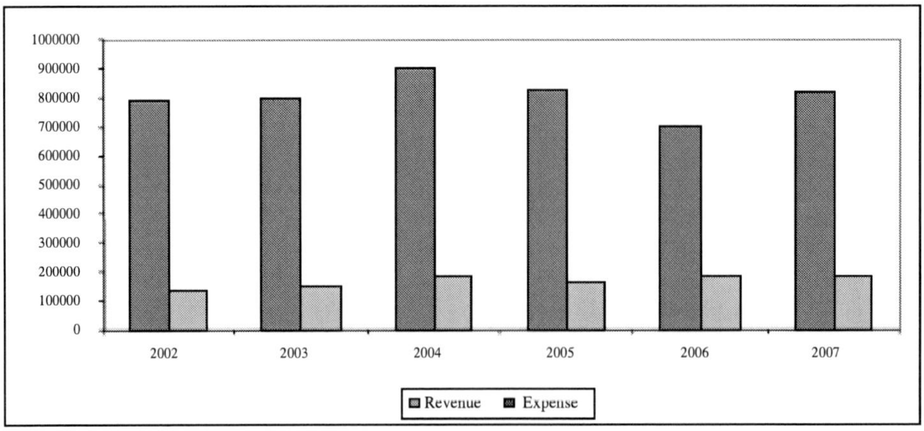

Figure 3. Development of Revenue and Expenses, 2002-2007.

In terms of size classes, high-level efficiency was held at Size 4. From our analysis Size 4 had the highest level of efficiency each year. Once again the reason for this was that post offices with Size 4 are located in major cities. Thus they can earn more revenue than other smaller sizes. This indicates that Size 4 uses their input factor more efficiently compared to other smaller sizes. The role of characteristic factors, such as population and the development of the region also contributed to the high level of efficiency. Later on we shall analyze this effect on the efficiency score. In terms of economic zone, a high level of efficiency was held by Zone 1, as the most populated and most developed regions. Post offices located in these regions are more efficient than in other zones. We shall also test some characteristic factors that might influence these zones.

The influence of other inputs, such as assets, technologies, vehicles, employees and government are relatively constant each year, but are found not to be so significant. Generally, the postal service has the challenges of remaining efficient, improving the management to be able to survive and competing, in order to receive public support continuously in an information technology age that is developing rapidly.

A. Government Support and IT Affects

The DEA model analysis identified around 179 units (2002-2007), with the value of efficiency scores varying in the interval 0.22 to 0.89. The efficiency level differs both across postal offices and over time. It is called time variant efficiency. It means 87% of post offices are inefficient in the production of postal services.

Table 5. Tobit Regression Analysis

Variables	Coefficient	Std error	P[|Z|>z]
Constant	0.2043	0.0210	0.000
Population	1.7232E-08	7.1142E-09	0.015
Geo coverage	1.2912E-06	3.0007E-07	0.000
Min Reg Wage	8.9101E-09	4.0675E-09	0.029
Gov_supp to rev	-0.0140	0.0204	0.494
Tech intensity sq	0.0010	0.0001	0.000
Tech intensity	-0.0871	0.0177	0.000
Sigma	0.1628	0.0033	0.000
Log likelihood	461.6720		

Table 5 shows that the estimated coefficient of government support and technology intensity has a negative sign in respect to inefficiency scores and this is in line with our expectation. However government support is not statistically significant. The technology intensity implies that an increase in IT capital is expected to result in an increase in the efficiency score.

This study uses technology squared to indentify the maximum amount of technology usage as optimal. But this study could not get an estimation of the maximum amount of technology usage. The study is similar to using the number of beds squared as an efficiency score to see the optimal size of a nursing home (Rosko et al., 1995).

The estimated coefficient of population, geographical coverage and minimum regional wage had a positive sign and was statistically significant. In real terms, the population of the region strongly affects the total revenue of the postal service. Nevertheless, in our study, we applied DEA under input-oriented. So the output is assumed constant. Therefore we can confirm that the population has no correlation to the efficiency score.

Findings from the Tobit regression show that an increase in the size of the population will lead to an increase in the number of input. As an illustration, the post offices which are located in more populated regions have to increase the number of vehicles or employees (capacity) to maintain a timely delivery of customer services. Geographical coverage also influences post office capacity, since bigger geographical coverage increases input factors such as the number of employees, assets and vehicles.

The number of post offices located in Zone 2 and Zone 3, are less compared to those located in Zone 1. On the other hand, the geographical coverage of Borneo Island (Zone 2) and Papua Island (Zone 3) is bigger than Java Island (Zone 1), so this test can explain why Zone 2 and Zone 3 are inefficient compared to Zone 1. A bigger geographical coverage will tend to generate a higher level of inefficiency.

Technology positively affects the efficiency of post offices; this implies that intense use of technology will affect positively the level of office efficiency. These findings can be a tool for policy makers to affect their investment decisions. However, we need to analyze further the issues of elasticity of technology before being able to recommend such investment actions by the public sector in the provision of better services.

B. Elasticity of Technology Use

We studied the elasticity of technology intensity usage in respect to production inefficiency in each of the different size classes and location zones. The elasticity of technology is the ratio of the amount of percentage change of technology (IT capital) translated to inefficiency of firms. The finding in Table 6 showed that elasticity of technology (IT capital) is negative in respect to inefficiency. It is interpreted as that investment in technology in order to provide postal services reduces the degree of inefficiency in the provision of postal services.

Table 6. Elasticity of inefficiency with respect to IT Capital

Description	Elasticity
2002-2007	-0.08631
Size1	-0.08624
Size2	-0.08656
Size3	-0.08660
Size4	-0.08668
Zone1	-0.08616
Zone2	-0.08631
Zone3	-0.08630

Conclusion and Policy Implication

Conclusion

This study measured the efficiency of postal services in Indonesia by using DEA and, in a two-stage procedure approach, identified and explained its determinants. Due to data limitations for output, in this study revenue represented aggregate service output. The finding shows that postal services located in developed regions were found to be more efficient compared to those located in other regions. We found that these offices were more profitable than those located in moderate or less developed regions.

In the second stage analysis, technology (IT capital) has a negative impact on inefficiency, in other words, it positively affects the efficiency of offices. Government support also has a positive correlation on efficiency but is not statistically significant. The other factors like population, geographical coverage and minimum regional wage also have no relation with the efficiency level of post offices.

This empirical study of postal services and the findings suggest that IT investment will improve the efficiency of offices only if it supports or increases the revenues. Otherwise, IT investment without increasing the revenue will make the organization vulnerable concerning future development, such as with the difficulties in raising the repayment of the investment loan for a long term and the yearly maintenance cost of IT investments. These factors will harm the organization. Thus, to solve this problem, IT investment must be applied to the sectors or businesses that will generate profit in the future. The investment must be prioritized for the developed regions, in particular Zone 1.

The study on the measurement of efficiency in the public sector, like the postal service, is useful research for a developing country to consider how to manage the performance of the public sector effectively. This study provides guidelines to the stakeholders or top management in order to help policymaking on effective management of the service. The Indonesian postal service requires strong support from the top management and government for innovative processes and the training of employees with outstanding IT knowledge who will utilize the benefits of IT in the organization.

Policy Implication

IT usage in postal services has positive effects on productivity and the efficiency of post offices. The decrease in efficiency over the 6 years of the study period indicates the urgent need for improvement in effective management of the post office. Investment in IT not only leads to increased revenue but also increases customer satisfaction. For instance, the postal process using IT will decrease time of delivery, will enable the service providers to give a precise time of delivery and allow the application of an effective tracking system in the postal service. IT usage in post offices also increases the opportunity for the development of new services and innovation which can be adapted to market demand. In addition, IT usage in the organization should be matched by the capability of its human resources with IT knowledge.

Given the resizing of the organization, followed by a lack of recruitment since 1995, the top management should consider outsourcing to satisfy postal service demand. This study could be useful for government since there is no performance measurement in the public sector in Indonesia. Thus, the efficiency measure could be a tool for government to make a valuable judgment on public sector performance and lead to a necessary restructuring of certain service activities. As we understand up to now the Indonesian Government has no performance index of the public sector where the taxpayer can see the performance of the Indonesian public sector.

REFERENCES

Abbot, M. and C. Doucouliagos (2003), The Efficiency of Australian Universities: A Data Envelopment Analysis, *Economics of Education Review*, No 22, pp. 89-97.

Ahmad, Allaa-Aldin and Steven D. Zink (1998), Information Technology Adoption in Jordanian Public Sector Organizations, *Journal of Government Information*, Vol 25, No 2, pp. 117-134.

Akdede, Sacit Hadi and Yigit Kazancoglu (2006), Efficiency in Turkish State Libraries a Data Envelopment Analysis Application, *International Conference on Human and Economics Resources,* Izmir.

Andrews, Rhys, George A. Boyne and Gareth Enticott (2006), Performance Failure in the Public Sector Misfortune or Mismanagement, *Public Management Review* Vol 8, No 2, pp. 273-296.

Asmild, Mette, Joseph C. Paradi, Vanita Aggarwall and Claire Schaffnit (2004), Combining DEA Window Analysis with the Malmquist Index Approach in a Study of the Canadian Banking Industry, *Journal of Productivity Analysis,* No 21, pp. 67-89.

Baily, M.N. (1986), What Has Happened to Productivity Growth, *Science,* Vol 234, pp. 443-451.

Barros, Carlos Pestana (2004), Measuring Efficiency in the Hotel Sector, *Annals of Tourism Research*, Vol 32, No 2, pp. 456-477.

Brynjolfsson, E. and Lorin M. Hitt (2000), Beyond Computation: Information Technology, Organization Transformation and Business Performance, *Journal of Perspectives*, Vol 14, No 1, pp. 339-376.

Borenstein, Denis and Joao Luiz Becker (2004), Measuring the Efficiency of Brazilian Post Office Stores Using Data Envelopment Analysis, *International Journal of Operations and Production Management*, Vol 24, No 10, pp. 1055-1078.

Boyne, George A. (2004), Explaining Public Service Performance: Does Management Matter?, *Public Policy and Administration*, Vol 19, No 4.

Boyne, George A. (2003), Sources of Public Service Improvement: A Critical Review and Research Agenda, *Journal of Public Administration Research and Theory*, Vol 13, No 3, pp. 367-394.

Charnes, A., W.W. Cooper and E.Rhodes (1978), Measuring the Efficiency of the Decision Making Unit, European Journal of Operating Research, Vol 2, No 6, pp. 429-444

Chung, Shu-Hsing, Amy Hsin-I Lee, He-Yau Kang and Chih-Wei Lai (2008), A DEA Window Analysis on the Product Family Mix Selection for a Semiconductor Fabricator, *Expert Systems with Application*, No 35, pp. 379-388.

Coelli, Timothy J., D.S. Prasada Rao, Christopher J. O'Donnell and George E. Battese (2005), *An Introduction to Efficiency and Productivity Analysis*, 2nd ed., New York: Springer.

Cooper, William W., Lawrence M. Seiford and Kaoru Tone (2007), *Data Envelopment Analysis A comprehensive Text with Models Applications References and DEA-Solver Software*, 2nd ed., New York: Springer.

Finger, Matthias, Ismail Alyanak and Patrick Mollet (2005), Postal Sector Overview and Dynamics, *MIR Report 2005-005*, Ecole Polytechnique Federale, Lausanne.

Fitriningrum, Andriati (2006), Indonesia Experience in Managing the State Companies, *OECD-Asian Roundtable on Corporate,* Singapore, May 15.

Gholami, Roghieh, Saeed Moshiri and Sang-Yong Tom Lee (2004), ICT and Productivity of the Manufacturing Industries in Iran, *The Electronic Journal on Information Systems in Developing Countries*, Vol 19, No 4, pp. 1-19.

Greene, William H. (2005), Econometric Analysis, 5th ed., New York: Prentice Hall, pp.871-874.

Heshmati, Almas and Wanshan Yang (2008), Contribution of ICT to the Chinese Economic Growth, *Techno-Economics and Policy Program*, Seoul, July 13.

Kirigia, Joses. M., Ali Emrouznejad, Luis G. Sambo, Nzoya Munguti and Wilson Liambila (2004), Using Data Envelopment Analysis to Measure the Technical Efficiency of Public Health Centers in Kenya, *Journal of Medical Systems*, Vol 28, No 2.

Kirjavainen, Tanja and Heikki A. Loikkanen (1998), Efficiency Differences of Finnish Senior Secondary Schools: An Application of DEA and Tobit Analysis, *Economics of Education Review*, Vol 17, No 4, pp 377-394.

Lee, Jeong-Dong, Won-Joon Kim, Tai-Yoo Kim (2003), The Role of IT, RandD in Industrial Productivity Growth: Evidence from Korea, *Evaluation Government Funded RandD Activities Conference (ZEW),* Vienna, May 15.

Maruyama, Shoji and Takanobu Nakajima (2002), Efficiency Measurement and Productivity Analysis for Japanese Postal Service, *Asia Conference on Efficiency and Productivity Growth (ACEP)*, Taipei, July 2002.

Matteuci, Nicola and Alessandro Sterlacchini (2005), ICT, RandD and Productivity Growth: Evidence from Italian Manufacturing Firms, February 2005, *EPKE Final Conference*, London, October 28-29, 2004.

Micheli, Pietro, Steve Mason and Mike Kennerley (2005), Public Sector Performance: Efficiency or Quality?, *Measuring Business Excellence*, Vol 9, No 2.

Pestieau, Pierre (2007), Assessing the Performance of the Public Sector, *CREPP Working Paper*, Vol 3.

Rosko, Michael D., Jon A. Chilingerian, Jacqueline S. Zinn and William E. Aaronson, (1995), The effects of Ownership, Operating Environment, and Strategic Choices on Nursing Home Efficiency, *Medical Care,* Vol 33, No 10, pp. 1001-1021.

Sánchez, Andrés Maroto and Luis Rubalcaba Bermejo (2007), Public Sector Performance and Efficiency in Europe: The Role of Public RandD, *Working Papers Institute of Social and Economic Analysis*, Vol 1.

Shao, Benjamin B.M. and Winston T. Lin (2002), Technical efficiency Analysis of Information Technology Investment: A Two-stage Empirical Investigation, *Information and Management*, Vol 39, pp. 391-401.

Shiu, Alice and Heshmati, Almas (2006), Technical Change and Total Factor Productivity Growth for Chinese Provinces: A Panel Data Analysis, *IZA Discussion Paper,* No 2133.

Smith, Peter C. and Andrew Street (2005), Measuring the Efficiency of Public Service: The Limits of Analysis, *Journal of Royal Statistical Society*, No 168, Part 2, pp. 401-417.

Stratoploulos, Theophanis and Bruce Dehning (2000), Does Successful Investment in Information Technology Solve the Productivity Paradox?, *Information and Management*, Vol 38, pp. 103-117.

Sung, Nakil (2007), Information Technology, Efficiency and Productivity: Evidence from Korean Local Governments, *Applied Economics,* Vol 39, pp. 1691-1703.

Yafee, Robert (2003), A Primer for Panel Data Analysis, *Connect Information Technology,* New York University.

In: Information and Communication Technologies… ISBN 978-1-60876-671-0
Ed: Almas Heshmati and Sun Peng

Chapter 13

UTILIZATION OF E-GOVERNMENT IN DELIVERY OF PUBLIC SERVICES IN ASIA

Almas Heshmati*[*]*, Malis Sun and JongEun Oh
Seoul National University

ABSTRACT

The purpose of this study is to compare the capacity or potential of governments in East and Southeast Asia in their utilization of E-government as an instrument to deliver public services to their citizens. The principal component analysis methodology is used to compute the E-government index. The index is used as a benchmark to compare the performance of developing and newly industrialized economies in delivery of public services. The overall index is compromised of three main components: ICT infrastructure, development information and finances indices. The E-government index level shows the capacity of each country's governments to deliver public services. The result is useful for identifying the weaknesses and strengths in their service provision. An attempt is made to suggest alternative approaches to achieve the goals and progress towards an advanced E-government-based service provision that enhances equality in opportunities.

Keywords: E-government; ICT; Principal Component Analysis, Asia.

1. INTRODUCTION

Information and communications technology (ICT) after the steam engine and electrical innovations are the third major technological breakthrough (Edquist and Henrekson, 2006). IT is one of the new major priorities that in recent years has played a very important role in the strategy of the development in all countries regardless of their levels of development.

[*] Orresponding author Email: heshmati@snu.ac.kr

ICT is seen as an important instrument in communication both within and between countries in a globalized world. It is not only a communication tool, but also a new high technology tool which has made the world smaller. Furthermore it is giving way to the emergence of new and fast growing digitalized and knowledge-based economies.

The use of information technology that is defined by the free movement of information which overcomes the physical bounds of traditional paper- and physical-based systems is E-government. In order to deliver an increasing number of services in a cost effective manner, the government is required to provide services increasingly. One of the greatest opportunities for a government to accomplish is increasing the efficiency of the delivery of public services to the citizens. It is important to examine the global scope of an E-government as well, because the relative development of these technologies in various countries will have a significant impact on the ability of these governments to function well.

The literature on E-government is growing rapidly. The development of the service is studied in Acrete, Pina and Torres (2005), Jaeger and Thompson (2003), Layne and Lee (2001), PCIP (2002), Relyea (2002), Reddick (2005), CDT (2002), UN (2004) and Yen and Evans (2005). Examples of evaluations are found in Christopher and Thompson (2002) for Japan, in Hwang, Choi and Myeong (1990) for Korea, in Ma and Thorson (2005) for China, in Moon (2002) focusing on municipalities, OECD (2003) in the case of OECD, and in Rieck and Tung (2005) for Singapore. Dedrick, Gurbaxani and Kraemer (2003) present a critical review of the empirical evidence on IT and economic performance. The organizational aspect is studied in Dekker and Shi (2002), while the public and private sector interest is investigated by Salem (2003).

Most industrialized and developed countries have used their technological and educational capabilities to create an E-government service structure. However, such development has been slow in many developing and less developed countries that use the basic technology, communication and education to create and to move towards an E-government system. Therefore a basic assessment of benefits and costs, the risk and opportunity of E-government still remains to be investigated. The literature on E-government and an evaluation of its functions is very poor. This study contributes to the growing ICT literature in respect of ICT utilization for public service provision. In particular by being based on data from many newly developing economies, our empirical result provides a major contribution to the literature.

The main objectives of this study are to measure and to compare the E-government performance of eleven countries in East and Southeast Asia. In particular, the emphasis is on: (i) quantifying the capacity or ability of those countries' governments to use E-government as a tool to deliver public services to their citizens; (ii) comparing the countries in their performances with respect to capacity building concerning E-government; (iii) evaluating the progress of those countries' governments in the use of ICT and human capital as indicators of their progress towards the achievement of a higher level of E-government in the future; (iv) using regression analysis to evaluate the impacts of ICT and E-government on the economic growth of the countries; and finally (v) suggesting measures and policies to enhance their progress in the formation and effectiveness of an E-government-based service delivery.

The organization of this study is as follows: Section 2 presents the literature review and viewpoints on E-government. Section 3 is on the methodology, models and data. Section 4 discusses the empirical results. The final Section presents the summary and conclusion of the results; it also suggests policy to enhance various E-government service deliveries.

2. Literature Review

In reviewing the literature on E-government we tried to identify aspects of the relationship between E-government, ICT infrastructure, development information, finances, and human capital indices, as well as to discuss the possible impacts of E-government on the welfare of citizens in those societies, or their causal relationships.

There are several recent studies that concern E-government, ICT and human capital and their interactions. Drawing from a study by Holman and McGregor (2004), E-government initiatives have prompted administrative agencies to use new communications and information technologies like the Internet and World Wide Web (WWW) to provide information, deliver services, and channel feedback from citizens, regulated industries, and other government entities. Akman et al. (2005) stated that "E-government is as the use of technology, particularly the internet, as a mean to delivery of services to citizens, businesses, and other entities. Operational benefits from the introduction of internet, for government and public sector, include the reduction in paper work, the provision of continuous services availability to contribute to the general increase in the efficiency of government."

Also we can find that there has been an increase in E-government, interactions between the government and citizens by using the internet and IT (Sharma and Grupta, 2002; and Relyea, 2002). E-government impacts government organizations by co-ordination and the elimination of waste and redundant elements of their work (Yen and Evans, 2006). Layen and Lee (2001) emphasized that E-government services can help the expansion of the opportunity for economic development by reducing the digital divide that countries lagging behind need to embrace in the form of digital, human, economic and social resources and relationships. But Acerete, Pina and Torres (2005) stated that E-government is important but the internet used by government should not be separated from other government activities as a whole.

From another report by the Pacific Council on International Policy (PCIP, 2002), we can find that E-government, as in the use of ICT, promotes a more efficient and effective government operation and better use of public resources. It allows greater public access to information and makes government more accountable to its citizens.

Several studies focus on the relationship between human capital and E-government. The research survey conducted by Jaeger and Thompson (2003) sheds light on the important relationship between education and E-government. This study shows a direct correlation between education in technology use and eventual technology usage and participation in E-government. In line with the survey, our research proves that, as the education level rises, the level of use of E-government increases.

The survey by Jaeger and Thompson (2003) suggests that the measure of E-government is dependent on the level of ICT and human capacity in each country. In order to enhance E-government, ICT investment and human capital play very important roles in maximizing the efficiency of delivering on-line public services between government and citizens. Therefore, predictions about the future of E-government depend on how each country defines it. It is rather difficult to predict the development of E-government, but it requires the interaction between governments, citizens and businesses (Jaeger and Thompson, 2003).

3. The Methodology and Data

The uncertainty in the capability requirement considering the ICT and human capability of those countries and how they use it for social welfare are crucial issues to the success of E-government. The E-government preparedness is one method that is frequently used to measure the E-government index to find out about the capability or potential of governments in a country that aims to utilize E-government in the delivery of service to its citizens. Kovacic (2005) discusses the reason why E-government readiness is important for monitoring the accessibility of ICT to the population and the regulatory framework on ICT use. The public reports from the United Nations (UN, 2003, 2004) and UN and ASPA (American Society for Public Administration, 2001) have measured the E-government index based on three main indicators. These include web presence, ICT infrastructures and Human capital. In the UN (2004) report, the measure of E-government index shows that the countries positioned in the higher rank of the E-government index all get a high score for their ICT infrastructure and human capital indices.

If we consider the E-government index, its construction requires a great amount of information to be assembled and processed. Most importantly, the exact valuation through an E-government readiness index can be obtained only when the development and movements of ICT infrastructure and human capability are fully identifiable and the necessary underlying information is attainable.

In this section we employ the parametric approaches to compute the E-government index. These include the computation of an index based on different infrastructure indices for development as well as regression analysis. In measuring the E-government index, we use the principal component analysis methodology. To summarize, this study consists of three main parts.

In the first part, the ICT infrastructure and human capital indices have been computed using different variables by principal component analysis methodology. In the second part, the E-government indices have been computed; and the correlation among the variables and index components that affect E-government over time and across countries are analyzed. Finally, in the third part, we estimate the effects of the E-government index on the economic development of the sample countries. Here by economic development, we mean measures like GDP per capita.

In addition, in part three we also discuss the results from parts one and two and establish the link between GDP and the computed indices in the sample countries and over time. Given the results and gained experience from other case studies in this paper we will provide recommendations on how to make E-government more effective in forming and building up capacity to develop and to deliver more effective public services.

3.1. The Principal Component Analysis

Principal component analysis is a multivariate technique for examining relationships between set quantitative variables. It is used to reduce the dimensions of the variables to a single one by constructing a single index out of several determinant variables. Depending on the number of variables used, a number of principal components are identified. The first component extracted accounts for a maximal amount of total variance explained in the observed variables.

This strategy for computing an index; using principal component analysis; was originally by Pearson (1901) and further developed by Hotelling (1933). Principal component analysis has been used in Kang (2002), computation of an environmental index in Heshmati (2006), Andersen and Herbertsson (2003) and Agenor (2003) for the computation of a globalization index. Heshmati and Oh (2006) also used the methodology to compute Lisbon's development strategy index.

Computation of the index is as follows. Given a dataset with p numeric variables, p principal components are computed. Each principal component is a linear combination of the original variables, with the coefficients equal to the eigenvectors of the correlation. The principal components are sorted by descending order of the eigenvalues, which are equal to the variances of the components. The eigenvectors are customarily taken with unit length. The first principal component has the largest variance of any unit length linear combination of the observed variables. In contrast, the last principal component has the smallest variance of any linear combination of the original variable. Principal component analysis is illustrated by:

$$Y = XB + E \qquad (1)$$

where Y is an $n \ x \ p$ matrix of the centred observed variables; X is the $n \ x \ j$ matrix of score on the first j principal components; B is the $j \ x \ p$ matrix of eigenvectors; E is an $n \ x \ p$ matrix of residuals, n is the number of observations, p is number of partial variables, and j is the number of variables or indicators of E-government index.

3.2. Data and Variables

The data used in this study is assembled from different international secondary databases, mainly from two sources including the International Telecommunication Union (ITU, 2003) and the World Development Indicators (WDI). It is a small balanced panel containing 20 variables or indicators and 11 countries from the Southeast and East Asia where each country is observed for 13 years during the period 1990 to 2002.

The data is used to compute the E-government index. The index consists of ICT infrastructure indicators and human capital components. The first component, ICT infrastructure, consists of a series of variables including: internet users, personal computers, mobile phones, telephone mainlines, television sets and main telephone lines in the largest city. The data are obtained from the ITU. All variables are expressed in number of users per 1,000 persons in the population. For instance, the internet users indicate connective persons per 1,000 people. The same is applied to other variables such as personal computers, mobile phones, telephone mainlines and television sets.

The second component of the E-government index is human capital. It consists of (i) development information indicators and (ii) finance indicators. The development information indicator is an integrated index of the eight variables or indicators. The variables are: vehicles, electric power consumption, Freedom of House Index, personal computers installed in schools, educational attainment of the total population, trade and urban population. The vehicles are defined as number of vehicles per 1,000 people. The electric power consumption is defined as kilowatts per capita. The education variable is defined as the percentage of adult people aged 15 years and over having attained at least upper secondary education as a proportion of the total population of the same age group. The finance indicators are obtained from variables: gross capital formation, general government's final consumption expenditure, inflation, or GDP deflators; they are defined as the percentage of GDP. The foreign direct investment (FDI) is defined as net flows as a share of GDP. The second index component, financial index variables are obtained from the World Bank Development Indicators dataset.

The missing observations in the data were imputed using lag and lead observations or alternatively by using averages over time for the same country. In addition we control country and time effects by adding time and country dummy variables when the data are pooled and used in regression analysis to evaluate the impacts of the indices on the economic development.

Summary statistics of the data including a brief definition and measurement unit is given in Table 1, where the variables are divided into: ICT, development information, and finances and other variables.

Table 1. Summary statistics of E-government indicators, n=143 obs.

Variables	Definition	Mean	Median	Minimum	Maximum
Year.	Years of obs	1990.00	1996.00	1990.00	2002.00
A. Information and communication technology index:					
itn	internet users	60.90	2.49	0.00	551.89
mp	mobile phone	124.05	22.57	0.00	942.47
pc	personal comp.	89.17	20.43	0.00	622.04
tm s	telephones mainline	203.13	86.96	0.35	589.02
tvs	television sets	249.95	201.79	7.55	784.71
mtlc	main tel. large city	2427524.44	1515737.00	4000.00	8895000.00
B. Development information index:					
ictxec	ICT exp. Per cap	569.22	65.70	2.00	3256.20
veh	vehicles	114.28	74.92	0.54	572.40
epc	electric power consumption	2406.91	1199.17	94.03	7446.72
fdhi	freedom of house	51.54	56.00	17.00	89.00
pcie	PC installed in education	250462.64	52657.00	1078.00	3555157.24
ays	education attendance	6.87	6.41	3.60	10.84
tgdp	trade GDP	104.71	80.94	15.92	296.01
upop	urban population	53.81	51.86	12.60	100.00
C. Finances index:					
gcf	gross cap. Formation	28.59	28.53	8.16	43.64

Variables	Definition	Mean	Median	Minimum	Maximum
Year.	Years of obs	1990.00	1996.00	1990.00	2002.00
gpcf	gross cap. Flows	27.64	11.22	2.30	179.17
fdi	foreign direct Investment	5378.75	2220.00	50.10	49308.00
igdpd	inflation gdp deflator	5.90	4.05	- 6.18	75.27
D. Other variables:					
mvgdp	manufacturing	23.17	24.89	4.71	35.39
gdpus	GDP million US dollar	554369.62	111452.76	1404.34	529171.80
gdpc	GDP million constant	676421.15	130274.86	2503.40	5725498.80
gdppc	GDP per cap const.	10049.90	2720.75	208.95	45029.48
ggcxe	general gov. cons. Exp.	10.22	10.12	4.59	17.84
hdi	human development	0.75	0.74	0.51	0.99

Despite regional effects, more homogenous samples of countries are taken, and there is a significant difference between the mean and media value of the ICT regionalism and development information variables suggesting the presence of extreme observations and high degree of skewness in the data. The correlation matrix among the e-government indicators is reported in Table 2.A.

With the exception of the Freedom of House Index, inflation and foreign direct investment, remaining relations to the indicators are positive and mostly statistically significant.

The correlation between the different indices and the economic development are found in Table 2.B. Most of the coefficients are larger than those among the indicators and most of the coefficients are positive and statistically significant.

4. Empirical Results

By looking at the principal components' computation results, we observe that the E-government index, based on previous research and current results, have been affected by the ICT infrastructure and human capital factors. As the result, the new industries like information and communications impact and determine the high rank of countries by the E-government index, because ICT and human capital are determinants of a higher level of development.

Table 2.A Pearson Correlation matrix among E-government indicators and economic development, n=143 obs

	gdpc	itn	mp	pc	tm	tvs	mtlc	ictxec	veh	epc	fdhi	pcie	ays	upop	fdis	gpcf	igdpd	gdppc	ggcxe
gdpc	1.00																		
itn	0.19a	1.00																	
mp	0.21b	0.98a	1.00																
pc	0.24b	0.90a	0.91a	1.00															
tm	0.47a	0.57a	0.66a	0.73a	1.00														
tvs	0.73a	0.44a	0.58a	0.56a	0.30a	1.00													
mtlc	0.78a	0.82a	0.89a	0.41a	0.66a	0.32a	1.00												
ictxec	0.61a	0.50a	0.60a	0.78a	0.36a	0.79a	0.54a	1.00											
veh	0.39a	0.40a	0.40a	0.49a	0.69a	0.38a	0.72a	0.78a	1.00										
epc	0.53a	0.60a	0.66a	0.30a	0.95a	0.38a	0.68a	0.92a	0.79a	1.00									
fdhi	-0.47a	-0.19c	-0.26b	-0.29b	-0.57a	-0.55a	-0.53a	-0.42a	-0.59a	-0.52a	1.00								
pcie	0.64a	0.81a	0.82a	0.26a	0.81b	0.57a	0.71a	0.85a	0.58a	0.88a	-0.16c	1.00							
ays	0.41a	0.42a	0.43a	0.58a	0.73a	0.66a	0.70a	0.54a	0.53a	0.69a	-0.74a	0.29b	1.00						
upop	0.25a	0.47a	0.56a	0.70a	0.39a	0.68a	0.46a	0.76a	0.49a	0.35a	-0.46a	0.11c	0.74a	1.00					
fdis	-0.47a	-0.19c	-0.26b	-0.29b	-0.57a	-0.55a	-0.53a	-0.12c	-0.88a	-0.13c	0.58a	-0.22b	-0.49a	-0.14c	1.00				
gpcf	-0.15c	0.25b	0.48a	0.46a	0.59a	0.23b	0.03	0.51a	-0.02	0.43a	-0.21c	-0.14c	0.87a	0.66a	0.08	1.00			
igdpd	-0.19c	-0.23b	-0.82a	-0.81b	-0.88a	-0.88a	-0.26b	-0.81b	-0.29b	-0.85a	0.27b	-0.22b	-0.23b	-0.24b	0.28b	-0.14c	1.00		
gdppc	0.76a	0.46a	0.54a	0.66a	0.33a	0.37a	0.66a	0.94a	0.35a	0.94a	-0.55a	0.89a	0.61a	0.75a	0.22b	0.40a	-0.30b	1.00	
ggcxe	0.68a	0.80b	0.80b	0.23b	0.84a	0.59a	0.54a	0.89a	0.64a	0.48a	-0.81b	0.57a	0.43a	0.80b	-0.21b	-0.11c	-0.24b	-0.47a	1.00

Note: less then 1% (a), 1-5% (b) and 5-10% (c) levels of significance.

Abbreviations: GDP in millions constant(gdpc), Internet users (itn), mobile phones (mp), personal computers (pc), telephone mainlines(tm), television sets (tvs), main telephone lines in largest city (mtlc), information and communication technology expenditure per capita (ictxec), vehicles (veh), electric power consumption (epc), freedom of house ranking (fhdi), personal computers installed in education (pcie), education attainment of the total population aged 15 over- (ays), trade (tgdp), urban population (upop), foreign direct investment (fdi)Gross private capital formation (gcf), gross private capital inflows (gpcf), inflation, gdp deflator (igdpd), gdp per capital (gdppc), and human development indices (hdi).

Table 2.B. Pearson correlation matrix among different indices and economic development, n=143 obs

	Year	gdppc	hdi	ict	dii	fni	egov
Year	1.000						
Gdppc	0.043	1.000					
Hdi	0.158c	0.831a	1.000				
ict	0.429a	0.802a	0.866	1.000			
dii	0.154c	0.926a	0.930a	0.866a	1.000		
fni	0.083a	0.454a	0.464a	0.679a	0.570a	1.000	
egov	0.244b	0.922a	0.932a	0.941a	0.980a	0.537a	1.000

Note: less then 1% (a), 1- 5% (b), 5- 10% (c) levels of significance. Abbreviations: GDP per capital constant (gdppc), human development index (hdi), finance indices (fni), information technology indices (ict), and development information indices (dii).

4.1. The Factors Analytical Results

In order to reduce the complexity of many of the indicators, the principal component is a better and less restrictive composite index than non-parametric ad-hoc weighted human development type indices; here we focus on the analysis of factors with eigenvalues larger than 1.

A. Factor Numbers and Corresponding Eigenvalues

In accordance with the Kaiser-Guttman criteria we focus on the main components only, where we chose those components that have an eigenvalue greater than *1* and where variables contribute more to the variance of the data than normally assumed. The eigenvalue of the first four components in the case of the general E-government model (2) are shown in Table 3.D. Those corresponding to smaller sub-indices (2), Development Infrastructure (2) and Finances (1) are reported in Tables 3.A, 3.B and 3.C. The number in parentheses indicates the number of eigenvalues exceeding 1.

From the maximum of 14 principal components, we will get the weighted average of the first 2 factors. The first factor has the largest eigenvalue (9.7214) followed by the second (1.7183) which are greater than 1.00. The proportion of the variance explained by the first factor is 69.44% and that of the second factor 12.24%, which suggest that the share total variance explained by the first two factors are 81.68%. See Table 3.D.

B. Variable Explanations and Corresponding Eigenvector

The eigenvectors show the four factors correlating with variances. The Tables 3.A to 3.D display the variables that have a factor loading greater than 0.30 in its absolute value and are marked by an asterisk (*). Notably at the threshold of 0.30, it will be selected as an important variable in the data sets to affect the factor loading.

The summary of principal components analysis for the ICT index is reported in Table 3.A. The first two eigenvalues are greater than 1 and they contribute to 91.24% of the variance. The first factor shows that all indicators contribute to the first factor, while in the second factor their contribution is much smaller and in two cases the effect is negative.

The corresponding information regarding the development information index is reported in Table 3.B. All indicators, i.e., PCs installed in schools, contribute positively, while Freedom House Index contributes negatively. In the case of the second factor, only PCs installed in schools and the urban population are contributors, the latter negatively.

Table 3.A. Summary of principal component analysis of 'ICT index', n=143 obs

Eigenvalues of the correlation matrix 'ICT index'				
	Eigenvalue	difference	Proportion	Cumulative
Prin 1	4.2756	3.0767	0.7126	0.7126
Prin 2	1.1989	0.9113	0.1998	0.9124
Prin 3	0.2876	0.1510	0.0479	0.9604
Prin 4	0.1365		0.0228	0.9831
Eigenvectors				
Variable	Prin 1	Prin 2	Prin 3	Prin 4
itn	0.4076*	-0.4393*	0.3399*	-0.0680
mp	0.4315*	-0.3543*	0.1980	-0.1457
pc	0.4452*	-0.2954	-0.2043	0.2464
tm	0.4287*	0.2036	-0.7149*	0.2605
tvs	0.3922*	0.4651*	-0.0183	-0.7663*
mtlc	0.3342*	0.5798*	0.5403*	0.5082*

Abbreviations: Internet users (itn), mobile phones (mp), Personal computers (pc), telephone mainlines (tm), television sets (tvs), Main telephone lines in largest city (mtlc).

Table 3.B. summary of principal component analysis on 'Development information index', n=143 obs

Eigenvalues of the correlation matrix 'Development information index'				
	Eigenvalue	difference	Proportion	Cumulative
Prin 1	4.4903	3.4579	0.6415	0.6415
Prin 2	1.0323	0.2344	0.1475	0.7890
Prin 3	0.7978	0.3743	0.1140	0.9029
Prin 4	0.4235	0.0605		0.9634
Eigenvectors				
Variable	Prin 1	Prin 2	Prin 3	Prin 4
ictxec	0.4141*	0.0428	0.4379*	-0.2268
veh	0.4015*	0.3117*	-0.0786	-0.5105*
epc	0.4469*	-0.0436	0.3010*	-0.1021
fdhi	-0.3347*	0.2147	0.6828*	0.2977
pcie	0.2106	0.8244*	-0.1225	0.4261*
ays	0.3948*	0.2140	-0.3747*	0.4899*
upop	0.3939*	0.3570*	0.2995	0.4088*

Abbreviations: infor. & communication technology exp. per cap. (ictxec) vehicles (veh), electric power consumption (epc), freedom of house ranking (fhdi), personal comp. Installed in edu. (pcie) Edu (pcie), attending of the total population age 15 over secondary school (ays), urban population (upop).

Table 3.C summary of principal component analysis on 'finances index', n=143 obs

Eigenvalues of the correlation matrix 'Finance index'				
	Eigenvalue	difference	Proportion	Cumulative
Prin 1	1.16358	0.6712	0.4090	0.4090
Prin 2	0.9646	0.2142	0.2412	0.6501
Prin 3	0.7504	0.1013	0.1876	0.8377
Prin 4	0.6490		0.1623	1.0000
Eigenvectors				
Variable	Prin 1	Prin 2	Prin 3	Prin 4
Fdis	-0.4339*	0.6801*	-0.4344*	0.4004*
gcf	0.4633*	0.6634*	0.0354	-0.5863*
ggcxe	0.5730*	0.1970	0.3801*	0.6987*
Igpd	-0.5182*	0.2415	0.8157*	-0.0868

Abbreviations: Foreign direct investment (fdi), Gross private. General government consumption expenditure (ggcxe), Gross capital information (gcf), gdp deflator (igdpd).

The results associated with the finances sub-index are shown in Table 3.C. Here only the first eigenvalue is greater than 1, suggesting only one factor component being extracted from the result.

All four indicator eigenvectors are bigger than 0.30, indicative of positive effects in the case of gross private capital formation and gross capital flows, while negative effects are related to those of foreign direct investment and inflation variables.

For the composite E-government index, the first component (factor) is the most important factor, which accounts for 69.4% of the total variance in the data, and it achieves a high loading with telephone mainline and electric power consumption. The most important factor we can call simply communications technology.

Table 3.D. summary of principal component analysis on 'E-government index', n=143 obs

Eigenvalues of the correlation matrix 'E-government index'				
	Eigenvalue	difference	Proportion	Cumulative
Prin 1	9.7214	8.0081	0.6944	0.6944
Prin 2	1.7133	0.8758	0.1224	0.8168
Prin 3	0.8375	0.0946	0.0598	0.8766
Prin 4	0.7429		0.0530	0.9297
Eigenvectors				
Variable	Prin 1	Prin 2	Prin 3	Prin 4
Itn	0.2099	0.5106*	-0.1858	0.2991
Mp	0.2325	0.4661*	-0.1737	0.2141
Pc	0.2610	0.4190*	-0.0461	0.0158
Tm	0.3076*	0.0056	0.0060	-0.2237
Tvs	0.2832	-0.1758	0.1795	0.2620
Mtlc	0.2372	0.2829	-0.1216	0.4465*
ictxec	0.2852	0.0259	0.3997*	-0.1318
Vch	0.2593	-0.2318	0.2415	0.3611*
Epc	0.3105*	0.0241	0.1911	-0.1258
Fdhi	-0.2016	0.3575*	0.4828*	-0.0424
Ays	0.2574	-0.1764	-0.5232*	-0.1328
upop	0.2711	0.0427	-0.0589	-0.5665*
gdppc	0.2958	0.1045	0.3406*	-0.0152
Hdi	0.2991	-0.0927	-0.0705	-0.2049

Abbreviations: Internet users (itn), mobile phones (mp), personal computers (pc), telephone mainlines(tm), television sets (tvs), main telephone lines in largest city (mtlc), infor.& communication technology exp. per capita (ictxec), vehicles (veh), electric power consumption (epc), freedom of house ranking (fhdi), education attendance (ays), urban population (upop), gdp per capita consumption (gdppc), human development index (hdi).

The second factor is underscored by information technology, and it is increased with a lower score then factor one. It includes internet use, mobile phone, personal computers and the Freedom House Index. This factor is very related to internet technology.

For the third factor, we find several indicators that contribute, but the eigenvalue is less than 1. We do not discuss the third and fourth factors further.

The principal component helps us organize the data into a few dimensions, therefore providing us with a general picture of the components that may underscore the E-government's index structure.

4.2. Variations in the E-Government Index

A. Variations in the Index Across Countries

By using the model in equations (1), the E-government index and its sub-components are calculated for each of the 11 countries and for thirteen years of data. The country mean values of all underlying indicators are presented in Tables 4.A, 4.B and 4.C and indices are computed and reported in Table 4.D.

Table 4.A shows the distribution of the ICT indicators across the sample countries. There is significant variation among the sample countries foremost with respect to internet use, mobile phones, and personal computers. Similar patterns are observed with respect to the human capital or development infrastructure variables (Table 4.B).

Table 4.A. Mean 'ICT index' variables by country

Country	itn	mp	pc	tm	tvs	mtlc
Japan	126.5	251.3	186.7	511.6	688.3	7504270
HongKong	129.8	258.8	208.0	535.6	398.8	3367162
Singapore	149.2	271.2	271.1	418.9	309.0	1542565
Korea Rep.	143.1	231.5	198.0	417.1	310.8	5289347
Malysia	79.2	110.1	55.9	161.6	173.1	298756
Thailand	16.4	48.1	18.2	65.7	218.6	2036173
Philippines	9.0	41.3	12.4	25.5	110.3	1235993
China	7.5	31.6	7.7	58.8	251.6	3631542
Indonesia	5.8	9.9	6.2	20.6	151.6	1514483
Vietnam	2.6	4.5	3.5	17.4	128.9	271995
Cambodia	0.3	5.7	0.7	1.4	8.0	10363

Abbreviations: Internet user (itn), mobile phone (mp), personal, Computers (pc), telephone mainlines (tm), Television sets (tvs), main telephone lines in largest city (mtlc).

Table 4.B. Mean 'Development information' variables by country

Country	ictxec	veh	epc	fdhi	pcie	ays	tgdp	upop
Japan	2211.8	535.1	6908.4	20.3	1161970	9.2	18.6	78.2
HongKong	446.0	75.6	4961.8	34.9	55266	9.3	272.2	99.9
Singapore	1738.6	149.5	5750.9	63.1	53384	6.5	156.1	100.0
Korea Rep.	495.7	189.1	3828.2	27.3	316544	10.5	68.6	78.7
Malysia	210.6	149.1	2022.7	62.2	63919	6.5	187.3	54.3
Thailand	67.5	87.2	1188.0	39.6	126169	6.1	95.6	19.4
Philippines	28.3	23.9	410.1	40.9	48592	7.8	87.0	54.7
China	24.8	16.9	665.0	60.8	5762	4.4	73.1	14.9
Indonesia	15.7	20.7	285.3	61.0	28406	4.5	61.0	36.7
Vietnam	12.3	5.2	191.3	74.0	12275	4.2	189.7	22.5
Cambodia	9.8	4.3	264.0	60.8	5762	4.4	73.1	14.9

Abbreviations: information and communication technology expenditure per capita (ictxec), vehicles (veh), electric power consumption (epc), freedom of house ranking(fhdi), edu. attendance (ays), PC installed in education (pcie), trade share of gdp (tgdp), urban population (upop).

Table 4.C. Mean 'finances index' variables by country

	Finance Index		
Country	gcf	igdpd	ggcxe
Japan	14.11	1.84	6.07
HongKong	38.40	5.53	12.56
Singapore	28.91	3.15	8.70
Korea Republic	24.89	4.36	7.75
Malysia	28.37	-0.01	15.25
Thailand	32.71	4.94	10.36
Philippines	33.74	3.31	12.10
China	21.91	8.60	11.60
Indonesia	32.95	1.25	10.07
Vietnam	33.37	3.66	10.37
Cambodia	25.24	1.30	7.68

Abbreviations: gross capital formation (gcf), inflation gdp deflator (igdpd), general government final consumption expenditure (ggcxe).

Table 4.D. Mean of different indices by countries, n=143 obs

	E-government indices					
	ICT infrastructure		Human Capital		E-government index	
Country	ict	dii	fni	hdi	egov	Rank
Japan	1.46	2.08	1.39	0.93	1.89	1
HongKong	1.06	0.97	-0.05	0.88	1.10	2
Singapore	0.80	0.73	-0.04	0.87	0.88	3
Korea Republic	0.86	0.88	0.55	0.85	0.84	4
Malysia	-0.29	-0.22	0.43	0.76	-0.25	5
Thailand	-0.44	-0.46	0.41	0.74	-0.45	6
Philippines	-0.67	-0.27	0.01	0.73	-0.48	7
China	-0.36	-0.72	0.70	0.68	-0.64	8
Indonesia	-0.66	-0.86	-0.69	0.66	-0.78	9
Vietnam	-0.78	-1.10	-1.52	0.65	-0.97	10
Cambodia	-0.95	-1.02	-1.26	0.55	-1.10	11

Abbreviations: infor. & commu. Tech (ict), development information (dii), finances (fni), Human development (hdi), E-government (egov).

The largest variations are associated with ICT expenditure per capita, vehicle density and electric power consumption. Relatively speaking, minor variations are found when looking at the financial variables (Table 4.C).

The indices result in Table 4.D shows that Japan is ranked first among the eleven countries which have the highest weighted score for the E-government index (1.89). The top rank is a result of the heavy weighting of each of the three ICT, development information and finances sub-indices. This shows that Japan has the highest capability and capacity to maximize its use of E-government in the delivery of public services to citizens.

Cambodia is a country in a critical situation. Cambodia has the lowest rank in the E-government index among the eleven countries (-1.10), as well as in the case of ICT, development information and human development indices. However, the position of Vietnam is the lowest in terms of its finances index.

The rank of countries differs somewhat, depending on the sub-indices studies, as these are based on different indicators where countries might be advanced in one area but not in others. The final rank shown in Table 4.D is based on the aggregate index labelled as E-government.

B. Variations in the Indices Over Time

Here the development of the mean of different indicators as well as the E-government and other sub-indices are reported over time in Tables 5A, 5B, 5C and 5D. The mean values have been computed for each year of observation from 1990 to 2002.

Development of the ICT indicators reported in Table 5.A show an increasing pattern in all variables. However, the direction of development is not always increasing in the case of the development of information variables reported in Table 5.B. For instance ICT expenditure per capita, vehicle density and electricity consumption increase over time while several other variables such as PCs installed in schools and trade share of GDP show a decreasing trend over time. The financial indicators change over time, but without any trend (Table 5.C).

The results show that the mean of indices over time differ and the highest value of the aggregate E-government index is attributed to year 2002 (see Table 5.D).

Table 5.A. Mean 'ICT infrastructure index' variables by year of observation

Year	itn	mp	pc	Tm	tvs	mtlc
1990	0.2	5.1	20.6	152.7	182.4	1634279
1991	0.3	7.7	24.3	161.0	191.1	1701460
1992	1.3	10.3	30.2	167.4	200.7	1775015
1993	2.5	14.4	36.3	176.2	212.8	1866749
1994	4.7	23.0	46.2	186.0	226.4	2028947
1995	8.0	39.2	58.6	196.3	243.5	2190996
1996	18.2	67.5	75.1	205.9	252.6	2398920
1997	36.0	108.3	92.1	216.9	261.8	2624903
1998	57.4	148.9	106.5	221.9	269.3	2713126
1999	98.3	208.4	129.3	230.8	279.4	2628658
2000	147.0	278.9	157.6	240.5	288.3	3003036
2001	191.8	323.3	177.6	242.0	293.8	3396787
2002	225.5	377.2	204.3	242.3	346.6	3394941

Abbreviations: internet user (itn), mobile phone (mp), personal computer (pc), Telephone mainlines(tm), television sets (tvs), main telephone lines in largest city (mtlc).

ICT and development information sub-indices are developing rapidly and are subject to major changes over time. The human development index is increasing steadily but very slowly from 0.72 in 1990 to 0.78 in 2002. The finances sub-index shows irregularities and negative signs in the beginning of the 90s and also in the post Asian Financial Crisis, 1997. However, there is a sign of recovery already in 2000.

Table 5.B. Mean 'development information index' variables by year of observation.

Year	ictxec	veh	epc	fdhi	pcie	ays	tgdp	upop
1990	332.3	86.0	1796.2	51.9	700062	7.24	126.2	56.7
1991	361.9	89.3	1879.8	50.6	531900	7.22	125.0	56.3
1992	392.3	94.2	1949.3	49.6	415717	7.12	128.6	55.8
1993	453.3	100.4	2041.2	29.5	334591	7.06	113.7	55.3
1994	504.9	107.4	2199.6	52.0	310464	7.07	114.2	54.8
1995	584.7	113.3	2301.4	53.3	250112	7.00	108.5	54.3
1996	664.3	119.4	2469.6	51.0	210911	6.93	103.8	53.8
1997	707.1	124.8	2610.8	52.3	175290	6.86	104.5	53.3
1998	677.3	125.1	2656.3	52.5	88208	6.76	97.0	52.8
1999	702.9	127.2	2721.5	51.5	69324	6.67	88.7	52.3
2000	765.6	129.4	2836.2	48.7	60624	6.56	85.8	51.8
2001	785.9	134.4	2911.7	53.3	56506	6.46	83.7	51.3
2002	466.8	134.3	2915.8	52.9	52306	6.38	81.1	50.8

Abbreviations: information and communication technology expenditure per capita (ictxec), vehicles (veh), electric power consumption (epc), freedom of house ranking(fhdi), PC installed in education (pcie), education attendance (ays), trade share of gdp(tgdp), urban population (upop).

Table 5.C. Mean 'finance index' variables by year of observation

Year	gcf	igdp	ggcxe
1990	23.8	9.55	11.12
1991	26.3	12.88	10.90
1992	35.0	7.25	10.36
1993	37.0	6.51	10.28
1994	32.1	7.02	10.02
1995	33.9	7.18	9.93
1996	27.8	4.78	9.96
1997	25.7	4.20	9.80
1998	26.8	11.40	10.01
1999	26.6	0.82	9.87
2000	29.3	1.84	10.13
2001	29.5	1.56	10.09
2002	28.9	1.77	11.46

Abbreviations: gross capital formation (gcf), inflation gdp deflator (igdpd), general government final consumption expenditure (ggcxe).

Table 5.D. Mean indices by year of observation

Year	hdi	ict	dii	fni	egov
1990	0.72	-0.48	-0.25	-0.17	-0.33
1991	0.73	-0.46	-0.22	-0.30	-0.30
1992	0.73	-0.42	-0.16	0.04	-0.25

Table 5.(Continued)

1993	0.74	-0.38	-0.13	0.06	-0.21
1994	0.75	-0.32	-0.09	0.02	-0.16
1995	0.75	-0.24	-0.03	0.01	-0.09
1996	0.76	-0.14	0.03	0.16	-0.01
1997	0.76	-0.01	0.06	0.20	0.04
1998	0.76	0.10	0.09	-0.42	0.09
1999	0.77	0.28	0.13	-0.04	0.18
2000	0.77	0.50	0.18	0.06	0.28
2001	0.78	0.68	0.22	0.15	0.37
2002	0.78	0.88	0.17	0.25	0.41

Abbreviations: infor. & commu. Tech (ict), development infor. (dii), finances (fni), Human development (hdi), E-government (egov).

4.3. Link between E-Government and Economic Development

Income is the most significant factor that is related to many factors in an economy. For instance, it is an indicator of economic activity, productivity, capability and welfare. Here we aim to study the correlation between income per capita to E-government, ICT, human development, development information- and finances components. A positive association will indicate that all three sub-indices, the aggregate E-government index, and human development index are increasing in levels over time.

Our important question is whether E-government and other factors have any impact on the economic development (GDP per capita), or are bidirectional causally related to income. In response to this question, a regression analysis is performed to test the following two main hypotheses which differ by aggregated vs. disaggregated e-government index and including vs. ignoring country effects:

- H_{1A}: An increase in urban population, FDI, and disaggregated E-government index components positively affects economic development, ignoring country effects.
- H_{1B}: An increase in urban population, FDI, and disaggregated E-government index components positively affects economic development, accounting for country effects.
- H_{2A}: An increase in urban population, FDI, and aggregated E-government index positively affects economic development, ignoring country effects.
- H_{2B}: An increase in urban population, FDI, and aggregated E-government index affects positively economic development, accounting for country effects.

A. Model Specification

Regression analysis is conducted to establish the link between the sub-indices computed and economic development. For this reason we have selected variables such as, urban population (defined as the share of the population residing in urban areas), net FDI share of GDP, trend, information and communications technology, human development, development information and finance sub-indices as a set of independent variables and economic development (GDP per capita) as a dependent variable.

The economic development models, where an attempt is made to capture the effects of different disaggregated sub-indices and aggregated e-government index on GDP per capita examined, are written as:

$$lGDP_{it} = \beta_0+\beta_1 lUPOP_{it}+\beta_2 lFDI_{it}+\beta_3 TREND_t+\beta_4 HDI_{it}+\beta_5 ICT_{it}+\beta_6 DII_{it}+\beta_7 FNI_{it}+\varepsilon_{it} \quad (2)$$

$$lGDP_{it} = \beta_0+\beta_1 lUPOP_{it}+\beta_2 lFDI_{it}+\beta_3 TREND_t+\beta_4 HDI_{it}+\beta_5 ICT_{it}+\beta_6 DII_{it}+\beta_7 FNI_{ii}+\mu_i+\varepsilon_{it} \quad (3)$$

$$lGDP_{it} = \beta_0+\beta_1 lUPOP_{it}+\beta_2 lFDI_{it}+\beta_3 TREND_t+\beta_4 EGOV_{it}+\varepsilon_{it} \quad (4)$$

$$lGDP_{it} = \beta_0+\beta_1 lUPOP_{it}+\beta_2 lFDI_{it}+\beta_3 TREND_t+\beta_4 EGOV_{it}+\mu_i+\varepsilon_{it} \quad (5)$$

where, for country i in year t; $lGDP_{it}$ is log GDP per capita; $lUPOP_{it}$ is log urban population; $lFDI_{it}$ is log foreign direct investment; and $EGOV_{it}$ *is* the aggregate E-government index; The aggregate *EGOV* is further disaggregated into four sub-index components. These are: HDI_{it} is the human development index; ICT_{it} is the information and communication technology index, DII_{it} is the development information index; FNI_{it} is the finance index; μ_i is the country effect; and ε_{it} is a random error term.

B. Estimation Results

The results from examining hypotheses H_1 and H_2 reported in Table 6 are described below. In what follows, we report the results from the fixed effect model regressions, emphasizing the findings of our analysis. In equations (2) and (4), we ignore the country effects, while in equations (3) and (5) we account for unobservable country effects.

The F-tests conducted suggest that the country effects should be included in the model specification, i.e. model A2 and B2 are the preferred model specifications. The models A2 and B2 are not tested and cannot be tested easily. In both cases the R2 is quite high and the effects are positive as expected but the development information index is insignificant. The aggregate e-government index suggests a clear positive effect, but the disaggregate model is more informative in the sense that it offers heterogeneous effects from different sub-index components on GDP.

The coefficient of log urban population is negative in Model A1 and Model B1, which was not expected and it is statistically and weakly significant at the 10% level of significance.

A positive relationship is expected because of higher average levels of education in urban areas, higher competition, better organization and infrastructure that support business and higher productivity. It indicates a negative relationship between the level of GDP and the level of urban population, but the relation turns out to be positive and statistically significant in Model A2 and Model B2 when we control for unobservable country effects.

Table 6. Regression analysis of the link between E-government indicators and economic development, n=143 obs

Variable	Model A1 Coeff.	Model A1 Std Dev.	Model A2 Coeff.	Model A2 Std Dev.	Model B1 Coeff.	Model B1 Std Dev.	Model B2 Coeff.	Model B2 Std Dev.
intercept	25.63a	1.357	18.56a	0.615	23.70a	0.835	19.59a	0.634
logupop	-0.392c	0.233	0.536c	0.243	-0.612b	0.210	0.803b	0.273
logfdi	0.410a	0.006	0.007	0.009	0.340a	0.065	0.006	0.011
trend	-0.410c	0.024	0.018b	0.006	-0.081b	0.021	0.029b	0.070
hdi	-4.163c	2.374	3.296a	0.694	-	-	-	-
ict	0.033	0.183	0.048c	0.025	-	-	-	-
dii	1.604a	0.276	0.010	0.060	-	-	-	-
fni	0.267c	0.107	0.056a	0.012	-	-	-	-
egov	-	-	-	-	1.484a	0.136	0.128c	0.07
China			4.018a	0.203			4.344a	0.232
Hong Kong			1.403b	0.514			1.881b	0.626
Indonesia			2.923a	0.212			3.054a	0.251
Japan			4.725a	0.492			5.446a	0.596
Korea Rep.			2.602a	0.443			3.116a	0.536
Malaysia			1.469a	0.320			1.842a	0.380
Philippine			1.529a	0.313			1.809a	0.372
Singapore			0.727	0.493			1.197c	0.602
Thailand			2.618a	0.153			3.230a	0.131
Viet Nam			1.187a	0.112			1.396a	0.121
R-square adjusted	0.7877		0.9982		0.7542		0.9976	
F-values	66.8500a		4411.4900a		88.1200a		3976.4300a	
Root MSE	0.8360		0.0766		0.8996		0.0884	
F-test	3.10				3.85			
F-critical value			2.34				2.34	

Note: less then 1% (a), 1-5% (b) and 5-10% (c) levels of significance. Abbreviation: urban population (upop), foreign direct Investment (fdi), human development index (hdi), information and communication technology index (ict), development information index (dii), finances index (fni), E-government index (egov).

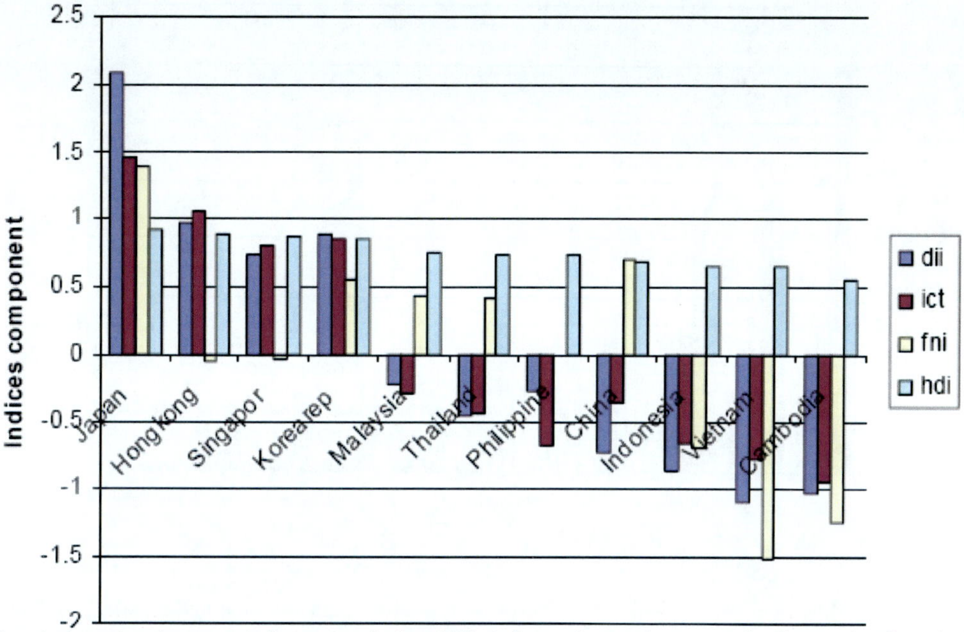

Abbreviation: development information index (dii), information and communication technology index (ict), finances index (fni), human development index (hdi).

Figure 1. Disaggregate E-government index components.

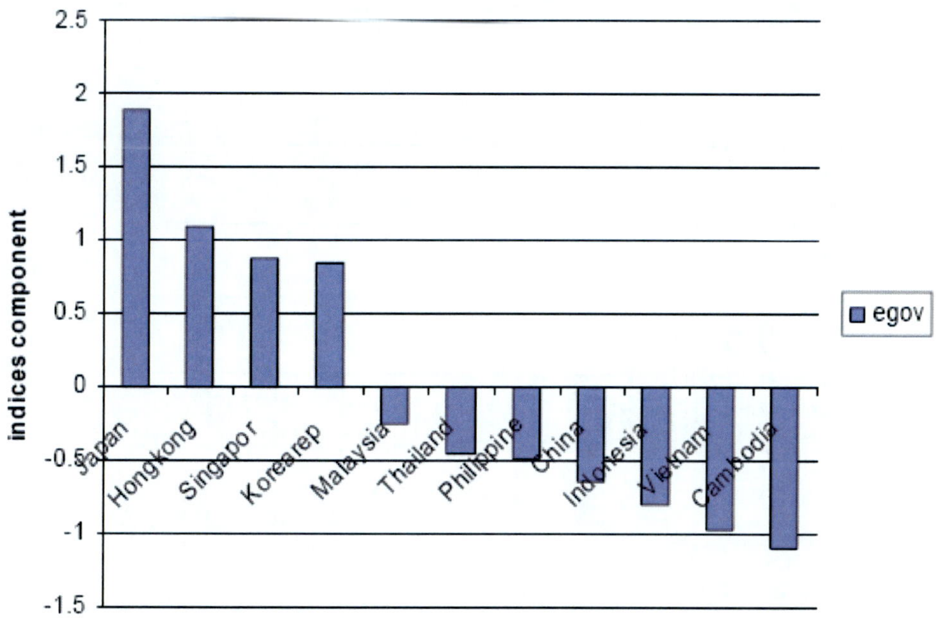

Abbreviation: E-government index (egov).

Figure 2. Aggregate E-government index.

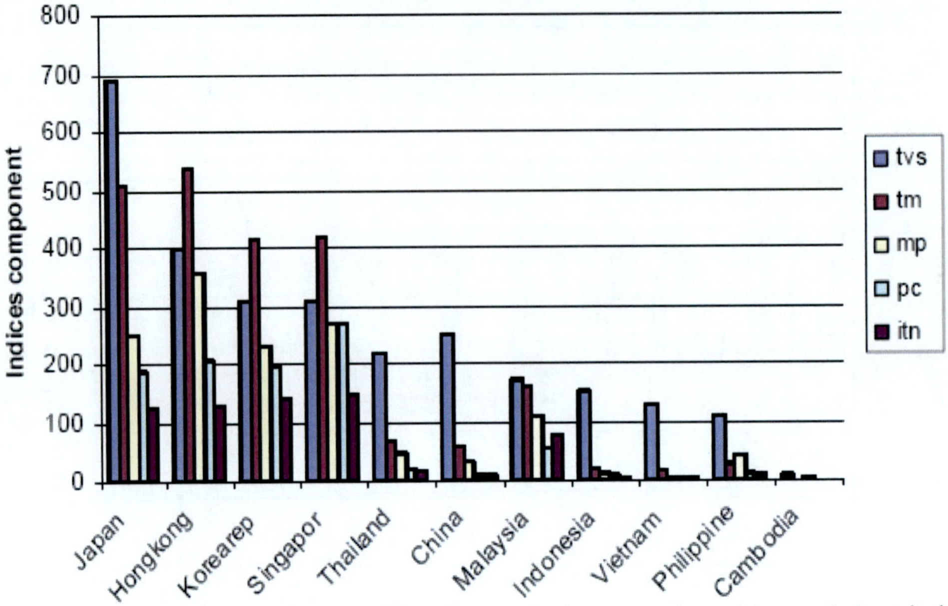

Abbreviation: Internet users (itn), mobile phones (mp), personal computers (pc), telephone mainlines(tm), television sets (tvs).

Figure 3. Components of information and communication technology index (ict).

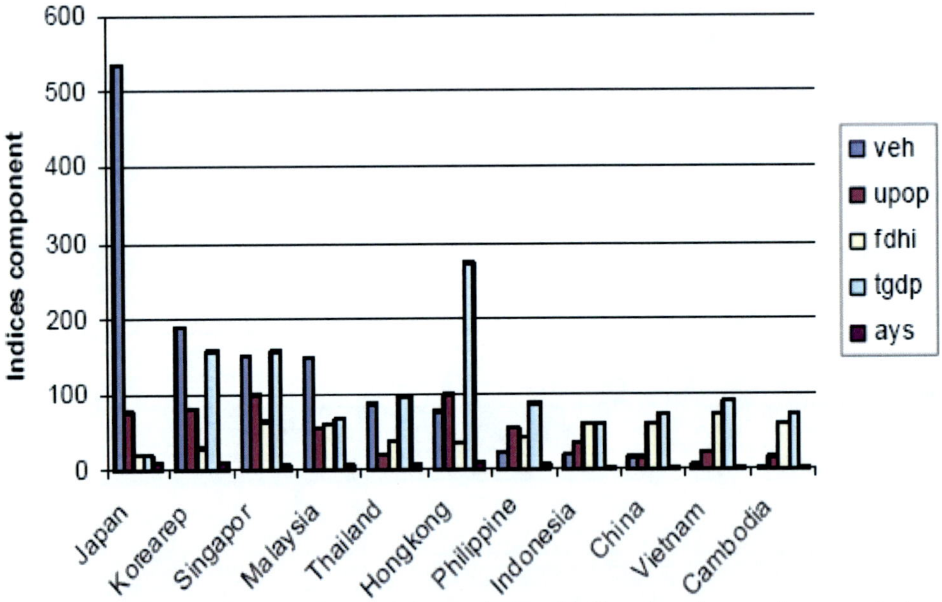

Abbreviation: vehicles (veh), freedom of house index (fhdi), education attainment of the total population aged 15 over-secondary school (ays), trade (tgdp), and urban population (upop).

Figure 4. Components of development information index (dii).

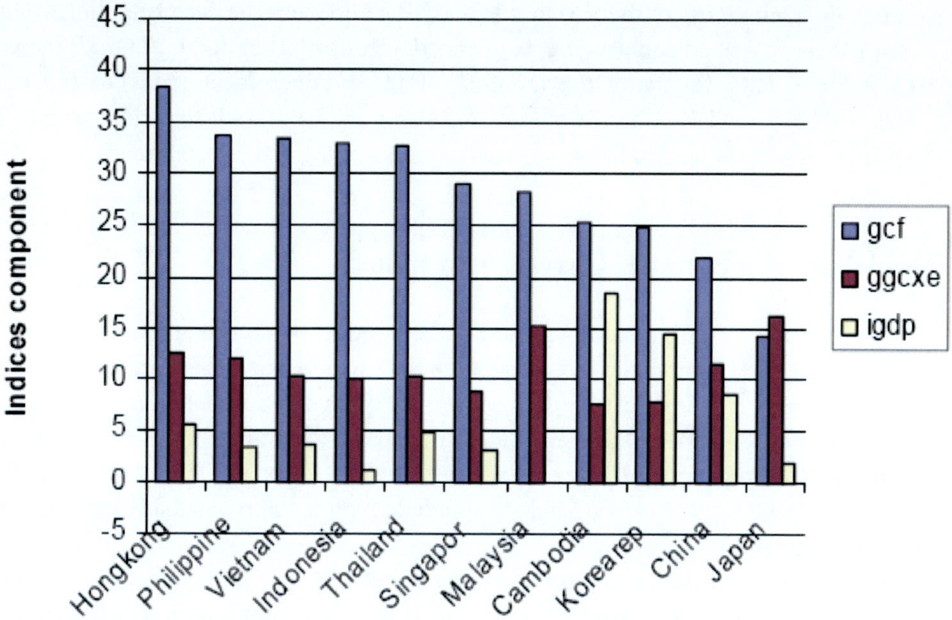

Abbreviations: gross capital formation (gcf), inflation gdp deflator (igdpd), general government final consumption expenditure (ggcxe).

Figure 5. Components of finances index (fni).

The coefficient of log FDI is positive and statistically significant at a level less then 1% for model A1 and B1, while it is insignificant in the models A2 and B2. Again the effect of FDI on economic development is sensitive to whether one controls for unobservable country effects or not. The sensitivity is due to systematic variation in the inflow of FDI among the sample countries, in which the effect is confounded by the country effect. In the models specified by ignoring country effects we observe a negative trend in GDP over time, but a positive trend in the models controlling for such effects.

Indicators such as human development, ICT infrastructure, development of information and finances have impacts on GDP per capita and are found to be statistically significant. However, with the exception of the financial index, their sign or significance changes according to model specifications. The aggregate e-government index has a statistically significant and positive effect on the level of GDP. However, the signs of urban population, FDI and trend variables change when country effects are accounted for.

In Models A2 and B2, all country effects in relation to the reference country (Cambodia) are positive and significant, except for Singapore where it is insignificant in Model A2. Contribution to GDP differs among the developing and newly industrialized economies. We can say that the level of development is positively associated with the level of effect. Looking at the F-values and F-test results, we reject both of the null hypotheses that the slopes or country effects are zero.

Our results seemed simple, but we still suspect that a negative relationship between the urban population and GDP in models A1 and B1 might be due to a misspecification of the model and measures used. In this study we show that GDP and E-government are positively correlated. A one percent investment in E-government will increase GDP per capita by 0.13% (Model B2). The model B1, estimated with and without the E-government index, shows that

E-government explains 21% of the variations in GDP per capita. The corresponding effect in the case of Model B2, when country effects are accounted for, is negligible. The R2 increases from 0.5441 to 0.7544 following the addition of the E-government index to the model specification. The overall conclusion is that E-government as a method of interaction does systematically reflect and lead to increased income and welfare across economies.

4.4. Guidelines to a Better E-Government Index

It should be noted that the results presented here are to be considered as a preliminary version of an E-government index. A more complete and better measured index requires incorporating a number of indicators that were omitted in the computation of the current index. The first improvement should be the identification of a complete list of indicators of an E-government index so that they cover its multidimensional aspects. The current sample of countries is small and needs to be expanded to include more countries outside the region and also other economic regions.

A well-defined index should incorporate several other relevant components. For instance, it should include some measurement of costs and benefits of information technology in the provision of services and its impacts on the social, economic, technology, governance, and ICT infrastructure among the sample countries. The index should be designed in such a way that it can further be used for international and regional comparisons, and in the evaluation of the impact of E-government on the welfare of nations and the sub groups of the population within countries and regions. The accounting for a regional distribution of connectivity and service provision should be a high priority in the construction of such an index.

Summary and Conclusion

This study addresses the computation and analysis of a composite E-government index. The index is calculated by using a principal component analysis method to reduce the dimensions of the index. The index is based on several indicators of E-government activities. It quantifies the level and the development of the E-government process and ranks countries based on the level of the generated index. The index is formed from three main components: ICT infrastructure, development information and finances. The latter two can be considered as human capital. Each sub-index component differs among the sample countries and it develops differently over time.

We observe significant heterogeneity among countries in their E-government level and how it develops over time. The result shows that low ranked countries are not greatly impacted by ICT infrastructure, development information and finances. Several developing countries for various financial, skill, management and governance reasons are unable to address in an effective way. This is due to their underdeveloped and insufficient ICT infrastructure and finances and their need to develop the entire sector. This means that they have a low and inadequate capability to provide online E-government service provision.

The regression results show that when we ignore country effects, the E-government index explains 21% of the variations in the economic development defined as GDP per capita among the Southeast Asian countries, but the effect is negligible when the country effects are taken into account. The level of urban population negatively affects the level of economic development. However, if one does account for the unobservable country effects, the urban population variable positively affects economic development. Other factors like ICT, development information and finance sub-indices are positively associated with economic development. We find that all country effects are positive and statistically significant in relation to the economic development in Cambodia, serving as a reference country.

The result from the measurement of E-government in this study is useful in the formation of a strategy for developing countries to consider and understand how to utilize E-government more efficiently in the delivery of public services to their citizens. Also to be considered by the government of a developing country are the identification of the main factors. Those factors should be given priority so that in the near future, governments will be able to use E-government services whenever they find it optimal to use them.

Last but not least, future research should attempt to improve our understanding of a number of issues as follows: (i) advances could be made along with identification of some factors or indicators that influence E-government and its contribution to economic growth, (ii) the study should be extended to consider the relationship between ICT and economic development or growth and aspects such as the digital divide should be investigated as well.

REFERENCES

Acerete B., Pina V. and Torres L. (2005). E-government developments on delivering public services among EU cities. *Government Information Quarterly* 20(3), 365-387.

Agénor P.R. (2003). Does Globalisation Hurt the Poor?, (unpublished manuscript), World Bank: Washington DC.

Akman I., Ali Yazici A., Mishra A. and Arifoglu A. (2005). E-government: A global view and an empirical evaluation of some attributes of citizens. *Government Information Quarterly* 22(5) 239-257.

Andersen M.T. and Herbertsson T.T. (2003). Measuring Globalization. *IZA Discussion Paper,* July 2003/817.

Center for Democracy Technology (2002). The three phases of E-government. *CDT Policy post* 8(26), November 25.

Christopher S. and Thompson S.C. (2002). Enlisting on line residents: Expanding the boundaries of e-government in a Japanese rural township. *Government Information Quarterly* 19(2), 173-187.

Dedrick J., Gurbaxani V. and Kraemer K. (2003). Information Technology and Economic Performance: A Critical Review of the Empirical Evidence. *ACM Computer Survey* 35(1), 1-28.

Dekker M. and Shi W. (2002). The contribution of Organizational Factors in the success of Electronic Government Commerce. *International Journal of Public Administration* 25(5), 629-657.

Edquist H. and M. Henrekson (2006), Technological Breakthroughs and Productivity Growth, *Research in Economic History* 24, 1-53.

Hwang S.D., Choi Y. and Myeong S.H. (1990). Electronic government in South Korea: Conceptual problems. *Government Information Quarterly* 16(3), 277-285.

Heshmati A. (2006), The Relationship between Income Inequality Poverty, and Globalization, in M. Nissanke and E. Thorbecke, *The Impact of Globalization on the World' s Poor*, Palgrave Macmillan, pp.59-93.

Heshmati A. and J-E. Oh (2006), Alternative Composite Lisbon Development Strategy Indices: A Comparison of EU, USA, Japan and Korea, *The European Journal of Comparative Economics* 3(2), 133-170.

Holman J. and M.A. McGregor (2004), Communication technology at the Federal Communications Commission: E-government in the public interest? *Government Information Quarterly*, 21(3), 268-283.

Hotelling H. (1933), Analysis of a complex of statistical variables into principal components. *Journal of Educational Psychology* 24:417-441 and 498-520.

ITU (2003), World Telecommunication Development Report: Access Indicators for the Information Society.

Jaenger T.P. and Thompson M.K. (2003). E-government around the world: Lessons, challenges, and future directions. *Government Information Quarterly* 20, 389-394.

Kang S.M. (2002), A Sensitivity Analysis of the Korean Composite Environmental Index. Ecological Economics 43, 159-174.

Kovacic J.Z. (2005). The impact of National Culture on Worldwide E-government readiness. *Informing Science Journal* 8, 143-158.

Layne K. and Lee J.W. (2001), Developing fully functional E-government: A four stage model. *Government Information Quarterly* 18,122-136.

Ma L. and Thorson S. (2005). E-government in China: Bringing economic development through administrative reform. *Government Information Quarterly* 22(5) 20-37.

Moon M.J. (2002). The revolution of e-government among municipalities: Rhetoric or reality? *Public Administration Review* 62(4) 424-433.

OECD (Organization for Economic Co-Operation and Development) (2003). OECD E-government studies: The E-government Imperative. The E-government Imperative- *ISBN 92-64-101117-9-OECD.*

Pacific Council on International Policy (2002). Roadmap for E-government in the developing world. *The working group on E-government in the developing world, April 2002.*

Pearson K. (1901), On Lines and Planes of Closest fit to Systems of Points in Space, Philosophical Magazine 6(2), 559-72.

Relyea H.C. (2002). E-government: Introduction and overview. *Government Information Quarter* 19(1), 9-35.

Reddick G.C. (2005). Citizen interaction with e-government: From the streets to servers? *Government Information Quarterly* 18(1) 122-136.

Tung L.L. and O. Rieck (2005). Adoption of electronic government services among business organizations in Singapore. *Journal of Strategic Information System* 14(4), 417-440.

Salem J.A. (2003). Public and Private sector interests in e-government: a look at the DOE's PubSCIENCE. *Government Information Quarterly* 20(3) 13-27.

Sharma S.K. and Gupta J.N.D. (2002). Transforming to E-government: A framework. *Proceedings of the 2nd European conference on e-government, U.K. Oxford, pp. 383-390.*

UN (United Nations, Division for public Economics and Public Administration) and ASPA (American Society for Public Administration) (2001). Benchmarking E-government: A Global Perspective.

UN (United Nations, Department of Economics and Social Affairs) (2003). World Public sector Report 2003: E-government at the crossroads. *ST/ESA/PAD/SER.E/49.*

UN (Untied Nations, Department of Economic and Social Affairs, Division for Public Administration and Development Management) (2004). UN Global E-government Readiness report 2004: Towards Access for opportunity. *UNPAN/2004/11.*

Yen C.D. and Evans D. (2006). E-government: An analysis for implementation: Framework for understanding cultural and social impact. *Government Information Quarterly* 23(2), 207-235.

In: Information and Communication Technologies...
Ed: Almas Heshmati and Sun Peng

ISBN 978-1-60876-671-0

Chapter 14

E-GOVERNMENT CHALLENGES IN CAMBODIA

Sinawong Sang*

National ICT Development Authority (NiDA), Office of the Council of Ministers of Cambodia and Seoul National University

ABSTRACT

So far there have been few studies dealing with e-Government in Cambodia, one of the Least Developed Countries (LDCs) with an emerging economy. This study can be considered as a first in the examination of e-Government challenges in Cambodia. The Government Administration Information System (GAIS), one of the leading e-Government projects in Cambodia, is a main setting for this study. The study categorizes e-Government challenges in LDCs into six main areas: infrastructure development; law and ICT policy; management; equity issues; the digital divide; and privacy and security. The findings indicate that even though the GAIS has been successful in its initiative objectives, it has faced various critical challenges as well. These challenges and a set of policy implications are discussed in the paper.

Keywords: E-Government, Government Administration Information System (GAIS), Least Developed Countries (LDCs), Cambodia.

1. INTRODUCTION

Since the adoption of a liberal political system and market economy in the late 1990's, Cambodia, one of the Least Developed Countries (LDCs) with an emerging economy (UN-OHRLLS, 2008), has enthusiastically pursued various political, economic and social reforms to accelerate its economic growth and help alleviate poverty in the country. As part of its reform instruments, the government has implemented e-Government – the Government Administration Information System (GAIS) – as a tool to improve the process of government

---

* E-mail: ssinawong@gmail.com

in order to meet a variety of governance challenges, including corruption, poor public administration, and lack of adequate transparency and accountability in the exercise of public decision-making powers, and the delivery of public services. So far, however, the utilization of the GAIS has not been widespread due to the fact that it still faces many barriers and challenges as it continues to develop. Therefore, this paper attempts to find out the challenges of the GAIS implementation and development in order to map out the policies and strategies for the successful use of e-Government in Cambodia.

This paper is organized into five sections including these introductory comments. Section 2 presents a literature review of the definitions and benefits of e-Government as well as e-Government challenges in LDCs. Section 3 presents and discusses e-Government challenges in Cambodia, followed by policy implications in Section 4. Section 5 brings this paper to a conclusion, including implications and suggestions for future research.

2. Literature Review

2.1. Definitions and Benefits of E-Government

Simply defined, e-Government is the use of information and communication technologies (ICTs) in general and the utilization of the Internet in particular to improve the efficiency, effectiveness, transparency, accountability, and activities of a public sector organization, with the goal of achieving better government (Song, 2006; OECD, 2003). Better government means delivering public services and processing internal tasks in the government in a much more convenient, customer-oriented, and cost-effective way (Song, 2006).

A more complex definition of e-Government given by the World Bank considers it "the use by government agencies of information technologies (such as Wide Area Networks, the Internet, and mobile computing) that have the ability to transform relations with citizens, businesses, and other arms of government. These technologies can serve a variety of different ends: better delivery of government services to citizens, improved interactions with business and industry, citizen empowerment through access to information, or more efficient government management" (World Bank, 2008).

Given the aforementioned definitions, the main goal of e-Government is not merely to computerize governmental records but to transform the government by enhancing administrative efficiency and effectiveness and increasing citizens' participation in, and the transparency and accountability of, the policy making process (Song, 2006; InfoDev, 2002; OECD, 2003). Successful e-Government is at most 20 percent technology and at least 80 percent about people, processes, and organizations (InfoDev, 2002). Hence, e-Government covers more than just technology. It challenges the ways in which public sector service providers and citizens interact.

E-Government can "contribute significantly to the process of making the government leaner and more cost-effective. It can facilitate communication and improve the coordination of authorities at different tiers of government, within organizations and even at the departmental level. Furthermore, e-Government can enhance the speed and efficiency of operations by streamlining processes, lowering costs, improving research capabilities, and improving documentation and record-keeping" (United Nations, 2008). The Economist magazine estimates that the potential savings of implementing e-Government could be as much as $110 billion and £144 billion in the U.S. and Europe, respectively (The Economist, 2008).

2.2. E-Government Challenges in LDCs

In general, LDCs are lagging behind in e-Government adoption compared to developed countries because they often face serious issues and challenges which are described in a number of articles (Song, 2006; OECD, 2003; Heeks, 2003; Heeks, 2006). In the study of e-Government challenges in Africa, Heeks (2002) considers e-readiness as the main key challenge to the implementation of e-Government. The e-readiness factors include (Heeks, 2002):

- Data system infrastructure (whether the management systems, data standards, records and work processes in place to provide the quantity and quality of data to support the move to e-Government);
- Legal infrastructure (the laws and regulations required to permit and to support the move to e-Government in place);
- Institutional infrastructure (e-Government can only progress if the institutions exist to act as a focus for awareness and to act as a means for facilitation of e-Government);
- Human infrastructure (the attitudes, knowledge and skills in place – especially within the public sector – that are required to initiate, implement and sustain e-Government initiatives);
- Technological infrastructure (computing and telecommunications infrastructure);
- Leadership and strategic thinking (an important pre-condition in successful e-Government is an e-champion or small group of e-champions: leaders with vision who put e-government onto the agenda, who set e-Government within a broader reform agenda, and who make it happen).

Among the factors above, technological infrastructure is the basic constraint for most e-Government implementation and development in LDCs. Many LDCs often have a poor technological infrastructure, i.e., there may not be consistent and reliable electricity, telecommunications, Internet connectivity, and low access to the necessary hardware (Tapscott, 1996; The Economist, 2008). They have struggled to develop a basic infrastructure in order to deploy e-Government services throughout their territories (InfoDev, 2002).

Moreover, the greatest challenges to e-Government in many LDCs are legislative and regulatory barriers. Indeed, the governments play an important role in ensuring a proper legal framework for the process of e-Government (Lau, 2003) because it is not sufficient simply to add ICT to government to have e-Government since fundamental transformations and changes will affect all layers of e-Government (InfoDev, 2008). For instance, if they are to be utilized in e-Government for the submission of electronic forms, including sensitive personal or financial information, it is very necessary to have the legal recognition of digital signatures (Lau, 2003).

E-Government challenges in LDCs may arise from a traditional government structure (vertical), modes of operation (command control), and a lack of coordination and cooperation between different levels of government (the inability of agencies to communicate with each other). These can have a significant impact on the success of e-Government efforts as it requires many agencies, departments, and policy makers to coordinate their efforts, in addition to preparing the technology and support infrastructure (Detlor and Finn, 2002; Jaeger and Thomson, 2003; Heeks, 2006; Lau, 2003).

In efforts to implement e-Government, governments in LDCs often face financial issues (Gant, 2008), thus, several e-Government projects in LDCs are usually driven by individual government departments that frequently depend upon on aid from donors. Once this financing stops, there is often inadequate funding to continue the project (Schware and Deane, 2003; Dada, 2006).

In LDCs, many ICT (e.g. e-Government) programs often leave women behind in gaining benefits from them (Heeks, 2003; Gant, 2008). Therefore, governments face the challenge of overcoming disparities in how men and women use and have access to ICTs (Gant, 2008). Hence, equity issues are presented. They are associated with differential access of women and traditionally disadvantaged groups (InfoDev, 2008). The challenges and barriers that may limit the opportunities to use ICTs and to realize fully the benefits of e-Government for women include (Gant, 2008):

- Physical access to the Internet may impact women differently from men;
- Few women and young women participate in vocational and college/university courses in ICT-related fields;
- Many women are less likely to find significant value in ICTs because they are less acquainted with the economic, social and psychological gain.

In addition to the equity issues, several people in LDCs do not have access to ICT, even if the infrastructure is available. Therefore, the digital divide is presented. It is the disparity between those who have access to and use of ICT versus those who do not (Yeo et al., 2004). There are three significant areas with barriers to ICT access (Yeo et al., 2004):

- Access to the ICT infrastructure (this includes access to hardware, software, and telecommunication links);
- Access to education and skills (it is necessary to be able to make use of ICT);
- Access to information media (it is restricted by the fact that the majority of digital media content is in English and therefore not comprehensible to the population that does not know the language.)

Indeed, it is common in LDCs that there is a large gap between the educated elite who can afford technology, and the uneducated poor who cannot (Basu, 2004). Thus, those without access cannot learn essential computer skills, cannot access information that can provide economic opportunities, and cannot share in the benefits of e-Government (InfoDev, 2002). Moreover, a person in a high-income country is over 22 times more likely to be an Internet user than one in a low-income nation (UNCTAD, 2008).

Though e-Government implementation can be considered in the early stages in many LDCs, privacy and security are also critical challenges (InfoDev, 2008). Privacy is about protecting the personal information the government collects about individuals, while security is about protecting e-Government sites from attack and misuse (InfoDev, 2002). Citizens are unlikely to use e-Government services without a guarantee of privacy and security (Lau, 2003). The governments in LDCs need to gain the trust of citizens. Moreover, "the challenge facing e-Government coordinators and implementers is to respect accepted privacy principles while allowing the benefits of the Internet and other technologies to flow to citizens. This balance is of particular importance when considering seamless government services involving data sharing among agencies" (Lau, 2003).

Given the literature review above, e-Government challenges in LDCs seem to fall into six main categories: infrastructure development; law and ICT policy; management; equity issues; the digital divide; and privacy and security (see Figure 1).

The infrastructure development deals with the development of basic telecommunications and ICT infrastructure. Law and ICT policy are concerned with the laws, rules, regulations, and policies, which must be implemented or changed in order to facilitate the development of both the new infrastructure and information services (Detlor and Finn, 2002; Jaeger and Thomson, 2003; Heeks, 2006).

Management includes strategic issues, human resource management, budget support and allocation, coordination and collaboration between agency leaders, and monitoring and evaluation of the projects. Equity issues are associated with differential access of women and traditionally disadvantaged groups.

The digital divide is about the gap between those who have access to and use of ICT versus those who do not. Privacy and security deal with the protection of personal information the government collects about individuals as well as the protection of e-Government sites from attack and misuse.

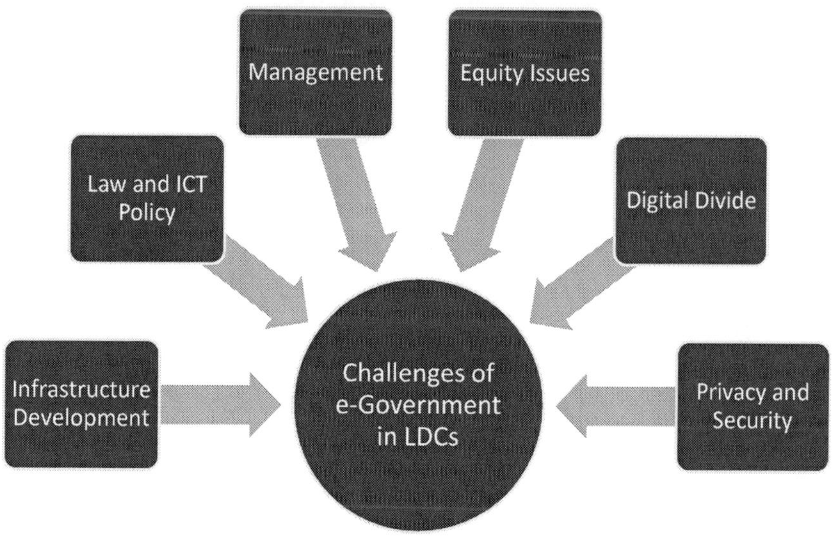

Figure 1. The Challenges of e-Government in LDCs.

3. E-Government Challenges in Cambodia

3.1. Government Administration Information System (GAIS)

The establishment of the National Information Communications Technology Development Authority (NiDA) in 2000 was the starting point for e-Government in Cambodia (Sang, 2008). The authority implemented the Government Administration Information System (GAIS) in 2002, through a concession loan and technical assistance from the Government of the Republic of Korea, along with the counterpart fund from the Royal Government of Cambodia (NiDA, 2003).

Revenue generation, along with better government image and services, was the main objective of the GAIS (Phu, 2003). The GAIS involves four practical applications (Phu, 2003): an electronic approval system, a vehicle registration system (for cars and motorbikes), a resident registration system, and a real estate registration system. The purpose of the electronic approval system is to allow ministries to exchange documents both internally and externally. It incorporates all traditional manual functions to allow easy use of the system. The vehicle registration system is used for managing basic vehicle data such as registration, ownership transfer, safety inspection, identification number, applicable taxes, vehicle certificates, and statistics. The resident registration system is used for managing basic resident data such as family composition, children of school age, change in family status due to marriage, divorce, birth or death, and other statistics, as well as information for ID card issuance, election administration, foreign residents, and applicable taxes. The real estate registration system is used for managing basic land records such as division and merger, ownership transfer, common land, applicable taxes, real estate certificates, and statistics.

Currently, the central government, including 7 districts and 76 communes, is fully connected. The connection allows all government offices to communicate electronically and to access the Internet and email at their convenience. The electronic approval system function has been in operation but it is not widely used. The vehicle, resident, and real estate registration functions are in operation and they are widely used in most parts of the city because of their convenience (Phu, 2003; Sang, 2008).

The GAIS project has achieved the initial objectives of revenue generation, better government image and services (Phu, 2003). The three core applications – the vehicle, resident, and real estate registration systems – have all generated revenue for the government through their respective services. On top of these three applications, the electronic approval system and the government homepage have contributed to better government image and services (Phu, 2003).

3.2. The Challenges of the GAIS

In the subsequent section, the challenges of the GAIS will be discussed in the light of the six categories mentioned in the literature review above, i.e.: infrastructure development; law and ICT policy; management; equity issues; the digital divide; and privacy and security.

3.2.1. *Infrastructure Development*

The telecommunication and ICT infrastructure of Cambodia has remained severely underdeveloped due to financial constraints, lack of technical equipment and know-how, and the fact that the government prioritizes support for other sectors (Moa, 2007; Sang, 2008).

The United Nations' Global e-Government Readiness Report put Cambodia in 139th place among the 182 countries surveyed in 2008 for the e-Government readiness index, which is a composite index comprised of the web measure index, the telecommunication infrastructure index, and the human capital index (United Nations, 2008). The e-readiness index trend for Cambodia indicates that the development of the telecommunication and ICT infrastructure there has been slow (see Figure 2) (United Nations, 2008).

Cambodia received a score of e-Government readiness index only 0.2989, which is below the world average (0.4267); Cambodia ranked eighth of the 11 countries in Southeast Asia (see Table 1) (United Nations, 2008).

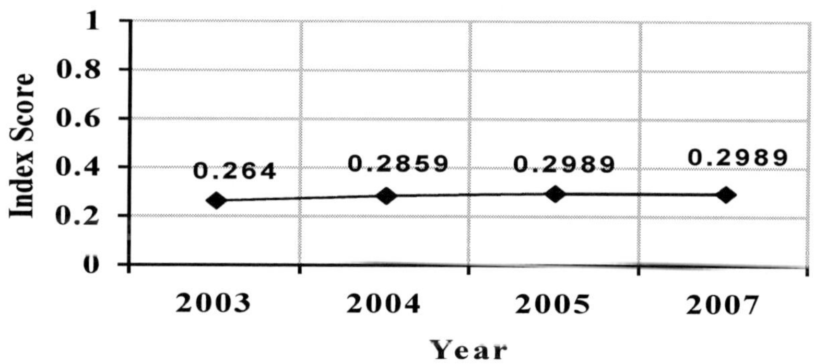

Figure 2. E-Readiness Index Trend for Cambodia.

Table 1. E-Government Readiness for Southeast Asia

Country	2008 Index	2005 Index	2008 Ranking	2005 Ranking
Singapore	0.7009	0.8503	23	7
Malaysia	0.6063	0.5706	34	43
Thailand	0.5031	0.5518	64	46
Philippines	0.5001	0.5721	66	41
Brunei Darussalam	0.4667	0.4475	87	73
Viet Nam	0.4558	0.3640	91	105
Indonesia	0.4107	0.3819	106	96
Cambodia	0.2989	0.2989	139	128
Myanmar	0.2922	0.2959	144	129
Timor-Leste	0.2462	0.2512	155	144
Lao PDR	0.2383	0.2421	156	147
World	0.4514	0.4267		

As shown in Table 2, Cambodia received a low score on the infrastructure index (0.0118); such a score is the main technical obstacle to adopting e-Government.

Table 2. E-Government Readiness for Cambodia

Web measure index	Infrastructure index	Human capital index	E-Government readiness index
0.1973	0.0118	0.6907	0.2989

The infrastructure index is a composite index of five primary indices relating to a country's infrastructural capacity as they relate to the delivery of e-Government services (United Nations, 2008). These are: Internet Users/100 persons; PCs/100 persons; Main Telephone Lines/100 persons; Cellular Telephones/100 persons; and Broadband/100 persons.

For the web measure index, which is based on a five-stage model known as emerging, enhanced, interactive, transactional, and connected, Cambodia obtained a score at only 0.197. This figure is below the world average which is 0.354 (United Nations, 2008).

From the figures above, it indicates that the basic challenge of e-Government development in Cambodia is due to the slow development of the telecommunication and ICT infrastructure.

3.2.2. Law and ICT Policy

In Cambodia, there is a lack of clear legal status for the government functioning, regulations, laws for online transactions (Moa, 2007). It has not yet developed well-defined ICT policies or strategies. There are only a few policies and laws related to ICT in Cambodia (see Table 3) (NiDA, 2003).

Table 3. Policy and Legal Framework Related to ICT Sector in Cambodia

Policy and Laws related to ICT	Status	Owner
ICT policy	In draft	NiDA
Royal decree on the establishment of NiDA	In effect	NiDA
Telecommunication sector policy statement	In effect	MPTC
Law on telecommunication	In draft	MPTC
Sub-decree on the creation of Telecom Cambodia as public enterprise	In effect	MPTC
Sub-decree on the creation of Telecommunications Regulator of Cambodia	In draft	MPTC
Law on electronic commerce	In draft	Ministry of Commerce
Policy and strategies on ICT in education	In effect	Ministry of Education, Youths and Sports
Law on copyright and related rights	In effect	Ministry of Commerce
Law on protection of patent, utility models and industrial designs	In effect	Ministry of Industry, Mine, and Energy
Law on trademarks and acts of unfair competition	In effect	Ministry of Commerce

In 2000, though the formation of NiDA - which currently has five divisions: infrastructure, policy, human resource development, enterprise, and content and applications - was initially intended to formulate ICT policy for short, medium and long-term development (NiDA, 2003), this responsibility clearly overlaps with the Ministry of Posts and Telecommunications of Cambodia (MPTC), which has resulted in conflict and confusion (Miyata, 2006). This conflict and confusion, however, has impeded the formation of ICT policies which is one of the key factors for the promotion and development e-Government in Cambodia.

Compared to ICT sector development in its neighboring countries and most other LDCs, Cambodia's ICT sector is developing at a slower rate due to a lack of decisive and progressive government action towards implementing a modern telecommunication and ICT policy and regulations, which in turn stems from a lack of progressive knowledge and expertise in the government teams in this rapidly growing field (Brian and Naomi, 2008) as well as from the conflict and confusion between NiDA and MPTC.

3.2.3. Management

The GAIS was implemented with total participation from each individual ministry, the state secretariats and the Phnom Penh municipality through its representative/s in the working group with the NiDA Secretariat as the focal point (Phu, 2003). This leads to some conflict among stakeholders, including design, platform, technology, role and participation (Sang, 2008). In addition to these conflicts, it is hard to retain government information technology staff due to uncompetitive pay and employment conditions as compared to the private sector organizations. This leads to a lack of public sector skills and qualified staff which are necessary conditions for the implementation and development of e-Government.

3.2.4. Equity Issues

In Cambodia, as in the study of e-Government for developing countries by Gant (Gant, 2008), widely held beliefs are evolving through various cultural norms that leave many women feeling that the Internet is more appropriate for men to use (Gant, 2008). Moreover, literacy, language and vocational skills create access barrier for many women (Gant, 2008). Most women tend to have less access to schooling in general. Relatively few women only participate in small numbers in vocational or college/university programs in computer science, information science, or other related fields in comparison with men (Gant, 2008). In addition, most of content of the Internet is dominated by English, which limits the extent to which women are attracted to go online. Consequently, many women in LDCs are falling behind in building specialized knowledge about ICTs (Gant, 2008).

3.2.5. The Digital Divide

The greatest challenge to maximizing the potential of e-Government in Cambodia is associated with the digital divide. According to Cambodia's Opportunity Index (OI) (Brian and Naomi, 2008), which uses 10 indicators to measure ICT capital (network infrastructure), ICT skills, ICT uptake or usage, and the intensity of ICT usage, grew from 20 in 2001 to 29 in 2005 – a growth rate of 42 percent. In 2005, Cambodia ranked 164th out of 183 countries. At first glance the growth rate might seem good. However, the speed at which ICT is developing throughout the world indicates that Cambodia is developing more slowly than most. To compare Cambodia with her neighbors (Brian and Naomi, 2008) : from 2001 to 2005 Myanmar's OI grew from 9 to 19 (ranking 177th), Lao PDR's OI grew from 24 to 39 (ranking 151st), Vietnam's OI grew from 44 to 77 (ranking 111th), and Thailand's OI grew from 75 to 99 (ranking 87th). The growth rates during these five years for Myanmar, Lao PDR, Vietnam and Thailand were 112 percent, 49 percent, 76 percent and 32 percent, respectively. Cambodia's ICT growth rate is lower than that of all of its neighbors except Thailand whose OI is three times that of Cambodia.

Access to ICT Infrastructure. In Cambodia computer penetration is virtually non-existent outside the capital city of Phnom Penh and outside major provincial towns. The limitation of the penetration of computers is because of the fact that computer operating systems and applications are not in Khmer (the Cambodian language), there is minimal Khmer content, non-availability or not reliable or expensive electricity and the cost of a computer is too high for most families (Moa, 2007).

Beside a low computer penetration, access to the internet – an essential prerequisite for the use of e-Government – is still limited in Cambodia. In 2007, the total internet subscribers were around 15,950 (see Table 3) (Moa, 2007).

Table 3. Internet Subscribers in Cambodia

Internet: Total of around 15,950 subscribers
Dialup service: 7,500 subscribers
Broadband services: - ADSL/Leased internet: 6,500 subscribers (8 companies) - Wireless broadband: 1,950 subscribers (6 companies)

The obstacles to Cambodian people accessing th einternet are due to the high price of the Internet in comparison to the income level of the people, inadequate infrastructure and lack of electricity, limitation of knowledge of computers and the internet for Cambodians, lack of local Khmer content on the internet, and the limitation of knowledge of foreign languages for Cambodians (Moa, 2007; Sang, 2008).

Access to Education and Skills. Since the GAIS has introduced the latest technology to Cambodia, it has shown that there existed capacity gaps between the NiDA Secretariat, all ministries and the Phnom Penh municipality (Phu, 2003). Indeed, the literacy rate of Cambodia is among the lowest in the region. According to the 2007/08 United Nations Development Program (UNDP) Human Development Report (HDR) (UNDP, 2008), the literacy rate for Cambodians aged 15 and over is 73.6 percent; within this figure, males and females account for 84.7 percent and 64.1 percent respectively. This literacy rate is a major concern for the development of e-Government in Cambodia.

Access to Information Media. Access to most computing tools, and to most internet and web content and services, requires some level of English literacy. Unfortunately, very few Cambodians can read English, which severely limits the number of people who can take advantage of ICT tools, content and services (Phu, 2003).

3.2.6. Privacy and Security

Though e-Government in Cambodia is still in the infancy stage, privacy and security is also one of the main challenges as the Cambodian citizens are wary about the government collecting their personal information such as health, education, employment, property ownership, income, and other sensitive matters and are even more concerned about it sharing that information.

Another concern is that cyber crime is quite a new phenomenon in Cambodia and the country is yet to adopt a law on anti-cyber crime (Moa, 2007). Moreover, the lack of human resources, experience and technology is the main factor in hindering the investigation process and limits the effectiveness of the operation on cracking down on cyber crime (Moa, 2007).

4. POLICY IMPLICATIONS

The challenges will remain the dominant issues in implementing the GAIS in Cambodia unless the issues and challenges highlighted above can be addressed and appropriate policies and strategies put in place. Policy and strategy implications for the success of e-Government implementation in LDCs like Cambodia are as follows:

4.1. Infrastructure Development

The poor infrastructure is the basic key challenge to e-Government implementation that must be addressed, i.e., telecommunication infrastructure will have to be upgraded and extended to where there is none right now. The government should develop projects that are compatible with its telecommunication infrastructure (InfoDev, 2002). Even with few financial resources, creative solutions can be found. The satellite revolution holds considerable promise for Cambodia in this regard (Moa, 2007). Wireless technology, such as cellular telephony, is already making a difference in some parts of the continent, and this could be exploited for the success of e-Government. Moreover, the government should introduce telecom competition and lift regulations on wireless and other digital technologies to accelerate their deployment (InfoDev, 2002).

4.2. Law and ICT Policy

In the case of Cambodia, in order to overcome the challenges of the lack of ICT policy due to the overlap between the MPTC and NiDA, the government should redefine the role of the MPTC and NiDA, i.e., NiDA's role is to promote and develop ICT while MPTC's role is the policy maker, regulator and operator of ICT and telecommunications. These will become a mechanism to create and promote the regulatory and ICT policy environment for the use of ICT and e-Government in particular.

In addition, the government needs to give legal status to online publication of government information and clarify laws and regulations (e.g. a legal digital signature, cyber crime protection, and authentication and security policies) to allow electronic filings with government agencies (InfoDev, 2002).

4.3. Management

The conflicts among stakeholders include political issues, design, platform, technology, role and participation, which can be tackled through the establishment of a high level steering committee (for resolving the political issues which may arise along the way or some conflicts of ministerial interests) and the establishment of a technical working group level (for resolving some conflicts in the design, platform, technology, role and participation among stakeholders) (Phu, 2003). Moreover, it is very important to hold regular meetings between e-Government policy leaders and the affected workforce so employees are active participants in the process (InfoDev, 2002). Furthermore, some workshops need to be conducted during the design and the implementation phases to resolve conflicts that might arise. Conflicts should be put to the workshop for comment and to find the best possible resolution acceptable by all (Phu, 2003).

To overcome the challenge with the higher turnover rates of government information technology staff, the government should develop an overall strategic compensation package to retain them in the workplace. These compensation packages such as: 1) put them in the right job; 2) provide them with the opportunities for international training through various forms of international co-operation; 3) provide them with some fees for the transportation and 4) allow them to have some part-time jobs.

4.4. Equity Issues

To be able to actively participate and benefit from government public services for anyone, at anywhere and anytime, and to prevent marginalization or the economic gap from widening and create a further burden on the society, the government should provide training in new skills on how to access or to acquire such services to vulnerable groups, such as women and children (Phu, 2003). Those new skills include how to use the computer to access government services and a good command of the English language to access the abundant content on the internet to improve their daily lives (Phu, 2003). Moreover, it is very important to localize the training content. It provides a unique opportunity to all Cambodians to acquire new knowledge without the difficulty of learning a new language. Localization is very important and necessary for women to be able to acquire new skills and to build their capacity (Phu, 2003).

4.5. The Digital Divide

To narrow the gap of the digital divide it is very important to implement an access-base policy. This policy is as follows.

Access to ICT Infrastructure. The government should promote internet access centers and network expansion to reduce the digital divide, particularly in rural areas. In addition to this, the Government should launch low cost computers under the e-Government national program in order to increase PC users. The main objective of this program is to give the opportunity to buy cheap and qualified computers and their complements to Cambodian citizens, especially low-income households. To do this, Cambodia should adopt laws on tax-free customs for computers and their accessories.

Access to Information Media. It is very important to ensure that the content of the government web portals are in Khmer and that interfaces are easy to use (Phu, 2003).

Access to Education and Skills. Information technology education for governmental and non-governmental organizations should be provided, targeting the underserved and remote groups (Phu, 2003). Furthermore, education needs to be structured so as to include ICTs in the early stages, i.e., educational curriculum from primary schools through to universities should include computer training. Women and youth, those left out traditionally, must also be targeted.

4.6. Privacy and Security

Government has a responsibility to provide leadership in developing a culture of privacy protection and security (Lau, 2003). It should provide this leadership through its roles in the development of public policy, as the owner and operator of systems and networks (Lau, 2003). In addition to this, to address the privacy issues, it is important to: 1) educate and train government officials in the importance of privacy; 2) design applications that integrate privacy protection; 3) follow "fair information practices"; 4) minimize the collection and retention of personal information; and 5) limit access to personally identifiable information so that it does not automatically allow employees to tap into databases of personally identifiable information (InfoDev, 2002).

Concerning the security issues, it is important to: 1) designate a senior official responsible for computer security; 2) continually assess systems to make sure that security precautions are being implemented; 3) backup information regularly and store backups in a separate location; 4) keep information collection to a minimum and not disclose personal information without express prior consent when it comes to personal information; 5) provide ongoing training about computer security to employees as well as cyber crime enforcers such as judges, lawyers and police officers and even educators and the general staff of ministries concerned; and 6) evaluate the performance of system managers in adhering to sound security practices (Moa, 2007; InfoDev, 2002).

In addition, privacy and security concerns need to be addressed through appropriate legislation and regulations (as well as in practice) before e-government initiatives can advance (Lau, 2003).

CONCLUSION

In this study, e-Government challenges in LDCs are grouped into six categories: 1) infrastructure development; 2) law and ICT policy; 3) management; 4) equity issues; 5) the digital divide; and 6) privacy and security. The findings reveal that Cambodia is still facing those six challenges in utilizing ICTs for delivering e-Government services.

The contribution of this study is to provide a literature review foundation for seeking e-Government challenges in LDCs, as it synthesizes much of the current research regarding e-Government challenges. In addition to this, it may serve as a research foundation for e-Government studies in Cambodia since there have been few such studies so far.

From a practical point of view, the findings of this study provide lessons in e-Government implementation to similar LDCs so that they can find the right policies and strategies to overcome those critical challenges for the successful utilization of e-Government services.

This study also has some limitations due to the lack of past research related to e-Government in Cambodia. Meanwhile, there are many directions that this research stream can take in the future. For instance, future research could extend this study by exploring other aspects of the e-Government acceptance and adoption.

References

Basu, S. (2004). "E-Government and Developing Countries: An Overview" *International Review of Law Computer and Technology, Vol. 18, No. 1*, 109-132.

Brian, U. and Naomi, R. ".kh Cambodia", May 2008, Available at: http://www.idrc.ca/en/ ev-127119-201-1-DO_TOPIC.html.

Dada, D. (2006). "The Failure of E-Government in Developing Countries: A Literature Review", *The Electronic Journal on Information Systems in Developing Countries, Vol. 26, No. 7* , 1-10.

Detlor, B., and Finn, K. (2002). *Towards a Framework for Government Portal Design: The Government, Citizen and Portal Perspectives*, Hershey: Idea Group Publishing.

Gant, J. P. (2008). *Electronic Government for Developing Countries*, Geneva: International Telecommunication Union (ITU).

Heeks, R. (2002). "eGovernment in Africa: Promise and Practice" *Working Paper,* Institute for Development Policy and Management, University of Manchester, Manchester, UK.

Heeks, R. (2003). "Most eGovernment-for-Development Projects Fail: How Can Risks be Reduced?" University of Manchester, UK.

Heeks, R. (2006). "Implementing eGovernment: Lessons Learned, Critical Success and Failure Factors", *Working Paper,* Development Informatics Group, University of Manchester, UK.

InfoDev. The E-Government Handbook for Developing Countries, November 2002. Available from: http://www.infodev.org/en/Document.16.pdf.

InfoDev, "E-Government Toolkit and Portal", May 2008, Available at: http://egov.sonasi.com.

Istvan, M. (2006), *Trust in E-Government Service*, Idea Group Inc.

Jaeger P. T. and Thomson, K.M. (2003). "E-Government around the World: Lessons, Challenges, and Future Directions" *Government Information Quarterly, Vol. 20*, 389-394.

Lau, E. (2003). "Challenges for E-Government Development, 5th Global Forum on Reinventing Government" Mexico: Organization for Economic Co-Operation and Development (OECD).

Miyata, M. (2006). "Situational Analysis of ICTD in Cambodia", *UNDP-Cambodia*, Phnom Penh.

Moa, C. (2007). "National Seminar on Internet Governance: Capacity Building in Public Policy of Internet Use for Business Development in Asia and the Pacific, Background Information and Main Consideration", *Telecom Cambodia (TC),* Phnom Penh.

NiDA (2003). "Research Report: Cambodia, E-Policy and Strategy for ICT Development" *National Information Communications Technology Development Authority (NiDA)*, Phnom Penh.

OECD (2003). "The e-Government Imperative" Paris: OECD Publications.

Phu, L. (2003). "Cambodia: The road to e-Governance", *National Information Communications Technology Development Authority (NiDA)*, Phnom Penh.

Sang, S. (2008). "The Influential Factors and Challenges in Implementing e-Government in Cambodia" *Proceeding Third 2008 International Conference on Convergence and hybrid Information Technology (ICCIT'08)*, IEEE Computer Society *Vol. 2*, 973-979.

Schware, R. and Deane, A. (2003). "Deploying e-Government Programs: The Strategic Importance of 'I' before 'E' ", *The Journal of Policy, Regulation and Strategy for Telecommunications, Vol. 5, No. 4*, 10-19.

Song, H.J. (2006). *E-Government in Developing Countries: Lessons Learned from Republic of Korea*, Communication and Information (CI) in Asia, UNESCO.

Tapscott, D. (1996). *The Digital Economy*, New York: McGraw-hill.

The Economists, "The Next Revolution: After E-Commerce, Get Ready for E-Government", May 2008, Available at: http://www.economist.com/l.cgi?f=20000624/index_survey.

UNCTAD, "The Digital Divide Report: ICT Diffusion Index", May 2008, Available at: http://www.unctad.org/Templates/webflyer.asp?docid=6994andintItemID=2068andlang=1.

UNDP, "Human Development Reports: 2007-2008", May 2008, Available at: http://hrdstats.undp.org/countries/data_sheets/cty_ds_KHM.html.

UN-OHRLLS, "Least Developed Countries: Country Profiles", May 2008, Available at: http://www.unohrlls.org/en/ldc/related/62/.

United Nations (2008). *UN E-Government Survey 2008: From E-Government to Connected Governance*, New York: United Nations.

World Bank, "Definition of E-Government", May 2008, Available at: http://go.worldbank.org/ M1JHE0Z280.

Yeo, G.K., et al. (2004). *ICT and Our Society*, Singapore: McGraw-Hill.

In: Information and Communication Technologies…
Ed: Almas Heshmati and Sun Peng ISBN 978-1-60876-671-0

Chapter 15

REVIEW OF TRADE POLICY AND ITS EFFECTS ON CHINA'S ECONOMIC GROWTH

Peng Sun[♣]
LiaoNing Entry-Exit Inspection and Quarantine Bureau of China
and Seoul National University

ABSTRACT

This study starts with a comprehensive literature investigation on the background of international trade theory, empirical studies of trade effects on economic growth and policies both in developed and developing countries. Then it focuses on the effects of instruments of trade policy, such as tariff, quota, and subsidy. The evolution of China's trade policy from the 1950s up to 2007 is also discussed, as well as the reform of the Chinese trade regime. WTO accession, which represents a new milestone in China's trade evolution, also provides China with the opportunity to share more and more advantages in the world market.

Finally, it provides a better understanding of the static and dynamic benefits from international trade which resulted from the reform of trade policy in China. It is found that China's specialization in assembly trade has given rise to a highly competitive and internationalized manufacturing sector, which has been the main channel of technology transfers, while the traditional export sector has lagged behind. The implication of policy and conclusions are drawn, concerning the determinants of China's trade regime as well. The future international trade patterns of China need to be adjusted to the change in the global market and domestic economic development.

Keywords: International trade policy, China, economic growth.

[♣] E-mail: sun_peng@temep.snu.ac.kr ; waterbrothersun@hotmail.com

1. Introduction

Economic growth is one of the most important objectives for economic study. Human beings have long been exploring ways to increase wealth. Marxist economics, neo-classical economics, development economics, growth theory and endogenous growth theory are no exception to exploration of the eternal problem: How to attain the goal of an increase in wealth and economic growth? Of course, as time changed, economic growth theory has evolved alongside it. Early in the closed economy, the major task is the accumulation of domestic elements which are primary land, labor, capital and other traditional factors of production. With the development of productivity and globalization, a country's economy is closely associated with external factors. In an open economy, the theory of economic growth is more concerned about the effects of openness on a country's economy.

International trade, as a major factor of openness, has made a more and more significant contribution to economic growth. It is defined as the exchange of capital, goods, and services across international borders or territories. In most countries, it represents a significant share of GDP. While international trade has been presented throughout much of history, its economic, social, and political importance has been on the rise in recent centuries. As a whole, international trade is one of the major sources of economic revenue for any nation that is considered a world power. Without international trade, nations would be limited to the goods and services produced within their own borders. As shown in a great number of studies many analysts believed that openness and ratios of international trade volumes were positively correlated with economic growth (Parikh and Stirbu, 2004).

International trade policy is the policy that governments adopt towards international trade with a number of different actions including taxes, subsidies and limits on trade volume or value. The policy of free trade and trade protection policy are the general principles. The adoption of a compromise between the two policies depends on national economic and social status. Developed countries have tended towards the policy of free trade, which brings efficiency with global specialization, but developing countries have always adopted some policies of trade protection at the initial stage of their openness for the promotion of domestic infant industry. In this paper, the effect of different trade policies on economic growth will be introduced. Implications will be drawn from the case study of Chinese trade policy evolution.

China's international trade has experienced rapid expansion together with its dramatic economic growth which has made the country target the world as its market. With fast growth China has become the No.3 economic entity in the world and ranks second in terms of international trade. Through international trade China achieved high growth rate of GDP, accompanied by enormous inflow of hard currency, increase in employment and advancement of technology. Chinese trade policy, which changed over time and imposed different effects on economic growth, will be introduced as well as the recommendation for its further development.

The organization of this study is as follows. In the second part of this paper, the international trade theory and empirical studies of trade effects on economic growth will be introduced. The various trade policies and instruments across countries and time are reviewed in the third part. In the fourth part a clear evolution of China's trade liberalization from protection to opening will be discussed, as well as exceptional trade performance. In the last two parts, the policy implications and conclusions will be reached respectively, according to the previous analysis.

2. LITERATURE REVIEW

With the emergence of the cross-border exchange of goods, people began to pay attention to the effects of international trade on economic growth. At first, international trade surplus was regarded as a source of national wealth. In 1776, Adam Smith, who was a strong advocate of free trade polices, first raised the point of absolute advantages and international specialization. Then, the Ricardian theory of comparative advantage, the international trade theory of Max, the factor-proportions theory of Heckscher-Ohlin and the engine effect theory of Ragnar Nurkse, etc. demonstrated the positive effects of international trade on economic growth to different degrees. Some economists, however, held opposing ideas. The theory of immiserizing growth and the terms of trade deterioration, which were so popular in the fifties and sixties, led to a pervasive application of the import substitution policy in so many developing countries. Moreover, some other scholars promoted the theory that assumed international trade is not the determinant factor of economic growth compared with endogenous factors, such as domestic consumption.

2.1. Theories of Trade For Economic Growth

2.1.1 Mercantilism is an economic theory originating in 15th century that holds that the prosperity of a nation is dependable upon its supply of capital, and that the global volume of trade is "unchangeable." Economic assets or capital, are represented by bullion (gold, silver, and trade value) held by the state, which are best increased through a positive balance of trade with other nations. Mercantilism suggests that the ruling government should advance these goals by playing a protectionist role in the economy, by encouraging exports and discouraging imports, especially through the use of tariffs. John Hales, William Stafford and Thomas Mun are the representative figures of Mercantilism. The main policies under Mercantilism can be listed as following: 1) bullion export forbidden, 2) trade monopoly, 3) export incentive and import limitation, and 4) manufacturing industry bias policy

Mercantilist ideas were the dominant economic ideology of all of Europe in the early modern period and most states embraced it to a certain degree. In the initial time of primitive accumulation of capital, the contribution of Mercantilism was significant. However, Mercantilism has its inherent defects such as: 1) That only bullion is regarded as the wealth under Mercantilism is rather superficial, 2) Mercantilism assumed that trade is the source of wealth. This is against the theory that production creates wealth and 3) Mercantilism regards trade as a "Zero Sum Game", which means that during international trade one country gains at the cost of another one. This neglects the effect of trade which can improve both participants' welfare. Finally, 4) the Free trade model is not applicable under mercantilism due to its strong barriers to trade.

2.1.2 Absolute advantage refers to the ability of a particular country to produce a particular good with fewer resources than another country. The idea of absolute advantage is generally attributed to Adam Smith who advocated free trade policy and international specialization. A country has an absolute advantage over another in producing a good, if it can produce that good using fewer resources than the other country. The benefits to nations from trading are contributed by specialization, which allows resources to be used more productively. Consequently, international specialization results in the increase of productivity with expansion from domestic market to global market and pushes the economy to develop at a high speed.

The positive effect of absolute advantage theory lies in the profound explanation of international trade by the productivity difference of countries. Free trade can bring benefits to both the participants, but the assumption that opportunity cost is constant is not reliable and it failed to explain the inter-trade between developing countries whose goods are inferior.

2.1.3 Comparative advantage refers to the ability of a country to produce a particular good at a lower opportunity cost than another country. Comparative advantage explains how trade can create value for both parties, even when one can produce all goods with fewer resources than the other (Krugman and Obstfeld, 2006; Hu S.G. et al, 2007). The net benefits of such an outcome are called gains from trade. Comparative advantage was first described by Robert Torrens in 1815 in an essay on the Corn Laws. He concluded that it was England's advantage to trade with Poland in return for grain, even though it might be possible to produce that grain more cheaply in England than Poland. However the term is usually attributed to David Ricardo who explained it in his 1817 book *On the Principles of Political Economy and Taxation*, as an example involving England and Portugal. So countries' specialization is determined by their comparative advantages. Ricardo believed that the laws hindering free trade constituted a burden to the agricultural economy. He supported the idea that free trade leads to an efficient allocation of resources and effective reduction of wage rates which are positively related to economy growth.

Essentially Ricardo's economic stance mirrors Adam Smith's teachings: the market, although imperfect, is best left untouched. Government action only prevents the economy from righting itself. But his theory is assumed on the condition of no movement of labor and resources between countries which is not the case in reality and it failed to explain the trade model between countries with similar comparative advantages.

2.2. Arguments Against Free Trade

2.2.1 The Deteriorating Terms of Trade theory was developed by David Ricardo, who thought that the world was composed of "centre" and "periphery". In the present world trade system the periphery produces primary goods to export to the center, and the centre produces secondary goods to export to the periphery. As technology improves the centre is able to retain the savings, since it can retain higher wages and profits through developed unions and commercial institutions. At the periphery companies and workers are weaker and have to pass on technical savings to their customers in the form of lower prices. The decline in the terms of trade between industrialized and non-industrialized countries, meant peripheral nations had to export more to get the same value of industrial exports. Through this trade system the centre would accrue all the benefits of technology and international trade.

2.2.2 Samir Amin developed the Dependency theory. He thought that because of the introduction of capitalism from outside, Third World economies were weak and national business groups in these countries were unable to launch and sustain industrialization. It is a central contention of the dependency theory that poor states are impoverished and rich ones are enriched by the way poor states are integrated into the "world system." This is based on the Marxist analysis of inequalities within the world system, but contrasts with the view of free market economists who argue that free trade advances poor states along an enriching path to full economic integration. As such, the dependency theory figures prominently in the debate over how poor countries can best be enriched or developed.

2.3. Empirical Study

Empirically there appears to be good evidence that international trade affects economic growth positively through capital accumulation, industrial structure upgrading, technological progress and institutional advancement. In addition, the benefits of international trade are mainly generated from the external environment, appropriate trade strategy and structure of trade patterns.

There are comprehensive empirical studies on the impact of trade on economic growth. Before the 1960s, the study on trade effects was limited to some specific countries. With the development of econometrics, many complicated methods based on mathematical models were introduced to analyze the interactive effect between trade and economic growth.

The OECD (2003) focused on the effect of trade level on the average income per population and got the result that the elasticity of international trade is 0.2 and statistically significant.

Maizels (1963) discussed the positive relationship between international trade and economic development by a rank correlation analysis among 7 developed countries. Kavoussi (1984) considered 73 middle and low-income developing countries and found a strong relationship of higher rate of economic growth with higher rates of export growth. He showed that the positive correlation between exports and growth holds for both middle- and low-income countries but the effects tend to diminish according to the level of development. Balassa (1986) and Dollar (1992) argued that outward-oriented developing economies really achieve much more rapid growth than the inward-oriented developing ones. Sachs and Andrew (1995) constructed a policy index to analyze economic growth rate and found that the average growth rate in the time period after trade liberalization is significantly higher than that in the period before liberalization.

Kraay (1999) investigated whether firms "learn" from exporting using a panel data of 2105 Chinese industrial enterprises between 1988 and 1992 and found "learning" effects are most pronounced among established exporters. Keller (2001) discussed the international trade contributed to the diffusion of technology by importing intermediate goods with a high quality. Most empirical studies supported the positive effect of openness on the improvement of total factor productivity. Through technology diffusion international trade could increase the absorbing capacity of trading countries and result in technology advancement (Krugman and Obstfeld, 2006).

3. Trade Policy and Instrument

3.1. Trade Policy

International trade policy is the policy that governments adopt toward international trade with a number of different actions including taxes, subsidies and limits on trade volume or value. It depends on the country specification and period. Each country has its own distinctive history and issues. When applying trade policy, these differences should be taken into consideration. Generally speaking, a country with a heavy reliance on an external economy would like to introduce a policy favoring export sectors. Similarly, a country with a strong power in the economy would like to implement a free trade policy across the world.

3.1.1 Trade policy in developed countries. From a perspective of history, we could find that most developed countries experienced trade policy evolution in the following sequence: export promotion in the Middle Ages, Trade Protectionism in the era of early capitalism, free trade combined with Trade Protectionism in the time of laissez-faire capitalism, ultra protective trade policy during the monopoly capitalism time, trade liberalization between WWII and the 1970s and New Trade Protectionism nowadays. The free trade policy advocated by developed countries is not purely free. While advocating a free trade policy, developed countries are most likely to protect their domestic industries by some less obvious means, such as non-tariff barriers.

3.1.2 Trade policy in developing countries. Most developing countries, which were colonies or semi-colonies of developed countries before, are located in Asia, Africa and Latin America. After WII the developing countries were struggling to develop industrialization with a diversified trade policy from primary goods export promotion, import substitution to export substitution.

After WWII many developing countries promoted their export sectors to outflow primary goods with low labor costs, which helped to accumulate foreign reserves and enhance the ability to develop their industries. However, due to fluctuating world prices and the control of developed countries, primary goods export promotion resulted in a diminishing return of capital and deteriorating trade terms.

Import substitution refers to an inward-oriented development strategy which was favored by so many developing countries in the early 1960s. During that time, many developing countries attempted to accelerate their development by limiting the imports of manufactured goods to foster a manufacturing sector serving the domestic market. Import substitution plays a positive role in the acceleration of industrialization and expansion in employment, but due to the strong protection, the substitution industry is often criticized for its lack of efficiency. Without global competition the use of resources by domestic industries is inefficient and with the strong reliance on the intermediate goods imported from developed countries the trade balance deteriorates.

To avoid the negative effect of import substitution from the 1960s many countries, including China, Singapore, Korea, Brazil, Mexico, Thailand and etc, changed their trade policy from inward-oriented to outward-oriented by promoting an export substitution policy. Manufactured goods, as the substitution of primary goods, accounted for the main component in exports. Many countries promoted their manufacturing sectors by tariff reduction, export subsidies, favorable tax policies, and primary resource allocation. Export substitution policies encouraged more and more developing countries to join the global specialization with their comparative advantages, which resulted in gains of both static and dynamic benefits from international trade. However, the heavy reliance on the global market brings an adverse effect to the domestic economy. The financial crisis in 1997 serves as a good example. In addition, the bias promotion for certain industries led to the unbalanced development of the industry structure, which in turn resulted in the restriction of national economic growth.

3.2. Trade Instrument

Trade instrument refers to a number of different actions adopted by the government of a certain country towards international trade which has specific taxes on some international transactions, subsidies for other transactions, legal limits on the value or volume of particular imports, and many other measures. By the application of different trade instruments, a country can conduct various trade policies.

Tariff, which serves as the main and simplest trade instrument, is a tax levied when a goods is imported. Specific tariffs are levied as a fixed charge for each unit of goods imported, while ad valorem tariffs are taxes that are levied as a fraction of the value of the imported goods. By imposing a tariff the domestic producers of a good gain, because a tariff raises the price they receive; the domestic consumers lose for the same reason. There is also a gain in government revenue. On one hand there is an efficiency loss, which results from the distortion in the incentives facing domestic producers and consumers. On the other hand there is a term of trade gain, reflecting the tendency of a tariff to drive down foreign export prices. In the case of a small country that cannot affect foreign prices, however, the second effect is zero, so that there is a unambiguous loss (Krugman and Obstfeld, 2006).

The analysis of tariff can be readily adapted to other trade policy measures, such as export subsidies, import quotas, and voluntary export restraints. An export subsidy causes efficiency losses similar to a tariff but worsens the terms of trade by lowering the price of the export in the foreign market. Import quotas and voluntary export restraints differ from tariffs in that government gets no revenue. Instead, what would have been government revenue accrues as rents to the recipients of import licenses in the case of a quota and to foreigners in the case of a voluntary export restraint.

4. Overview of Chinese Trade Policy and Performance

China's international trade has experienced rapid expansion as well as a speeding economic growth rate. With the target of the world market China has successfully converted from an inward-oriented country to an outward-oriented country. International trade, as a main factor of the domestic economy, plays an important role in driving economic growth. China's international trade policy stance has shifted dramatically several times since 1949, the year of the establishment of the People's Republic of China. Since then China has experienced evolution periods, such as dependence on the Soviet Union, absolute isolation, and opening doors to the world. An inspection of China's trade policy history and current performance could help to get a better understanding of how the country has been transformed from an isolated economy to a highly open society with rapid growth.

4.1. Evolution of China's International Trade Policy

4.1.1 The initial phase (Before 1978) In the 1950s, the decade after the establishment of the Republic, China experienced an international trade pattern with high dependence on the Soviet Union due to the American coastal blockade and shortages of food in urban areas. Practically China at that time needed the alliance with the USSR to protect the nation and to build domestic industry. With the trade policy in favor of the USSR, international trade in this period was mainly conducted with the USSR and other socialist countries. China's imports consisted mainly of capital goods, such as heavy machines and equipment during the 1950s, while it exported primary raw materials including agricultural and mineral products. In 1950 China's trade volume was only 1.135 billion Yuan and it was ranked 17th in the world.

Wang (2007) pointed out that the 1960s was a period of isolation and emerging pragmatism in China's international trade. With the end of dependence on the Soviet Union, China turned the country economically inward and maintained a relatively autarkic approach to development in the next 12 years. During this time, China's international economic agreement and interaction with the rest of the world were at the lowest level in its history. China did, however, import great amounts of grain and other basic consumer goods in the early 1960s due to 3 consecutive years of natural disasters. The import share of consumer goods jumped from 4.3% in 1959 to 44.5% in 1964. In the mean time, China also started to diversify its trade partners. Japan, Europe and Hong Kong became the main trade partners of China with a supply of industrial equipment.

In the 1970s China adjusted its international relationship with the rest of the world. Between 1970 and 1972 relations were normalized with Canada, West Germany and Japan. The US president Nixon also visited China in 1972 and China gained entry into the United Nations in the same year. As political and economic influence increased, Chinese trade expanded dramatically in the following years: The trade between U.S. and China increased from 5 million USD in 1971 to more than 800 million USD in 1973. From then on, the West, mainly including Japan, the United States, Western Europe, together with Hong Kong and Singapore, became China's top trading partners in the following three decades.

In summary before 1978 the planned economic strategy and the inward-oriented policy resulted in the subordinate status of international trade in the Chinese national economy. China conducted minimal trade with the outside world, exporting just surplus raw materials and simple manufactured goods to cover payments for imported goods, including strategic minerals and other necessities not available at the domestic market. In 1950 the total trade volume of China was 1.135 trillion Yuan and it jumped to 13.433 trillion Yuan in 1976. Its rank in international trade, however, dropped from No.17 to No.34, which showed the big gap between China and the world. An import substitution policy, which was oriented to the domestic market, was implemented at that time. The organization of foreign trade was completely controlled by the state through central government. By imposing a high tariff rate and the overvaluation of the exchange rate, China controlled the import sectors very strictly and protected the infant industry in order to promote industrialization. The dominant import substitution policy was carried out to increase the supplies of machinery and equipment, industrial raw materials and intermediate goods to meet its physical production targets for the domestic industry. At that time China mainly imported the means of production, such as steel, chemical raw materials, rubber, machine tools, tractors, vehicles, fertilizer, oil, etc. As for consumer goods, foodstuffs, sugar, cotton and animal and vegetable oils were the primary imports. As for exports, the primary goods accounted for a large amount with the increasing share of manufactured goods.

The planed economy and import substitution policy optimized the export structure by driving the growth of domestic industry at the initial time. A number of national industries were established to promote economic growth. But due to the lack of competition, the optimization of resource allocation could not be achieved and the dynamic benefits from international trade, such as competition effect, efficiency effect and technology improvement effect, made no sense in the economics of Chinese international trade.

4.1.2 Trade reform from 1978 to 2001 There is no doubt that China has conducted trade liberalization since 1978 to a large extent, which is almost unparalleled in the world and China has gained tremendous benefits from its integration into the global trade system. The political line and open-door economic strategy determined by the Third Plenary Session of the Party's 11th Central Committee has initiated a new phase in China's economic relations with foreign countries. Since 1978, with the establishment of the socialist marketing economy and the transition of the economy and society in China, great changes have taken place in the society. The openness of China has been improved, step by step, from coastal cities to inland ones. With the sustained development of the national economy and the increase of the average income, there is a great need for international trade which accounts for a more and more significant contribution to economic growth.

Deng Xiaoping's policy of opening up to the outside world induced a steady increase in China's trade with the world (Wang, 2007). Under this strategy the system of foreign trade planning was gradually dismantled in the 1980s, and the framework of a decentralized, market-oriented system was gradually established.

One of the most significant reforms was the diversification of trading rights. During the pre-reform period, trading rights were exclusively limited to a small number of specialized foreign corporations. In the 1980s and 1990s, a great number of other companies were authorized to conduct foreign trade. The growth of companies which were authorized to conduct international trade from 1986 to 2001 (Figure 1) was rapid. Within 5 years the number of authorized companies in China has increased by 30 times.

In the perspective of the import regime China was devoted to reducing the trade barriers and enhancing its openness to the world. At the beginning in the early 1980s tariffs on many products were set to block the flood of foreign products into the Chinese market. Chinese government canceled its import substitution list in the 1980s to encourage the market mechanism to achieve effective resource allocation with less intervention from government. The initial tariff was set at the high rate of 56% in 1982.

In the following two decades, China launched a massive tariff cut at least ten times, reducing the average tariff rate to 15% in 2001 and below 10% in 2007 (Figure 2). In the meantime, a broad array of non-tariff barriers, such as licenses and quotas, were reduced massively.

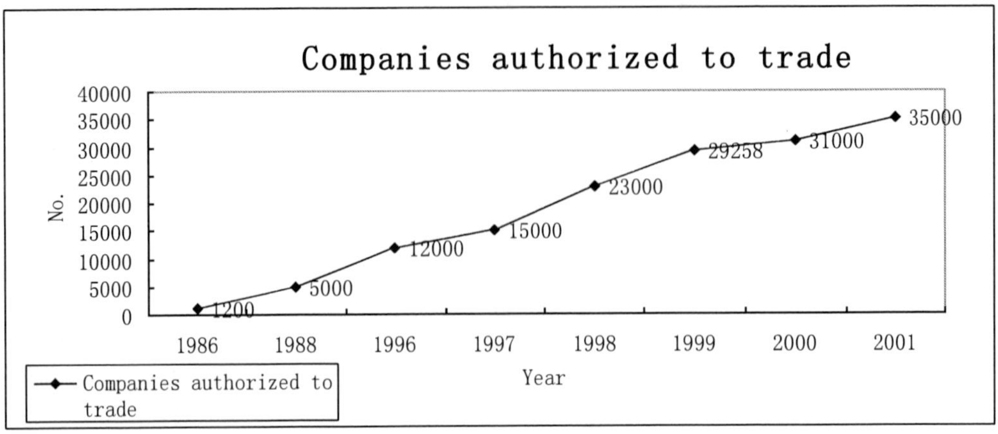

Figure 1. Companies Authorized to Trade.

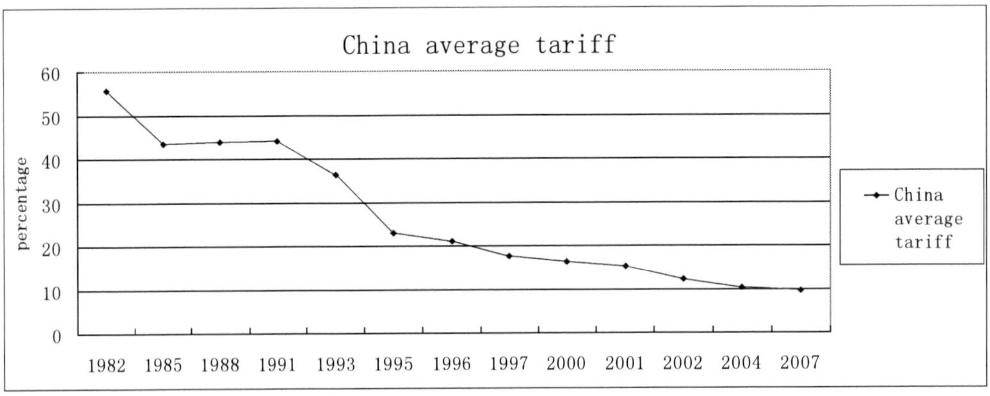

Figure 2. China Average Tariff.

The export quota was reduced from 227 (in 1992) to 66 (in 2001) and the import quota from 53 (in 1992) to 33 (in 2001) respectively. After the relaxation of pervasive and complex import and export controls in the 1980s, the value of imports exceeded that of exports as a result of the promotion of domestic manufacturing industry by importing capital goods. During 1989-1992, the demand for imports fell below that of exports.

4.1.3 WTO Accession (from 2001) After 15 years of endeavor, China formally became the 143rd member of the WTO at the 4th WTO Ministerial Meeting held in Doha, capital of Qatar on December 11, 2001. Entering the WTO was a strategic decision made by Chinese government under the condition of economic globalization, marking a new stage of China's opening-up. With its huge political influence, a giant economy and its status as a top global trader, China's accession to the WTO will help to strengthen and improve the multilateral trade system, promote world economic and trade development, and establish a new, open and just international economic order.

To meet the requirements for joining the WTO China started to modify and improve laws and administrative regulations, including foreign trade and economic cooperation, in 1999. Laws and regulations not in compliances with WTO regulations were revised or nullified. By the end of 2001 relevant departments of the State Council had revised 2,300 related laws and regulations and a list of 221 administrative regulations annulled by the State

Council had been published. In 2001 the National People's Congress of China (NPC) revised the Copyright Law, Trademark Law, and Law on Joint Ventures with Chinese and Foreign Investment. Together with the Law on Chinese-Foreign Cooperative Ventures, Law on Foreign-funded Enterprises and Patent Law revised in 2000, China had revised six laws directly related to China's WTO entry.

The tariff reductions planned by China in the context of its WTO accession are the continuation of a longstanding trend. This trend is reflected in the decreasing level and dispersion of tariffs and the continued reduction in NTBs, especially since the early 1990s. On January 1, 2004, China lowered its average tariff rate by 0.6 percent to 10.4 percent and in 2007, the average tariff rate was below 10%. In the meantime, China agreed to eliminate import quotas, licenses, designated trading practices and other non-tariff barriers.

In contrast with the continuity in tariff reductions, China's commitments on trade in services represent a milestone. Plans include the opening of key service sectors where foreign participation was previously nonexistent or marginal, such as telecommunications, financial services and insurance. In those sectors, full access will eventually be guaranteed to foreign providers through transparent and automatic licensing procedures. China will also remove restrictions on trading and domestic distribution for most products.

Increased overseas market access is the most immediate benefit from WTO accession for China. China is permanently granted most-favored-nation (MFN) treatment by other WTO members, a significant step toward normalizing its trade relations. Also, upon accession, several trading partners eliminated many of their restrictions on imports from China. Easier access to foreign markets is likely to boost China's labor-intensive exports in a number of sectors, including electronics. In particular, China's WTO accession will lead to the removal of quotas against its textiles and clothing exports. It is expected that this removal will generate a significant boost to China's exports.

China will also benefit from the treatment of future trade conflicts within the multilateral dispute settlement procedures under the WTO (Rumbaugh and Nicolas, 2004). This should help China better promote its trade interests, benefit from greater reciprocity in trade conflict resolution, and limit the scope for other WTO members to unilaterally impose antidumping protection against its products.

However, China's accession protocol incorporates provisions that could constrain its export market gains in the coming years, with respect to textiles and clothing. It allows other WTO members to impose restraints on any type of Chinese exports (embracing industrial goods, including textiles and apparel, and agricultural goods) if a surge causes or threatens "market disruption" to domestic producers, the threshold will be made lower than that required by ordinary safeguard measures under the WTO rule, and will be available for twelve years after China's accession.

4.2. China Trade Performance

China's international trade has expanded steadily since the opening of the economy in 1978. Exports and imports have grown faster (Figure 3) than world trade for more than 20 years and China's share in global trade has increased steadily since 1979 (Figure 4).

With broader trade reforms and its export promotion policy, China has maintained a sustained a trade surplus from 1994 till now, which contributed to the accumulation of large amounts of foreign reserves (1.68 trillion $ in 2008 Aug).

Since the reform of 1978, the outward-oriented policy improved economic growth and international trade expansion. Nowadays China has achieved an average 10% GDP growth rate, and a 15% international trade expansion rate. China became the No.2 trading nation ranked after the US. The dependence on foreign trade, however, has increased dramatically from 17.4% in 1984 to 65.7% in 2007, which indicates the increasing reliance on the external economy (Figure 5).

China's overall trading structure has experienced obvious changes with the rapid growth of foreign trade (Lemoine and Deniz, 2004). As for ordinary and processing exports, China's foreign trade expansion has relied mainly on processing operations with the share of more than 50%.

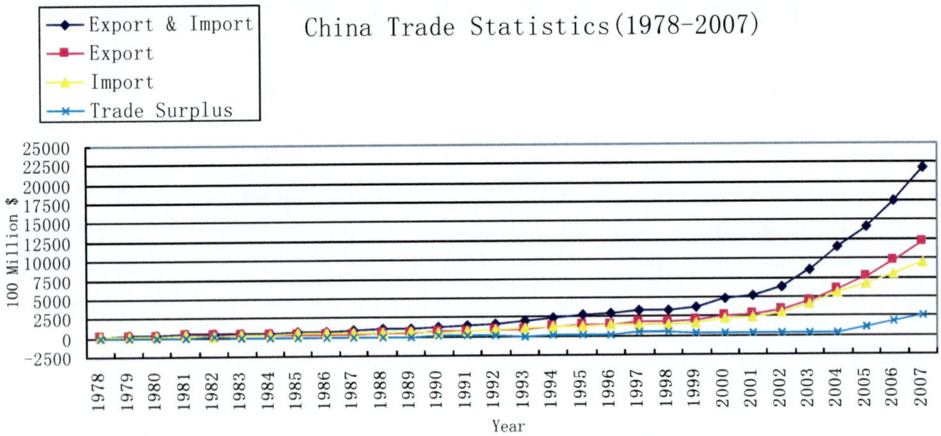

Figure 3. China Trade Statistics (1978-2007).

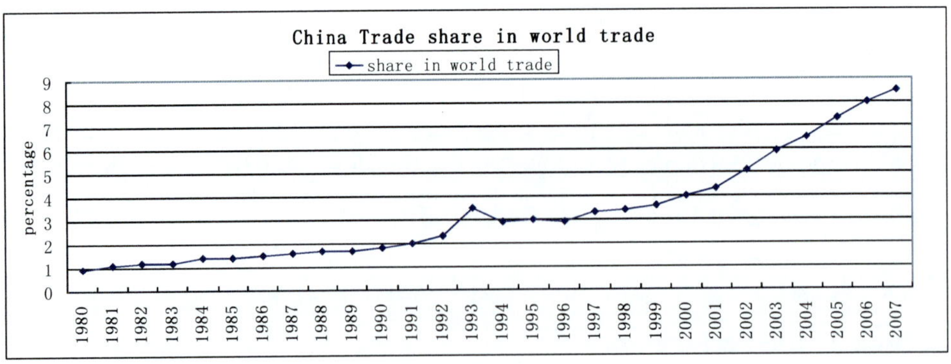

Figure 4. China Trade Share in World Trade.

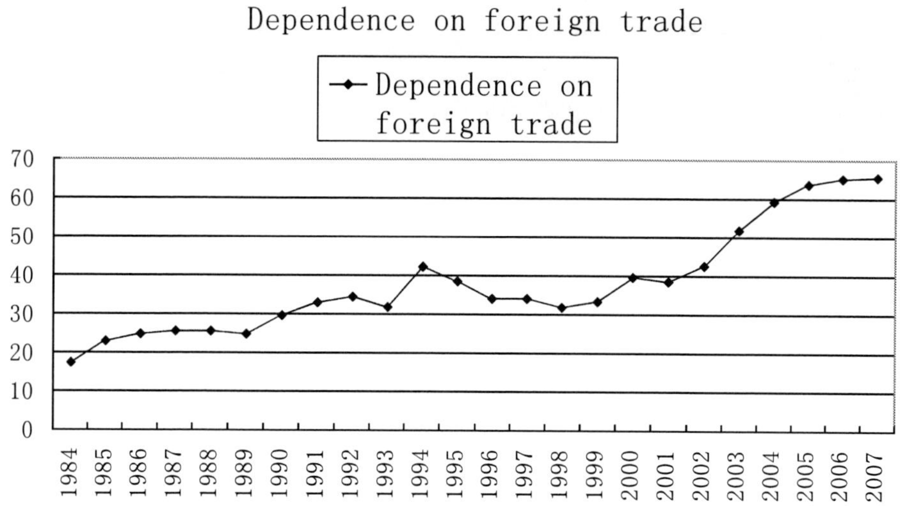

Figure 5. Dependence on Foreign Trade.

Table 1. China's Foreign Trade by Customs Regimes (in percentage)

Year	Total Export	Ordinary Export	Exports after processing	Other Export	Total Import	Ordinary Import	Imports after processing	Other Import
1992	100	51.40	46.60	2.00	100.00	41.70	39.10	19.20
1993	100	47.10	48.20	4.70	100.00	36.60	35.00	28.40
1994	100	50.70	46.50	2.80	100.00	33.20	41.10	25.70
1995	100	47.90	49.50	2.60	100.00	32.80	44.20	23.00
1996	100	41.60	55.80	2.60	100.00	28.30	44.90	26.80
1997	100	42.70	54.50	2.80	100.00	27.40	49.30	23.30
1998	100	40.40	56.90	2.70	100.00	31.10	48.90	20.00
1999	100	40.60	56.90	2.50	100.00	40.50	44.40	15.10
2000	100	42.20	55.20	2.60	100.00	44.50	41.10	14.40
2001	100	42.00	52.10	5.90	100.00	46.60	38.60	14.80
2002	100	41.83	55.26	2.91	100.00	43.74	41.40	14.86
2003	100	41.54	55.19	3.27	100.00	45.47	39.48	15.05
2004	100	41.06	55.28	3.66	100.00	44.21	39.50	16.28
2005	100	41.35	54.66	3.99	100.00	42.37	41.52	16.11
2006	100	42.95	52.67	4.37	100.00	42.08	40.62	17.30
2007	100	44.22	50.71	5.07	100.00	44.84	38.55	16.62

Source: China Statistical Yearbook.

The import of ordinary goods has also experienced an increase since 1992 (Table 1). As for primary and manufactured goods, in 1980 primary goods accounted for 50.3% of total exports, while manufactured goods accounted for 49.7%. In 2007, primary goods' share was only 5.1%, while manufactured goods increased their share to a dominant level of 94.9% (Table 2).

Table 2. China Export Structure (in percentage)

Year	Primary Goods	Manufactured Goods	Machinery Goods	High-tech Goods
1980	50.3	49.7		
1981	46.7	53.3		
1983	43.3	56.7		
1984	45.6	54.4		
1985	50.5	49.5	6.1	
1990	25.6	74.4	17.9	
1995	14.4	85.6	29.5	6.8
1998	11.2	88.8	36.2	11.0
1999	10.2	89.8	39.5	12.7
2000	10.2	89.8	42.3	14.9
2001	9.9	90.1	44.6	17.5
2002	8.7	91.3	48.2	20.8
2003	7.9	92.1	51.9	25.2
2004	6.8	93.2	54.5	27.9
2005	6.4	93.6	56.0	28.6
2006	5.5	94.5	56.7	29.0
2007	5.1	94.9	57.6	28.6

Source: China Statistical Yearbook.

Table 3. China Import Structure

Year	Primary Goods	Manufactured Goods	Machinery Goods	Percentage High-tech Goods
1980	34.8	65.2		
1985	12.4	87.6	43.6	
1990	18.5	81.5	40.2	
1995	18.5	81.5	44.8	16.5
1998	16.4	83.6	45.6	20.8
1999	16.2	83.8	46.8	22.7
2000	20.8	79.2	45.7	23.3
2001	18.8	81.2	49.5	26.3
2002	16.7	83.3	52.7	28.1
2003	17.6	82.4	54.5	28.9
2004	20.9	79.1	53.8	28.8
2005	22.4	77.6	53.1	30.0
2006	23.6	76.4	54.0	31.2
2007	25.4	74.6	52.2	30.0

Source: China Statistical Yearbook.

Thanks to technology advancement and innovation incentives, from the 1990s the export share of electromechanical products and high-tech goods increased at a high speed, which indicated the transformation of China's trade structure from labor intensive industry to capital and technology intensive industry. Similar to exports, from the 1990s the share of capital and technology imports demonstrated an increasing trend (Table 3). China's trading structure changed from primary products to light-industry and textile products in the early 1990s and to machinery and electronic goods with high tech now.

We could divide China's main export into 4 groups according to their factor intensity. PP, LT, MT and HT refers to primary products, low-tech products (labor intensive products), medium-tech products (capital intensive products), and high-tech products (technology intensive products). Table 4 and Figure 6 show the main export share in China's trade volume and world trade volume. The primary and labor intensive goods demonstrate a significant declining trend while the capital and technology intensive goods show a strong increasing trend.

Table 4. China Export Share

Year	Share in China Trade				Share in World Trade			
	PP	LT	MT	HT	PP	LT	MT	HT
1978	60.0	32.0	5.2	1.3	1.9	3.0	0.4	0.2
1985	55.0	33.5	7.4	2.8	5.3	9.9	1.4	1.0
1993	16.2	57.6	15.4	10.1	5.9	29.1	5.3	4.3
1998	12.5	49.4	17.7	19.4	7.1	32.5	7.5	8.0
2006	11.6	30.5	19.0	33.7	4.1	20.2	6.6	20.1

Source: China Statistical Yearbook.

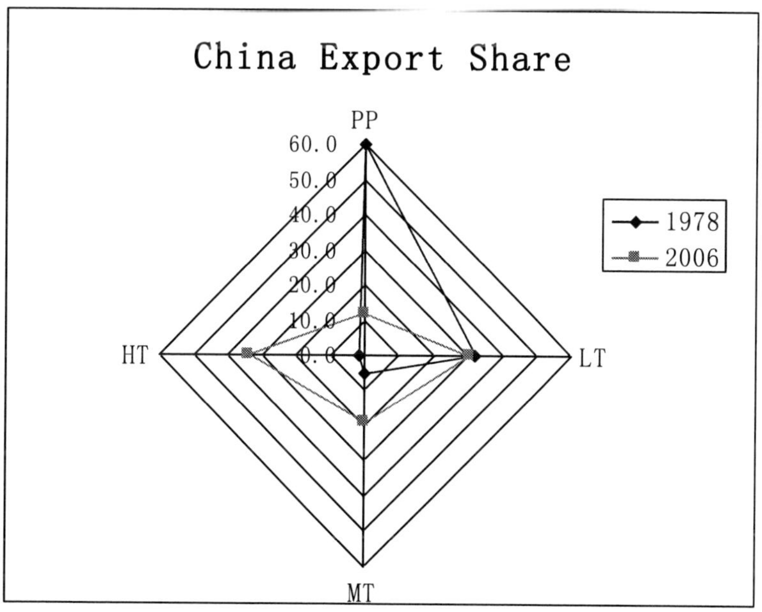

Figure 6. China Export Share.

We can also find more information from the TCI index which reflects the competitiveness of exported goods as a flowing function:

$$TCI = (X_i - M_i)/(X_i + M_i) \quad (1)$$

where Xi and Mi refer to export and import in a certain industry. This index shows the competitiveness of export goods from -1 to 1. -1 indicates the zero export and infant industry protection phase and 1 signifies the zero import and industry mature phase. If TCI is below 0, exports are less than imports and vice versa. Figure 7 shows the TCI of the main exported goods from 1980 to 2006. The TCI of primary goods increased to its peak at 0.47 in 1985 and dropped dramatically after that, which reflects the decreasing export and increasing import of primary goods.

Labor intensive goods maintain a high stable competitiveness level across time until 2002 when there is a slight drop. Capital and high technology goods show a relatively low level of competitiveness before 1990, but an obvious rise after that, which shows the potential catch-up capacity. With the background of fast growing high-tech trade, the competitiveness of high-tech goods is becoming more and more important for economic growth. Table 5 shows the high-tech products share in the exports and imports of China. We can find a significant rising trend in the high-tech goods in both the export and import sectors. The TCI of high-tech goods is shown in Table 6. The index number was negative before 2004 with an increasing trend and reached 0.049 in 2006, which indicates the increasing competitiveness in high-tech goods.

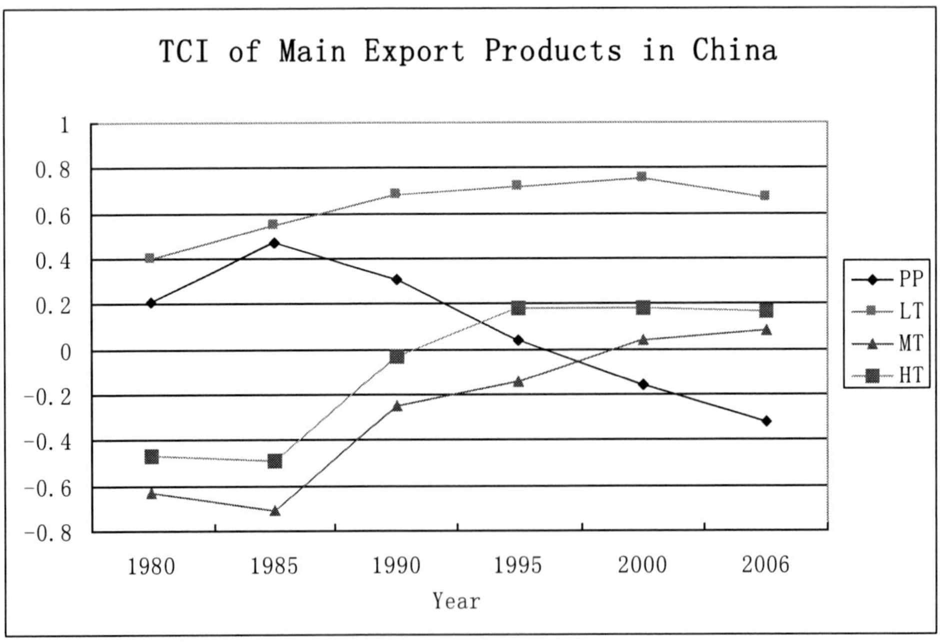

Figure 7. TCI of Main Export Products in China.

The indices of Computers and telecommunications, Life science technologies, Opto-electronics, and Biotechnology goods are positive, but still under development, while the TCI in other high-tech industries, such as Computer-integrated manufacturing and Electronics, are still negative, which shows a heavy reliance on imports.

Arora and Vamvakidis (2004) discussed the effects of trading partner on economic growth. They indicated that industrial countries benefit from trading with developing countries, which have a rapid growth, while developing countries gain benefit from trading with developed countries, which have relatively high incomes.

Table 5. National Imports and Exports of High-tech Products

100 million $

	2001	2002	2003	2004	2005	2006
Exports of high-tech products	464.5	678.6	1103.2	1653.6	2182.5	2814.5
Share in total exports (%)	17.5	20.8	25.2	27.9	28.6	29.0
Share in industrial manufactured exports (%)	19.4	22.8	27.3	29.9	30.6	30.7
Imports of high-tech products	641.1	828.4	1193.0	1613.4	1977.1	2473.0
Share in total imports (%)	26.3	28.1	28.9	28.7	30.0	31.2
Share in industrial manufactured imports (%)	32.4	33.7	35.1	36.3	38.6	40.9

Source: Web of the Ministry of Science and Technology.

Table 6. TCI of High-tech Products in China

	1999	2000	2001	2002	2003	2004	2005	2006
Total	-0.207	-0.173	-0.160	-0.099	-0.039	0.012	0.049	0.065
Computers and telecommunications	0.073	0.134	0.211	0.323	0.390	0.458	0.492	0.522
Life science technologies	-0.071	-0.091	-0.139	-0.130	-0.101	-0.079	0.010	0.105
Electronics	-0.474	-0.536	-0.614	-0.639	-0.649	-0.614	-0.609	-0.567
Computer-integrated manufacturing	-0.829	-0.835	-0.835	-0.852	-0.834	-0.842	-0.777	-0.745
Aerospace	-0.695	-0.587	-0.786	-0.771	-0.759	-0.729	-0.721	-0.688
Opto-electronics	0.064	0.027	-0.048	-0.024	-0.096	0.083	0.354	0.267
Biotechnology	0.425	0.369	0.431	0.136	0.288	0.339	0.307	0.249
Materials	-0.647	-0.427	-0.653	-0.731	-0.711	-0.548	-0.534	-0.520
Other technologies	-0.436	-0.641	-0.443	-0.270	-0.468	-0.029	0.206	0.163

Source: Web of the Ministry of Science and Technology.

Zhu (2007) analyzed the China's trade with 26 OECD members and found both intra-industry trade and inter-industry trade are critical in China's international trade patterns. As for China, OECD members remained the major trading partners of China from an early time. The share of relevant trade with OECD demonstrated a slightly drop from 73.3% in 1998 to 65.5% in 2006. The top 10 trading partners of China are shown in Table 7, which indicated that the US is China's primary exporting destination and Japan is the main origin of imports.

China is a huge country which possesses one fifth of the world's population and has a vast territory of some 9.60 million square kilometers with 22 Provinces, 5 Municipalities, 4 Autonomous Regions and 3 Special Administrative Region. However, China's economic growth experienced rapid development with a special characteristic of its regional disparities, as well as its trade performance.

Table 7. Value of Imports and Exports by Country (Region) of Origin/Destination (%)

2007				2006			
Exp Share Rank		Imp Share Rank		Exp Share Rank		Imp Share Rank	
United States	19.11	Japan	14.01	United States	21.00	Japan	14.62
Hong Kong, China	15.15	Korea Rep.	10.85	Hong Kong, China	16.03	Korea Rep.	11.34
Japan	8.38	Taiwan, China	10.57	Japan	9.46	Taiwan, China	11.00
Korea Rep.	4.61	United States	7.26	Korea Rep.	4.59	United States	7.48
Germany	4.00	Germany	4.75	Germany	4.16	Germany	4.79
Netherlands	3.40	Malaysia	3.00	Netherlands	3.19	Malaysia	2.98
United Kingdom	2.60	Australia	2.70	United Kingdom	2.49	Australia	2.44
Singapore	2.43	Philippines	2.42	Singapore	2.39	Thailand	2.27
Russia	2.34	Thailand	2.37	Taiwan, China	2.14	Philippines	2.23
India	1.97	Russia	2.06	Italy	1.65	Singapore	2.23

Source: China Statistical Yearbook.

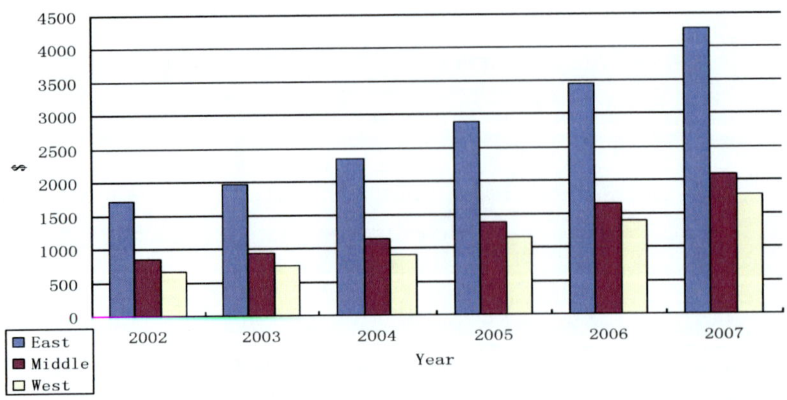

Figure 8. GDP per Capita by Region.

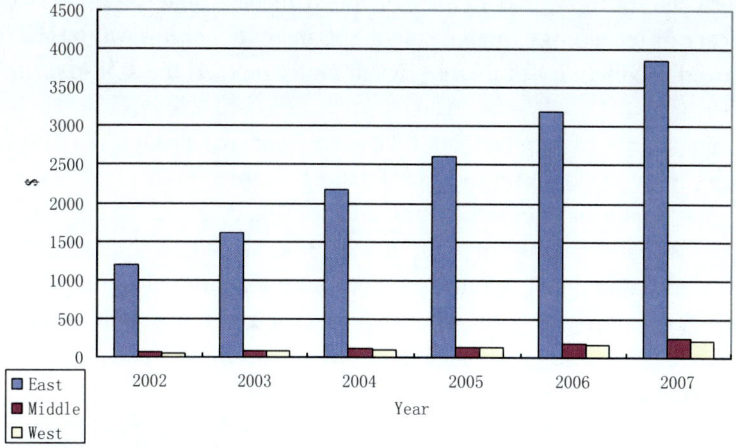

Figure 9. Trade per Capita by Region.

According to Chinese government we could group the Chinese provinces into 3 parts by location and economic development. The East region, which refers to the eastern coastal area, comprising 11 provinces, including ShangHai, GuangDong and JiangSu, is endowed with a more developed infrastructure and technology, and much higher levels of labor force skills due to its favorable geography conditions and for historical reasons. These all helped to attract more foreign investment, technology spillover, and opportunities for international trade, which contributed to its considerable economic growth. As compared with the East region, the Central region, which includes 8 provinces neighboring the East region, and the West region, which covers 12 provinces in the interior western area, are less developed with lower productivity and economic growth rate. Figure 8 shows that the GDP per capita varies from the eastern region to the western side.

Figure 9 describes the different trade per capita among the East, Middle, and West regions of China. The East region shows a relatively larger amount both in GDP per capita and trade per capita compared with the Central and West regions.

4.3. Trade Contribution to China's Economic Growth

China's integration with the global economy has contributed to sustained growth in its economy. China has joined the global specialization in the industries with comparative advantages. With the adequate supply of skilled labor at a low cost, China mainly exported labor intensive goods at the initial time to get enough hard currency to import capital-intensive and high-tech intensive products, which promoted domestic industrialization. Through international trade, not only the static benefit, but also the dynamic ones, such as competition effect and upgrade of industry structure have been obtained by China.

Exports play an important role in China's industrialization. Before 1992, the static benefit of international trade was brought in by the expansion in employment and the accumulation of a great amount of foreign reserves. After that, with the implementation of an outward-oriented strategy and the deepening of market mechanism reform, more dynamic benefits from international trade have been induced. The competition effect, scale economy effects and efficiency effects are more and more developed in the Chinese export sectors. Thanks to the advancement of technology, management and institutional innovation, Chinese export enterprises improved productivity to a large extent and promoted the spill-over across sectors.

Imports, as the main source of capital and high-tech intensive products, provided a continuous and adequate supply to domestic industrialization. Before 1992, under the policy of import substitution, the foreign hard currency gained by primary goods exports was the main source for import production means. Imports at that time played an important role in driving economic growth and after 1992, with more and more capital and high-tech goods imports, technology transformation was brought to Chinese conventional industries. Most domestic enterprises achieved technology advancement through learning by doing, imitation and innovation which resulted from the dynamic effects of international trade.

From the perspective of dynamic benefits, international trade also helped to improve the industry structure upgrade in China. The industry structure decides the trade structure. With the deepening of industrialization, manufactured goods account for the main share of exports. Previous analyses show that China's industry structure, which varies according to the change of resource endorsement and external market demand, shifted from primary products to manufactured products and from labor intensive products to capital and technology intensive products. With the global market provided by the integration of the world, China conducted its industrialization successfully.

In addition, international trade advanced technology development dramatically. Firstly, technology imports are the main driving source of domestic innovations. Without technology trade and a large amount of investment in R&D, a company like Lenovo (previously known as Legend), which became large and profitable enough to purchase IBM's personal computer business, would never have come into being. Also the spillover and learning by doing effects are also associated with the dynamic benefits from trade. Thirdly, fierce competition in the world market forced every participant to reach the technology frontier to be more effective and efficient.

Finally, international trade leads to institutional changes. China, as a large country in economic transition, is learning to apply market power more efficiently with less intervention from government. Through international trade, not only goods are traded by countries, but also ideas on market mechanisms. Especially with joining the WTO China should fulfill its commitment to the international rules in world games which surely will bridge the gap between China and the world.

5. Policy Implication

In light of the study of Chinese trade above, the conclusion that foreign trade exerts a great positive effect upon China's economic growth could be drawn. China, however, is facing some serious problems, such as degradation of its trade structure, deterioration of the terms of trade, the negative impact of trade on the environment, and trade friction with partners. All of them impose a negative impact on the sustainable development of China's foreign trade. Therefore, to achieve sustained economic growth, China should pay more attention to the proper and appropriate trade strategies and policies.

Firstly, Chinese government should pay attention both to comparative advantage and competitiveness. During the last decades, the abundant labor supply contributed to the rapid economic development in China dramatically. Trade liberalization has strengthened China's specialization in the sectors in which it has a comparative advantage, for example labor intensive industries. The export of labor intensive goods, such as textiles, helped China to take part in the global specialization and gain enough capital goods to develop industrialization. The accelerated expansion of labor intensive industries also helped to contain the rise of unemployment which has become the most serious problem of China's economy since the end of the 1990s. However, the development model, narrowly based on the comparative advantage, could result in the deterioration of the terms of trade. Therefore, in the meantime, Chinese government should take great efforts to help enterprises enhance their competitiveness through incentives in R&D, education and preferential loans. The policy should be adjusted according to the change in the factor endowment and global market structure.

Secondly, the foreign trade structure should be upgraded step by step. On one hand, the production and export of high-pollution, high-energy-consumption, low-value-added, and labor-intensive goods should be reduced and high-tech, environmentally-friendly, high-value-added goods should be promoted for export by incentives from government, such as tax deductions and currency policies. On the other hand, Chinese government should carry out policies focusing on the regional gap elimination between the east, central and west regions of China. The production of labor intensive goods could be transferred to the less developed regions, such as the west and centre.

Thirdly, the ability of assimilation and dissemination of domestic firms should be enhanced to a large extent by R&D investment, education, and infrastructure construction. The rise in the quality of human resources will result in the enhancement of innovation creation accordingly. Therefore, Chinese government should also pay a great deal of attention to the innovation and creation ability of each export sector. Through the promotion of the absorptive capability of domestic firms, the competitiveness of Chinese products could be enhanced enormously.

Fourthly, China should take an active part in the global trade rules making and solving trade friction. The multilateral trade rules of GATT/WTO have weakened government administration and interfered with trade and investment powers. The government providing support to domestic industries should know at which point the protection should be terminated, although this is not always easy. However, the rules of global trade play more and more imperative roles in solving the trade friction between countries. Especially after China enters WTO, most enterprises directly face the international market and more frequently apply all kinds of international trade laws than ever. Hence, the decision, still under consideration by the Chinese authorities, to take the initiative to formulate the international trade rules would be another step towards leveling the playing field of global standardization.

CONCLUSION

This study of trade policy and its effects on China's economic growth has amply shown that China's outstanding performance in rapid economic growth can be traced back to its involvement in the global trade market and dynamic trade policy. International trade has been considered as an important factor contributing to China's economic growth. China clearly has embarked on the road of trade liberalization for decades since 1978, when Chinese government began to reduce tariffs, expand trading rights, reform the pricing of traded goods, and adopt market-oriented exchange rate policies. Since the implementation of the opening policy in 1978, China focused on an outward-oriented policy, which encouraged export sectors to join the global specialization. Driven by the domestic and world market, China has achieved the optimization of resource allocation and enjoyed static and dynamic benefits from trade. Consequently, China has experienced a continuous upgrading of the trade structure from primary goods and labor intensive goods exports to manufactured goods and capital or high-tech intensive goods exports during industrialization. WTO accession, which represents a new milestone in China's trade evolution, also provides China with the opportunity to share more and more advantages in the world market. Under these WTO commitments, China has reduced its average tariff rate to below 10% and has also eliminated import quotas, licenses, designated trading practices and other non-tariff barriers considerably.

During the transformation of China's trade liberalization, Chinese government played a vital role in setting economic and industrial policy to grant privileges to exporting firms, guiding foreign investment, designing the pace and sequencing of liberalization and balancing the development of the state-owned sector and the private sector. With globalization, however, it is essential to point out that an industrial policy supporting domestic economic sectors should not be turned into permanent protectionism. On one hand, China could pay more attention to the conventional industries with comparative advantages, such as the textile industry and other labor intensive industries, to help to contain the rise of unemployment and reinforce industrialization. On the other hand, the government should be devoted to increasing the competitiveness of domestic firms by R&D investment, basic education and infrastructure construction which enable them to assimilate and disseminate foreign technologies and to enhance their own innovative capacities. After almost three decades of reform and integration into the world economy, many domestic enterprises and industries should be ready to stand normal competition in both domestic and international markets.

REFERENCES

Arora V. and Vamvakidis A. (2004), How much do trading partners matter for economic growth?, *IMF Working Paper*, 04/26, (Washington: International Monetary Fund).

Balassa B. (1986), Policy responses to exogenous shocks in developing countries, *American Economic Review*, 1986(5) 77.

Dollar D. (1992), Outward-oriented developing economies really do grow more rapidly: Evidence from 95 LDCs, 19761985, *Economic Development and Cultural Change*, 1992 (40) 523-544.

Hu S.G., Men S.L. and Zhang F. (2007), *International Economics*, 2nd Ed, 2007.

Kavoussi R.M. (1984), Export expansion and economic growth, *Development Economics*, 1984(14) 241-250.

Keller W. (2001), Knowledge spillovers at the world technology frontier, *NBER Working Paper*, 8150, 2001.

Kraay A. (1999), Exports and economic performance: Evidence from a panel of Chinese enterprises, *Revue d' Economique du Developpement*, 1999 (1-2),183-207.

Krugman P.R. and Obstfeld M. (2006), *International Economics, Theory and Policy* 7th Ed, Pearson Education, Inc.

Lemoine F. and Deniz U. (2004), Assembly trade and technology transfer: The case of China, *World Development* 2004, Vol.32, 5, 829-850.

Maizels A. (1963), *Industrial growth and World Trade*, Cambridge University Press.

OECD (2003), *The Source of Economic Growth in OECD Countries*, Paris: Organization for economic cooperation and development, 2003.

Parikh A. and Stirbu C. (2004), Relationship between trade liberalization, economic growth and trade balance: An econometric investigation, *HWWA Discussion Paper*, 2004-282.

Rumbaugh T. and Nicolas B. (2004), China: international trade and WTO accession, *IMF Working Paper 04/36 March* (Washington: International Monetary Fund).

Sachs J.D. and Andrew W. (1995), Economic reform and process of global integration, *Brookings Papers on Economic Activity*, 1995(1), 1-118.

Wang J.Y. (2007), The evolution of China's international trade policy: development through protection and liberalization, *Economic Development Through World Trade*, 191-213.

Zhu Z.G. (2007), A gravity model of China's trade flows, *Recent Developments in the Chinese Economy*, 135-172.

In: Information and Communication Technologies... ISBN 978-1-60876-671-0
Ed: Almas Heshmati and Sun Peng

Chapter 16

REGULATORY POLICY FACTORS IMPACTS ON INDUSTRIAL TECHNOLOGY DEVELOPMENT IN NEPAL

Tek B. Ghimire [*]
The Office of the Attorney General of Nepal and
Seoul National University

ABSTRACT

Nepal is one of the least developed countries in the world with a minimal input to national development from its industrial sector. The pace of industrialization depends on the quality and the approaches followed by the nation in its implementation of designated policies. This paper tries to analyze the policy implementation achievement in three major factors that are identified as key factors impacting industrial economics of Nepal. These are intellectual property rights (IPR), foreign direct investment (FDI) and technology transfer. The three factors are both interrelated and interdependent. In this study we provide a descriptive analysis of the available data. This will include the current status of the policies and their implementation, identification of weaknesses in policy implementation. In addition provide recommendations for the way forward in the dealing with the existing problems concerning IPR, FDI and technology transfer in Nepalese context.

Keywords: IPR, FDI, RandD, technology transfer, compatible regulation and codified knowledge.

1. INTRODUCTION

Regulation directly affects the innovative process, while innovation and technical change have significant impacts on regulation (Firth and Mellor, 1999). To be successful, regularity

---

[*] E-mail: teksnu@gmail.com

reform efforts must take into account the linkages between regulation and innovation. There are three types of regulations. Economic regulation is intended to improve the efficiency of markets in delivering goods and services which influences the innovative process. Social regulation protects the environment and the safety and health of society at large and its design can encourage or discourage innovation. Administrative regulation governs the practical functioning of the public and private sectors which set some basic conditions for technological advancement.

The existence of an effective regulator within a stable regulatory environment encourages higher levels of investment. It enables fair competition, and it accelerates the rate at which services are opened to competition (UNIDO, 2002). Regulation can maintain a certain level of openness or competition in product markets which provides the necessary conditions for research and innovation (Mytelka and Smith, 1977). Economic regulation is intended to ensure the efficiency of markets, partly through promoting adequate competition among actors in the market-place. In the social sphere, regulations can place technical demands on industries and act as focusing devices for their research efforts. It aims to promote the internalization of all relevant costs by these actors. Regulations have also spawned the creation of new industries and products as in the case of the "environment industry" (OECD, 1996). Administrative regulation can be said to aim at ensuring the smooth functioning of public- and private-sector operations. It ensures there are fair "ground rules" for all economic actors in the innovative process, as in the case of intellectual property rights protection.

Regulations can have both positive and negative effects on the innovation process. The regulatory process must take into account the effects of regulation on innovation as well as the implications of technical change for the rationale and design of regulations. The regulation-innovation interface is mutual and dynamic. Regulatory decision makers, therefore, must rely on their abilities to understand, predict, and direct technological change (OECD, 1996).

The rest of the study is organized as follows. Section 2 elaborates the technology development sphere. The theoretical model is presented in Section 3. In Sections 4 and 5 intellectual property rights and its protection are discussed. Foreign direct investment, technology transfer and technology licensing are discussed in Sections 6-8. Section 9 is on the impacts of IRPS protection on FDI and technology transfer. Finally, a discussion of the issues of challenges, opportunities and policy recommendation is found in Section 10-11.

2. Technology Development Sphere

There are three inter-related terms in the technology development sphere: research and development (RandD), technology innovation and regulation. Research and development is the most important input for technology development. Regulation widens the financial opportunity to RandD and commercialization of industrial technology products. Regulation often helps to adopt an integrated approach for technology innovation. Fostering competitive markets to promote an efficient supply of good quality of industrial products, the advancement of the next generation technology, and the efficient price of products are the main contributions of regulation to make ample financial opportunity for further development of technology. Finally, financial outcomes of those regulatory functions go to research and development. Regulation prevents abuses of market power, such as with excessive pricing and anti-competitive behavior by dominant firms and suppliers where competitive markets do not exist or fail. In addition regulation promotes confidence in industrial production markets through a transparent regulatory management and licensing process.

3. Theoretical Model

The theoretical model used in this study is illustrated in Figure 1. In this model, the regulatory stimulus is perceived by industry as requiring some change in the nature of industrial production (Ashford and Heaton, 1983).

Regulations (economic, administrative and social) have considerably controlled and regulated different aspects of technology development (LaPierre, 1997). It is believed that, in the absence of government intervention, industries would be characterized by excessive entry, unstable prices, inefficient services, costly technology development, duplication of facilities and inadequate investment in innovation. Regulations are, to some extent, a reflection of the desires of society rather than the narrow interests of an agency administrator. The format and timing of regulations will affect the outcome. Regulations relying on detailed specification standards may leave little room for innovation in compliance (Ashford and Heaton, 1983). Regulatory strictness appears to be the most important factor influencing the extent of the technological response.

Regulated industry comprises those industrial sectors that are legally bound to comply with regulations as well as those so closely related to the legally bound sector that the regulations are effectively imposed on them (OECD, 1996). Governments have regulated some sectors more than others in terms of entry, prices and services due to perceived natural monopolies, the need to correct market failures and the desire to promote universal access to networks.

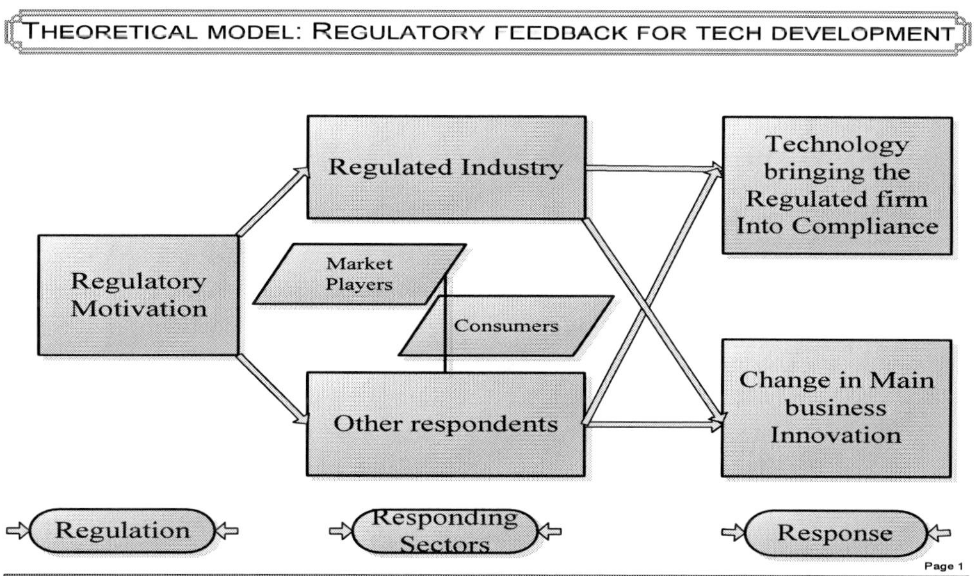

Figure 1. Theoretical Model of regulatory feedback for technology development.

Regulation creates new markets and transforms existing ones, which establishes a set of incentives. The obvious new market created by regulation is in the field of compliance technology. The transformation of existing markets occurs by virtue of requirements that decrease the attractiveness of an existing product or process relative to its potential substitutes. Thus, regulation creates a new competitive environment in which some firms or industries are relatively advantaged and others relatively disadvantaged. In this new environment, some firms may perceive regulation as a market constraint, whereas others will certainly see it as a market opportunity.

4. Intellectual Property Rights

Intellectual property rights (IPR) are the rights awarded by society to individuals or organizations principally over creative work: inventions, literary and artistic works, and symbols, names, images, and designs used in commerce. They give the creator the right to prevent others from making unauthorized use of their property for a limited period. Intellectual property (IP) is categorized as Industrial Property (functional commercial innovations), and Artistic and Literary Property (cultural creations) (IPR Commission, 2002).

IP creates a legal means to appropriate knowledge – one person's use does not diminish another's right to use or right to information. Moreover, the extra cost of extending use to another person is often very low. From the social point of view, the more people use knowledge, the better it is because each user gains something from it at low or no cost, and society is in some sense better off. Economists therefore say that knowledge has the character of a non-rival public good (Stiglitz, 1999). IP means property from original thought protected by law. It is the original creative work manifested in a tangible form that can be legally protected in the form of a patent, trademark and design.

5. Intellectual Property Rights Protection and Technology Development

Intellectual property is codified knowledge which is a stimulus to creation and fosters competition in a healthy way. This is necessary to allow countries to develop their own processes of technological innovation, and to enable them to absorb technologies developed abroad effectively. Strengthening national innovation systems is an important way to address the problem of developing industrial technology either in developing or in developed countries. IP rights can contribute to promoting effective national systems of innovation by giving input to research and development which is a base line of technology development. A strong IPR regime provides economic assistance to RandD. Research and development fosters return investments to technology patenting as an intangible input for process innovation, efficient market management and increasing quantity and maintaining quality of industrial products as well.

5.1 Intellectual Property Rights Regime in Nepal

The evolution of IPR in Nepal dates back to the Patent, Design and Trademark Act 1937. Later the Act was replaced with another Act with the same name in 1965 and it was amended in 1987, 1991 and 2005.

It has been now modified, upgraded and improved for the promotion and protection of Industrial Property with TRIPS agreement compatible (Gyawali and Bhatta, 2006). Even though the new Act is more comprehensive than the earlier one, people are not much more aware about the compliance of intellectual property rights.

5.2. Legal and Policy Structures Relating To IPRs in Nepal

5.2.1. National Instruments and Organizations

1. Patent, Design and Trademarks Act, 1965
2. Industrial policy 1992
3. Foreign Investment and Technology Transfer Act 1992
4. Copyright Act, 2002 and Copyright Rules, 2004
5. Ministry of Industry, Commerce and Supplies
6. Department of Industry (DOI) is full responsible authority for the administration and implementation of Patent, Design and Trademark Act 1965 as well as Foreign Investment and technology transfer Act 1992. DOI also maintains the record of the approved agreements for foreign investment as well as the technology transfer agreements
7. Department of Cottage and Small Industries (DCSI)
8. Nepal Academy of Science and Technology (NAST)
9. Nepal Agriculture Research Center (NARC)
10. Council for Technical Education and Vocational Training (CTEVT)
11. Nepal Copyrights Registrar's office
12. Industrial Enterprise Development Institute (IEDI)
13. Intellectual Property Attorneys
14. Cottage and small Industries Development Board (CSIDB)
15. Federation of Nepal Cottage and small Industries (FNCSI)

5.2.2. International Instruments

1. Trade Related Aspects of Intellectual Property Rights (TRIPS) Agreement 1994 from 2003
2. Paris Act, 1883 from 2004
3. Berne Convention for the Protection of Literary and Artistic Works 1886, form 2006
4. Paris Convention, 1981
5. Besides the instruments above, there are governments, bilateral and multi-lateral organizations involved in technology transfer and the skill development sector. The World Intellectual Property Organization (WIPO) has started to provide support in the examination of national patents before registration. The department of industry sends the patent document to WIPO for examination services. The title to any patent,

design or trademark registered in a foreign country, if not registered in Nepal, shall not be valid in Nepal. However, foreign patents, which are registered in their home country, may be registered directly without any examination process as per the provisions of the Patent, Design and Trademarks Act 1965.

5.3. Patent, Industrial Design and Trade Marks

The duration of the patent in Nepal is for seven years from the date of registration and it can be renewed for two periods of seven years each. The graph shown in Appendix 1 indicates the annual registration pattern of patent in Nepal.

The owner of the design in Nepal has his/her right to the design for a period of five years from the date of registration. It can be renewed for two periods of five years within 35 days of the date of expiry of the registration period. The graph (Figure 3) presented in Appendix 1 indicates the annual registration pattern of design in Nepal.

The registered trademark holder shall have his/her right to the trademark for a period of seven years from the date of registration and it shall be renewed any number of times within 35 days from the date of expiry of the trademark. The graph (Figure 4) shown in Appendix 1 illustrates the annual registration pattern of design in Nepal. An integrated data sheet (annual registration number of patent, trademark and design) is also included (Table 1) in Appendix 1 as resource data for figure 2, 3 and 4.

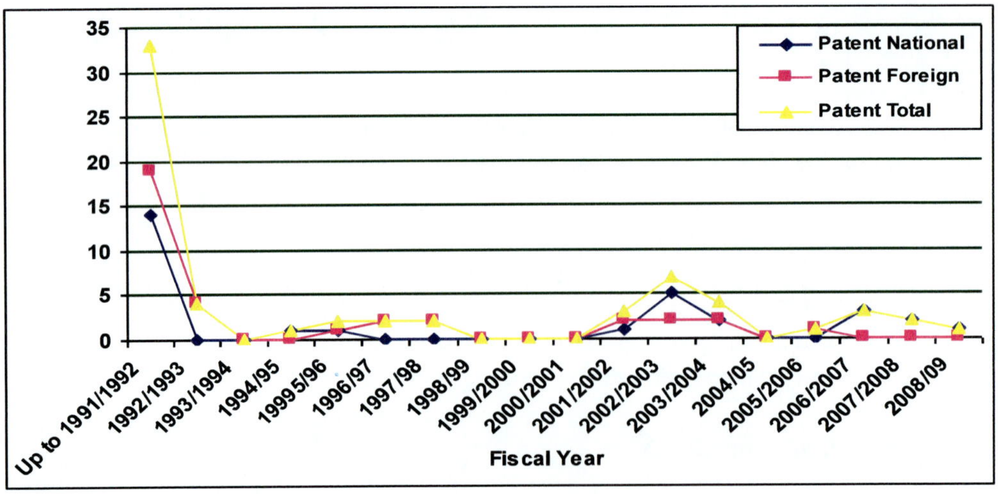

Source: Department of Industry, Government of Nepal.

Figure 2. Annual Registration Pattern of Patent.

5.4. Punishment for Infringement of IPR Regulation

The Patent, Design and Trademark Act had the provision of a nominal fine for breaching IPR rules. After the third amendment of the Act, it increased the punishment and penalty as "fine up to NPR 500,000 (approximately $6,500) depending upon the extent of violation along with confiscation of related goods" if the patent regulation is violated, "fine, up to NPR 100,000 (approximately $1,300) depending upon the extent of violation along with confiscation of related goods" if the trade mark related regulation is violated, "fine, up to NPR 50,000 (equivalent to $650 approx.) depending upon the extent of violation along with confiscation of related goods" if the design related regulation is violated (Patent, Design and Trademark Act, 1965 , third amendment 2005).

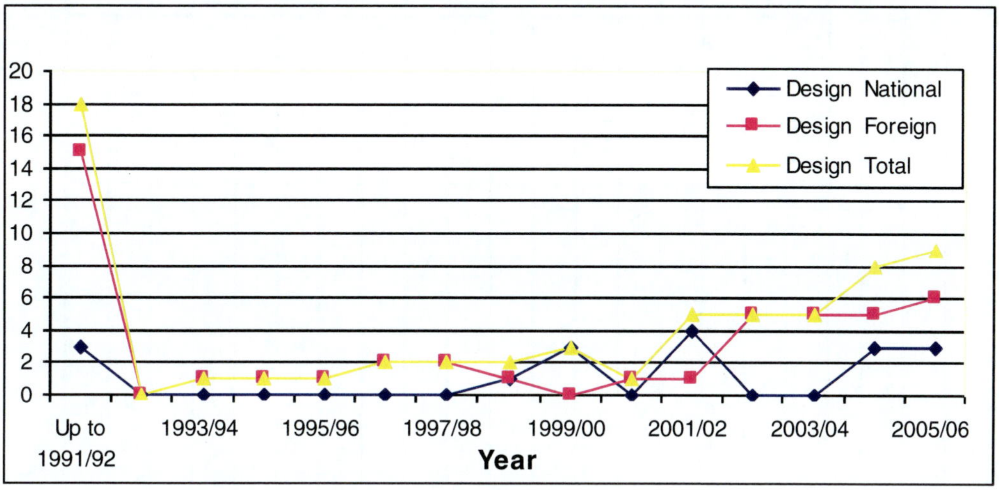

Source: Department of Industry, Government of Nepal.

Figure 3. Annual Registration Pattern of design.

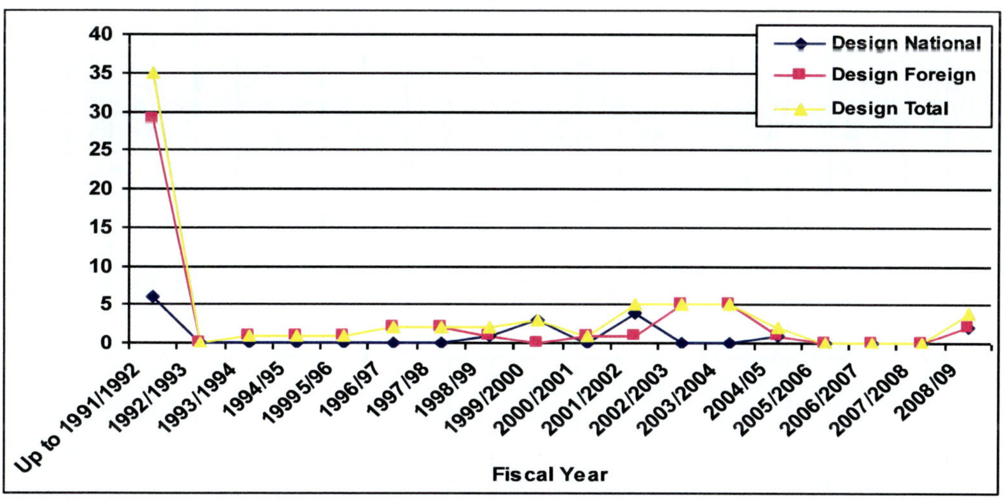

Source: Department of Industry, Government of Nepal.

Figure-4. annual registration pattern of trademark.

Table 1. Integrated data sheet (annual registration number of patent, trademark and design)

Fiscal Year	Trade Mark			Patent			Design		
	National	Foreign	Total	National	Foreign	Total	National	Foreign	Total
Up to 1991/92	4982	3675	8657	14	19	33	6	29	35
1992/93	512	170	682	0	4	4	0	0	0
1993/94	369	244	613	0	0	0	0	1	1
1994/95	393	471	864	1	0	1	0	1	1
1995/96	403	617	1020	1	1	2	0	1	1
1996/97	423	411	834	0	2	2	0	2	2
1997/98	442	377	819	0	2	2	0	2	2
1998/99	429	454	883	0	0	0	1	1	2
1999/00	574	588	1162	0	0	0	3	0	3
2000/01	678	485	1163	0	0	0	0	1	1
2001/02	660	518	1178	1	2	3	4	1	5
2002/03	804	557	1361	5	2	7	0	5	5
2003/04	1255	396	1651	2	2	4	0	5	5
2004/05	949	367	1516	0	0	0	1	1	2
2005/06	609	565	1174	0	1	1	0	0	0
2006/07	585	419	1004	3	0	3	0	0	0
2007/08	420	303	723	2	0	2	0	0	0
2008/09	612	529	1141	1	0	1	2	2	4
Total	15099	11146	26445	30	35	65	17	52	69

Source: Department of industry, Government of Nepal.

Table 2. Number and category of Projects with foreign collaboration in Nepal

Category	Number of Projects	Equity only	Equity + technology	Technology only	Scale		
					Small	Medium	Large
Manufacturing	419	338	39	42	269	98	49
Agro-based	14	13	0	1	9	5	0
Energy based	14	14	0	0	2	1	10
Construction	17	15	2	0	8	5	3
Mineral-based	3	1	1	1	1	0	2
Services	186	176	3	7	141	32	13
Tourism	206	196	6	4	154	22	30
Total	859	753	51	55	584	163	107

Source: Department of Industry, government of Nepal.

Table 3. Budget allocation by the Government on RandD in science and technology

Fiscal year	GNP (in million of Rs.)	RandD (in million of Rs.)	Percentage of GNP
1995/96	254349	686	0..270
1996/97	204899	655	0..327
1997/98	214939	703	0..327
1998/99	225894	752	0..333
1999/00	236771	801	0..338
2000/01	247573	851	0..347
2001/02	258306	901	0.349

Source: RONAST, 1998.

6. Foreign Direct Investment

Foreign Direct investment (FDI) contributes to the development of a host country by increasing the country's investment level beyond what would be permitted by domestic saving alone. In addition, FDI enhances entrepreneurial capability when the foreign firm brings with it some firm-specific knowledge (in the form of technology, managerial expertise, and marketing know-how) that cannot be effectively leased or purchased on the market by the host country. FDI allows new local entrants to learn about export markets; it provides training for workers, and stimulates competition with local firms. The later potential cumulative benefits of FDI can be far greater than the direct benefit in the form of augmenting domestic investment alone (Maskus, 1997). FDI is a flow of long-term capital based on long-term profit considerations that, once, received, is not likely to be quickly withdrawn. Thus, in comparison to portfolio and other types of investment flows, FDI is like to be a relatively stable source of funds (Mytelka and Smith, 2001).

6.1. FDI Policy in Nepal

Nepal opened the door for foreign investment and foreign technology in 1981 with the promulgation of Foreign Investment and Technology Transfer Act and one window policy. This act was replaced by a new policy and Act in 1992 (Pradhan and Rajbamshi, 2006).The Industrial Policy of 1992 identifies foreign investment promotion as an important strategy in achieving the objectives of increasing industrial production to meet the basic needs of the people, create maximum employment opportunities and pave the way for an improvement in the balance of payments. The foreign investment and one window policy aims:

1. To build a strong and dynamic economy by generating additional opportunities for income and employment through expanding productive activities
2. To increase the participation of the private sector in the process of industrialization
3. To increase productivity by mobilizing internal resources and materials in the productive sectors and by importing foreign capital, modern technology, management and technical skills
4. To increase the competitiveness of Nepalese industries in international markets (Industrial policy 1992).

Nepal encourages foreign investment either as joint venture operations with Nepalese investors or as 100 percent foreign-owned enterprises. The broad areas open for foreign investment include manufacturing industries, energy based industries, tourism industries, mineral resource based industries, agro-based industries and service industries.

Foreign investment is expected to supplement domestic private investment through foreign capital flows, transfer of technology, improvement in management skills and productivity and providing access to international markets. In this context, Government is encouraging foreign investment and transfer of foreign technology in Nepal by providing incentives and facilities within a liberal and open policy.

The Act of 1992 opened up foreign investment in all sectors, except in some industries such as defense, cigarettes and alcohol. Development of hydropower was also opened to foreign investment. The Act guaranteed 100 percent repatriation of equity invested, dividends obtained from foreign investment and amount received as payment of principal and interest on foreign loans in convertible currencies. The Act also made provisions for easing visa problems and the settlement of disputes.

The annual inflow of FDI on an amount basis, category of industry basis, scale of industry basis and the present status of industries approved for FDI are shown in Figures 5, 6, 7 and 8 respectively and the Table 4, 5, 6 and 7 are included as resource data of these figures (Appendix 1).

Table 4. Summary sheet of foreign Investment in Nepal- up to F/Y 2008-09

Fiscal year	# of Industries	Total Project Cost	Total Fixed Cost	Foreign investment	Employment
Up to 1989	59	542592	4581. 82	466. 84	10586
1989/90	30	2438.19	2139.6	398.51	9515
1990/91	23	863.56	690.74	406.28	2974
1991/92	38	3508.17	2902.1	597.84	5615
1992/93	64	17836.22	16210.81	3083.67	13873
1993/94	38	3733.23	3175.66	1378.76	4734
1994/95	19	1627.28	1247.85	477.59	2386
1995/96	47	10047.47	9398.54	2219.86	8032
1996/97	77	8559.25	6629.15	2395.54	9347
1997/98	77	5569.38	5142.32	2000.28	4336
1998/99	50	5324.42	4380.17	1666.42	2146
1999/00	71	2669.09	1910.24	1417.61	4703
2000/01	96	7917.62	6122.49	3102.56	6880
2001/02	77	3318.53	1559.59	1209.65	3731
2002/03	78	4923 .74	3775. 86	2764. 82	3572
2003/04	77	4309.65	3762.17	2755.4	2144
2004/05	64	1801.10	1150. 89	1639 .52	5576
2005/06	116	4121.08	3296.95	2606.31	7358
2006/07	188	3425.57	2650.56	3226.79	7389
2007/08	121	2690. 21	2123 .54	2453 .12	5398
2008/09	139	16057	13664.93	7968.10	6604
Total	1549	116217.3	96515.98	44235.47	122165

Source: Department of Industry, Government of Nepal.

Table 5. Number of Industries approved for FDI (by category) up to F/Y 2000-09

Category	No of Industries	Total Project Cost	Total fixed cost	Foreign investment	Total Employment
Agriculture	24	525.85	446.49	175.11	1344
Construction	35	3026.54	2286.36	2355.62	2647
Energy-based	26	26660.42	24947.6	5935.06	5477
Manufacturing	572	42434.76	30765.4	15517.24	69426
Mineral	5	2436.02	1980.70	1634.70	1461
Services	393	21179.05	17558.7	9691.66	22170
Tourism	368	16948.45	16004.6	5490.30	18959
Total	**1423**	**113211.10**	**93989.8**	**40799.68**	**121484**

Source: Department of Industry, Government of Nepal.

Table 6: Number of Industries for FDI (by scale) UP to F/Y 2007-08

Category	Number of Industries	Total project cost (Rs millions)	Total Fixed Cost (Rs millions)	Foreign Investment (Rs millions)	Employment
Large	141	85621.41	75493.92	27694.48	36232
Medium	196	14052.98	10037.37	5408.97	25859
Small	1086	13536.71	8458.58	7696.24	59393
Total	1423	113211.1	93989.87	40799.69	121484

Source: Department of Industry, Government of Nepal.

Table 7. Summary sheet of FDI in Nepal (Status-wise) from the beginning to January 2005

Status	Number	Total Project Cost (Rs. In millions)	Total Fixed Cost (Rs. In millions)	Foreign investment (Rs. In million)
Operational	401	47062.28	39836.57	10892.86
Under construction	33	5373.74	3866.24	1260.97
Licensed	122	13040.53	10388.09	3838.58
Approved	286	13348.05	10213.68	6966.5
Closed	21	1570.46	1329.68	442.67
Cancelled	72	8508.2	7380.43	2280.09
Total	935	88903.26	73014.69	25681.67

Source: Department of Industry, Government of Nepal.

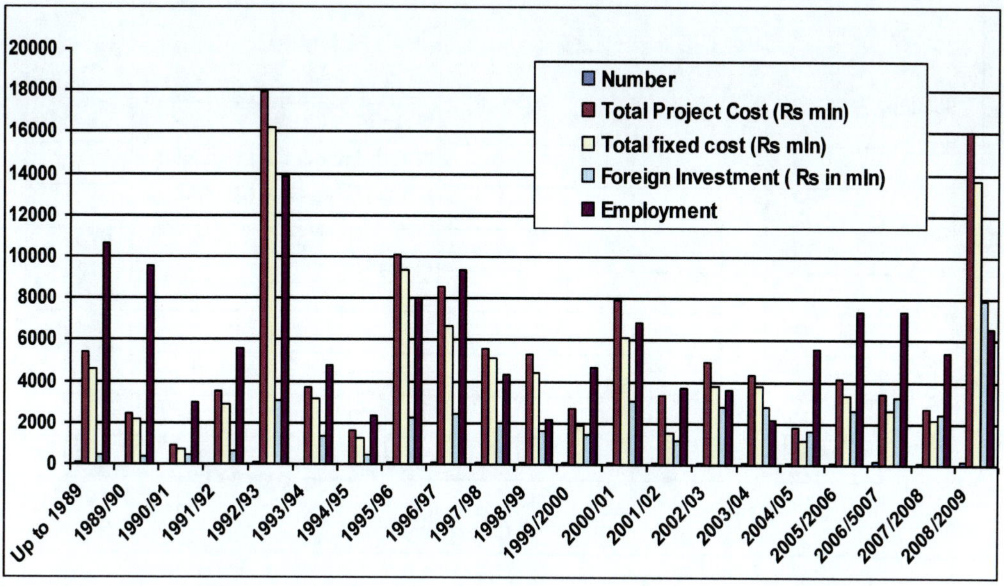

Source: Department of Industry, Government of Nepal.

Figure 5. summary chart of FDI in Nepal (year wise)

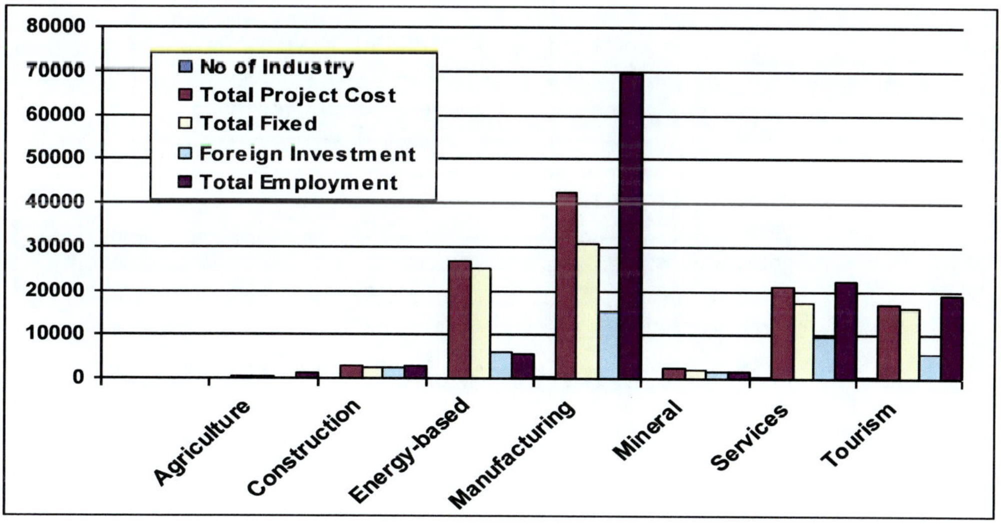

Source: Department of industry, Government of Nepal.

Figure 6. Number of Industries approved for FDI (by category) as of FY 2007/08.

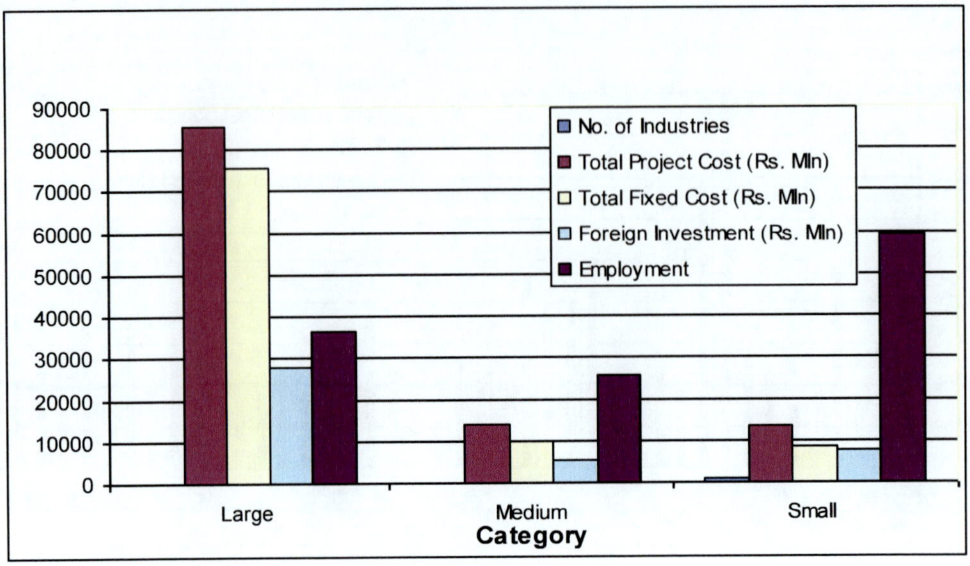

Source: Department of industry, , Government of Nepal.

Figure 7. Number of Industries approved for FDI (scale wise) as of FY 2007/08.

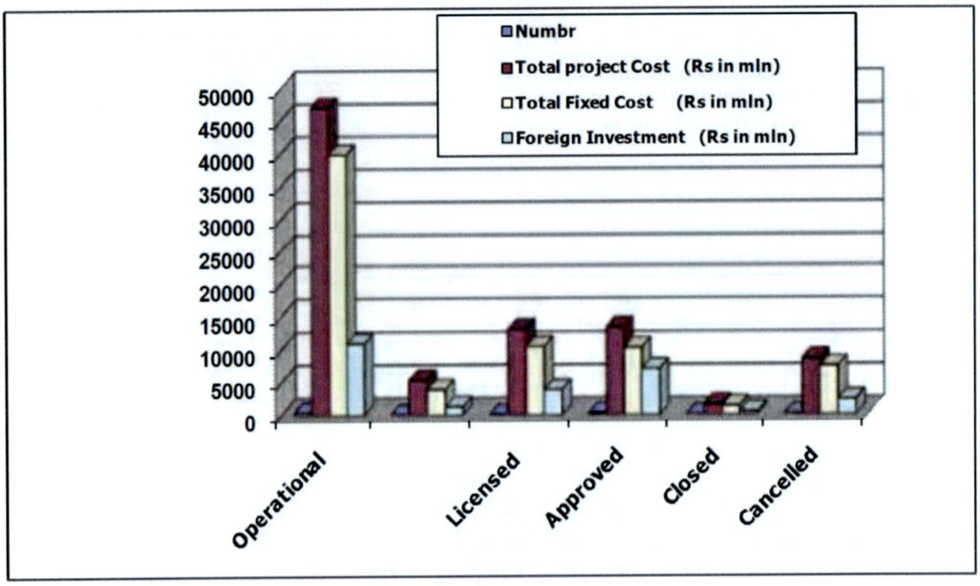

Source: Department of industry, Government of Nepal.

Figure 8. summary chart of FDI in Nepal (status wise) from the beginning to January 2005.

7. Technology Transfer

Technology transfer is the use of knowledge and when we talk about the transfer of technology, we really mean the transfer of knowledge. Transfer does not mean movement or delivery; transfer can only happen if technology is used. So, it is the application of technology considered as a process by which technology developed for one purpose is used either in a different application or by a new user. Technology transfer is usually considered as dissemination of information, matching technology with needs and the creative adaptation of items for new uses. In many LDCs the concept of technology has to be made clear among concerned stakeholders.

Government is encouraging foreign investment and transfer of foreign technology in Nepal by providing incentives and facilities within a liberal and open policy. Stronger IPR could have both market expansion effects, which enable rights holders to better exclude imitators and enjoy a larger market for their technologies, and market power effects, which in theory could enable rights holders to increase the rents earned on their technologies by constraining the quantity supplied.

Technology Transfer has been defined in the Foreign Investment and Technology Transfer Act 1992 as any transfer of technology to be made under an agreement between an industry and a foreign investor on the following matters reported in (FDI Act, 1992):

1. Use of any technological right, specialization, formula, process, patent or technical know-how of foreign origin.
2. Use of any trademark of foreign ownership
3. Acquiring any foreign technical, consultancy, management and marketing service.

Foreign individual, firm, company or corporate body including foreign government and international agencies involved in foreign investment or technology transfer are recognized as foreign investors. Under the Foreign Investment and Technology Transfer Act, if any dispute arises between the foreign investor or foreign technology supplier and Nepalese Firm or Company, the Department of industry tries to mediate so that they can come to an amicable settlement. Failing this, the parties go to arbitration or take the case to court The number and categories of projects with foreign collaboration in Nepal are shown in Table 2 (Appendix 1).

8. Technology Licensing

Technology licensing is a contractual arrangement, in which the licensor's patents, trademarks, service marks, copyrights, trade secrets of other intellectual property may be sold or made available to a license for compensation that is negotiated in advance between the parties. Technology licensing can also be used to acquire foreign technology such as cross-licensing agreements or grant-back clauses awarding rights to improved technology developed by a licensee (Paik S-M, 2007).

Under the Foreign Investment and technology transfer Act 1992 and One-Window Policy, approval and licensing procedures were simplified, with the aim to approve investment applications within a stipulated time period of 30 days following the receipt of the application. After the third amendment of patent, design and trademark Act, 1965 in September 2005, the provision for licensing of patent, design and trademark for use has been possible. Before that only transfer of ownership was possible. The licensing has to be approved by the Department of Industry.

9. The Impact of IPR Protection on FDI and Technology Transfer

There are three main channels through which IPR protection can affect FDI (Ang, 2007). The first channel regards the impact of host countries' IPR protection on the technology transfer motive behind the demand or FDI inflows. The second channel regards the competition reduction effect of host countries IPR protection on the multinational corporations (MNCs) which are patent holders. The third channel refers to the impact of home countries IPR protection on their FDI outflow. In general, stronger IPR protection in the home countries encourages more technological innovations there, and here the destination countries are likely to rely more on the FDI inflows from home countries to reap international technology spillovers. As a result, the demand for FDI from these countries with higher IPR protection is higher

The first channel mentioned above centers on the technology transfer motive in the demand for FDI inflow. In the absence of IPR protection policies, host countries with strong imitative abilities have substantial room to benefit from the advanced technology embodied in the FDI inflows as they can freely imitate the foreign technology. Nevertheless, in the presence of strict IPR protection policies, technology imitation is largely restricted or becomes very costly. This substantially reduces the extent to which these countries can benefit from technology transfer through FDI inflows. As a result, the technology transfer demand for FDI inflow is weakened.

The second channel through which IPR protection affects FDI is related to the completion reduction impact of IPR protection. Stronger IPR protection in the host countries raises the incentives of multinational corporations to operate there, as the foreign firms are less threatened by the increased completion from domestic firms caused by technology leakages and spillovers, and it creates a better legal system for the protection of technology ownership. We can call this incentive given by the host countries to encourage FDI the "FDI-supply-generating effect (pulling effect) (Ang, 2007) of IPR protection in the host countries.

The third channel that drives the relationship between IPR protection policies and FDI lies in the motive of the host countries to search for technology transfer from countries which are suppliers of advanced technology. As strong IPR protection usually breeds technological innovations, the demand for FDI from countries with stronger IPR protection tends to be higher. We call this "FDI-Home country-bias (source-country bias) of IPR protection in the home countries" (Ang, 2007)[1].

10. Challenges and Opportunities

10.1. Legal Provisions and Assessment Mechanisms

Legally speaking the only law that governs technology transfer (from foreign countries) in Nepal is the Foreign Investment and Technology Transfer Act 1992, which has laid down

[1] The term "home bias" is using different from the general use of it in international portfolio investment which means the inventors tend to invest more in the domestic countries than they should be based on standard risk and return analysis.

the regulations and rules governing foreign investment and technology transfer. But the Act appears to be more focused on foreign investment than on technology transfer as such. The Act does not spell out the technology transfer process and facilities which could be instrumental in transferring and developing technology in the country.

Technology transfer is not only related to the purchase of hardware or the contractual agreements for supply of technology, but also linked to the country's existing socio-economic environment (Mytelka and Smith, 2001).The process of technology transfer, thus, must be seen within a larger framework, which incorporates the historical and socio-economic context as well because technology is applied in a productive system, in which hardware interacts with knowledge or methods of operating it, i.e. the software part of the system. Furthermore, a social structure and organization appropriate to the level and characteristics of the technology used are also considered. Without any of these three components, imported technology cannot be efficiently absorbed, diffused and assimilated in the system. In the Nepalese context, there is a need for an appropriate mechanism for technology adaptation, reproduction/modification, innovation and absorption which, in the long run, help to build the nation's own technological capability.

There is no effective system and institutions for performance evaluation of technology transfer function. The Department of Industry has performed the dual responsibility (handling the technology transfer administration and a self evaluation of performance). A new model of technology transfer as a process with a feedback loop (Putranto, Stewart and Moore, 2003) could be a milestone for the effective implementation of industrial technology policy in Nepal.

10.2. Insufficient RandD Input

The ultimate purpose of a technology transfer policy must be to enhance the indigenous technological capability in the long run. Once a suitable technology has been imported, a process of adaptation of this technology should take place in order to absorb it efficiently. This calls for RandD in the country level and/or industry level. Adaptation of imported technology and innovation of new technology is not happening in the Nepalese industrial sector due to a lack of enough initiation and facilities in RandD. Technology transfer and development is an area where a lot of investment is needed because it requires an adequate infrastructure and a long duration to develop and test the technology. It is contextual to look at the investment made by the Government in RandD activities in the field of science and technology. Table-3 shows that the importance of investment in RandD is virtually not realized by the Government despite all the positive policy formulation. (RONAST, 1998)

10.3. Challenges and Opportunities in IPR Protection

There is not much initiative with regard to protecting IP rights because of the lack of skilled manpower as well as a lack of an IP rights protection culture particularly in SMEs (Nepal, Karki and Niraula, 2003) which constitute more than 90 percent of industries in Nepal. In addition, there seems to be a lack of knowledge about the importance of IP rights and access to IP information as well. Hence, protection of IP rights has emerged as one of the major challenges to them. Industries in Nepal do not have adequate funds for RandD for increasing competitive capacity of their industries. Besides, the government has also not given adequate attention to establishing research laboratories in different industrial districts, since, countries like Nepal have a paucity of means and resources to carry out those activities. Furthermore, Nepal, despite being a member of WTO and WIPO, could not obtain technical assistance at the necessary level from these institutions under TRIPs arrangement since these arrangements are not mandatory. Because of the reasons mentioned above, Nepal has to face severe challenges in its implementation of the activities related to IPR effectively.

A judicial mechanism for IPR dispute settlement seems non-compatible with a legacy of the conservative approach of jurisprudence. The Department of Industry has a semi-judicial function with respect to IPR dispute settlements in Nepal. It exercises the power of a trial (District) Court. Whoever is not satisfied with the decision by DOI can take the case to the Appeals Court. If the Appeals Court decision is in line with the DOI decision, it cannot be taken up further to the Supreme Court (see Appendix 2). The process of law enforcement is also lengthy.

There are no formal educational and training institutions for the study of intellectual property to create an awareness in Nepal. In addition, there is no formal institution and separate law for the administration of traditional knowledge, folklore, genetic resources, geographical indication and biodiversity.

Nepal is rich in traditional arts and handicrafts, natural and cultural heritage as well as bio-diversity. Most of the production of SMEs is related to traditional arts, style and culture, which utilizes the artisans knowledge and imagination at a higher level. Hence, it is very urgent to protect the IP of these industries. These industries will get an adequate opportunity to grow from IP protection. Nepalese traditional pictures, *Thankas* and other artistic products from these industries can be protected by copyright. The pattern of carpet and model of ornaments and handicraft products can be protected by registering them as designs. Nepalese indigenous (original) products such as: the apple of Mustang and Jumla, *Khukuri* (sword) of Bhojpur, Tea of Ilam etc. can be protected under Geographical Indication, and can be exported to foreign countries.

There is the greater possibility of taking advantage of patent registration of different types of ayurvedic medicines based on herbs and vegetation which is available in local areas such as *Panch Aule* (Orchis Latifolia) and *Yarcha Gumba* (Cordyceps sinensil). Food production processes and recipes can be protected as trade secrets.

SMEs can enjoy collective rights at a minimum cost by registering a collective trademark. The utility model is quite beneficial to the country. Since its registration does not require more time and cost as patent registration. Handicraft products can be protected under the utility model.

11. Policy Recommendations

1. To establish an institute for Intellectual Property Training is a must.
2. Public awareness programs through electronic media could be effective ways to increase awareness.

3. Periodic assessments and evaluations of policy impacts must be ensured, making them a routine exercise
4. As the experience in many other countries shows, what is important for attracting FDI is not so much the level of fiscal and tax concessions, but ensuring an attractive enabling environment where the costs of doing business are transparent and predictable, where business-related decisions can be transacted with efficiency and speed.
5. Eradicating graft and corruption will help significantly as accountability; transparency, participation and competition etc are the core features of good governance. This will definitely give foreign investors the sense of a guarantee.
6. The information technology policy has been formulated to create a conducive environment to making information technology accessible to the general public and increasing employment through this means. It also emphasizes the building of a knowledge-based society and establishing knowledge-based industries. The policy has already been made effective. However, effective implementation of the policy is a must.
7. Civil service reforms toward creating a technocracy at the central level (based on open autonomous bureaucracies with the transfer of excess civil servants at the center to district administration). Emphasis on a specialist-led administration instead of the prevailing generalist-led administration which functions at present.
8. A special Judicial Reform Commission should be established to modernize commercial rules and regulations as well as make regulatory bodies fully transparent, accountable and participative with stakeholders in the true spirit of the market economy and democracy.
9. A separate Commercial court for settlement of commercial disputes is needed.
10. The process of law enforcement should not be cumbersome.
11. To develop our own technological capability to absorb and adapt the imported technology rather than to look for short-term solutions.
12. Increase the budget in the public RandD sector for building capability to select, assimilate, adapt, improve and create new technology.

APPENDIX

Case Studies

Kiran Shoes Manufacturer further took the case to the Supreme Court including request for stay order for the decision of the Court of Appeal. The Supreme Court provided the stay order as requested on 22 September 2003. Two judges of the Supreme Court had different views on the case and it was recommended to be considered by the full bench. After legal hearings from both the sides together with the examination of the products, it was decided that the Court of Appeal had not analyzed the similarity of the trademarks. The trademarks applied by Basnet Footwear were found similar to the trademarks registered on the name of Kiran Shoes to such an extent that can create confusion to the consumers and harm the reputation of Kiran shoes, if registered. On this ground, the Supreme Court gave its verdict to reverse the decision of the Court of Appeal.

REFERENCES

Ang, Z. (2007), The Impact of Home and Host Country's Intellectual Property Rights Protection on Foreign Direct Investment, dissertation submitted to the Department of Economics and Finance , City University of Hong Kong.

Ashford, N.A., and Heaton, G.R., (1983), Regulation and Technological Innovation in Chemical Industry, *Law and Contemporary Problems*, Vol. 46, No. 3, PP. 110-157, Duke University School of Law.

Firth, L. and Mellor, D. (1999), The Impact of Regulation on Innovation, *European Journal of Law and Economics*, Vol. 8 No. 3 PP. 199-205.

Foreign Direct Investment and Technology Transfer Act 1992, Nepal.

Gyawali, M.P. and Bhatta, T.R. (2006), A country report of present status of Intellectual Property in Nepal, paper presented in WIPO/ ESCAP Colloquium on intellectual property, 6-8 November 2006, Bangkok, Thailand.

Industrial Policy 1992, Government of Nepal.

Integrating Intellectual Property Rights and Development Policy (2002), Report of the Commission on Intellectual Property Rights, London.

LaPierre*, D. Bruce (1977),* Technology-Forcing and Federal Environmental Protection Statutes*,* 62 Iowa Law Review.

Maskus, Keith E. (1997) The Role of Intellectual Property Rights Encouraging Foreign Direct Investment and Technology Transfer, Paper prepared for the Conference Public-Private Initiatives after TRIPS: Designing a Global Agenda, Brussels.

Mytelka, L.K., and Smith, K. (2001), Innovation Theory and Innovation Policy: Bridging the Gap, Paper presented to DRUID Conference, Aalborg.

Nepal C, Karki B. R. and Niraula, K.P. (2003), Technology Transfer in SMEs: Problems and issues in the Context of Nepal, paper presented at the National Seminar on building Capacity for Technology Transfer for Small and Medium Enterprises in Least Developed Countries: A Case in Nepal's Development, Kathmandu, Economic and Social Commission for Asia and the Pacific, United Nations.

OECD (1996), Regulatory Reform and Innovation.

Paik, S-M,(2007), Technology licensing, paper presented in CALS- May Workshop on Technology licenses and contracts, south Korea, Seoul.

Patent, Design and Trademark Act, 1965 (third amendment 2005), Nepal.

Pradhan, R.S. and Rajbamshi D.L. (2006), A country Report on Industrial Property System in Nepal, Paper presented in symposium on Intellectual Property Rights and its implication for Developing countries, New Delhi, India.

Putranto, K., Stewart D. and Moore G. (2003), International Technology Transfer and Distribution of Technology Capabilities: The Case of Railway Development in Indonesia, *Technology in Society* Vol. 25, pp 43-53.

Royal Nepal Academy of Science and Technology (RONAST), (1998), *RandD Investment in Nepal* unpublished, Kathmandu.

Stiglitz, J. (1999), Knowledge as a Global Public Good, in I. Kaul, I. Grunberg, and M. Stern, eds., *Global Public Goods: International Cooperation in the 21st Century*, New York, Oxford University Press.

UNIDO (2002), An analytical report on industrial Development perspective plan: vision 2020, Prepared for His Majesty's Government of Nepal, Ministry of Industry, Commerce and Supplies.

Online References

www.moics.gove.np

LIST OF CONTRIBUTORS
"Information and Communication Technology Policies and Practices"

Editors: Almas HESHMATI and Peng SUN
NOVA Science Publishers

Editors:

1. Almas HESHMATI, Professor of Economics, at Technology Management, Economics and Policy Program, College of Engineering at Seoul National University and Research Fellow member of Institute for the Study of Labor (IZA), Bonn. His earlier positions include Professor of Economics at the MTT Economic Research, Helsinki, Finland and Research Fellow at the World Institute for Development Economics Research (WIDER), The United Nations University (UNU), Helsinki during 2001-2004. From 1998 until 2001, he was Associate Professor of Economics at the Stockholm School of Economics.

   Homepages: http://temep.snu.ac.kr/ and http://www.iza.org/

   Address: College of Engineering, TEMEP, #37-306-1, Seoul National University, San 56-1, Shilim-dong, Kwanak-gu, Seoul 151-742 Korea, Phone: 0082-(0)2-880-5845, Fax: 0082-(0)2-886-8220, Email: heshmati@snu.ac.kr

2. Peng SUN, Vice Section Chief, LiaoNing Entry-Exit Inspection and Quarantine Bureau of China and Researcher, Seoul National University, Contact: Office Address: No.81, RenMin Road, DaLian City, LiaoNing Province, China PC:116001, Email: sun_peng@temep.snu.ac.kr, waterbrothersun@hotmail.com

Contributors: BY THE ALPHABETICAL ORDER OF THEIR LAST NAMES

1. BORJA-BARRERA, Sergio M., Adviser, Presidency of the Republic of Colombia, Contact: Office Address: Calle 7 # 6 – 54 Bogotá – Colombia, South America Email: sergioborja@presidencia.gov.co

2. CHEANG, Sopheak, Deputy Head, Cambodia Computer Emergency Response Team (CamCERT), NiDA, Office of the Council of Ministers and Researcher, Seoul National University, Contact: House 17A, Street 328, Sangkat Toul Svay Prey 1, Khan Chamkarmorn, Phnom Penh, Cambodia, Email: sopheak@temep.snu.ac.kr

3. EL-RHINAOUI, Rachid, Engineer, Ministry of Industry, Commerce and New Technologies, Morocco, Contact: Office Address: 1, Av My EL HASSAN, Rabat, Morocco, Email: r.elrhinaoui@technologies.gov.ma

4. GHIMIRE, Tek B., Deputy Attorney, The office of the Attorney General of Nepal and Researcher, Seoul National University, Contact: The Office of Attorney General of Nepal Ramshah Path, Kathmandu, Nepal, Email: teksnu@gmail.com

5. IMAN-SANTOSO, Hertadi, Head of e-business project, PT. POS Indonesia, Contact: Office Address: Jl. Gedung Kesenian No. 2 Jakarta 10710 Indonesia Email: hertadi40500@gmail.com
6. KHAYYAT, Nabaz T., Senior Advisor, Ministry of Water Resources, Federal Region of Kurdistan, Iraq, and Researcher, Soul National University, Contact: Office Address: Iraq-Erbil- Ministry of Water Resources, Email: nabaz.tahir@mowr-krg.org
7. KIM, Yongil, Researcher, Seoul National University, Contact: TEMEP, College of Engineering, #36-302, Seoul National University, 599, Gwanang-ro, Gwanak-gu, Seoul 151-744, Korea, Email: napacificy@temep.snu.ac.kr
8. LEE, Daeho, Researcher, Seoul National University, Contact: Building #37, Room #413, Seoul National University, San 56-1, Sillim-dong, Kwanak-gu, Seoul, 151-742, South Korea, Email: dealfish@temep.snu.ac.kr
9. MANANDHAR, Shisir P., Division Chief, Kathmandu Metropolitan City, Nepal and Researcher, Seoul National University, Contact: Kathmandu Metropolitan City P.O. Box 8416, Bagdurbar, Kathmandu, Nepal, Email: spmanandhar@hotmail.com
10. MUKHRUMBAEV, Zafar M., Business Manager, ISTEDOD Foundation of the President of the Republic of Uzbekistan and Researcher, Seoul National University, Contact: 171, Almazar street, Tashkent city, Republic of Uzbekistan, Email: zafarmm1978@yahoo.com
11. OH, Jongeun, Researcher, Seoul National University
12. SANG, Sinawong, Deputy Director, National ICT Development Authority (NiDA), Office of the Council of Ministers of Cambodia and Researcher, Seoul National University, Contact: Villa #42, St. 199, Sangkat Tuol Svay Prey I, Khan Chamkamorn, Phnom Penh, Cambodia, Email: ssinawong@snu.ac.kr
13. SUN, Malis, Researcher, Seoul National University
14. TRAN-QUY, Nam, Official, Ministry of Information and Communication of Vietnam and Researcher, Seoul National University, Contact: Office Address: No.18, Nguyen Du Street, Hanoi, Vietnam, Email: tqnam@temep.snu.ac.kr
15. WANG, Shaofei, Vice Division Chief, State-owned Assets Supervision and Administration Commission of the State Council, China, Contact: Office Address: No. 26, Xi Da Jie, Xuan Wu Men, BeiJing, China, PC:100053, Email: sdwangshaofei@temep.snu.ac.kr

INDEX

A

B

C

D

E

F

G

H

I

J

K

L

M

N

O

P

T

U

V

W

Z